Caring for the Disabled Elderly

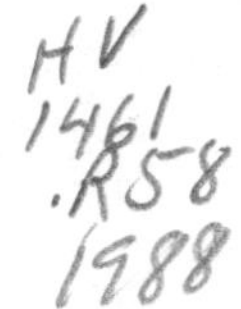

Caring for the Disabled Elderly

Who Will Pay?

Alice M. Rivlin
& Joshua M. Wiener
with Raymond J. Hanley and Denise A. Spence

THE BROOKINGS INSTITUTION
Washington, D.C.

1775 Massachusetts Avenue, N.W., Washington, D.C. 20036

Library of Congress Cataloging-in-Publication data:

Rivlin, Alice M., 1931–
Caring for the disabled elderly: who will pay? / Alice M. Rivlin and Joshua M. Wiener with Raymond J. Hanley and Denise A. Spence.
p. cm.
Includes index.
ISBN 0-8157-7498-2 ISBN 0-8157-7497-4 (pbk.)
1. Aged—Long-term care—United States. 2. Aged, Physically handicapped—Long-term care—United States. 3. Insurance, Long-term care—United States. I. Wiener, Joshua M. II. Title. III. Title: Disabled elderly.
HV1461.R58 1988
362.1′6′0973—dc19 88-10528
CIP

9 8 7 6 5 4 3 2

The paper used in this publication meets the minimum requirements of the American National Standard for Information Sciences—Permanence of Paper for Printed Library Materials, ANSI Z39.48-1984.
∞

Set in Linotron Galliard
Composition by Monotype Composition
Baltimore, Maryland

Printed by R.R. Donnelley and Sons, Co.
Harrisonburg, Virginia

THE BROOKINGS INSTITUTION

The Brookings Institution is an independent organization devoted to nonpartisan research, education, and publication in economics, government, foreign policy, and the social sciences generally. Its principal purposes are to aid in the development of sound public policies and to promote public understanding of issues of national importance.

The Institution was founded on December 8, 1927, to merge the activities of the Institute for Government Research, founded in 1916, the Institute of Economics, founded in 1922, and the Robert Brookings Graduate School of Economics and Government, founded in 1924.

The Board of Trustees is responsible for the general administration of the Institution, while the immediate direction of the policies, program, and staff is vested in the President, assisted by an advisory committee of the officers and staff. The by-laws of the Institution state: "It is the function of the Trustees to make possible the conduct of scientific research, and publication, under the most favorable conditions, and to safeguard the independence of the research staff in the pursuit of their studies and in the publication of the results of such studies. It is not a part of their function to determine, control, or influence the conduct of particular investigations or the conclusions reached."

The President bears final responsibility for the decision to publish a manuscript as a Brookings book. In reaching his judgment on the competence, accuracy, and objectivity of each study, the President is advised by the director of the appropriate research program and weighs the views of a panel of expert outside readers who report to him in confidence on the quality of the work. Publication of a work signifies that it is deemed a competent treatment worthy of public consideration but does not imply endorsement of conclusions or recommendations.

The Institution maintains its position of neutrality on issues of public policy in order to safeguard the intellectual freedom of the staff. Hence interpretations or conclusions in Brookings publications should be understood to be solely those of the authors and should not be attributed to the Institution, to its trustees, officers, or other staff members, or to the organizations that support its research.

Foreword

Because people are living longer, the question of how to pay for long-term nursing home and home care for the disabled elderly has become increasingly urgent. The cost of care can be far beyond the resources of the average family and at present is not normally covered by either private insurance or medicare. Elderly people must rely on their own or their family's income and assets to pay for care or, when these are depleted, turn to welfare.

This study analyzes the major options for reforming the way long-term care is financed. It first explores the potential market for private long-term care insurance and other private sector initiatives. Then it turns to the advantages and disadvantages of various public sector programs. The study recommends both a greatly expanded role for the private sector in financing long-term care and a new public insurance program.

Alice M. Rivlin and Joshua M. Wiener are senior fellows in the Brookings Economic Studies program. Raymond J. Hanley and Denise A. Spence are senior research analysts in that program. David L. Kennell and John F. Sheils, of ICF Incorporated, were equal partners with the authors in developing the Brookings-ICF Long-Term Care Financing Model and provided invaluable help in formulating and analyzing the simulated options. The authors wish to thank Sheila E. Murray, who assisted in the analysis and the preparation of the manuscript; Diana L. Coupard, Deborah A. Ehrenworth, and Ronald R. Hopkinson, who provided research assistance; Robert W. Davis II, Joseph P. Fennell, Ellen J. Hope, Carole H. Newman, Peter Robertshaw, and Piraphong Suppipat, who supplied computer programming assistance; Caroline Lalire, Jeanette Morrison, and Brenda B. Szittya, who edited the manuscript; Victor M. Alfaro, Carl L. Liederman,

Carrie L. Manning, and Almaz S. Zelleke, who verified the factual content; Susan L. Woollen, who prepared the manuscript for typesetting; and Nancy L. Abner, E. Carole Hingleton, Sara C. Hufham, Valerie M. Owens, Jane R. Taylor, and Marian S. White, who provided secretarial assistance.

Special thanks are extended to the Brookings Advisory Panel on Long-Term Care (listed on pages ix and x) for their expert guidance on the study and for their comments on various drafts. The authors also thank James P. Firman, formerly of the Robert Wood Johnson Foundation, for conceiving the original idea of the study. Comments by many others greatly improved the final manuscript. In particular, the authors wish to thank Henry J. Aaron, Robert M. Ball, Bruce L. Boyd, Charles R. Byce, Judith Feder, James P. Firman, Peter D. Fox, Robert B. Friedland, Susan Van Gelder, Terri Gendel, Mary Jo Gibson, Jay N. Greenberg, Bruce Jacobs, Korbin Liu, Steven R. McConnell, Mark R. Meiners, Ronald F. Pollack, John C. Rother, Rose M. Rubin, Louise B. Russell, Kenneth M. Scholen, Charles L. Schultze, David D. Strachan, and Valerie S. Wilbur.

Funding for this study was provided by the Robert Wood Johnson Foundation, the Villers Foundation, the Retirement Research Foundation, the Greenwall Foundation, the John A. Hartford Foundation, the John D. and Catherine T. MacArthur Foundation, and the U.S. Department of Health and Human Services. In addition, the following representatives of these organizations gave help and encouragement to the authors: John L. Duggan, Jr., Paul D. Gayer, Ina G. Guzman, Marilyn M. Hennessy, Jeffrey C. Merrill, Judith R. Peres, Laura A. Robbins, Richard A. Sharpe, and Stephen A. Somers. Brookings is very grateful for this support.

The views expressed here are those of the authors and should not be attributed to the persons or organizations whose assistance is acknowledged, or to the trustees, officers, or other staff members of the Brookings Institution.

BRUCE K. MACLAURY
President

April 1988
Washington, D.C.

The Brookings Advisory Panel on Long-Term Care

CHARLES D. BAKER
Professor, Northeastern University (formerly Under Secretary, U.S. Department of Health and Human Services)

CYRIL F. BRICKFIELD
Former Executive Director, American Association of Retired Persons

ELAINE M. BRODY
Director of Human Services, Philadelphia Geriatric Center

ROBERT N. BUTLER, M.D.
Chairman, Department of Geriatrics, Mt. Sinai Medical Center

JAMES J. CALLAHAN
Professor, Brandeis University

JACOB CLAYMAN
President, National Council of Senior Citizens

DAVID F. DURENBERGER
U.S. Senate

PAUL M. ELLWOOD, JR.
Chairman, Interstudy, Inc.

CARROLL L. ESTES
Professor, University of California at San Francisco

SHELDON L. GOLDBERG
Executive Vice President, American Association of Homes for the Aging

VAL J. HALAMANDARIS
President, National Association for Home Care

H. JOHN HEINZ
U.S. Senate

ELMA L. HOLDER
Executive Director, National Citizens' Coalition for Nursing Home Reform

JOHN K. KITTREDGE
Former Executive Vice President, Prudential Insurance Company

JAMES G. MACDONALD
Former Chairman and Chief Executive Officer, Teachers Insurance and Annuity Association–College Retirement Equities Fund

BARBARA P. MATULA
Director, Division of Medical Assistance, North Carolina Department of Human Resources

Contents

TABLES

FIGURES

PART I
Overview

Chapter One

Introduction and Summary

It is time for Americans to face a serious problem—how to organize and pay for long-term care for the disabled elderly. More and more Americans are living past 75, 85, and even 95. As they age, the elderly suffer not only acute illnesses requiring care in hospitals and by physicians, but chronic disabling conditions that require long-term care either at home or in nursing homes.*

Alzheimer's disease, osteoporosis, heart disease, and stroke predominate among the many diseases that cause chronic disability in the elderly. The toll is not only physical but emotional as people experience and relatives watch a decline in the ability to do things that most of us take for granted. Long-term care is the help needed to cope, and sometimes to survive, when physical or mental disabilities impair the capacity to perform the basic activities of everyday life, such as eating, toileting, bathing, dressing, and moving about.[1]

Most long-term care services are provided by family members and friends of the disabled person, often at considerable personal sacrifice. Paid services are offered by nursing homes, home health care workers, homemaker and personal care workers, adult day care centers, and respite programs for family caregivers. Costs can be high. Paying for a long stay in a nursing home, at an average cost of $22,000 a year, is beyond the financial capacity of most families.[2]

At present the United States does not have, either in the private or the public sector, satisfactory mechanisms for helping people anticipate

* Although people can require long-term care at any age, this study is concerned with physically and cognitively impaired persons aged 65 and over. It does not include the mentally ill, developmentally disabled, or nonelderly physically disabled—all important populations with pressing needs, but beyond the scope of this study.

and pay for long-term care. The disabled elderly and their families find, often to their surprise, that the costs of long-term care are not covered to any significant extent either by private insurance or by medicare, the federal health care program for the aged. Instead, most rely on their own resources or, when these have been exhausted, turn to medicaid, the federal-state welfare program that finances health services for the poor.

The aging of the baby boom generation combined with rapidly falling mortality rates for the aged will lead to sharply increased demand for long-term care that will require substantially greater public and private spending far into the next century. One premise of this book is that these rising costs of long-term care should not come as an unpleasant surprise. Chronic disability is a normal risk of growing old that can be anticipated and planned for, both publicly and privately. A second premise is that neither the public nor the private sector can handle these rising costs alone. Major new efforts are needed in both the public and private sectors to improve the organization and financing of long-term care.

We hope this book will stimulate and clarify public debate on financing care for the disabled elderly. To this end we reviewed the available information on long-term care and, with ICF Incorporated, constructed a computer simulation model to project the population of disabled elderly over the next three decades and to estimate their financial resources and likely use of long-term care. We used the Brookings-ICF Long-Term Care Financing Model for three purposes: first, to anticipate likely future strains on the system of paying for long-term care if current policies remain unchanged; second, to evaluate the potential contribution of private long-term care insurance and other private sector initiatives; and, third, to estimate the costs and effects of changes in federal government policy, both incremental changes in existing programs and new coverage for long-term care under medicare.

Our analysis leads us to recommend two general directions of reform. First, private long-term care insurance and other private sector risk-pooling mechanisms should be strongly encouraged and should expand to finance a more substantial part of long-term care than they do now. Second, a public insurance program should also be enacted, by adding long-term care coverage to medicare, and should replace medicaid as the principal public mechanism for financing long-term care.

Long-Term Care in the 1980s

Most older people are physically active, able to care for themselves, and not in need of long-term care. Of the 28.6 million Americans aged 65 and over in 1985, less than a quarter (6.3 million) were disabled (table 1-1). Of this group, 2.6 million were severely disabled.*

The prevalence of disability rises steeply with advancing age. Only about 14 percent of people aged 65–74 were disabled in 1985, but that proportion rises to 58 percent for people aged 85 and over. Today the fastest growing age group in the population is the very elderly, the group most likely to need long-term care.[3] Largely because women live longer than men, the disabled elderly are disproportionately very old widows.

WHO PROVIDES LONG-TERM CARE?

Although many people identify long-term care with nursing homes, the predominant provider of long-term care in the United States is the family. The elderly express strong preferences for remaining in their own homes as long as possible and for being cared for by relatives.[4] Only about 21 percent of the disabled elderly were in nursing homes in 1985. The rest were in the community, mostly in their own homes. Those with more severe disabilities were more likely to be in institutions, but even among the severely disabled considerably less than half were in nursing homes.

Nearly 90 percent of the disabled old people who were not in nursing homes received assistance from relatives and friends, sometimes supplemented by paid services.[5] The majority of unpaid caregivers are women relatives of the disabled, usually wives, daughters, or daughters-in-law.[6]

Families devote enormous time and energy to the care of elderly relatives, often at considerable emotional and physical cost. One study estimates that more than 27 million unpaid days of informal care are provided each week.[7] Other studies suggest the large emotional and physical strain on families caring for elderly relatives.[8]

The strong role of the family in long-term care runs counter to the myth that American families, who supposedly took care of their aging relatives at home "in the good old days," are now "dumping" them in

* Severely disabled is defined as needing assistance with three of the six activities of daily living—eating, toileting, bathing, dressing, getting in and out of bed, and getting around inside.

TABLE I-1. *Number and Distribution of Disabled Elderly, by Place of Residence, 1985*

Category	Total number of elderly (millions)[a]	Disabled elderly: Nursing home		Disabled elderly: Community		Disabled elderly: Total[b]		Disabled elderly as a percent of number of elderly in each category		
		Number (millions)	Percent	Number (millions)	Percent	Number (millions)	Percent	Nursing home	Community	All disabled
Age										
65–74	16.9	0.2	15.4	2.1	41.9	2.3	36.5	1.3	12.3	13.6
75–84	9.1	0.5	38.5	2.0	40.9	2.5	40.0	5.6	22.1	27.7
85 and over	2.7	0.6	46.2	1.0	19.7	1.6	25.0	22.1	36.1	58.2
Sex										
Male	11.4	0.3	23.1	1.7	35.3	2.1	33.2	2.9	15.2	18.2
Female	17.2	1.0	76.9	3.3	66.2	4.3	68.0	5.7	19.1	24.8
Race[c]										
White	25.9	1.2	92.3	4.2	84.0	5.4	85.9	4.7	16.1	20.8
Black	2.3	0.1	7.7	0.6	13.0	0.7	11.6	3.5	27.6	31.2
Number of ADL dependencies[d]										
Fewer than three	...	0.4	28.5	3.3	67.0	3.7	58.9	1.3[e]	11.6[e]	12.9[e]
Three or more	...	0.9	71.5	1.6	33.2	2.6	41.3	3.3[e]	5.7[e]	9.0[e]
TOTAL	28.6	1.3	100.0	4.9	100.0	6.3	100.0	4.6	17.3	21.9

SOURCES: 1982 National Long-Term Care Survey; Esther Hing, "Use of Nursing Homes by the Elderly: Preliminary Data from the 1985 National Nursing Home Survey," *Vital and Health Statistics* (advance data), no. 135 (Hyattsville, Md.: National Center for Health Statistics, Department of Health and Human Services, May 14, 1987), p. 2; U.S. Bureau of the Census, "Projections of the Population of the United States, by Age, Sex, and Race, 1983 to 2080," *Current Population Reports,* series P-25, no. 952 (Washington, D.C.: Department of Commerce, May 1984), table 6; and National Center for Health Statistics, "Health Statistics on Older Persons, United States, 1986," *Vital and Health Statistics,* series 3, no. 25 (Hyattsville, Md.: DHHS, June 1987), p. 15. Figures are rounded.

a. Includes disabled and nondisabled elderly.
b. Sum of the number of elderly in nursing homes and the estimated number of noninstitutionalized disabled elderly on an average day.
c. Numbers may not add because the number of elderly of other race or unknown race is not included.
d. Inability to perform the activities of daily living—eating, bathing, dressing, toileting, getting in and out of bed, and getting around inside.
e. Percent of total elderly.

nursing homes. In fact, in the past, few families cared for an elderly parent because relatively few people lived long enough to experience a prolonged period of disability.[9] Because of increased longevity, the odds of being called upon to provide parent care are much higher now than in the past.

Although nursing homes serve less than a quarter of the disabled elderly, they dominate long-term care financing. In 1985 there were 19,100 nursing homes with 1.6 million beds, more beds than in acute care hospitals.[10] In 1987 dollars, average annual expenditures for nursing home care for the elderly in 1986–90 are estimated to be $33 billion.* Estimated expenditures for paid home care are much smaller—only about $8.6 billion in 1986–90—although nearly twice as many people will be served.†

HOW ARE THE BILLS PAID?

The striking fact about long-term care financing is that such a trivial portion of the bill is paid by any form of insurance. Most private health insurance policies do not cover long-term care; about 1 percent of total long-term care expenditures are paid by private insurance.[11] Medicare covers short stays in skilled nursing facilities, but medicare spending amounted to less than 2 percent of nursing home expenditures in 1985.[12]

The disabled elderly who use long-term care pay for it out of their own or their family's income and assets—or they turn to welfare. Out-of-pocket spending accounts for a little more than half, and medicaid for a little less than half, of all spending for nursing home care. The proportion of all costs of nursing home care paid out-of-pocket has increased somewhat over the past decade.[13] Medicaid is the dominant source of public funding for long-term care, accounting for 71 percent of government spending for nursing home and home care in 1986–90.[14]

Because the cost of an extended stay in a nursing home exceeds the financial resources of most elderly, it is not surprising that 54 percent of all newly admitted nursing home patients in 1986–90 and even more patients who stay longer than a year must ultimately depend on welfare to help pay for their care.[15] While many nursing home patients are not

* Brookings-ICF Long-Term Care Financing Model. See table 1-3 below. Expenditures are averaged over a five-year period and can be conceived as the annual experience for the midpoint year (for example, 1988).

† Brookings-ICF Long-Term Care Financing Model. See tables 1-2 and 1-3 below. Some home care services are provided to the elderly who are not chronically disabled.

poor when they enter the nursing home, they become poor by depleting their income and assets paying for care, a process known as "spending down."[16] Many beneficiaries of medicaid financing of long-term care find their unexpected status as welfare patients demeaning.

Because medicaid is intended for the needy, eligibility is strictly limited to those who meet the means test.[17] In 1988 individuals are not eligible for medicaid if they have more than $1,900 in assets, generally not counting the value of the home. Nursing home residents who meet the asset test and whose medical expenses exceed their ability to pay must contribute all of their income to help pay for their care after deducting a small personal needs allowance (usually $30 a month) to pay for personal items.[18] Only then will medicaid help pay the bills. In some cases, medicaid eligibility rules can leave the spouse of a medicaid nursing home patient with very few resources on which to live.

Problems of the Current System

The current method of paying for long-term care in the United States is makeshift and inadequate. Neither the public nor the private sector has developed ways of pooling the risks of long-term care or spreading the costs over time. Families and governments are simply coping with the rising costs of long-term care as best they can. The result is a system that satisfies no one and whose problems are severe.

First, the burden falls heavily on persons unlucky enough to need extensive long-term care and on their families. Incomes are strained; life savings used up. The pain and anxiety inherent in becoming disabled and in caring for a disabled relative are compounded by worries over how to pay for care without turning to welfare.

Second, public costs are rising rapidly, primarily in medicaid, which was not originally intended as a mechanism for paying for long-term care for the elderly. Poor families with children now compete with the disabled elderly for limited medicaid funding.

Third, the dependence on out-of-pocket spending and medicaid for long-term care financing perpetuates a two-class system of long-term care, especially with respect to nursing home care, which in turn exacerbates concern about the quality of care. Although many long-term care facilities provide high-quality care, some provide fair or poor care, and many provide only mediocre care. Nursing homes whose patients are mostly private generally provide higher-quality care than facilities dependent on medicaid patients.

Fourth, access to care is often limited. Nursing home occupancy rates averaged 92 percent in 1985, and waiting lists are common.[19] Because nursing homes charge private patients much more than medicaid pays, private patients are usually preferred over medicaid patients. As a result, medicaid patients often have difficulty gaining access to nursing homes. Similarly, since severely disabled patients require more expensive care than the average patient does, fewer nursing homes will accept them.

Fifth, because financing is more widely available for nursing home care than for home care, especially under medicaid, home care services are limited in supply. Despite the strong preference of the elderly for remaining in their own homes as long as possible, only 25 percent of the disabled elderly in the community receive any paid in-home services.[20] Total expenditures for long-term care are overwhelmingly for nursing home rather than for home care, especially in the public sector. While medicare does cover some home health care, it is restricted to medically oriented services of limited use to most disabled elderly. Hardly any home care services are covered by medicaid.

Finally, although public spending for home care is not large, many programs and agencies at the federal, state, and local levels fund some home care services, creating a highly fragmented financing and delivery system. At the federal level, funding for elderly home care services is available from medicare, medicaid, the social services block grant, the Veterans Administration, and the Older Americans Act. Each program has its own eligibility requirements, benefit coverage, regulations regarding provider participation, administrative structure, and service delivery mechanisms. The result is that it is difficult to coordinate a comprehensive set of home care services.

Increasing Strains on the System

Pressure on the long-term care financing system is bound to grow as the population of disabled elderly increases. To illustrate what is likely to happen if long-term care services and financing continue unchanged, we used our model to create a "base case."* The results of

* The base case projections assume that use of long-term care services remains constant by age, sex, marital status, and disability status. If use rates were to rise—perhaps because

TABLE I-2. *Thirty-Year Projection: Number of Elderly, Finances, and Use of Long-Term Care, 1986–90 to 2016–20*[a]

	1986–90				2016–20			
		Age				Age		
	All elderly	65–74	75–84	85 and over	All elderly	65–74	75–84	85 and over
Number of elderly (millions)[b]								
In the population	31.3	17.5	10.3	3.5	50.3	28.4	14.6	7.2
Age distribution (percent)	100	56	33	11	100	57	29	14
In a nursing home[c]	2.3	0.4	0.9	1.0	4.0	0.7	1.3	2.1
Age distribution (percent)	100	18	40	42	100	16	32	51
Receiving home care services[d]	4.0	1.2	1.7	1.1	6.4	1.8	2.3	2.2
Age distribution (percent)	100	31	43	26	100	29	37	34
Median family income (1987 dollars)[e]	9,314	10,806	8,657	6,837	17,210	23,203	14,956	7,999
Median family assets (1987 dollars)[f]	59,230	67,764	52,106	40,143	79,050	94,449	73,300	56,410
Housing	35,532	42,643	29,611	17,764	47,383	50,347	47,381	42,640
Financial	13,799	20,840	9,473	6,425	26,518	40,227	21,372	8,634

SOURCE: Brookings-ICF Long-Term Care Financing Model. Figures are rounded.

a. Five-year averages.

b. Elderly aged 65 and over.

c. Persons in a nursing home at any time during the year.

d. Persons using paid home care services at any time during the year, including the nonchronically disabled elderly.

e. Family income is joint income for married persons and individual income for unmarried persons. Income sources are social security, pensions, supplemental security income, individual retirement accounts, wages, and asset earnings. Families and individuals without income are included.

f. Includes families without assets.

TABLE 1-3. *Thirty-Year Projection: Long-Term Care Spending, 1986–90 to 2016–20*[a]
Billions of 1987 dollars

Payment source	1986–90	2016–20	Percent increase
		Nursing home services	
Medicaid	14.1	46.2	227
Medicare	0.6	1.6	168
Patient out-of-pocket	18.3	50.3	175
TOTAL	33.0	98.1	197
		Home care services	
Medicaid	1.2	2.4	95
Medicare	3.1	7.7	149
Other payers[b]	2.7	7.2	170
Patient out-of-pocket	1.6	4.6	182
TOTAL	8.6	21.9	154

SOURCE: Brookings-ICF Long-Term Care Financing Model. Figures are rounded.

a. Average annual expenditures. Nursing home and home care inflation is assumed to be 5.8 percent a year. General inflation is assumed to be 4.0 percent a year; long-term care inflation in excess of general inflation is assumed to be 1.8 percent a year.

b. Other payers include state and local expenditures, social services block grants, Older Americans Act and Veterans Administration home care funds, charity, and out-of-pocket expenditures by persons other than the service recipient.

this simulation for the three decades between 1986–90 and 2016–20 are summarized in tables 1-2 and 1-3.

The number of older people will grow rapidly; the number of very elderly even faster. Because they will be older, more of the population over 65 will be disabled. The increase in the number of disabled elderly will mean more users of long-term care, especially nursing home care. While the number of people over 65 is projected to increase 61 percent, the nursing home population will increase 76 percent. Nursing home residents will also be older—51 percent of them will be 85 or over in 2016–20, compared with 42 percent in 1986–90.

Older people will be significantly better off financially by the end of the period, but the income and assets of the younger elderly will increase much more rapidly than those of the very old. Real incomes of people aged 65–74 will more than double over the three decades because of higher pensions and increases in social security benefits and income from assets. Incomes of the 85-and-over group, who are most likely to be users of nursing homes and home care, will go up only

of decreased availability of family caregivers—total spending would be higher, as would the burden on medicaid. If use rates were to fall—perhaps because of a breakthrough in the treatment of Alzheimer's disease—total spending would be lower, as would the burden on medicaid.

about 17 percent in real terms. Members of this group are already 50 years of age or older and will not benefit as much as younger cohorts from expected increases in pension availability and labor force participation by women.

Long-term care spending will increase rapidly, especially for nursing homes.* If nursing home costs rise 5.8 percent a year (compared with a 4.0 percent increase assumed for the general price level), nursing home spending for the elderly will triple, climbing from $33 billion in 1986–90 to $98 billion (in constant 1987 dollars) by 2016–20.

Finally, medicaid spending will rise faster than total long-term care spending, and the proportion of nursing home patients dependent on medicaid will not decline. This is a surprising finding. Because the overall economic well-being of the elderly is expected to improve substantially by 2016–20, one would expect them to become less dependent on a program intended for the poor. The reason they do not is that long-term care costs are projected to rise faster than the incomes of the very elderly, the group most likely to use long-term care. Those most likely to need care will actually be worse off in the future in terms of their ability to pay for it.

Choosing Options for Reform

The best solution to the long-term care problem would be medical breakthroughs that reduced the prevalence of disability among the aged and diminished their need for care. Both public and private funding should be directed to biomedical research to reduce the incidence of disabling diseases and to develop techniques for managing them better. However, success is not assured. Advances in medical knowledge are inherently unpredictable and can have the effect of postponing death while lengthening periods of disability.[21]

Even with rapid medical advances, it is likely that the number of disabled elderly will increase for many decades to come. It is also likely that both private and public expenditures will rise rapidly and that the

* Both total nursing home spending and the proportion covered by medicaid are extremely sensitive to assumptions about the extent to which nursing home costs increase more rapidly than the general price level. If nursing home costs increase only 10 percent faster than the consumer price index, the proportion paid by medicaid would fall—substantially more elderly would be able to finance their own care without going on welfare. Such a low rate of inflation in nursing home costs, however, implies either large increases in the productivity of nursing home workers, which seems unlikely, or declines in their relative wages, which would make recruiting difficult and threaten the quality of care.

fraction of long-term care patients dependent on welfare will not shrink. Public policy must be predicated on these assumptions.

OBJECTIVES OF REFORM

One objective of reform should be to reduce the uncertainty and anxiety that now surround paying for long-term care. Some combination of public and private financing mechanisms should be developed to give older people the security of knowing how they will pay for long-term care if they need it.

Another objective should be to enable older people to remain at home as long as possible. Reform should reduce the current bias toward nursing home care by providing financing for reasonable amounts of home care, adult day care, and other such services. It should ease the burden on families without creating incentives to substitute paid for unpaid care.

Reform of the financing system should also aim to improve the quality of care and the flexibility and efficiency of the delivery system. It should encourage experimentation with new ways of organizing care designed to increase patient satisfaction and avoid nursing home placement.

At the same time, reforms should not greatly exacerbate the expected rise in long-term care expenditures or add to the inflationary pressures on the long-term care industry. As usual, the objective of ensuring more and better care conflicts with the objective of minimizing public and private costs, and policymakers must find the appropriate balance.

FOUR SPECIAL CHARACTERISTICS OF LONG-TERM CARE

When alternative means of financing are considered, four characteristics of long-term care take on special importance. First, only a minority of the elderly have large long-term care expenses. On the average day, only 4.6 percent of the elderly are in nursing homes (table 1-1). Moreover, only between 35 and 50 percent of the elderly will spend any time in a nursing home before they die.[22] Over 40 percent of all admissions to nursing homes are for 90 days or less.[23] Because relatively few people face long stays that involve a large outlay of funds, long-term care lends itself to insurance and risk pooling, whereby many people contribute to a fund to cover the extraordinary expenses of the few.

Second, if people wait until retirement age to begin buying insurance or accumulating assets to pay for care, the premium payments or level of savings required is large. To reduce the cost, people should begin early in their working years to protect themselves against a risk that will not be significant for another thirty to fifty years. Human nature makes it difficult, however, to convince young and middle-aged workers, or their employers or unions, to pay for protection against a contingency that—if it occurs at all—lies in the remote future.

Third, the rising cost of long-term care presents special problems. The price of nursing home and home care is likely to rise faster than general inflation. Over the thirty or more years during which people might provide for their long-term care needs, the real cost increases can accumulate to very large sums. That cumulative cost increase not only raises the amount that people of working age have to save to provide reasonable protection in old age; it also magnifies the financial risks for both the user and the supplier of insurance. If the long-term care insurance provides only a fixed dollar benefit (for example, $50-a-day in a nursing home), the buyer is at risk for the unplanned inflation in the cost of care. If nursing home fees increase 5.8 percent a year, a $50-a-day indemnity payment needs to grow to more than $271 a day to maintain its purchasing power after thirty years. If the insurance provides a service benefit (that is, the actual cost of care minus any cost-sharing), the insurance company or the government is uncertain how much should be charged for premiums or taxes to cover expenses in future years.

Finally, because such a large fraction of long-term care services are now performed voluntarily by relatives, use of paid services may increase significantly once third-party financing is available. The principal effect of insurance or other such financing mechanisms is to reduce the net cost of a service. People tend to buy more of a service when it costs less out-of-pocket. In designing and financing a long-term care program, both private insurance companies and the government must take such "moral hazard" into account.

In this study moral hazard is considered in two ways: first, as it affects the estimated cost of both private and public financing mechanisms and, second, as it affects program design. Increases in service use, and thus cost, can be limited by requiring beneficiary cost-sharing, restricting eligibility to the severely disabled, requiring preauthorization of services, and so on.

It is difficult to judge precisely the extent of the moral hazard problem. The disabled elderly are overwhelmingly cared for by relatives and not by paid providers. About 41 percent of the disabled elderly were receiving paid home care or nursing home care in 1985.[24] Many additional people who could "medically qualify" for paid services are not receiving any. The increase in use could especially be a problem if families stopped providing care and depended on paid services to fill the gap. Some studies have found use of nursing home care to be quite sensitive to price.[25]

While the greater availability of third-party financing would surely increase use, the likely increase is probably not as great as some fear. The overwhelming majority of elderly want to stay out of nursing homes if at all possible.[26] Canada and other countries that pay for long-term care through social insurance systems have not found use to increase to unacceptable levels.[27] Although most disabled elderly are receiving only unpaid services from families, the extent of paid assistance varies by degree of disability. For example, 58 percent of the severely disabled elderly already receive paid services.[28] Thus well-circumscribed eligibility criteria would limit the extent to which use could increase. Finally, most evidence suggests that families do not withdraw care when paid services are provided.[29]

On balance, the increase in nursing home use induced by expanded availability of third-party payments is likely to be modest. In the case of home care services, however, the increase in use is likely to be substantial.

PUBLIC VERSUS PRIVATE FINANCING

At present both the public and private sectors play a role in financing long-term care. Views differ strongly on how much relative emphasis should be put on public and private efforts in the future. Some believe that the primary responsibility for care of the elderly should fall on individuals and their families, and that the government should act only as a payer of last resort for those who are unable to provide for themselves. The opposite view is that the government should take the lead in ensuring comprehensive care for all older people, regardless of financial need, either by providing care directly or by compulsory social insurance. In this view, there is little or no role for the private sector. Between these polar views many combinations of public and private responsibility are possible, and most people would probably opt for some middle ground.

The choice of emphasis between public and private programs depends not just on differences in political ideology, but also on differences in perceptions of what private initiatives are feasible and affordable and whom they would benefit. For example, if it were demonstrably possible to market private long-term care insurance that would protect a large majority of the elderly population from hardship and reduce dependence on medicaid, then many people would see little need for new kinds of government intervention. Conversely, if private initiatives were not to prove feasible, then the case for an expanded public role would be stronger.

GIVING PRIORITY TO THE PRIVATE SECTOR

In picking options to analyze, we began with the private sector options. Reliance on the private sector reflects the American tradition of individuals taking responsibility for their own lives and needs. Moreover, the huge federal deficit and general concern with the level of public expenditures have made large-scale expansions in any public programs difficult to enact. In the case of long-term care, they have fed the hope that private sector initiatives could hold down public spending on medicaid. The marked improvement in the financial position of the elderly in the past twenty years has also made it more plausible to argue that private sector financing might be widely affordable in the future. Although currently only a tiny part of the market, private sector financing mechanisms are growing in popularity, and it seemed useful to begin by examining the feasibility and limits of such mechanisms.

In our simulations, we made optimistic assumptions about the willingness of consumers to buy private insurance or participate in other private sector financing initiatives. Our purpose was to establish an upper bound for the effect of these options, so that we could determine what part of the problem would remain unsolved even if heavy reliance was put on the private sector.

Exploring the Potential of the Private Sector

Private sector initiatives involve two general strategies. One, which we believe holds the greater promise, involves bringing people together in various ways to pool the risk of high long-term care expenditures. Examples of this approach include private long-term care insurance, continuing care retirement communities, and social/health maintenance organizations. The other approach aims at improving the ability of people to pay for their own long-term care out of their accumulated savings. Examples of this approach include individual medical accounts and home equity conversions.

PRIVATE LONG-TERM CARE INSURANCE

Private long-term care insurance is the clearest private sector opportunity for spreading the cost of high long-term care costs across a broad group of the population. Private insurance is widely used in American society for pooling the risk of expensive, but relatively infrequent, misfortunes such as fire, theft, automobile accidents, and hospitalization. Indeed, two-thirds of the elderly in 1977, including substantial proportions at low-income levels, purchased health insurance to supplement medicare.[30]

The market for long-term care insurance is burgeoning. More than 400,000 private long-term care insurance policies are currently in force, up substantially over the past four years.[31] Most major insurers are offering policies, at least on an experimental basis. And many market surveys show that elderly people are interested.

Insurers, however, remain fearful of large financial losses. To lessen the risk, current policies screen out applicants likely to need long-term care, exclude mental illness from coverage, require that care take place only in certain types of nursing homes, and provide reimbursement only in cases of prior hospitalization. Insurers' concern about losses due to increased use of long-term care or to future inflation is also reflected in high deductibles, limited coverage of care, and restriction of almost all policies to a fixed indemnity not indexed for inflation.

Despite limitations, premiums for long-term care insurance are high relative to the cost of medicare supplemental insurance and to the income of many elderly people. An average "high-option" long-term care insurance policy costs $684 a year if initially purchased at age 65 and rises to $1,496 if first purchased at age 79 80.*

Group insurance, especially if sold to the nonelderly population, could lower premiums by reducing marketing and administrative costs and by allowing people to pay premiums over their entire working careers. Although employers are increasingly interested in offering long-term care insurance, they seem unwilling to help pay for it.

* A high-option policy is defined as having the shortest period before insurance coverage begins, maximum length of nursing home coverage, and $60 a day reimbursement for skilled nursing care. Joshua M. Wiener, Deborah A. Ehrenworth, and Denise A. Spence, "Private Long-Term Care Insurance: Cost, Coverage and Restrictions," *Gerontologist,* vol. 27 (August 1987), p. 488.

Employers face some tax barriers to prefunding these benefits, and premiums for group policies can still be quite high, even for younger people.

CONTINUING CARE RETIREMENT COMMUNITIES (CCRCS)

Continuing care retirement communities are residential complexes for older people with apartments or cottages and an array of medical, nursing, and social services on the premises. Approximately 680 CCRCs serve some 170,000 residents.[32] In exchange for often substantial entry and monthly fees, the continuing care retirement communities guarantee residents care appropriate to their needs for the rest of their lives. In concept, such communities combine both risk pooling and the notion that the availability of a continuum of care—from occasional home care to full nursing home care—is a more efficient way to provide care than the current system, with its bias toward nursing home care. Ideally, CCRCs combine comprehensive long-term care insurance with improvements in the delivery of services.

In practice, continuing care retirement communities, mostly geared to quite affluent people, have limited potential to finance long-term care. First, CCRC residents must move out of their homes and into an organized setting, something most elderly do not want to do. Second, while much of the appeal of CCRCs is the financial protection they can offer, more than half of the existing communities require substantial out-of-pocket payments for use of long-term care services, and more communities are adopting this policy. Third, they prefer the healthy elderly and tend to exclude those most likely to need long-term care services. And fourth, in some relatively rare but highly publicized cases, continuing care communities have been financially unsound and have gone bankrupt. Those with the most extensive long-term care coverage tend to be in worse shape financially than those with only minimal guarantees.[33]

SOCIAL/HEALTH MAINTENANCE ORGANIZATIONS (S/HMOS)

Social/health maintenance organizations extend the health maintenance organization concept of comprehensive, prepaid financing for acute care to include a variety of long-term care services. The principal premises are that a continuum of care will be cost-effective and that there can be enough savings on acute care to help finance expanded long-term care services. A demonstration of this concept is currently under way in four cities with about 15,000 elderly enrolled.[34] The demonstration projects offer a moderate amount of home care benefits, but limited nursing home care.

An empirical question to be answered by the demonstration is whether there can be enough substitution of long-term care for acute care and home care for nursing home services to make the S/HMOs financially feasible. A problem in the demonstration sites is that all but one had a hard time recruiting participants, which has adversely affected their financial position and raised questions about their long-run workability.

INDIVIDUAL MEDICAL ACCOUNTS (IMAS)

Individual medical accounts, a proposed variant of individual retirement accounts (IRAs), would be personal savings accounts specifically earmarked for long-term care that would receive favorable income tax treatment by the federal government. A person would contribute up to a maximum amount each year to an IMA, deducting the contribution from current income for tax purposes (or, in some versions, obtaining a tax credit). Neither the principal nor the interest would be taxed until used, if at all.

It is appealing to think that IMAs could encourage people to save enough to pay for their own long-term care and to purchase the care most suited to their needs, but the extremely high level of savings required are out of most people's reach. Experience with IRAs suggests that less than a fifth of all taxpayers are likely to establish any tax-favored savings account, and that at least part of the tax-protected savings may replace rather than add to other forms of savings.[35] Because use of IMA funds would be restricted to long-term care services or insurance, participation would be expected to be lower than for IRAs, which can be spent on anything. IMA participation, like that of IRAs before the Tax Reform Act of 1986 reduced their attractiveness to higher-income taxpayers, would most likely be concentrated among higher-income and older people.

Tax revenue lost to the government because of IMAs would probably exceed what the government would save in lower medicaid spending. Ironically, if many people actually did put substantial amounts of money into IMAs to cover the possible cost of their own long-term care, it would result in massive oversavings because most people will never have a long stay in a nursing home.

FIGURE 1-1. **Private Sector Approaches: Key Simulation Assumptions for Major Options**

- *Long-term care insurance ($30, $40, and $50 nursing home daily benefit).* All nondisabled individuals and couples aged 67 with $10,000 or more in nonhousing assets buy policies if the cost of the premiums is 5 percent or less of their income. The policy provides six years of nursing home care after a 100-day elimination period at $30, $40, or $50 a day (in 1986 dollars) depending on what the person can afford. The indemnity benefit level is moderately indexed for inflation for ten years after initial purchase. A prior hospitalization requirement allows 75 percent of the people who meet the elimination period to receive benefits.
- *LTC insurance ($50 nursing home daily benefit).* The same policy as above, except that individuals buy policies only if they can afford the $50 a day indemnity benefit for nursing home care.
- *Continuing care retirement communities.* Continuing care retirement communities are modeled as comprehensive long-term care insurance mechanisms. Physically fit individuals and couples are assumed to join CCRCs if they have 130 percent of the income needed for the monthly payment and if they have enough total assets to pay the entry fee and have at least $10,000 in assets left over. Of the disabled elderly who qualify financially, half are assumed to pass health screening requirements and join. Because of the reluctance of the elderly to move, only 50 percent of qualifying individuals and couples are assumed to join CCRCs. Individuals join CCRCs at age 76.
- *Social/health maintenance organizations.* Modeled on one of the demonstration sites, the plan covers $7,500 (in 1986 dollars) of long-term care services annually. Policies are purchased if the cost is less than 5 percent of household income. Disabled persons may purchase policies. Reflecting the organizational development and enrollment barriers, only 50 percent of the elderly who can afford social/health maintenance organizations actually buy policies.
- *Individual medical accounts.* Ninety percent of individuals at the individual retirement account maximum contribute up to $1,000 a year to an individual medical account to be used exclusively for long-term care.
- *Home equity conversions.* All individuals and married couples with $25,000 or more in home equity take out a home equity loan at age 75. Repayment of the loan is postponed until after the homeowner's death, and all appreciation on the home accrues to the mortgage company.

HOME EQUITY CONVERSIONS (HECS)

Home equity conversions change the illiquid assets invested in home ownership into cash that can be used to meet long-term care or other needs. Typically, the bank makes a loan that is paid to the homeowner in monthly installments. At some time in the future, often after death, the homeowner or his heirs repay the loan with interest, using the proceeds from the sale of the house.

HECs are an attractive potential source of long-term care financing because nearly three-quarters of the older population own their homes.[36] Even among low-income elderly, about half are homeowners.[37] Most elderly homeowners have paid off their mortgages; average homeowner equity now exceeds $50,000, while few older people have liquid assets of this size.[38]

Nevertheless, obstacles to widespread use of HECs are serious. In fact, as of 1987 only about 2,000 have been written.[39] The homestead has a mythic quality in American society, and the elderly are generally unwilling to "let go" of their homes. Moreover, the home is already largely an excluded asset under medicaid. Turning to home equity conversions that use up the principal asset of the elderly to prevent medicaid from using less important assets would seem contradictory. For their part, lending institutions have been reluctant to enter into nontraditional relationships with the elderly under circumstances in which the elderly might live longer than actuarially expected. When they do, the banks must either foreclose or postpone being repaid. Banks do not like waiting to be repaid, and foreclosing on elderly widows in wheelchairs conjures up the worst possible image of bankers.

PRIVATE SECTOR SIMULATION RESULTS

Simulations using the Brookings-ICF Long-Term Care Financing Model show that private sector financing mechanisms for long-term care could grow substantially. Indeed, since as few as 600,000 elderly currently participate in the whole range of private sector approaches, there is no place to go but up. A multibillion dollar market is almost entirely untapped. Its growth is highly desirable and should be encouraged.

Nevertheless, even under generous assumptions about who would participate, private sector financing options cannot do the whole job. Figure 1-1 summarizes the assumptions we used for our simulations of the most important private sector options, and table 1-4 summarizes

TABLE 1-4. *Private Sector Approaches: Key Simulation Results for Major Options, 2016–20*[a]

Option	Percent of elderly participating[b]	Percent of total nursing home expenditures paid by option[c]	Percent change from base case medicaid nursing home expenditures[d]	Percent change from number of base case medicaid nursing home patients[e]
Private insurance				
$30, $40, or $50 nursing home benefit	45.03	11.69	−4.94	−4.52
$50 nursing home benefit	25.41	7.04	−1.18	−1.37
Continuing care retirement communities	18.24	13.68	−2.60	−2.77
Social/health maintenance organizations	26.32	10.30	−7.77	−5.59
Individual medical accounts	28.19	2.97	−1.25	−1.84
Home equity conversions	66.61	n.a.	2.02	2.39

SOURCE: Brookings-ICF Long-Term Care Financing Model.
n.a. Not available.
a. Options are independent and cannot be summed.
b. Because age at initial participation varies by option, the denominators (elderly population) are different for each option. Participation for the two long-term care insurance policies is expressed as the percent of elderly aged 67 and older. Participation in social/health maintenance organizations and individual medical accounts is the percent of elderly aged 65 and older. Continuing care retirement communities participation is the percent of elderly aged 76 and over. Home equity conversion participation is the percent of elderly aged 75 and older.
c. Total nursing home expenditures vary under each option.
d. Medicaid nursing home expenditures under the base case are $46.2 billion.
e. The number of medicaid nursing home patients under the base case is 2.34 million a year; it includes all persons who are eligible for medicaid at any time during the year.

our results. Private sector approaches are unlikely to be affordable by a majority of elderly, to finance more than a modest proportion of total nursing home and home care expenditures, or to have more than a small effect on medicaid expenditures and the number of people who spend down to medicaid financial eligibility levels. For example, by 2016–20 optimistic estimates are that private long-term care insurance aimed at older people may be affordable by 25–45 percent of the elderly, may account for 7–12 percent of total nursing home expenditures, and may reduce medicaid expenditures and the number of medicaid nursing home patients compared with the base case by 1–5 percent (table 1-4). These general conclusions also apply to individual medical accounts, continuing care retirement communities, and social/health maintenance organizations. Home equity conversions are the only option in which a substantial majority of the elderly might participate. However, while such conversions could be used to help pay for private long-term care insurance, they have limited potential, by themselves, for paying large long-term care bills directly.

Why do private sector options have so little effect? One reason involves two of the characteristics of long-term care noted earlier. The long time that might elapse between the purchase and use of long-term care insurance and the possibility of increased use rates by the insured lead insurers to reduce their risk by offering policies with only limited financial protection. People can have private insurance, for example, and still have large out-of-pocket costs.

The other reason is that private sector initiatives that offer substantial coverage are simply too expensive for most elderly. Because people who would otherwise spend down to medicaid cannot afford private options, those options cannot materially affect public expenditures. Although the financial position of the elderly will improve with time, inflation will increase the cost of long-term care coverage nearly as rapidly, lessening the prospect that comprehensive private sector financing will become much more affordable.

The problem is that improved coverage and affordability are trade-offs. Coverage improvements are likely to make products more expensive, thus reducing affordability. For example, indexing the indemnity levels to a 5 percent inflation assumption would probably increase insurance premiums at initial purchase by 30 percent to 40 percent.[40]

Public Sector Options

Although the potential market for private initiatives is large, private financing cannot stop public spending for long-term care from growing rapidly over the next three decades and beyond. The private sector can neither substantially reduce medicaid spending for long-term care nor appreciably decrease the number of people spending down to medicaid eligibility. Hence it is important to address the question: should the nation continue to finance long-term care largely with a means-tested welfare program, or should it enact a new program of social insurance?

RESTRICTING THE PUBLIC SECTOR

Some people believe that the tax burdens of the current system are already too large. They would increase family financial responsibility for medicaid nursing home patients and would convert medicaid and other long-term care programs to a block grant to the states to minimize public sector costs. These approaches would retain a welfare-based strategy and make it more difficult to obtain benefits.

Block Grants

A long-term care block grant could reduce federal financial responsibility for long-term care and provide the states with broad flexibility to design their own programs. Reducing federal payments to the states for long-term care would force them to choose between generating more revenue or cutting back on benefits. Some argue that states could avoid this choice by improving the effectiveness of service delivery, especially by substituting home care for institutional care, but there is little evidence to support this claim. Cutting back on funding for long-term care without developing an alternative source of funding seems likely to exacerbate the burdens on moderate-income elderly, a group unlikely to be able to afford private financing.

Family Responsibility

The cost of medicaid and other programs also could be held down by making the financial eligibility rules more stringent. One possibility would be to require spouses and adult children to contribute to the cost of nursing home care for medicaid patients. Medicaid patients, however, are unlikely to have especially affluent relatives, and efforts to track down possible contributors are likely to have low financial payoffs. Moreover, extending family responsibility under medicaid conflicts with the norm of adult independence, which generally holds that adults are legally, financially, and socially independent unless voluntarily joined together by marriage or responsibility for minor children.

INCREMENTAL EXPANSIONS OF THE PUBLIC SECTOR ROLE

A second set of proposals involves incremental expansion of the existing public role. Aiding family caregivers, increasing government funding for home care, and liberalizing the medicaid program are examples of this approach.

Support for Family Caregivers

Unpaid caregivers provide the vast bulk of care for the disabled elderly, and their efforts deserve support. Although tax incentives for family care would symbolize societal regard for caregivers, they would be either expensive, because a great many people would qualify, or too small to be of significant help—or both. Providing cash payments directly to caregivers under strictly limited circumstances has become an increasingly popular approach at the state and local level. Such cash subsidies can help to make life easier for unpaid providers and the disabled relatives.

Expanded Home Care

By expanding home care services, the service delivery system can more closely conform to the elderly's stated desires for care. Past efforts to expand home care at the federal level have been blocked by opponents' fears of uncontrollable costs due to increased use. But program design features, such as cost-sharing, case management, eligibility restrictions, and limits on the type or number of visits, can keep use levels reasonable. Because current public spending for home care is relatively low, substantial expansion is possible without dramatically changing aggregate long-term care expenditures.

Liberalized Medicaid

Making the means test less onerous and reimbursement rates more adequate would make life better for those elderly who have to depend on medicaid, but would retain the fundamental welfare character of the program. Desirable changes include increasing the personal needs allowance and the level of protected assets for patients and raising the amount a medicaid patient's spouse is allowed to retain for living expenses.

The principal argument for this approach is that medicaid, despite its many deficiencies, does meet the most urgent needs of the low-income disabled elderly population at minimal cost to the taxpayer. The spend-down requirements ensure that medicaid finances only the part of the care that is beyond the resources of the elderly. While targeted on the poor, medicaid also provides a safety net for middle-class people with high long-term care expenses.

Although incremental improvements in medicaid are attractive and not inconsistent with more fundamental restructuring of the public role in financing long-term care, public charity always carries some stigma, and efforts to reduce taxpayer costs are likely to perpetuate a two-class system with inferior care and status for medicaid patients. Moreover, it is an odd welfare program whose eligibility requirements are met by a majority of the people using services. In other U.S. welfare programs, such as aid to families with dependent children and supplemental security income, only a small minority of the population is expected to be financially eligible.

PUBLIC INSURANCE

The last strategy, the one we support, is to cover long-term care under a general social insurance program like medicare. This approach would provide near-universal coverage for the elderly and would explicitly recognize that using long-term care is a normal, insurable risk of growing old. Everyone should contribute to public long-term care insurance and earn the right to needed benefits without having to prove impoverishment.

Social insurance coverage should not make long-term care free, or even nearly free, to beneficiaries. Substantial cost-sharing is appropriate to control increases in service use that might occur if financing was newly available to the many disabled elderly who do not now receive paid care. Indeed, with respect to home care, limiting benefits to the severely disabled, strictly defined, would also be desirable. Under such a system, the private sector can and should play a much larger role than it does now in financing care.

Two basic approaches to public insurance should be considered. Each implies a different way of relying on the private sector. The first would provide coverage of nursing home and home care for elderly people who become disabled, but require significant cost-sharing for all users. The basic model here is the current medicare program. The role of private sector financing would be substantial but supplementary—to provide greater financial protection and services for those who desire them. The second approach would rely on a greatly expanded market for private insurance to provide long-term care coverage for a defined period (one to two years), with public insurance covering the costs of care only for nursing home and home care patients who required care for longer periods. This approach requires substantial faith in the private sector to provide the insurance to cover the one to two years of care. The federal government would provide coverage for truly catastrophic costs and retain a residual medicaid program for those who could not afford private financing. Subsidies for the purchase of private insurance for moderate- and low-income elderly would be highly desirable.

Public costs and the taxes necessary to pay for a public insurance program would be substantial, but need not be unmanageable. Figure 1-2 presents the assumptions of two prototype public insurance programs

FIGURE 1-2. **Public Insurance Strategy: Key Simulation Assumptions for Two Illustrative Options, MODCO and CATINS**

MODCO

- *Medicaid and medicare benefits.* Medicaid separate program with no improvements; medicare long-term care benefits maintained.
- *Nursing home benefits.* Unlimited coverage of skilled nursing and intermediate care facilities; deductible 100 days; coinsurance 25 percent.
- *Home care benefits.* Beneficiary must have three or more deficiencies in activities of daily living (eating, bathing, dressing, toileting, getting in and out of bed, and getting around inside); skilled and unskilled services; deductible one month; coinsurance 20 percent.
- *Reimbursement rates.* Nursing home: 115 percent of medicaid rate; home care: 115 percent of weighted average cost per visit for all noninstitutional services.

CATINS

- *Medicaid and medicare benefits.* Medicaid separate program with no improvements; medicare long-term care benefits maintained.
- *Nursing home benefits.* Unlimited coverage of skilled nursing and intermediate care facilities; deductible two years; coinsurance 10 percent.
- *Home care benefits.* Current medicare and medicaid home health benefits; no new benefits.
- *Reimbursement rates.* Nursing home: 115 percent of medicaid rate; home care: same as current rates.

that we modeled. These simulations are for illustrative purposes only and are designed to provide a range of possible costs. Assuming a 20 percent increase in nursing home use and a 50 percent increase in home care use, we estimate that the near-term (1986–90) public costs of a fully implemented public long-term care insurance would range from $33 billion to $42 billion, compared with $22 billion under current policies (table 1-5). It would require an average 2.2 percent to 2.9 percent payroll tax (no cap on taxable salaries and employer and employee contribution combined) to finance the program, compared with 1.6 percent if current public long-term care programs were financed on a payroll tax basis. The incremental tax can and should be reduced by retaining some state contributions, estate or inheritance taxes, and excise taxes.

TABLE 1-5. *Public Insurance Strategy: Simulation Results under Base Case and Two Illustrative Options, MODCO and CATINS, 1986–2050*
Billions of 1987 dollars

Option	Expenditures 1986–90	Expenditures 2016–20	Average payroll tax, 1988–2050[a]
		Total expenditures[b]	
Base case[c]	41.602	120.003	2.84
		Public expenditures	
Base case[c]	21.720	65.096	1.59
MODCO[d]	42.175	121.959	2.94
CATINS[e]	33.373	93.465	2.22

SOURCE: Brookings-ICF Long-Term Care Financing Model.
a. Represents percent of payroll with no cap on taxable salary and both employer and employee contributions.
b. All public and private expenditures for nursing home and home care. Public expenditures are medicaid, medicare, and other payers.
c. The base case projects what will happen under current programs and policy.
d. Assumes a 20 percent increase in nursing home use and expenditures and a 50 percent increase in home care use and expenditures.
e. Assumes a 20 percent increase in nursing home use and expenditures but no expansion of home care coverage and no increase in home care use.

Conclusion

Five themes emerge from this study and shape its recommendations.

First, Americans should recognize that the need for long-term care is a normal risk of growing old that needs to be anticipated. Almost all elderly are insured against hospital and physician expenses under medicare, and most carry supplemental private insurance that helps pay the costs of acute illness not covered by medicare. By contrast, long-term care is not covered to any significant extent either by medicare or by private insurance. The disabled elderly who seek long-term care must rely on their own or their families' resources or turn to welfare.

Second, risk pooling is appropriate to long-term care financing. Elderly people who are severely disabled for a long time incur costs that outstrip most families' resources. Only a minority of the elderly, however, use large amounts of paid care. Pooling the risk of high long-term care expenses through private or public insurance or some other risk-pooling mechanism provides protection against unforeseeable individual need for long-term care at a far lower cost than having each family bear the risk itself.

Third, both public and private efforts are needed to finance long-term care. A large untapped market exists for private long-term care insurance and other private initiatives. Development of that market by the private sector with encouragement from the government can and should make long-term care much more affordable for a substantial fraction of the population. However, even with maximum likely development of private options, public spending for long-term care, mostly under medicaid, will increase rapidly for the foreseeable future. It is not realistic to envision the private sector supplanting public spending.

Fourth, the primary source of public sector financing for long-term care should be a social insurance program rather than a welfare program. At present, most public spending for long-term care is treated as a form of social charity requiring severe means tests. Hospital and physician care, by contrast, is covered by social insurance to which most people contribute and from which they are entitled to draw benefits without the stigma of a means test. There is no cogent rationale for this distinction.

Fifth, private and public sector financing can fit together in a variety of ways to cover long-term care. A public insurance program could provide basic coverage with substantial cost-sharing or only catastrophic coverage for those who need care over a long period.

Chapter Two

The Model and the Base Case

The first task in evaluating alternative policies for financing long-term care was to construct a model that could be used to project the size and status of the elderly population, showing their likely numbers, by age, sex, and other characteristics; their expected use of long-term care of various sorts; and their financial resources to pay for it. With that information in hand, the cost of financing long-term care both under current policy and under new public and private financing mechanisms can be projected. The model can also estimate how new mechanisms would affect different groups in the elderly population and spending from existing private sources and public programs, such as medicaid.

This chapter first describes the Brookings-ICF Long-Term Care Financing Model. We explain the methodology in general terms (more details can be found in the Technical Appendix), highlight key assumptions, and point out some of the limitations of the model. In the second part of the chapter, we discuss the "base case," or what is likely to happen if current policies are continued. Finally, we show how the findings of the model are sensitive to different economic and demographic assumptions.

The Model

Our first objective was to construct a model of the elderly population that would project likely changes in their numbers, ages, income and assets, prevalence of disability, and so forth. To that end, we worked with ICF Incorporated to develop a computer simulation model of the older population known as the Brookings-ICF Long-Term Care Financing Model.

The model is a microsimulation model, meaning that it starts with a sample of actual people and simulates what happens to each of them. The model begins with a nationally representative sample of the adult population, with a record for each person's age, sex, income, assets, and other characteristics. It simulates changes in the population from 1986 through 2020, indicating for each person both general changes, such as in age and economic status, and changes specific to long-term care, such as the onset and recovery from disability, use of care, and method of paying for care. More aggregate projections are made through 2050.

These changes can be simulated, as in the base case, on the assumption that current public programs and private financing mechanisms remain unchanged. The changes can also be simulated assuming additional private financing, such as increased purchase of private long-term care insurance or new public financing programs. In all cases these simulations will be greatly affected by the choice of assumptions about the economic environment, such as the rate of growth of the overall economy, and human behavior, such as rates of nursing home use.

STRUCTURE OF THE MODEL

The detailed model consists of six major components.

Population data base. Using data from the Current Population Survey, the first part of the model contains information on a representative sample of adults of all ages in 1979. This 1979 data base was chosen because it contains social security earnings histories for each person in the sample.

Income simulator. Using ICF Incorporated's Pension and Retirement Income Simulation Model (PRISM), the second part of the model simulates labor force activity, marital status, income, and assets for each person. The model estimates retirement income from private sector defined-benefit pension plans, public pension plans, private sector defined-contribution plans, individual retirement accounts, and Keoghs. Using data from the Survey of Consumer Finances, the model also simulates assets, including the value of home equity.

Disability of the elderly. Using probabilities estimated primarily from the 1982 National Long-Term Care Survey and the 1977 National Nursing Home Survey, this part of the model simulates the onset of and recovery from disability for people aged 65 and over. The model does not routinely distinguish among levels of disability, although it can be adjusted to do so.

Use of long-term care services. This part of the model uses probabilities estimated primarily from the 1977 National Nursing Home Survey to simulate admission to and length of stay in a nursing home. For disabled people not in nursing homes, it also simulates use of paid home care services using probabilities derived from the 1982 National Long-Term Care Survey.

Sources and levels of payment. The next part of the model simulates the sources of payment and the level of expenditures for every person receiving either nursing home or home care services. The model incorporates the eligibility and coverage provisions of medicare and medicaid and the spend-down of persons to medicaid.

Aggregate expenditures and service use. The final part of the model accumulates medicare, medicaid, and private expenditures and service use for the simulated persons for each year.

The model uses a Monte Carlo simulation methodology to enable the computer to age this sample year by year, simulating changes in demographic, economic, and other characteristics of the older population. In the model, persons die or get older, become disabled, use home care services, enter nursing homes, use up their assets, become eligible for medicaid, and so on. The probabilities of these events happening are estimated from existing data and assumptions about future trends, such as declines in mortality rates and increases in pension income. The model simulates each of these changes in status by drawing a random number between zero and one and comparing it with the probability of that event occurring for a person with particular socioeconomic characteristics. For example, the annual probability of death for an 85-year-old woman is 0.09 (that is, nine out of every one hundred women aged 85 are expected to die each year). If the random number drawn for an 85-year-old woman in the data base is less than or equal to 0.09, she is assumed to die during that year. If the number drawn lies between 0.09 and 1.0, she is assumed to live.

ASSUMPTIONS

Because all projections depend on assumptions about future trends and behavior, it is important to keep the assumptions clearly in mind when evaluating the projections. We have tried to pick realistic assumptions about the basic factors affecting the demand and supply of long-term care and, in some cases, have explored the sensitivity of results to alternative assumptions.

Death and Disability

In general our projections are based on the Social Security Administration's mid-range mortality assumptions, called Alternative II-B. Projected mortality rates decline substantially. Disability rates are assumed to remain constant by age, sex, and marital status. Controlling for these variables, we assume that the population becomes neither sicker nor healthier.*

* There are two polar theories regarding the future health status of the elderly—compression of morbidity and mortality and expansion of morbidity. One theory, advanced by Fries, contends that morbidity will be increasingly compressed into a smaller and smaller part of life. James F. Fries, "Aging, Natural Death and the Compression of Morbidity," *New England Journal of Medicine,* July 17, 1980, pp. 130–35; and James F. Fries, "The Compression of Morbidity," *Milbank Memorial Fund Quarterly: Health and Society,* vol. 61 (Summer 1983), pp. 397–419. Citing evidence that all major organs show a linear functional decline that starts early in life and is not due to disease but to biochemical properties of senescence, he argues that these changes can lead to "natural death" without disease. In this optimistic scenario, the morbidity and mortality curves will become more rectangularly shaped as people live longer, healthier lives and then die quickly after only short periods of disability.

At the other extreme, Gruenberg and Kramer both suggest that disability levels will radically increase in the future. Ernest M. Gruenberg, "The Failures of Success," *Milbank Memorial Fund Quarterly: Health and Society,* vol. 55 (Winter 1977), pp. 3–24; and M. Kramer, "The Rising Pandemic of Mental Disorders and Associated Chronic Diseases and Disabilities," *Acta Psychiatrica Scandinavica Supplementum,* vol. 62, supplement 285 (1980), pp. 382–97. They argue that medical advances have reduced mortality but have not changed the age of onset of morbidity—a result of the medical emphasis on clinical management of diseases rather than on their prevention. This theory views medical care as "pulling people back from the grave" and leaving them in a disabled state for an extended period of time. Proponents of this theory pessimistically predict a rising "pandemic" of chronic disorders and ironically characterize that as the "failure of the success" of the medical care system.

Which of these theories accurately describes the past and predicts the future has generated a great deal of controversy. In general, the evidence is mixed and does not strongly support either a very optimistic or a very pessimistic view of the future health status of the elderly. Overall, there is little data to support the rectangularization of mortality. Rosenwaike and others report that recent mortality rates have dropped fastest for those aged 85 and older. Ira Rosenwaike, Nurit Yaffe, and Philip C. Nagi, "The Recent Decline in Mortality of the Extreme Aged: An Analysis of Statistical Data," *American Journal of Public Health,* vol. 70 (October 1980), pp. 1074–80. Their finding is inconsistent with Fries's notion that the oldest old have reached their naturally endowed lifespan, which would imply that mortality rates should drop faster for younger age groups.

Evidence is available to support both the contention that the elderly are becoming more disabled and the contention that they are becoming less disabled. On the one hand, using data from the Health Interview Survey, Colvez and Blanchet and Verbrugge found increases in disability among the aged. Alain Colvez and Madeleine Blanchet, "Disability Trends in the United States Population, 1966–1976: Analysis of Reported Causes," *American Journal of Public Health,* vol. 71 (May 1981), pp. 464–71; and Lois M. Verbrugge, "Longer Life but Worsening Health? Trends in Health and Mortality of Middle-Aged and Older Persons," *Milbank Memorial Fund Quarterly: Health and Society,*

Economic Assumptions

We also use the Alternative II-B economic assumptions, which call for moderate, steady growth in the economy and in inflation. Over the long run, the consumer price index (CPI) increases 4.0 percent a year. Real wage growth (that is, net of inflation) is 1.6 percent a year, and real growth in fringe benefits is 0.2 percent a year.

Long-Term Care Use

Another crucial assumption is the extent to which the disabled elderly actually use long-term care. In general we assume that nursing home and home care use rates remain constant by age, sex, marital status, disability, and (for home care) income. Despite recent efforts by states to cut costs by constraining the nursing home bed supply, we assume that the long-run increase in demand will be so great as to make this strategy untenable. Thus nursing home and home care supply is assumed to keep pace with demand. Since use of long-term care, especially home care, is likely to be affected by the availability of financing, we have made estimates in some places of the impact of higher use rates on the cost of financing, especially of public long-term care insurance (see chapter 16).

---

vol. 62 (Summer 1984), pp. 475–519. For example, Verbrugge found that over the period 1958 to 1980, total restricted activity days and bed disability days for the elderly population rose for both men and women.

On the other hand, Shanas found several indicators for which there were reduced disability rates between 1962 and 1975. Ethel Shanas, *National Survey of the Aged,* (OHDS) 83-2045 (Washington, D.C.: Department of Health and Human Services, December 1982), pp. 95–125. Again, using Health Interview Survey data, Palmore argues that the health of the elderly improved a fair amount between 1961–65 and 1976–81 relative to the health of all noninstitutionalized Americans. Erdman B. Palmore, "Trends in the Health of the Aged," *Gerontologist,* vol. 26 (June 1986), pp. 298–302.

After examining data on morbidity and health expenditures to assess recent trends in health status among the elderly, Poterba and Summers conclude that the historical evidence is inconsistent. James M. Poterba and Lawrence H. Summers, "Public Policy Implications of Declining Old-Age Mortality," in Gary Burtless, ed., *Work, Health, and Income among the Elderly* (Brookings, 1987), pp. 19–51. The nursing home institutionalization rate for the elderly has fallen somewhat in recent years, consistent with the notion that their health is improving. Nevertheless, the amount of medicare expenditures per person for those aged 85 and over relative to the expenditures per person for 65-year-olds has not changed. The authors interpret this as evidence that medical progress has improved the health of the elderly who would have survived under earlier higher mortality rates by about enough to offset the expected decline in health arising from the growing number of frail elderly who remain alive solely because of recent reductions in mortality.

Reimbursement Rates and Public Program Eligibility

Reflecting the heavy labor component of long-term care services, nursing home and home care reimbursement rates are assumed to increase by the consumer price index plus the Social Security Administration's projection of real wage and fringe benefit growth (in the long run, 5.8 percent a year). Adjusting for general inflation, nursing home and home care rates increase 1.8 percent a year. We assume that nursing home and home care wages and other benefits must increase at a rate comparable with that of the rest of the economy.* Public program benefits and eligibility rules are assumed to remain constant except for inflation, unless changes in public programs are explicitly being simulated.

Detailed projections are made only through 2020, a time well before the peak of the baby boom's need for long-term care. The period is sufficiently long to permit evaluation of the relative effect of different policy options.† It is not, however, adequate to develop estimates of the financing necessary to pay for various public insurance options. Thus a simple methodology was developed to extrapolate long-term care expenditures in each year through 2050. Inflation-adjusted, age-specific long-term care costs are multiplied by the number of elderly

* The cost of a unit of nursing home and home care is likely to increase faster than the overall CPI, partly because of the different inputs used and partly because of changes in the intensity of services provided (for example, staffing increases). The increase in the costs of medical care, as a rule, have been much higher than the general inflation. Between 1975 and 1985 the average yearly percentage change in the medical care component of the CPI was 10.3 percent, compared with 8.2 percent for the overall CPI, a difference of 2.1 percentage points. U.S. Bureau of the Census, *Statistical Abstract of the United States, 1987* (Washington, D.C.: Department of Commerce, 1987), table 775. Longitudinal data on the overall price of nursing home and home care are not available. However, in their mid-range projections of the long-run costs of the medicare program, Health Care Financing Administration actuaries assume that the cost of skilled nursing facilities and home health agencies will increase at least 2.5 percent and 3.0 percent a year, respectively, faster than the CPI. *1986 Annual Report of the Board of Trustees of the Federal Hospital Insurance Trust Fund,* pp. 67–68. The cost increases for nursing homes and home care agencies that provide less medically intense services would probably be somewhat lower.

† Longer-range projections were not done, for both practical and conceptual reasons. As a practical matter, the model "ages" the adult population in 1979, and after 2020 there is virtually no one left in the sample to turn age 65. Results after 2020 would be incomplete. Conceptually, uncertainty about income, inflation, mortality, disability, and long-term care use rates over the next thirty-four years is already great; uncertainty is considerably larger over the next sixty-four years. Thus we did not feel comfortable making detailed projections over the longer time period. A feeling for what would happen after 2020, however, can be gleaned by examining the results for the early baby boom cohort, which will be aged 65–74 during 2016–20.

in each age category for each year through 2050. To estimate payroll taxes required to finance various programs, we projected total payroll by multiplying inflation-adjusted data on wages and salaries by the number of projected workers in various age and sex categories for each year through 2050. To estimate the additional personal income tax required to finance various programs, we assumed that federal income tax revenues increased in accordance with the Alternative II-B assumption about real wage growth.

POSSIBLE SOURCES OF ERROR

The model's projections could be wrong for many reasons. One obvious source of error is that the economic environment of the future—income levels, inflation, and so forth—could turn out to be quite different from that assumed in the model. Individual behavior—death and disability rates, use of nursing homes, and so forth—could also turn out to be at variance with our estimates.

For some estimates it was necessary to rely on relatively old data, such as the 1977 National Nursing Home Survey. In other instances, we had to use cross-sectional data, such as the 1982 National Long-Term Care Survey, to make estimates of longitudinal probabilities, always a problematical set of inferences. In other cases, quite arbitrary assumptions were made because little basis existed for estimating responses to major change, such as the response of long-term care supply to substantial increases in demand or the sensitivity of use rates to new financing initiatives.

While much uncertainty exists, the model provides for the first time a way of projecting simultaneously many characteristics of the older population that will affect their need for and use of long-term care, together with the financial resources likely to be available to them to pay for it. It provides a way of comparing the costs and effects of different schemes on a consistent basis. These comparisons can provide insight into the relative advantages and disadvantages of various financing approaches even if some economic or behavioral assumptions prove invalid.

One of the advantages of this type of simulation model is that it is possible to change many of the assumptions of the model and investigate the sensitivity of the results to alternative assumptions. Changing economic assumptions, for example, is quite easy; changing behavioral characteristics, such as use rates, is somewhat more difficult, but still feasible.* It is our hope that this model will prove a flexible tool for those interested in long-term care financing and that the model can be used to analyze the effects of alternative assumptions and of other policy instruments, both public and private.

A GUIDE TO INTERPRETING THE SIMULATIONS

In interpreting the results from the simulations, several features of the model must be kept in mind. First, all tables present information only on the elderly population. Nursing home and home care expenditures and use for the nonelderly population are not included, nor are expenditures and use by residents of intermediate care facilities for the mentally retarded. Second, all expenditures in *constant 1987 dollars* are adjusted to eliminate the effect of general inflation but not the extra increase in costs of nursing home wages and fringe benefits. Nominal amounts would be dramatically higher. Third, most tables are presented for the time period 2016–20. This period, which is the latest to which the full model projects, presents the option being analyzed in a relatively mature period and takes advantage of the projected increased income of the elderly between 1986 and 2020.

Two types of tables are presented. The first gives overall long-term care expenditures by source of financing and number of medicaid beneficiaries averaged over a five-year period (for example, 2016, 2017, 2018, 2019, and 2020). The results can be conceived as the annual experience for the midpoint year (in this case, 2018). The second type disaggregates expenditures by social and economic characteristics and presents the data on an "admission cohort" basis for the entire length of stay in a nursing home or use of home care. In other words, it identifies all people who started using long-term care services during

* There are several reasons for the difficulty in simulating moral hazard. First, source of payment for nursing home care is derived only after the person has entered the nursing home. Second, in the model a person's chance of dying partly depends on whether he or she is admitted to a nursing home. More admissions to nursing homes would result in higher overall mortality rates, a result that is not likely. Third, as explained elsewhere, this inability to explore fully the effects of moral hazard is only a minor problem for evaluating private sector options (see chapter 3). For public sector options, where assumptions about moral hazard are critical, hand calculations of model output allow us to take increased use into account. Fourth, while all assumptions in the model are theoretically changeable, in practice some assumptions are easier to change than others. Computer time necessary to run the model makes changes in mortality, wages, and nursing home use relatively difficult, while changes in medicare and medicaid program rules, nursing home and home care inflation, and private and public sector financing mechanisms are relatively easy to do.

TABLE 2-1. *Average Annual Number of Elderly, by Age, Selected Periods, 1986–2020*
Millions

Age group	1986–90		2001–05		2016–20	
	Number	Percent	Number	Percent	Number	Percent
65–74	17.494	55.9	17.810	48.2	28.442	56.6
75–84	10.315	32.9	13.277	35.9	14.577	29.0
85 and over	3.492	11.2	5.864	15.9	7.234	14.4
TOTAL	31.302	100.0	36.952	100.0	50.253	100.0

SOURCE: Brookings-ICF Long-Term Care Financing Model. Figures are rounded.

a specific five-year period (for example, 2016–20) and follows them until they are discharged from the nursing home or stop using home care services. Their expenditures are totaled for each day they use nursing home or home care. For example, for persons who stay in a nursing home for four years, this second type of table aggregates their expenditures for all four years, not just for one year. Thus expenditures for long-stay patients are more dominant in the second set of tables than they are in the first.

The Base Case

The base case projects what will happen if there are no changes in the way long-term care services are organized, used, and reimbursed. Alternative financing options discussed in subsequent chapters are compared with what will happen under this scenario.

DEMOGRAPHIC AND ECONOMIC CHARACTERISTICS OF THE ELDERLY

There will be more elderly people in the future, especially more aged 85 and over (table 2-1). The number of elderly is projected to grow from 31.3 million in 1986–90 to 50.3 million in 2016–20, an increase of 61 percent. The number of elderly aged 85 and over is projected to grow from 3.5 million in 1986–90 to 7.2 million in 2016–20, an increase of 106 percent. That remarkable increase is partly a result of expected large decreases in mortality rates for this age group. Higher mortality rates than assumed would reduce the projected number of people surviving to age 85 and beyond.

The financial position of the elderly as reflected in their income and assets should improve markedly by 2020. Family income is defined here

TABLE 2-2. *Median Annual Family Income, by Age, Selected Periods, 1986–2020*[a]
1987 dollars

Age group	1986–90	2001–05	2016–20
65–74	10,806	15,795	23,203
75–84	8,657	9,364	14,956
85 and over	6,837	6,697	7,999
TOTAL	9,314	10,902	17,210

SOURCE: Brookings-ICF Long-Term Care Financing Model.
a. Family income is joint income for married persons and individual income for unmarried persons. Income sources are social security, pensions, supplemental security income, individual retirement accounts, wages, and asset earnings.

as joint income for married persons and individual income for single persons. It does not include income of family members with whom the elderly might reside. People in nursing homes and those without any income or assets are excluded from most published Census and other data, but are included in our figures.

The median income of the elderly in constant 1987 dollars is projected to almost double, from $9,314 in 1986–90 to $17,210 in 2016–20 (table 2-2). That jump is due both to projected substantial growth in the number of families receiving pensions and to projected higher pension, social security, and asset income. Consistent with the improved financial position of the elderly, the number of families receiving supplemental security income payments will decline.

Total income growth is greatest for the 65- to 74-year-old age group, conspicuously less for the 85-and-older age group. Moreover, the income disparity between the young-old and old-old grows over time. People who will be in the oldest age group in 2016–20 were already aged at least 51 in 1986 and are least likely to benefit from improved pension availability, individual retirement accounts, or increased labor force participation by women. This income discrepancy is important because the oldest age group has the highest rates of nursing home and home care use.

Conversely, the baby boom population may be much better off financially than earlier cohorts when it reaches age 85 because of higher earning histories and better pension coverage. To the extent that this is true, the baby boom cohort may be better able to afford private long-term care financing mechanisms and to pay for long-term care out-of-pocket. However, this projected increased income must be viewed with caution. Almost all the work histories of the baby boom population are simulated rather than based on actual experience, making

TABLE 2-3. *Median Family Assets, by Age and Asset Type, Selected Periods, 1986–2020*[a]
1987 dollars

Age group	1986–90	2001–05	2016–20
		Total assets	
65–74	67,764	77,492	94,449
75–84	52,106	65,020	73,300
85 and over	40,143	51,420	56,410
TOTAL	59,230	66,268	79,050
		Housing assets	
65–74	42,643	47,381	50,347
75–84	29,611	46,194	47,381
85 and over	17,764	35,527	42,640
TOTAL	35,532	45,400	47,383
		Financial assets	
65–74	20,840	27,292	40,227
75–84	9,473	16,952	21,372
85 and over	6,425	5,210	8,634
TOTAL	13,799	18,094	26,518

SOURCE: Brookings-ICF Long-Term Care Financing Model.
a. Includes families without assets.

the results highly dependent on the Social Security Administration's assumptions about real wage growth. A recent study of the baby boom population suggests that those assumptions about real wage growth may be too optimistic.[1]

Assets of the elderly are also expected to grow over the next three decades (table 2-3). Including families with no housing or financial assets, median total assets for the elderly are projected to grow from $59,230 in 1986–90 to $79,050 in 2016–20 in constant 1987 dollars. For all age groups, home equity accounts for the majority of assets.

LONG-TERM CARE USE

Older people will use more long-term care in the future because many more will be living to ages at which use rates for long-term care are high (table 2-4).* The number of elderly in nursing homes at any time during the year is projected to increase 76 percent, from 2.3 million

* Unlike most estimates of use, which count the number of people in nursing homes on a given day, these figures report the total number of people using nursing home or home care at any time during the year. Thus our estimates include many short-stay nursing home and home care patients who are underrepresented in "snapshot" cross-sectional counts. For a further discussion on measuring use, see Korbin Liu and Yuko Palesch, "The Nursing Home Population: Different Perspectives and Implications for Policy," *Health Care Financing Review,* vol. 3 (December 1981), pp. 15–23.

TABLE 2-4. *Average Annual Nursing Home and Home Care Populations, by Age, Selected Periods, 1986–2020*[a]
Millions

Age group	1986–90		2001–05		2016–20	
	Number	Percent	Number	Percent	Number	Percent
			Elderly in nursing homes			
65–74	0.404	17.7	0.390	11.9	0.659	16.4
75–84	0.913	40.0	1.216	37.2	1.295	32.2
85 and over	0.968	42.4	1.666	50.9	2.067	51.4
TOTAL	2.285	100.0	3.272	100.0	4.021	100.0
			Elderly using home care			
65–74	1.235	30.8	1.306	24.2	1.840	28.9
75–84	1.715	42.8	2.295	42.7	2.330	36.6
85 and over	1.059	26.4	1.803	33.4	2.190	34.4
TOTAL	4.009	100.0	5.404	100.0	6.359	100.0

SOURCE: Brookings-ICF Long-Term Care Financing Model. Figures are rounded.
a. Persons in a nursing home or using home care services at any time during the year.

in 1986–90 to 4.0 million in 2016–20, compared with a 61 percent increase in the overall number of elderly. The average age of elderly nursing home residents will also increase. The proportion of nursing home residents aged 85 and older will rise from 42 percent in 1986–90 to 51 percent in 2016–20.

As with nursing home care, the home care estimates are for the total number of users during the course of the year. They also include all elderly medicare home health users, including those who are not chronically disabled. The number of home care users is projected to rise from 4.0 million in 1986–90 to 6.4 million in 2016–20, an increase of 60 percent. As with nursing homes patients, the proportion of home care users 85 and older increases over time.

LONG-TERM CARE EXPENDITURES

Consistent with the expected increases in use, total long-term care expenditures will rise substantially from $41.6 billion in 1986–90 to $120.0 billion in 2016–20 in constant 1987 dollars (table 2-5). Assuming a 5.8 percent annual nursing home and home care inflation rate, nursing home expenditures for all elderly are estimated to increase from $33.0 billion in 1986–90 to $98.1 billion (in constant 1987 dollars) in 2016–20 (table 2-5). While the number of nursing home patients is projected to less than double, total nursing home expenditures are projected to triple. Thus nursing home cost increases in excess of general inflation

TABLE 2-5. *Total Expenditures for Nursing Home and Home Care, by Source of Payment, Selected Periods, 1986–2020*[a]
Billions of 1987 dollars

Payment source	1986–90	2001–05	2016–20	Percent increase, 1986–90 to 2016–20
Nursing homes				
Medicaid	14.129	30.732	46.192	227
Medicare	0.602	1.012	1.612	168
Patients' cash income	10.675	16.075	27.888	161
Patients' assets	7.576	13.079	22.423	196
TOTAL	32.982	60.901	98.117	197
Home care				
Medicaid	1.223	1.644	2.385	95
Medicare	3.097	4.919	7.699	149
Other payers[b]	2.669	4.741	7.208	170
Out-of-pocket payment	1.630	3.132	4.593	182
TOTAL	8.620	14.435	21.886	154

SOURCE: Brookings-ICF Long-Term Care Financing Model. Figures are rounded.

a. Average annual expenditures. Nursing home and home care inflation is assumed to be 5.8 percent a year. General inflation is assumed to be 4.0 percent a year; long-term care inflation in excess of general inflation is assumed to be 1.8 percent a year.

b. Other payers include state and local expenditures, social services block grants, Older Americans Act and Veterans Administration home care funds, charity, and out-of-pocket expenditures by persons other than the service recipient.

are as responsible for rising expenditures as are the size and age composition of the elderly population.

Medicare and medicaid account for 49 percent of total nursing home expenditures in 2016–20, up slightly from 1986–90, with cash income and assets accounting for the balance. Despite the overall increase in the income and assets of the elderly, medicaid expenditures increase even faster than total expenditures. The reason is that the cost of the nursing home care increases faster than income for people aged 85 and older, who will make up an increasing proportion of the nursing home population. Indeed, in relation to the cost of nursing home care, the elderly aged 85 and older in 2016–20 will be financially worse off than they are now.

For those people who enter a nursing home, out-of-pocket expenditures will average over $29,000 in constant 1987 dollars for the entire stay by 2016–20 (table 2-6). Over half of all nursing home patients will pay more than $5,000 out of income and assets; almost a fifth will pay more than $50,000. For highest-income groups, who finance almost all their own care out of income and assets, average nursing home out-of-pocket costs exceed $59,000.

Home care expenditures are expected to increase from $8.6 billion

TABLE 2-6. *Out-of-Pocket Expenditures for Nursing Home Care, by Demographic and Income Groups, Assets, and Length of Stay, 2016–20*

Category	Average payments (1987 dollars)	Patients with payments over $5,000 (percent)	Patients with payments over $25,000 (percent)	Patients with payments over $50,000 (percent)
Total out-of-pocket	29,224	54.4	28.1	17.1
Age				
65–74	37,580	59.6	33.3	23.4
75–84	29,923	56.6	31.2	17.9
85 and over	24,754	50.3	23.4	13.7
Sex and marital status				
Male	36,749	61.8	36.0	21.8
Married	48,511	68.2	45.0	28.9
Unmarried	29,618	58.0	30.5	17.5
Female	25,333	50.8	24.3	14.9
Married	32,961	64.0	34.7	22.6
Unmarried	23,395	47.7	21.9	13.1
Family income[a]				
Under 7,500	8,520	33.3	6.9	2.6
7,500–14,999	22,507	61.0	32.0	13.7
15,000–19,999	34,465	65.7	37.7	22.7
20,000–29,999	42,619	66.7	41.4	28.2
30,000–39,999	59,840	74.8	50.0	39.8
40,000–49,999	66,054	74.4	53.8	38.5
50,000 and over	59,533	63.5	43.9	36.5
Assets[b]				
Under 15,000	11,246	39.3	10.7	4.1
15,000–49,999	28,177	68.4	39.8	18.0
50,000 and over	55,580	68.8	47.7	36.6
Length of stay (months)				
1 or less	1,435	0.0	0.0	0.0
1–2	3,529	34.1	0.0	0.0
2–3	5,779	61.4	0.0	0.0
3–12	14,299	71.2	22.9	0.0
12–24	32,414	78.4	50.0	38.1
24–36	51,409	84.5	56.0	44.0
36–48	66,756	90.7	69.5	50.0
48–60	69,516	85.2	64.2	39.5
60 or more	106,959	94.8	80.2	60.5

SOURCE: Brookings-ICF Long-Term Care Financing Model. Figures are rounded.

a. Family income is joint income for married persons, individual income for unmarried persons. Income sources are social security, private pensions, supplemental security income, individual retirement accounts, wages, and asset sources.

b. Assets exclude home equity.

TABLE 2-7. *Total and Public Expenditures for Long-Term Care as a Percentage of Gross National Product, Total Payroll, and Total Federal Personal Income Tax, Selected Periods, 1988–2050*[a]

Period	Total expenditures as percent of: GNP	Total expenditures as percent of: Total payroll	Total expenditures as percent of: Income tax	Public expenditures as percent of: GNP	Public expenditures as percent of: Total payroll	Public expenditures as percent of: Income tax
1988–90	0.87	1.59	10.02	0.45	0.83	5.23
2001–05	1.17	1.91	11.95	0.62	1.02	6.35
2016–20	1.42	2.48	14.51	0.78	1.36	7.95
2026–30	1.72	3.18	17.97	0.94	1.74	9.85
2036–40	2.12	4.06	23.19	1.21	2.32	13.23
2046–50	2.32	4.67	26.35	1.42	2.87	16.18
1988–2050	1.55	2.84	16.63	0.87	1.59	9.31

SOURCES: Brookings-ICF Long-Term Care Financing Model; and U.S. Congressional Budget Office, *Economic and Budget Outlook: An Update* (Washington, D.C., August 1987), p. 38. Figures are rounded.

a. Percentages shown are average annual percentages. The GNP figures assume a 2 percent real annual growth rate. Public expenditures include medicare, medicaid, and (for home care) other payers.

in 1986–90 to $21.9 billion in constant 1987 dollars in 2016–20 (table 2-5). Medicare and medicaid account for approximately half of all home care expenditures; out-of-pocket payments account for approximately one-fifth; and other payers account for a bit less than a third. Other payers include state and local expenditures, charity, social services block grant funds, Veterans Administration programs, Older Americans Act funds, and out-of-pocket expenditures by persons other than the service recipient.

While expenditures will be growing, so will the U.S. economy (table 2-7). In general, between 1988–90 and 2046–50 the financial burden of long-term care as a percentage of gross national product, total payroll (wages plus salaries), or federal personal income tax will roughly triple. For example, total long-term care expenditures as a share of GNP will increase from about 0.87 percent in 1988–90 to 2.32 percent in 2046–50. Similarly, public expenditures will increase from about 0.45 percent of GNP in 1988–90 to 1.42 percent in 2046–50. Although this increase will clearly strain public and private resources, the burden does not appear unsupportable, at least from an economic perspective.

EXPENDITURES BY SOCIODEMOGRAPHIC GROUPS

Total and medicaid nursing home expenditures are heavily concentrated among the unmarried, women, and the 85-and-over age group (table 2-8). Total nursing home expenditures are also concentrated among people with relatively modest means. By 2016–20 two-thirds of total nursing home expenditures will be for people whose family

TABLE 2-8. *Total and Medicaid Expenditures for Nursing Home Care, by Demographic and Income Groups, and Length of Stay, 2016–20*[a]
Billions of 1987 dollars

Category	Total expenditures		Medicaid expenditures	
	Amount	Percent of total	Amount	Percent of total
Total share	100.231	100.0	47.557	100.0
Age				
65–74	19.291	19.2	5.683	11.9
75–84	35.152	35.1	15.698	33.0
85 and over	45.788	45.7	26.176	55.0
Sex and marital status				
Male	33.528	33.4	11.104	23.3
Married	16.676	16.6	5.540	11.6
Unmarried	16.852	16.8	5.564	11.7
Female	66.704	66.6	36.453	76.6
Married	12.717	12.7	4.821	10.1
Unmarried	53.987	53.9	31.632	66.5
Family income (dollars)[b]				
Under 7,500	30.510	30.4	25.249	53.1
7,500–14,999	24.795	24.7	14.123	29.7
15,000–19,999	10.636	10.6	3.850	8.1
20,000–29,999	12.635	12.6	3.185	6.7
30,000–39,999	8.012	8.0	0.793	1.7
40,000–49,999	4.998	5.0	0.202	0.4
50,000 and over	8.645	8.6	0.155	0.3
Length of stay (months)				
1 or less	0.878	0.9	0.078	0.2
1–2	1.122	1.1	0.195	0.4
2–3	0.949	0.9	0.220	0.5
3–12	8.878	8.8	2.806	5.9
12–36	22.746	22.6	9.795	20.6
36–60	27.879	27.8	14.759	31.0
60 or more	37.780	37.7	19.704	41.4

SOURCE: Brookings-ICF Long-Term Care Financing Model. Figures are rounded.

a. Five-year average of total nursing home expenditures for entire stays with 5.8 percent annual inflation of nursing home per diem charges. Expenditures are net of general inflation. These data are based on the total payments for an admission cohort over the entire length of their stays in a nursing home. For example, for a person who is admitted to a nursing home in 2016–20 for a two-year stay, we totaled two years worth of nursing home expenditures. We then calculated the proportion of those expenditures paid by medicaid.

b. Family income is joint income for married persons, individual income for unmarried persons.

incomes are projected to be less than $20,000. Fully 30 percent of total expenditures will be for people with family incomes of $7,500 or less. Because very elderly widows, who are the main users of long-term care, have quite low income and assets, this finding is not surprising.

Although most nursing home patients stay only a fairly short time, nursing home expenditures are heavily concentrated among long-stay patients. While 66 percent of total nursing home expenditures in 2016–20 are for nursing home patients who stay three years or more, only 20 percent of patients stay that long. As a result, financing and organizational options for reform that aim to affect the bulk of nursing home expenditures must concentrate on patients with long lengths of stay.

Medicaid expenditures exhibit the same general pattern, but are skewed even more strongly toward the 85-and-older age group, unmarried women, those with long lengths of stay, and the low-income population. As would be expected for a means-tested welfare program, over half of all medicaid expenditures in 2016–20 are for the elderly with family incomes of $7,499 or less; 83 percent are for elderly with family incomes of $14,999 or below. While some medicaid nursing home patients may have been middle class when they were working or when they first retired, may be psychologically middle class, or may have middle-class children, they are likely to have very modest incomes by the time they enter nursing homes.

Sensitivity Analyses

By using alternative assumptions, the model can show how sensitive the results are to the assumptions chosen. Three key assumptions regarding long-term care financing concern the nursing home and home care inflation rate, the proportion of the elderly with disabilities, and the overall growth in the economy.

NURSING HOME AND HOME CARE INFLATION

Nursing home and home care expenditures are very sensitive to the projected long-term care inflation rate. Using a 4.4 percent or a 7.2 percent annual nursing home inflation rate produces expenditure levels that are substantially different from that produced with a 5.8 percent inflation rate (table 2-9). Indeed, subtracting general inflation, under a 7.2 percent annual nursing home inflation rate, total expenditures are more than twice what they would be under the 4.4 percent inflation assumption in 2016–20. At that time medicaid expenditures under the high-inflation assumption will be almost four times as large as those under the low-inflation assumption.

Lowering nursing home and home care inflation will not be easy. Long-term care is extremely labor intensive, and so much of it involves hands-on, personal services that opportunities for substantial productivity gains are probably few. Thus reducing nursing home inflation to a rate that approximates the consumer price index would mean substantially reducing wages of nursing home employees relative to

TABLE 2-9. *Expenditures for Nursing Home Care, by Source of Payment under High and Low Inflation Assumptions, Selected Periods, 1986–2020*[a]
Billions of 1987 dollars

Payment source	1986–90	2001–05	2016–20	Percent increase, 1986–90 to 2016–20
		7.2 percent inflation assumption		
Medicaid	14.582	41.871	84.131	477
Medicare	0.609	1.251	2.426	298
Patients' cash income	10.672	15.861	26.780	151
Patients' assets	7.766	15.994	32.026	312
TOTAL	33.630	74.980	145.366	332
		4.4 percent inflation assumption		
Medicaid	13.680	22.154	23.597	72
Medicare	0.594	0.817	1.065	79
Patients' cash income	10.692	16.122	27.154	154
Patients' assets	7.378	10.272	14.277	94
TOTAL	32.345	49.367	66.095	104

SOURCE: Brookings-ICF Long-Term Care Financing Model. Figures are rounded.
a. Average annual expenditures. Expenditures are net of general inflation.

the rest of the work force. It is doubtful that people could be recruited to work for such low wages, and quality of care could be adversely affected. Indeed, advocates for improving the quality of care argue that nursing home employees need to be better trained and more highly paid than they are now.[2] Moreover, some evidence suggests that nursing home patients have become more disabled over time, and the new medicare hospital prospective payment system should accentuate that trend by encouraging earlier discharge of sicker patients from hospitals to nursing homes and home care.[3] As a result, staffing levels and their associated costs will most likely increase in order to cope with these more disabled patients.

DISABILITY RATES

A key variable in determining the future demand and cost of long-term care services is the health of the future elderly. Will they live longer but more disabled lives? Or will they live increasingly healthy lives? The evidence is unclear.

To assess the effect of varying disability rates on long-term care expenditures and use, three different scenarios were simulated. Under the high-disability scenario, elderly disability rates increase at the same rate that Alternative II-B mortality rates decline.* In this scenario,

* The methodology for performing this analysis was as follows. The average percentage

TABLE 2-10. *Expenditures for Long-Term Care under Different Disability Assumptions, 2016–20*[a]
Billions of 1987 dollars

Assumption	Total long-term care	Nursing home care	Home care
High disability rates	149.951	120.853	29.098
Constant disability rates	120.003	98.117	21.886
Low disability rates	92.805	73.977	18.828
	Percent change from constant disability rates		
High disability rates	24.9	23.2	33.0
Low disability rates	−22.7	−24.6	−14.0

SOURCE: Brooking-ICF Long-Term Care Financing Model. Figures are rounded.
a. Average annual expenditures. Expenditures are net of general inflation.

people live longer but more disabled lives. Under a no-change disability scenario (base case), disability rates remain constant on the basis of age, sex, and marital status. In this scenario, people will live longer but will face no higher risk of disability at a given age. Under a low-disability scenario, disability rates decline at the same rate that mortality rates decline.* In this scenario, people will live longer and less disabled lives.

The effects of varying the disability rates are significant, but expenditures and use of services increase substantially even under the more optimistic assumptions. The low-disability assumptions result in total long-term care expenditures 38 percent less than those of the high-disability scenario (table 2-10). But even with the low-disability assumptions, long-term care expenditures by 2016–20 are projected to be more than double those in 1986–90.[4] In the low-disability scenario the total number of people who use nursing homes and home care in 2016–20 is lower by 31 percent than in the total high-disability scenario (table 2-11). Home care use and expenditures are less strongly affected by different disability assumptions because some medicare home care use is by people who are not chronically disabled.

change in mortality for individuals in each of the sex and five-year age groups is calculated on the basis of Social Security Administration Alternative II projections. Because the mortality improvements are provided by single year of age, a weighted average of the mortality changes for the five-year age groups is calculated. Weighted percentage change is calculated separately for each year through 2025. These weighted average percentage changes are then applied to the disability prevalence rates to generate a new set of disability rates for each year between 1985 and 2025. These percentage changes are applied uniformly to both married and unmarried persons within each age and sex group.

* The same methodology as for the higher-disability scenario is used.

TABLE 2-11. *Number of Elderly Using Long-Term Care Services under Different Disability Assumptions, 2016–20*[a]
Millions

Assumption	Total long-term care	Nursing home care	Home care
High disability rates	12.90	5.02	7.88
Constant disability rates	10.38	4.02	6.36
Low disability rates	8.91	3.03	5.88
	Percent change from constant disability rates		
High disability rates	24.2	24.9	23.9
Low disability rates	−14.2	−24.6	−7.5

SOURCE: Brookings-ICF Long-Term Care Financing Model. Figures are rounded.
a. All nursing home and home care users during the course of the year.

GROWTH IN THE ECONOMY

Although the number of disabled elderly likely to use long-term care will grow dramatically by 2050, the economy will grow as well. The financial burden of long-term care will largely depend on how fast it grows (table 2-12). Under a low-growth assumption (1 percent real growth a year), total long-term care expenditures increase from 0.89 percent of GNP in 1988–90 to 4.22 percent in 2046–50, almost a fivefold increase. In contrast, under a high-growth assumption (3 percent real growth a year), total long-term care expenditures grow from 0.85

TABLE 2-12. *Total and Public Expenditures for Long-Term Care as a Percentage of Gross National Product, by Different Growth Rates, Selected Periods, 1988–2050*[a]
Percent of GNP

Period	Total expenditures			Public expenditures[b]		
	Low growth[c]	Medium growth[d]	High growth[e]	Low growth[c]	Medium growth[d]	High growth[e]
1988–90	0.89	0.87	0.85	0.46	0.45	0.45
2001–05	1.37	1.17	1.00	0.73	0.62	0.53
2016–20	1.92	1.42	1.05	1.05	0.78	0.57
2026–30	2.57	1.72	1.15	1.41	0.94	0.63
2036–40	3.51	2.12	1.29	2.00	1.21	0.73
2046–50	4.22	2.32	1.28	2.59	1.42	0.78
1988–2050	2.28	1.55	1.09	1.28	0.87	0.61

SOURCES: Brookings-ICF Long-Term Care Financing Model; and CBO, *Economic and Budget Outlook*, p. 38.
a. Percentages shown are averages of annual percentages.
b. Public expenditures include medicaid, medicare, and (for home care) other payers.
c. Low growth is 1 percent real growth in GNP a year.
d. Medium growth is 2 percent real growth in GNP a year.
e. High growth is 3 percent real growth in GNP a year.

percent of GNP in 1988–90 to 1.28 percent in 2046–50, barely a 50 percent increase. High economic growth rates could minimize the burden of increased expenditures for long-term care.

Conclusion

Future long-term care use and expenditures for the elderly will be influenced by the aging of the population, changing mortality rates, public and private financing sources, disability rates, use patterns, income and asset levels, health services inflation, and many other variables. The interaction of these forces will determine the social costs of long-term care over the next thirty years and beyond. The Brookings-ICF Long-Term Care Financing Model simulates that interaction to permit assessment of a variety of financing options.

The base case and the sensitivity analyses indicate that long-term care expenses will impose an increasing burden on society despite continued economic growth. Indeed, the base case is discouraging for those who had hoped that rising future incomes would make it easier for the elderly to afford long-term care. Although the income and assets of the elderly will increase substantially in the future, the increase in income for the 85-and-older population will be far less than that for younger elderly cohorts. Since long-term care costs will almost surely rise faster than the general price level, people in that age group may be less able to cover the cost of nursing home and home care in the future then they are now. The analysis also shows that, through 2020, increasing costs of long-term care will probably be at least as important in causing a growth in real expenditures as will the growing number of elderly.

PART 2
Private Sector Strategies for Reform

Chapter Three

Introduction to Private Sector Strategies

Interest in private sector approaches to financing long-term care is fairly new but has grown substantially over the last six years. Although still in their infancy, private sector approaches tend to dominate current public policy discussions of long-term care reform. These initiatives are of two sorts. Some options, such as individual medical accounts and home equity conversions, encourage people to save or to use their assets in new ways to pay for their own long-term care needs. Other options, such as private long-term care insurance, continuing care retirement communities, and social/health maintenance organizations, pool the costs associated with long-term care over a broad population, most of whom will never incur substantial long-term care expenditures. Thus the risk pooling reduces the cost of long-term care to any one person.

Despite considerable public policy, media, and academic interest in private sector approaches, they are only a tiny part of current long-term care financing. In all, less than 2 percent of the elderly participate in any private long-term care financing mechanism. There are about 400,000 people with private long-term care insurance; 150,000 in continuing care retirement communities; 15,000 in social/health maintenance organizations; 2,000 with home equity conversions; and no one contributing to individual medical accounts.[1]

Reasons for Interest in Private Sector Financing

Private sector approaches are appealing because they reflect the American tradition of individuals taking responsibility for their own lives.* The classic virtue of the competitive private market is that it has the flexibility to adapt to individual needs and wants and to local conditions. Moreover, private sector approaches potentially offer the happy combination of reducing both catastrophic health care costs for the elderly and medicaid outlays at the same time. All other things being equal, Americans usually prefer private to public programs. Some advocates contend that the private sector is more likely to do a better job than the public sector in controlling costs.[2] Yet despite these attractions, earlier studies of long-term care financing options never gave serious consideration to the idea of a major role for the private sector initiatives.[3] In those studies the "private sector" was limited to out-of-pocket expenditures. Why is there now such strong interest in private sector alternatives?

One reason is that the Reagan revolution, ideologically, and the large federal budget deficits, practically, have made large-scale increases in public programs difficult to enact, at least for the next few years. The expected large increases in spending for long-term care under existing programs strongly clash with the generally tight fiscal constraints at all levels of government.[4] How to obtain the money to pay for the increasing costs of long-term care is now the dominant public policy issue.

This assessment of the limits of the public role has led many to look for alternative sources of financing. Advocates of private sector solutions argue that if middle- or upper-class medicaid nursing home patients could purchase insurance or accumulate enough additional assets, both their impoverishment and their medicaid expenditures on nursing homes could be avoided. A key question about private sector approaches is whether they can reach far enough down the income distribution to include the people who would otherwise spend down to medicaid (that is, use up their incomes and assets) and incur substantial public expenditures.

A second reason for the interest in private sector approaches is that the financial position of the elderly has improved markedly over the last twenty years. Historically the elderly have been disproportionately poor; in 1966 their poverty rate was 28.5 percent, compared with 14.7 percent for the total population.[5] Thus private sector financing mech-

* There are, of course, other American traditions. Government has been used to promote transportation, help the development of industry, protect the family farm, and provide a wide variety of arrangements for personal security.

anisms that required substantial out-of-pocket payments for insurance premiums, for example, were simply out of the question.

Controlling for different factors, most evidence suggests that the elderly are now roughly as well off as the rest of the population. The poverty rate of the elderly declined to 12.6 percent in 1985, a figure comparable to that for the nonelderly.* Danzinger and others found that after adjustments are made for the lower tax rates, the availability of asset income, and living arrangements, the elderly on average have about 90 percent of the income of the nonelderly.[6] Hurd and Shoven found that between 1970 and 1980 the real incomes of the elderly increased faster than the incomes of the rest of the population.[7] Most forecasts of income of the elderly project an improved financial position.[8] Our own projections suggest that the real median income of the elderly will almost double between now and 2020. In addition, many elderly have substantial assets, most often in the form of home equity; even among the poor, about one-half of low-income elderly are homeowners.[9] Although few elderly are rich, a significant number are clearly quite well off financially. Thus it is now plausible to argue that private sector financing of long-term care might be affordable for the majority of the elderly.

The interest in private sector approaches to long-term care comes from many groups, with their own distinct goals and expectations. There are ideological conservatives for whom it is axiomatic that the private sector does things better than the public sector. There are liberals who hope that by getting the middle class off the medicaid rolls and allowing the program to focus on the "truly needy," public support of programs for the poor will increase. The liberals also despair of the current unwillingess of people to pay higher taxes and hope that private funds can be used to develop an improved delivery system. There are elderly advocates trying to protect the dignity and assets of the middle class from pauperization. There are government officials desperately looking for a way out of large-scale increases in public expenditures for long-term care. There are nursing home and home care providers who doubt the willingness of government to finance a large growth in medicaid expenditures and are looking for a way to

* It should be noted that the poverty rate among the elderly remains considerably higher than for other adult age groups. For instance, the poverty rate among people aged 45–54 was only 8.4 percent in 1985. U.S. Bureau of the Census, "Money Income and Poverty Status of Families and Persons in the U.S., 1985," *Current Population Reports* (advance data), series P-60, no. 154 (Washington, D.C.: Department of Commerce, 1986), p. 27.

increase their revenues. And, finally, there are businessmen who hope to make money by offering new financing instruments. Because of these differing perspectives, the perceived success of private sector approaches will depend on the goal chosen. What may be a success by one criterion will be a failure by another.

Simulation Strategy

In using the Brookings-ICF Long-Term Care Financing Model to evaluate private sector options, we addressed four major questions. First, what proportion of the elderly might be able to participate in those options? Though largely a measure of affordability, the participation rate also reflects some judgments about other determinants of the supply of and demand for private sector financing mechanisms. Second, what proportion of nursing home and home care expenditures might these options finance? And how does that proportion vary with sociodemographic characteristics? Third, what effect would the options have on medicaid and other public expenditures? Fourth, what effect could the options have on out-of-pocket long-term care expenditures? Also, taking the number of medicaid nursing home patients as a rough proxy of the number of persons reduced to poverty by long-term care, what effect could the options have on the number of elderly who incur truly catastrophic costs?

In developing specifications for the simulations, we deliberately chose assumptions favorable to private sector options. Our strategy was to establish upper-bound estimates of the potential participation in and effect of those options.* Many of our assumptions could therefore be criticized for exaggerating the affordability and effectiveness of the options in meeting the need for long-term care. Indeed, we would argue that some of our assumptions may not be true predictors of future behavior. For example, we assume that the elderly purchase long-term care insurance at age 67, even though current anecdotal experience suggests that most long-term care insurance is purchased at ages 70 and older, when premiums are higher and less affordable. We assume that *all* people buy long-term care insurance if they can afford

* In addition, while there is some consensus on what constitutes relatively generous assumptions about future participation, there is no consensus on what constitutes a "realistic" set of assumptions. Thus less generous assumptions, or our "best guess" of what really would happen, could generate arguments that our assumptions are too conservative and that if we just liberalized them a little bit, the results would be substantially different.

it for 5 percent of their income and have $10,000 in assets, even though that would mean a very substantial increase in out-of-pocket health care costs for most elderly. We also assume that the contributions to individual medical accounts are entirely new savings, even though many economists believe that contributions to comparable individual retirement accounts largely come from existing or already planned savings.

In developing assumptions for the simulations, we had to address two other issues. First, exactly which financing mechanisms should be modeled and what should be their price? Considering the newness of the market, advocates of private sector financing mechanisms argue that, after a shakedown period, future products will provide better coverage at lower prices than what is currently available. After gaining some experience, they suggest, companies will not need so many restrictions or price their products to include such a large cushion for potential increased use.

To address that issue, we adopted the following strategy. First, for most simulations, we tried to approximate the coverage, restrictions, and prices of the private sector products actually on the market. While products may change in the future, existing products are the current reality of private approaches, and no one knows what future products will be like. Moreover, it is not at all clear that existing products are priced too high. Experience may, in fact, show them to be priced too low to return a profit to the seller. At this point, there is no way to tell. Second, we used the better products on the market, usually offered by companies or organizations with relatively extensive experience. Presumably, their experience should be partly reflected in their prices. Third, for private insurance and individual medical accounts, we also used a set of premium and contribution levels for innovative prototype policies estimated by the Social Security Administration actuaries for the Technical Work Group on Private Financing of Long-Term Care for the Elderly.[10] Thus we were not entirely dependent on currently marketed products.

The second main issue was how to address moral hazard, the increased use of long-term care services induced by the insurance coverage. As part of our general strategy of making assumptions favorable to private sector initiatives, we did not assume any increase in use, even though at least some would be expected. Since any additional use would include at least some people who would spend down to medicaid and since virtually all would incur out-of-pocket costs, the unchanged utilization assumption generates the largest possible estimates of the effect on medicaid expenditures, the number of medicaid nursing home patients, and out-of-pocket costs. Although an assumption of increased use would raise the estimate of the proportion of total expenditures paid by private sector initiatives, it would reduce the effect on medicaid. Moreover, any increased use could result in a misleadingly high estimate of the role that private sector mechanisms could play in financing long-term care for those who would be expected to use services in the base case. Thus, while assuming away moral hazard is not "realistic," it seemed the best way to answer the questions asked in this study.*

Conclusion

The results of our review of private sector financing mechanisms and the simulations of the options suggest both a large potential for expansion of private approaches and limits to their ability to replace public spending. On the one hand, private sector options should be encouraged and are likely to increase substantially. Since at present market penetration hardly exists, they have nowhere to go but up. From an investor's perspective, a potentially multibillion market is almost entirely untapped. And people who can afford the products will be substantially better protected against catastrophic costs than they are now.

On the other hand, from a public policy perspective, private sector approaches cannot be the total solution. Even with generous assumptions about private sector participation, our simulation results suggest that only a minority of the elderly could afford private financing mechanisms by 2016–20. Further, private financing mechanisms are unlikely to finance more than a modest proportion of total nursing home and home care expenditures and will not have much effect on either medicaid expenditures or the number of medicaid nursing home patients. Lower-income and most moderate-income elderly will be almost entirely untouched by private sector activities. Thus private sector options probably have their brightest future in combination with a broadened public program.

* Assumptions of moral hazard would be critical to any effort to estimate premiums or required contributions for any of these private sector financing mechanisms.

Chapter Four

Private Long-Term Care Insurance

American society widely uses insurance to protect against loss from potentially catastrophic events such as hospitalization, automobile accidents, home fires, theft, and early death.* Insurance against the potentially devastating costs of long-term care, however, is relatively rare. To date, only about 423,000 long-term care insurance policies have been sold.[1] And in 1985 private insurance covered only about 1 percent of total nursing home expenditures.[2]

Despite these small numbers, private long-term care insurance is a rapidly changing market. The number of insurance products more than tripled between 1983 and 1987, so that sixty different products were on the market as of mid-1987.[3] Some of the newer products are offering improved benefits. Most of the large insurance companies, including Prudential, Aetna, Travelers, and Metropolitan Life, are now offering policies, at least on an experimental basis. And several government agencies have recently issued reports encouraging long-term care insurance.[4]

Although the use of private insurance is likely to spread substantially, none of our simulations suggest that it will become the dominant form of long-term care financing. A reasonably optimistic estimate would be that by 2016–20 a third of the elderly could afford a moderately comprehensive freestanding insurance product. Even in the two simulations with the most generous purchase assumptions, a third or more of the elderly could not afford insurance. Moreover, the effect of

* Americans have eagerly bought acute care insurance. Indeed, they have shown such a willingness to buy insurance, rather than to pay even routine medical costs out-of-pocket, that the prevalence of health insurance has become a cause of concern. The pervasiveness of third-party payment for acute care is thought to contribute to an excessive use of care and higher costs.

insurance on medicaid expenditures and on the number of people who spend down (use up their assets and income) to medicaid is modest at best.

Long-term care insurance does not play a bigger role, because premiums are too expensive for most elderly. Furthermore, products contain mechanisms that limit the degree of financial protection offered. These include exclusions for preexisting conditions, health screenings, prior hospitalization requirements, restrictions on covered levels of care, and indemnity payments that are not indexed for inflation. Thus people may have insurance but may have only part of their bills paid by the policy.[5]

The problem is that improved coverage and affordability are trade-offs. That is, improvements in coverage are likely to make products more expensive, thus reducing their affordability. Premiums could be lowered without loss of coverage by selling policies to younger people, by offering insurance on a group rather than individual basis, or by merging long-term care benefits with acute care benefits. To have a greater effect on out-of-pocket and medicaid expenditures, insurers need to minimize restrictions and expand benefits.

Description of Current Insurance Policies

To assess currently available private long-term care insurance, we analyzed thirty-one policies offered by twenty-four different insurance companies during March to June 1986. We evaluated the policies with respect to premium costs, exclusions or restrictions on purchasing policies, levels of long-term care services covered, and length of coverage.[6]

PRICE

Long-term care insurance can be expensive for the elderly living on a limited income, and the price climbs rapidly with age. An average low-option policy costs $318 a year for persons aged 65 and rises to $728 for persons aged 79 to 80. An average high-option policy costs $684 a year for persons aged 65 and rises to $1,496 for persons aged 79 to 80.* After initial purchase, premiums usually remain level as a

* A low-option policy provides the longest deductible period offered, a minimum of one year nursing home coverage, and $40 a day reimbursement for skilled nursing home care. A high-option policy provides the shortest deductible period offered, the maximum length of nursing home coverage offered, and $60 a day reimbursement for skilled nursing home care.

person ages. Individuals cannot be singled out for premium increases, although companies retain the right to raise premiums from year to year for a "class" of people.

PURCHASE RESTRICTIONS

Through application questions relating to illnesses, prior nursing home use, and disability limitations, insurance companies identify and exclude persons who are likely to use long-term care services. In addition to formal screenings, policies are almost always sold through face-to-face interactions with potential buyers. Insurance agents can thus informally screen out people who are disabled and who they expect will use services. In general, policies are not sold to persons over age 80, because that group has such a high risk of using long-term care.

Most policies guarantee renewability until the insured dies or exhausts benefits, although some companies reserve the right to cancel all of their policies in a state. That might occur, for example, if an insurance product became unprofitable.

COVERAGE

Covered services vary greatly from one long-term care insurance policy to another. Nursing home care, especially skilled nursing care, is by far the predominant kind of institutional coverage. Recently coverage has expanded to include intermediate nursing care and custodial care. Differentiating among the levels of nursing home care is difficult because they are seldom clearly defined.* Home care is not covered extensively.

Almost all insurance companies cover skilled nursing home care only if it occurs within fourteen to thirty days after the patient has been hospitalized for at least three consecutive days. This restriction excludes many residents who enter a nursing home from places other than a

* Nursing homes are commonly categorized by levels of care based on the amount and type of care provided (skilled versus intermediate care) and the disability level of the patients. Long-term care insurance policies do not usually cover all levels of nursing home care, or at least do not cover all equally. For each level of care there are restrictions on the type of facility in which the care can be provided (for example, only skilled nursing facilities, only medicare-certified skilled nursing facilites, or intermediate care facilities) or, in the case of home care, the type of person delivering the service (for example, licensed professional or registered nurse). Some levels of care are also limited by the length of coverage. Coverage periods are positively related to the level of skill, so that the longest length of coverage is for skilled nursing services—the highest level of care.

hospital.[7] Usually the medical reason for a skilled nursing home stay must be the same as that for the previous hospitalization. For intermediate and custodial nursing home care to be covered, the insured must often have a prior hospitalization or skilled nursing home stay. Home care services must usually be preceded by a nursing home stay.

Medical conditions existing before the purchase of insurance are not usually covered until after a six-month waiting period. Most policies also exclude coverage of mental and nervous disorders unless they have demonstrable organic causes. Most insurers will not sell policies to patients with Alzheimer's disease, but may cover the disease if a person contracts it after purchasing a policy.

Most policies have a deductible period ranging from 20 to 100 days before insurance coverage begins. A choice of deductible periods is usually offered, with higher premiums for shorter deductibles. Long deductible periods can result in substantial out-of-pocket costs for the consumer. For example, a 100-day deductible can easily entail a $6,000 out-of-pocket expense. And long deductible periods do not cover short-stay residents. About 41 percent of all nursing home entrants stay for 90 days or less.[8]

PAYMENT LEVEL

Almost all policies offer a fixed indemnity rather than a service benefit. Service benefits cover the entire cost of a service minus any cost-sharing, whereas indemnity benefits pay a fixed amount per day or per visit, regardless of the actual cost of the service. Policies normally offer a choice of indemnity payments of anywhere from $10 to $120 a day. Indemnity payments do not increase over time to adjust for inflation, and the amount usually varies with the level and type of care. A few new policies are now offering service instead of indemnity benefits.[9] Service benefits are likely to be more expensive, since the benefits rise with inflation.

Financing Potential

The ability of private long-term care insurance to have an important role in financing long-term care depends on the demand for and the supply of insurance. On the one hand, the decision to buy long-term care insurance is influenced by the price of policies, the income of the elderly, and their interest in policies. Long-term care insurance could build on the willingness of the elderly to purchase private insurance to supplement medicare. About 65 percent of the noninstitutionalized elderly in 1977 had medicare supplemental insurance.[10] On the other hand, the insurer's decision to offer policies depends on the insurability of long-term care, the ability to price premiums accurately, the profitability of policies, and regulatory barriers.

MARKET DEMAND

Elderly people are interested in acquiring long-term care insurance to protect income and assets, to remain independent, and to ensure access to care.[11] A survey conducted for the American Association of Retired Persons (AARP) showed that about half of its members wanted to learn more about nursing home insurance. In other surveys between 40 percent and 70 percent of the elderly expressed various levels of interest in purchasing such insurance.[12]

Despite this rising curiosity, the current demand for private long-term care insurance is still low. The reasons for this are hard to disentangle, but the most important are the inability and unwillingness to pay, the lack of awareness of the risk of using long-term care services, misinformation on current medicare and private insurance coverage, and possibly the availability of medicaid to pay for long-term care services.

Ability and Willingness to Pay

Long-term care insurance premiums add significantly to the substantial health care costs already incurred by the elderly. Excluding nursing home costs, out-of-pocket health care costs averaged $1,800 per elderly person in 1986.[13] For some elderly, long-term care insurance means at least a doubling or a tripling of what they currently pay for medicare supplemental policies. So they may not be able or willing to pay for long-term care insurance unless it replaced some acute care insurance coverage.[14] Surveys show that high premium costs are one of the most important reasons for not buying policies, and that lower-income elderly are less interested than upper-income elderly in purchasing long-term care insurance.[15] The majority of those interested in buying long-term care insurance in 1982 said they would pay no more than $360 a year, less than the market price of the average policy.[16]

Even if they could afford the policies, older people may not be willing to buy current products, which often do not cover the services most desired. For example, the elderly strongly prefer home care coverage to nursing home coverage even if they have to pay more for it.[17] Hence the relative lack of home care coverage in existing policies is a deterrent to the purchase of insurance.

Unawareness of the Risk of Using Long-Term Care Services

Lack of awareness of the need for this type of coverage is a strong barrier to purchasing insurance. In a survey of AARP members, "lack of need" was cited as a major reason for not purchasing a long-term care insurance policy.[18] Several other surveys show that the elderly do not believe they will need long-term care, that relatively few have used long-term care services, and that most do not think about entering a nursing home, much less how to pay for it.[19] People seem to accept the possibility that they will someday get sick and visit a doctor or enter a hospital, but few seem willing to accept the risk of their becoming seriously disabled and using expensive home care or nursing home services.

Awareness of long-term care risks may heighten over time as people witness the increasingly common long-term care experiences of their relatives. Indeed, purchasers of the AARP-Prudential policy were more likely than nonpurchasers to have had a relative or friend in a nursing home.[20] As Brody suggests, improvements in longevity will make having a seriously disabled elderly relative an increasingly normal life experience.[21] Public awareness of the potential financial consequences of long-term care has increased over the past few years, in large part because of media coverage of proposed federal legislation to improve catastrophic acute care coverage.[22]

Misinformation

A serious barrier to the expansion of long-term care insurance is that many elderly mistakenly believe medicare or medicare supplemental insurance already covers long-term care. In a widely cited 1984 survey of AARP's membership, 79 percent of the respondents thought medicare would cover extended nursing home stays.[23] That is factually incorrect: medicare does not cover extended nursing home stays. More recent surveys have found that between 25 percent and 54 percent of the elderly thought medicare or their private supplemental insurance already covered long-term care.[24] Again, media coverage of federal legislation on catastrophic acute care coverage has probably had a salutary effect.

Availability of Medicaid

Some observers have argued that the availability of medicaid to pay for nursing home care is a deterrent to the purchase of private insurance. Indeed, the Health Insurance Association of America's Task Force on Long-Term Care identified medicaid as a competitor of private insurance.[25] This seems unlikely, since most elderly are not even aware that medicaid covers long-term care services.[26] Moreover, because of its "welfare" stigma and requirement that people use almost all their income and assets before becoming eligible, medicaid may actually motivate people to purchase private insurance.

SUPPLY-SIDE BARRIERS

On the supply side, insurers face the following dilemma. On the one hand, insurers are attracted by the opportunity for increased premium revenue from a virtually untapped market. Individual companies fear that if they do not enter the market, their competitors will capture it. On the other hand, insurers are afraid of large potential financial losses and are cautious about entering the market. They worry that only persons who need long-term care will buy policies and that the availability of insurance will induce large increases in nursing home and home care use. Insurance companies may also be disillusioned by past financial losses incurred with other types of health insurance.[27]

These fears have a real basis. While there is great potential for market growth, there are also substantial financial risks. It will be difficult to develop affordable policies that give people what they want and that can be administered in a way that keeps costs below premiums. In recent years the supply of long-term care insurance has steadily increased, but only one company offers policies on a nearly national basis.[28] Where they do offer policies, insurers have built in features that minimize their financial risks, at the cost of reducing the financial protection given consumers.

Insurability of Long-Term Care

Although the insurance industry increasingly agrees that the use of nursing home services is an "insurable event," the insurability of home care remains controversial.[29] The quintessential insurable event is a major home fire that, excluding criminal arson, is rare, unpredictable, and financially devastating and is not created or desired by the insured.

There are three main components of insurability. One is the extent to which the event being insured against is under the control of the insured. More precisely, to what extent will there be moral hazard, or increased use induced by insurance coverage? Several factors lead insurers to worry about moral hazard in long-term care. First, social, not strictly medical, considerations are the key determinants of using long-term care. Partly as a result, there is not much agreement about who should use services or how much they should use them. Nursing home utilization rates among the elderly over age 75, for example, varied by a factor of four among states in 1980.[30] Second, an important function of insurance is to lower the out-of-pocket price of services. People usually buy more of a good or service when the price is lower.

In addition, many disabled elderly who might medically qualify for long-term care services do not receive any. Thus, with insurance, admissions to nursing homes and use of home care may rise. The reluctance of the elderly to enter nursing homes, however, reduces the likelihood of a large increase in nursing home use. But the inherent desirability of some home care services means that their use is likely to increase substantially if covered by insurance. Who, after all, would not want a homemaker today to help clean the house and prepare meals?

Insurers typically try to protect themselves from moral hazard by imposing high deductibles, focusing coverage on skilled nursing home care, requiring prior hospitalization before nursing home coverage, and including only minimal home care.[31] These elements help to narrow coverage to the patients with medically intense care needs, who presumably have less choice about whether they will use services. Insurers also build substantial increases in use into their premiums.

The second component of insurability is whether people can easily predict their need for the insured benefits. In this instance, if people can predict whether they will use long-term care services, those most in need of those services may disproportionately purchase the insurance. This adverse selection could drive use beyond expected levels and force the company to raise premiums. That in turn would cause low-risk persons to drop their policies, pushing average use even higher. To protect against adverse selection, insurers usually screen for health problems, exclude people over age 80, and prohibit coverage for preexisting conditions and most mental illness.[32]

The third component is whether the total costs associated with the event are predictable for the population as a whole, a prediction necessary to establish insurance premiums. With respect to long-term care, the difficulty of prediction is greatly heightened by the long period that may elapse between the acquisition of insurance and the use of benefits. If a policy is underpriced, insurers will not know for perhaps fifteen to twenty years, too late to adjust the price for that cohort.

Insurers argue that the lack of data on costs and use makes long-term care relatively hard to insure.[33] Developing long-term care financing mechanisms depends on an accurate assessment of the expected risk and cost of nursing home and home care. Ideally, calculations of long-term care premiums would be made with data accumulated under insurance covering such risks for an extended period (that is, "insured lives"). Because of the newness of the products and the proprietary nature of this information, actual claims data are not likely to become publicly available. States can, however, encourage data collection, as Florida has done, by requiring nursing homes to report data documenting the experience of private pay patients.[34] The National Association of Insurance Commisioners (NAIC) Advisory Committee on Long Term Care has called for greater cooperation between private insurers, state agencies, and researchers to provide data on the use and costs of nursing home and home care services.[35]

Another difficulty in foreseeing costs is the likelihood but unpredictability of substantial long-term care inflation. Current policies cope with this problem by offering only a fixed-indemnity benefit that does not increase over time. By not reimbursing on a cost or charge basis, insurers reduce the risk associated with unknown and possibly high future inflation.

Fixed-indemnity policies present a major problem in that a payment level adequate today will not be adequate in the future. For example, at 5.8 percent annual nursing home inflation, a nursing home indemnity policy with a $50 a day benefit purchased at age 65 needs to pay more than $150 a day at age 85 to have comparable purchasing power. In a review of thirty-one long-term care insurance policies, only one indemnity policy had any inflation protection, and the adjustment was very modest and limited to ten years.[36]

Automatically adjusting the indemnity level for inflation will make insurance policies significantly more expensive and therefore less affordable. Because benefits are normally paid much later than premiums are received, premiums must be upwardly adjusted from the beginning to accommodate future inflation costs. Estimates developed by the Actuarial Research Corporation show that "at older issue ages, the beginning premium for a 5 percent inflation assumption is in the range of 30 to 40 percent higher [than an unindexed benefit]. At younger issue ages the necessary adjustment is dramatically higher—by a factor of between four to six times greater [than the premium for an unindexed benefit]."[37] Part of the difficulty is that the earnings on reserves that could reduce premiums are largely eroded by nursing home inflation. The dilemma is that policies purchased at younger ages are more affordable than if purchased later, but that inflation protection is more important for those younger age groups.

Although many of these characteristics of nursing home and home care arguably cast doubt on the insurability of long-term care, some also apply to acute health care, which our society treats as clearly insurable. For example, the extremely wide geographic variations in hospital use for acute care also largely result from lack of consensus on who should receive care and how much they should receive.[38] However, the insurability of long-term care differs in several ways from that of acute care. First, the long time that may elapse between purchase of long-term care insurance and use of services greatly increases uncertainty. Second, the possibility of widespread substitution of paid for unpaid care greatly increases the chances for moral hazard. Third, acute care insurance is typically sold to groups rather than individuals, so that adverse selection is less likely. In addition, premiums can be more accurately estimated from the groups' previous use of services. Because of these differences, insuring long-term care will be more difficult than insuring acute care.

The High Cost of Individual Insurance and Barriers to Group Insurance

Unlike most acute health care insurance, almost all long-term care insurance is sold on an individual rather than on a group basis. Moreover, those insured must pay all the premiums themselves. By contrast, most acute care group insurance is employment based and largely paid by the employer. Only about 10 percent of the elderly, however, are still working, and only a minority have any employer-sponsored retiree health benefits.[39] Although it is possible to market long-term care insurance to groups other than employers (for example, to senior citizen groups), that has generally not been done. The main exception is the policy developed by Prudential, which is being marketed as a group policy to members of the AARP.

The overwhelming dominance of individual products substantially increases the overhead costs. Administrative and marketing costs are high because sales have to be made one at a time. Advertising material must be developed and viewed by a large number of people, most of whom may never buy the product. Insurance representatives report that it takes an average of three to four separate visits with potential purchasers to sell a long-term care insurance policy.[40] Thus agent commissions must be high per policy sold.

Group insurance especially geared to the nonelderly population would potentially address the problems of high cost and adverse selection. Premiums should be lower in employer-based group policies because administrative and marketing costs are lower and people would be able to contribute over their entire working careers, allowing reserves to build. Adverse selection would also be reduced because the under 65 age group has a very low disability level and both high- and low-risk people would be covered by the insurance. Several insurance companies, including Aetna and Travelers, are experimenting with offering long-term care insurance through employers.[41] As of December 1987 a few employers had instituted policies, including American Express, the Alaskan state government, Procter and Gamble, and Ford and General Motors in a demonstration project.[42] The federal government is planning to offer a long-term care insurance policy to its employees.[43]

Employers' interest in offering long-term care insurance is growing, but their interest in paying for the insurance is not.[44] Employers see long-term care insurance as financially risky because the costs are uncertain, potentially large, and sure to grow as the baby boom population ages. Moreover, benefits are not likely to be used until employees have been retired for twenty or more years and have little, if any, connection with the firm. Nevertheless, as employers face labor shortages caused by the changing age structure, they may begin to offer new benefits to keep older employees in the work force.[45] Employer-based long-term care insurance, however, is not likely to exceed that of employer-sponsored acute care insurance, which covers only a substantial minority of the elderly and is concentrated among former employees of large corporations or governments.[46]

In addition, because of the lack of awareness of the need for long-term care, few employees and unions have bargained for long-term care insurance.[47] Furthermore, many labor unions are having difficulty holding onto the benefits they have instead of expanding into new areas. But employee interest may be rising. A survey of 1,000 employees in large companies found that 5 percent of those surveyed were very interested and 32 percent somewhat interested in trading some current fringe benefits for new nursing home benefits.[48]

Even if employers were so inclined, there are many barriers to employer-financed long-term care benefits. First, insurance premiums can still be high, despite discounts for large groups of younger people.[49] For example, the Social Security Administration actuaries estimate that the annual premium for a policy that after a 90-day deductible paid an inflation-indexed nursing home benefit of $50 a day up to a maximum of six years would be $412 if issued at age 30, and would rise to $950 if issued at age 60.[50]

Second, in part because of recent efforts to shift some medicare costs to employers and because of court cases involving retiree health benefits, the general movement has been to restrict rather than to expand elderly health benefits. Both the Tax Equity and Fiscal Responsibility Act of 1982 and the Consolidated Omnibus Budget Reconciliation Act of 1985 make medicare the second payer for the employed elderly, increasing the share of elderly health care costs paid by employers. Courts have ruled both for and against employers on discontinuing or modifying health benefits for retired employees.[51] Where they have ruled against employers, the implication is that retirees have vested rights to health insurance and that employers cannot unilaterally alter or terminate those benefits.

A third barrier pertains to the difficulties of prefunding retiree health benefits. In financing health plans, in contrast to pension plans, employers are not required by law to prefund benefits; instead they generally use a pay-as-you-go strategy. As a result, there is a very large unfunded liability for health benefits for current retirees and workers aged 40 and over, the value of which was $98 billion in 1983.[52] Companies fear that the Financial Accounting Standards Board may change reporting requirements so that future liabilities for retiree health benefits are reflected in the annual financial statement, a change that could make some large corporations look financially unstable.[53]

Very few companies prefund their retiree health benefits, partly because the tax code does not provide incentives to do so. The two principal vehicles for prefunding postretirement medical benefits under the Internal Revenue Code are 501(c)(9) welfare trusts (so-called voluntary employee benefit trusts, or VEBAs) and 401(h) trusts in pension plans. The Deficit Reduction Act of 1984 placed many restrictions on VEBAs. Although employer contributions to future retiree health benefits are tax deductible, earnings on investment income are taxable.[54] In 401(h) trusts, income from employer contributions does accumulate tax free. But the potential for prefunding long-term care benefits under 401(h) is limited; only 25 percent of the aggregate employer contribution to the pension plan can be for "incidental benefits," including life insurance, death benefits, disability insurance, and health insurance.[55] For most employers these limits are too low to adequately cover existing incidental benefits, much less long-term care benefits. Other ways of prefunding long-term care benefits are through defined-contribution plans or tax-deferred savings arrangements such as 401(k) plans. Obviously, employers could prefund health and long-term care insurance without specific tax advantages, but the marginal cost would be higher.

Regulatory Barriers

Although insurance companies face some regulatory obstacles to developing and selling long-term care insurance, regulation is not a major impediment to growth. Long-term care insurance is typically regulated by state insurance departments under provisions for other types of insurance such as medicare supplemental, general medical, and disability insurance.[56] The problem for state insurance regulators is how to strike a balance between protecting consumers and nurturing a new product. Proponents of regulation fear that if tough regulations are not imposed, consumers will not be protected against inferior products and fraud. They recall the scandals that resulted from the federal government's failure to set minimum standards for medicare supplemental insurance policies.[57] Opponents of strict regulation argue that officials do not have enough information or experience to regulate intelligently and that flexibility is needed to prevent financial losses that may discourage the insurance industry.[58]

As private long-term care insurance has grown, so has regulatory activity, both in providing greater flexibility and in imposing mandatory minimum standards.[59] Many more states can be expected to consider new laws and regulations based on the NAIC's recently adopted Long Term Care Insurance Model Act. In general, the act seeks to promote a positive regulatory environment, alleviating barriers to market growth and diversification.

The principal areas of regulatory concern are benefit levels, policy restrictions and exclusions, loss ratios, and policy renewability.[60] Current long-term care insurance policies have many limits on who and what will be covered by the policies. To protect consumers from buying policies with little or no value, some states have tried to set minimum benefits or to prohibit certain restrictions.[61] Opposing such requirements, insurers argue that they need those restrictions to manage risk, control use of services, and reduce premiums. Accordingly, the NAIC model act discourages mandated benefits, allows companies to exclude specific diseases and preexisting conditions as defined in the model act, and allows prior insitutionalization requirements with minor limitations.[62]

To prevent the sale of contracts not worth buying because of their limited benefits, regulators have developed a general measure, the loss ratio, to evaluate an insurance policy's economic value. The loss ratio is the proportion of total premiums paid out in benefits to consumers during the year. Typically, high loss ratios are thought to be a sign of a good product. Although little is known about long-term care insurance loss ratios, some states have set loss ratio minimums in the range of 50 percent to 60 percent.[63]

Unfortunately, interpretation of simple loss ratios applied to long-term care insurance is not straightforward and may be misleading. Computed loss ratios may be very low in the early years of long-term care policies, since premiums are usually collected several years in advance of expected benefit payments.[64] Thus initial payouts to the consumer may be quite low, whereas the long-range liability of the insurer may be substantial. The buildup of reserves for the younger age population is a crucial element in lowering premium costs, but the application of annual minimum loss ratios does not take that into account. With these limitations in mind, the NAIC advisory committee recommends that no specific minimum loss ratio be set and that regulators evaluate loss ratios over the entire period for which rates are calculated.[65]

Currently, insurers are allowed great flexibility in deciding whether to renew policies. Since insurers are often collecting premiums far in advance of expected payout, such decisions could become a serious consumer protection problem. Most policies are guaranteed renewable. For those that are not, it is technically and legally possible to collect premiums, put them in reserve, and then cancel all the policies in a state. The NAIC model act allows policies to be conditionally renewable instead of guaranteed renewable. Specifically, renewal can be declined by class, by geographic area, or for other reasons except age or deterioration of the insured's mental or physical health.[66] The model

FIGURE 4-1. **Simulation Assumptions for LOWBEN Insurance Policy**

- The policy is similar to a currently marketed policy with a 100-day deductible period and a $30, $40, or $50 a day indemnity benefit, depending on what the person can afford. The benefit is increased by $1.50, $2.00, and $2.50 a year for ten years for the $30, $40, and $50 benefit, respectively. The maximum length of covered nursing home care is six years. Seventy-five percent of the insured who use nursing home care are assumed to meet the three-day prior hospitalization requirement. The policy also provides persons with a limited home care indemnity benefit after a nursing home stay.
- Individuals and couples buy the insurance only if they can afford it for less than 5 percent of their income and if they have $10,000 or more in nonhousing assets. Couples purchase policies only if they can afford two policies.
- In 1986 people aged 67 to 81 are eligible to purchase the policy. After 1986 people purchase the policy starting at age 67.
- Only the physically fit are allowed to start to purchase the policy. People who become disabled after buying the policies will be able to keep them.
- For purchases after 1986, the initial premium and indemnity level are increased by 5.8 percent a year to reflect nursing home and home care inflation.
- The premium for the policy is based on the person's age at initial purchase. In 1986 the annual premiums for the $50 indemnity benefit range from $584 for persons aged 67 to $1,642 for persons aged 81. Premiums for the $30 and the $40 indemnity benefit are 60 and 80 percent, respectively, of the $50 indemnity benefit premiums.
- If the income of an individual or couple declines over time after purchase of the policy, they will keep buying the policy as long as the premium is less than 7 percent of income and they have $10,000 in nonhousing assets.

act would prohibit any policy from being optionally renewable, that is, that an insurance company could cancel a policy arbitrarily.

Model Results

To assess the financing potential of private long-term care insurance, we modeled five different policies.[67] Detailed assumptions for these simulations are presented in figure 4-1 and table 4-1.

The first two alternatives, BIGBEN and LOWBEN, are based on a recently marketed policy offered by a major insurer in the field. They cover up to six years of nursing home care after a 100-day deductible and a prior hospitalization, providing a fixed-indemnity payment with a limited inflation adjustment. Home care is covered only after a

TABLE 4-1. *Coverage and Purchase Criteria for Private Long-Term Care Insurance Options*
1987 dollars

Insurance option	Coverage criteria						Purchase criteria
	Age start	Indemnity benefit (dollars a day)	Indemnity inflation index[a]	Deductible period (days)	Coverage period (years)	Prior hospitalization	
BIGBEN	67	50	A	100	6	Yes	5 percent or less of family income plus 10,000 in nonhousing assets
LOWBEN	67	30, 40, or 50	B	100	6	Yes	5 percent or less of family income plus $10,000 in nonhousing assets
MEDIGAP	67	50	C	90	1	No	Same proportion of elderly population as now purchases medigap insurance
YOUNGINS	30	50	C	90	1, 2, 4, 6, or unlimited	No	Age 65 or under, as much as 1 percent of income buys; ages 65–80, 3 percent of income plus $10,000 in assets
PENSIONS	65	50	C	90	2	No	$500 minimum annual pension

SOURCE: Rose M. Rubin, Joshua M. Wiener, and Mark R. Meiners, "Private Long Term Care Insurance: Simulation of an Emerging Market," Brookings, August 1987, table 1.

a. A: For ten years after purchase, indemnity increases by 5 percent of initial coverage, or $2.50 a year.
B: For ten years after purchase, indemnity increases by 5 percent of initial coverage, or $2.50 a year for $50 indemnity, $2.00 a year for $40.00 indemnity, and $1.50 a year for $30.00 indemnity.
C: Indemnity increases yearly by nursing home inflation rate of 5.8 percent.

nursing home stay. Following general industry practice and the specific requirements of the modeled insurance policy, no disabled person and no one over the age of 81 may buy a policy. The initial nursing home indemnity level for BIGBEN is $50 a day, and for LOWBEN $30, $40, or $50 a day, depending on what the person can afford. Since a $30 a day nursing home payment is less than half the average nursing home daily rate, a substantial out-of-pocket payment is required.

To estimate the maximum affordability and effect of this approach, all individuals or couples who can afford the policy for 5 percent or less of their income and who have at least $10,000 in nonhousing assets are assumed to purchase a policy at age 67. Age 67 was chosen because most elderly have left the work force by then and are living on their retirement income. In 1987 only 25 percent of men and 14 percent of women aged 67 were in the labor force.[68] Since the elderly already spend about 12 percent of their income on health care, the 5-percent-of-income test would mean a significant increase in out-of-pocket medical care costs for the elderly and is an assumption favorable to private insurance. The $10,000-asset test assumes that few elderly will purchase insurance unless they have at least a modest level of assets to protect.

In 1986 LOWBEN and the BIGBEN premiums for a $50 nursing home indemnity level ranged from $584 a year for those aged 67, up to $1,642 for those aged 81. LOWBEN's additional $40 and $30 indemnity levels require premiums that are 80 percent and 60 percent, respectively, of the $50 indemnity level premium. In both options once a policy is purchased, premiums remain constant over time. For new purchasers after 1986, the initial premium and benefit are assumed to increase 5.8 percent a year.

A third simulation, MEDIGAP, tests the idea that the elderly who purchase medicare supplemental insurance (medigap) would also buy insurance for long-term care. Like BIGBEN and LOWBEN, this policy is assumed to be marketed to the elderly as an individual rather than a group policy. The objective of this alternative is to introduce a potential link between acute care and long-term care insurance. People who purchase medicare supplemental insurance are assumed to buy a policy that covers one year of nursing home care after a 90-day deductible period and that pays $50 a day (indexed for inflation) for nursing home care. There is no affordability test, as such, for this simulation. Thus this option primarily extends medicare supplemental insurance to encompass short- or medium-term nursing home care. We used a one-year policy because many medicare supplemental insurance policyholders would be unable to afford more extensive coverage. Social Security Administration actuaries estimate that in 1986 these policies would cost $362 a year at issue age 65.[69]

The fourth policy alternative, YOUNGINS, attempts to mitigate the problems of adverse selection and affordability by including insured persons of working age. At younger ages relatively few people are disabled, and prefunding reduces annual premiums by lengthening the period of contributions and accumulation of interest earnings. Persons starting at age 30 and over are assumed to buy as much nursing home insurance (in terms of years of covered care) as they can afford for 1 percent of their income. Again, premiums were estimated by Social Security Administration actuaries and vary from $127 a year at age 30 for a policy that covers one year of nursing home care to $3,135 a year at age 80 for a policy that covers unlimited nursing home care.[70]

The final policy simulated, PENSIONS, assumes that private long-term care insurance is provided to all persons aged 65 and over who get at least $500 in annual pension benefits. Qualifying persons receive a long-term care insurance policy that provides a $50 a day inflation-adjusted two-year nursing home benefit after a 90-day deductible period. The objective of this alternative is to test the addition of long-term care insurance as a retiree benefit for those receiving at least a minimal pension. This type of plan might be offered to retirees in lieu of some pension benefits.

PARTICIPATION

The proportion of elderly projected to buy long-term care insurance in 2016–20 ranges from a quarter of the elderly for BIGBEN to nearly two-thirds of the elderly for MEDIGAP (table 4-2). Although the BIGBEN policy reaches only 25 percent of the elderly aged 67 and over, the LOWBEN alternative results in coverage of 45 percent of the elderly aged 67 and over. Improved affordability is obtained by reducing the indemnity level purchased. Thus BIGBEN and LOWBEN are affordable by a substantial minority, but not a majority, of the elderly, even with generous purchase assumptions. Under an assumption of 4.4 percent rather than 5.8 percent annual nursing home and home care inflation, 57 percent of the elderly aged 67 and over could hold LOWBEN policies in 2016–20. A significantly lower inflation rate

TABLE 4-2. *Elderly Participation in Private Long-Term Care Insurance Options, Selected Periods, 1986–2020*[a]
Numbers in millions

Option	1986–90[b]		2001–05		2016–20	
	Number of elderly with insurance	Percent of elderly population	Number of elderly with insurance	Percent of elderly population	Number of elderly with insurance	Percent of elderly population
BIGBEN[c]	2.716	10.0	6.810	20.7	11.064	25.4
LOWBEN[c]	5.587	20.6	12.485	37.9	19.607	45.0[d]
MEDIGAP[c]	5.092	18.8	17.303	52.5	27.719	63.7
YOUNGINS[e]	4.218	13.5	10.942	29.6	31.420	62.5
PENSIONS[e]	1.753	5.6	10.035	27.2	20.756	41.3

SOURCE: Brookings-ICF Long-Term Care Financing Model. See table 4-1 for a description of the options.
a. Assumes that nursing home expenditures rise at an annual rate of 5.8 perent.
b. The MEDIGAP, YOUNGINS, and PENSIONS options do not include 1986.
c. Ages 67 and over.
d. At 4.4 percent annual nursing home inflation, 57.0 percent of the elderly age 67 and over could have LOWBEN in 2016–20.
e. Ages 65 and over.

increases but does not dramatically change the proportion of elderly who might participate in private insurance.

The MEDIGAP option covers 64 percent of the elderly aged 67 and over by 2016–20, reflecting the present proclivity of the elderly to purchase medicare supplemental policies. Since even a one-year policy would probably double the cost of existing medigap policies, the percentage of elderly likely to choose this additional coverage would be less than our assumption.

The policy aimed at younger people, YOUNGINS, has a relatively high coverage of 63 percent of the elderly 65 and over. This reflects the somewhat lower premiums for persons who bought some coverage before age 65. Even beginning at younger age groups, however, many people would have to pay more than 1 percent of their income to buy any long-term care insurance.

The PENSIONS option covers 41 percent of the elderly aged 65 and over, slightly fewer people than LOWBEN. This moderate coverage reflects the fact that many elderly do not have pensions or that some pensions are too low to pay for long-term care insurance. Another restriction is that coverage is provided to individuals, not families, with pensions.

PROPORTION OF TOTAL EXPENDITURES

In the future, private insurance will account for a larger proportion of nursing home expenditures. Under the policies simulated, by 2016–

TABLE 4-3. *Total Expenditures for Nursing Home Care, by Source of Payment, Base Case and Private Insurance Options, 2016–20*[a]
Billions of 1987 dollars; percent change from base case

Option	Total	Medicaid	Medicare	Insurance	Patients' cash income	Patients' assets
Base case	98.117	46.192	1.612	...	27.889	22.423
BIGBEN	98.461	45.645	1.612	6.930	24.597	19.674
Percent change	0.35	−1.18	0.00	...	−11.80	−12.26
LOWBEN[b]	100.107	43.903	1.612	11.699	24.745	18.145
Percent change	2.03	−4.95	0.00	...	−11.27	−19.08
MEDIGAP	101.642	37.684	1.612	17.929	25.108	19.308
Percent change	3.59	−18.42	0.00	...	−9.97	−13.89
YOUNGINS	100.470	40.465	1.612	16.979	23.224	18.187
Percent change	2.40	−12.40	0.00	...	−16.73	−18.89
PENSIONS	100.545	40.497	1.612	14.826	23.978	19.631
Percent change	2.47	−12.33	0.00	...	−14.02	−12.45

SOURCE: Brookings-ICF Long-Term Care Financing Model.
a. Average annual expenditures. Assumes that nursing home expenditures rise at an annual rate of 5.8 percent.
b. For LOWBEN, at 4.4 percent annual nursing home inflation, medicaid expenditures would be reduced by 9.5 percent, cash income by 17.4 percent, and assets by 25.9 percent from the base case. Nursing home payments by insurance would be $12.040 billion, or 17.8 percent of total nursing home expenditures.

20 private long-term care insurance would account for between 7 percent and 18 percent of total nursing home expenditures (table 4-3). Even under a lower nursing home and home care inflation assumption (4.4 percent), the LOWBEN policy would still account for only 18 percent of total nursing home expenditures. Although these results suggest that the role of private insurance in financing nursing home care will grow, they do not suggest that private insurance will be the dominant form of long-term care financing.

As a whole, private insurance is a more important source of financing for the young old (ages 65 to 74), married couples, males, and higher-income persons (table 4-4). The principal exception to this pattern is MEDIGAP, which reflects an extensive participation in medicare supplemental policies that does not vary dramatically by demographic and income characteristics.

EFFECT ON PUBLIC EXPENDITURES

Medicaid nursing home expenditures under the different insurance options are between 1 percent and 18 percent less than they would be under the base case in 2016–20 (table 4-3). While private insurance may lower medicaid expenditures modestly, they will still roughly triple over the simulation period.

TABLE 4-4. *Private Long-Term Care Insurance Expenditures for Nursing Home Care, by Demographic and Income Groups, 2016–20*[a]
Percentage of total payments for nursing home services

Category	BIGBEN	LOWBEN[b]	MEDIGAP	YOUNGINS	PENSIONS
Total insurance share	6.7	11.3	18.1	15.4	15.0
Age					
65–74	11.3	19.0	17.3	28.2	15.0
75–84	7.8	13.0	17.0	17.0	15.2
85 and over	3.9	6.8	19.1	8.6	14.9
Marital status					
Married	10.5	17.2	18.7	18.3	17.5
Unmarried	5.1	8.9	17.8	14.2	14.0
Sex					
Male	8.3	14.7	18.5	20.6	21.9
Female	5.9	9.6	17.8	12.8	11.6
Family income (dollars)[c]					
Under 7,500	0.0	0.8	17.7	6.4	7.1
7,500–14,999	0.5	4.9	17.5	12.7	14.0
15,000–19,999	2.0	13.1	21.2	18.8	19.8
20,000–29,999	8.2	20.8	17.2	23.2	21.1
30,000–39,999	18.3	25.1	19.1	25.0	19.8
40,000–49,999	29.0	29.0	17.0	24.3	23.4
50,000 and over	27.3	27.4	17.9	25.2	21.5

SOURCE: Brookings-ICF Long-Term Care Financing Model.

a. These data are based on the total payments for an admission cohort over the entire length of their stays in a nursing home. For example, for a person who is admitted to a nursing home in 2016–20 for a two-year stay, we totaled two years' worth of nursing home expenditures. We then calculated the proportion of those expenditures paid by private long-term care insurance. We assume that nursing home expenditures rise at an annual rate of 5.8 percent.

b. At 4.4 percent annual nursing home inflation, LOWBEN would account for 17.5 percent of nursing home payments.

c. Family income is joint income for married persons, individual income for unmarried persons.

The freestanding, relatively comprehensive nursing home policies aimed at the elderly (BIGBEN and LOWBEN) reduce medicaid expenditures by between 1 percent and 5 percent and therefore have little effect on public expenditures. Under a 4.4 percent nursing home and home care inflation assumption, LOWBEN reduces medicaid expenditures by 10 percent. These options simply do not reach far enough down the income distribution to include those persons who would spend down to medicaid. By contrast, the option that links long-term care coverage to medigap coverage (MEDIGAP) reduces medicaid expenditures by a fairly significant 18 percent, even though it provides only one year of nursing home coverage. The relatively high proportion of lower-income elderly who are assumed to purchase this policy accounts for the relatively large effect.

The two options oriented more to long-term care insurance as a

TABLE 4-5. *Number of Elderly Medicaid Patients in Nursing Homes, Base Case and Insurance Options, Selected Periods, 1986–2020*[a]
Millions of patients; percent change from base case

Option	1986–90	2001–05	2016–20
Base case	1.334	2.006	2.343
BIGBEN	1.333	1.987	2.311
Percent change	−0.07	−0.90	−1.37
LOWBEN	1.333	1.952	2.237[b]
Percent change	−0.07	−2.69	−4.52
MEDIGAP	1.332	1.940	2.144
Percent change	−0.15	−3.29	−8.49
YOUNGINS	1.334	1.965	2.148
Percent change	0.00	−2.04	−8.32
PENSIONS	1.334	1.955	2.143
Percent change	0.00	−2.54	−8.54

SOURCE: Brookings-ICF Long-Term Care Financing Model.
a. Ever in a nursing home during the course of a year; assumes that nursing home expenditures rise at an annual rate of 5.8 percent.
b. At 4.4 percent annual nursing home inflation, there would be 1.80 million medicaid nursing home patients, a 9.1 percent reduction from the base case of 1.98 million.

fringe benefit, YOUNGINS and PENSIONS, both reduced medicaid expenditures by 12 percent. The relatively modest effect of YOUNGINS partly reflects the fact that 1 percent of income may be an inadequate contribution to purchase insurance and that many older elderly still do not have insurance by 2016–20.

EFFECT ON PRIVATE EXPENDITURES

Although private insurance does not substantially reduce public expenditures, it has a greater effect on private out-of-pocket expenditures. Private long-term care insurance reduces nursing home payments from cash income by 10 percent to 17 percent, and from assets by 12 percent to 19 percent (table 4-3). Under a lower long-term care inflation assumption (4.4 percent), payments from cash income are reduced by 17 percent, and payments from assets are reduced by 26 percent.

As a rough proxy of the ability of private sector options to reduce the incidence of catastrophic long-term care costs, the effect of different options on the number of medicaid nursing home patients is shown in table 4-5. Private insurance reduces the number of medicaid nursing home patients in 2016–20 by between 1 percent and 9 percent below the base case. Thus the total effect of private insurance on the number of people who impoverish themselves down to the levels of medicaid financial eligibility is fairly small.

Conclusion

Private long-term care insurance is a rapidly changing and developing market that is still in its infancy. Although the number of policies sold has increased significantly in recent years, only slightly more than 1 percent of the elderly have policies. The potential future market for such insurance is large, but primarily confined to upper- and upper-middle-income people not currently relying on medicaid. Hence private long-term care insurance has limited potential for reducing future public costs. Its potential could be improved by making policies more affordable.

There are basically four ways to bring down the price of private insurance. First, insurance companies could offer less comprehensive benefits than they do now. That, of course, would leave people vulnerable to the catastrophic costs for which they purchase insurance in the first place. So this strategy makes most sense in combination with some form of public insurance.

Second, policies could be sold to persons under age 65 in order to spread the risk over more people and to provide more time to build up reserves. But even though more people could then afford this type of insurance, nursing home and home care inflation would largely erode the interest earnings on the reserves, leaving the premiums at a fairly high level even at younger ages. Furthermore, market interest by persons under 65 is low.

Third, employers could help pay for long-term care insurance by making it a fringe benefit of employment and reducing the out-of-pocket cost to the insured of working age. This approach is, after all, critical to the affordability of acute care insurance. Many fewer people would have acute care insurance if they had to pay for it all themselves. But employers are especially reluctant to take on payment for long-term care insurance because of the unknown and potentially high costs and their already large unfunded liability for acute care retiree health benefits.

The cost of insurance policies could be reduced if the interest on premium reserves was allowed to accumulate tax free, as in life insurance. Because long-term care insurance currently does not fit neatly into insurance benefit categories under the tax law, its tax treatment is unclear. Insurers argue that, as in whole life insurance, an integral part of long-term care insurance products is the accumulation of funds over time to pay for benefits. Long-term care insurance also fulfills an asset and income protection function similar to life insurance.[71]

Fourth, long-term care insurance could be combined with acute care insurance, perhaps with reduced acute care coverage in exchange for broader long-term care coverage. The difficulty with this approach is that, as shown by their extensive purchase of medigap policies, the elderly strongly prefer comprehensive acute care coverage and may be very reluctant to give it up. Alternatively, life insurance or other fringe benefits could be traded in for long-term care insurance.

For long-term care insurance to expand to cover a significant proportion of the elderly and to provide a substantial amount of financial protection, several other barriers must be overcome. On the demand side, both the elderly and nonelderly must become better informed about their risks and potential financial liabilities regarding long-term care. People must learn that medicare and most private supplemental insurance do not cover much nursing home or home care. Older Americans must also be informed about what private long-term care insurance does and does not cover. On the supply side, insurers must overcome their fears of losing money on this insurance.

Chapter Five

Continuing Care Retirement Communities

Continuing care retirement communities (CCRCs), or "lifecare" communities, are residential campuses consisting of independent apartments and cottages and a variety of social and health services in one setting. Usually a nursing home is on or near the campus. In exchange for often large entry and monthly fees, CCRCs agree to provide care to residents for the rest of their lives.

CCRCs are simultaneously residential settings, health and social service providers, and insurers. They offer housing that enables older Americans to live close to their peers in a setting with services available.[1] CCRCs guarantee access to, and usually provide, nursing home care and other health care services, and have strong incentives for cost containment. By providing the kinds of services that elderly people need at different stages of disability, this arrangement may shorten or eliminate their stays in nursing homes.[2] At the same time, some CCRCs act as insurance mechanisms, since they guarantee to provide at least basic long-term care services in exchange for the entry and monthly fees. These CCRCs pool their residents' financial risks of long-term care.

In 1987 there were about 680 lifecare communities, each with an average of 245 residents.[3] The combined facilities serve less than 1 percent of the aged population. Almost all CCRCs are nonprofit organizations, although more for-profit CCRCs have entered the market in recent years.[4] Most do not provide full health care guarantees. The majority of facilities require substantial out-of-pocket payments for nursing home use and do not cover home health care in their contracts.

The ones that do pool the financial risk of long-term care tend to charge higher entry and monthly fees.

Simulation results suggest that comprehensive CCRCs have considerable market potential, but mostly for people at the top quarter of the income and asset distributions. Consequently, CCRCs can reduce medicaid and other public expenditures significantly only if developers devise far less expensive versions.

A new variant of the lifecare option attempts to lower two strong market barriers—the expensiveness of CCRCs and the unwillingness of the elderly to move from their homes. Developed by researchers at Brandeis University, the "lifecare at home" (LCAH) concept offers the same financial and health security of a CCRC at a substantially reduced cost to the elderly who prefer to remain in their own homes.[5] Essentially, LCAH is a prepaid long-term care insurance policy linked to its own delivery system. Entry and monthly fees are lower than for traditional CCRCs because the housing component is excluded. It differs from a social/health maintenance organization by providing more extensive long-term care services and no acute care services, and by requiring a large payment up front. The feasibility of LCAH is being tested in a demonstration project sponsored by the Robert Wood Johnson Foundation.

Although discussed here as a private sector financing option, CCRCs would fit easily into a public insurance program as a provider of services or as a supplemental insurer. This approach is currently used by the medicare program with health maintenance organizations.

CCRC Characteristics

Communities vary greatly in both long-term care services covered and fees charged. These and other characteristics have been reported in two national surveys: one conducted in 1986 jointly by the American Association of Homes for the Aging (AAHA) and Ernst and Whinney of roughly 400 communities, and another by the Wharton School in 1982 of 200 CCRCs.[6]

HEALTH CARE GUARANTEES

Although access to a broad range of services is an element that attracts people to CCRCs, many contracts cover only limited long-term care services. All CCRCs in the AAHA–Ernst and Whinney survey guaranteed access to nursing home care. More than a quarter

(28 percent) guaranteed access only, offering "fee-for-service" contracts under which residents pay full per diem rates for long-term nursing home care. A third (33 percent) provided "all-inclusive" contracts, under which the monthly fee is not increased when a resident enters a nursing home. Even under "all-inclusive" contracts, however, only half (52 percent) of the CCRCs included home health care in the monthly fees, and less than half included physical therapy (35 percent), prescription drugs (31 percent), or physician services (41 percent). Most of the full-service contracts did cover social services (79 percent) and Alzheimer's disease treatment (67 percent). The last third (31 percent) of communities surveyed offered "modified" contracts, under which the CCRC provides some nursing home care without raising the monthly fee substantially but charges either a discounted or full per diem rate for a lengthy nursing home stay.

Although access to a broad range of services is available in all these communities, the trend is away from prepaid coverage and toward charging fees for use of long-term care services.[7] Some communities, however, are beginning to offer supplemental private long-term care insurance to their residents.

ENTRY FEES

Most CCRCs require a lump-sum fee to be paid upon entry, which many people finance by selling their homes.[8] Part of the plan behind the entry fee is to prefund services that residents may use in later years as they age. Typically, entry fees vary according to the type and size of living unit (for example, studio, one-, two-, or three-bedroom apartment, cottage), square footage of the living unit, and number of persons occupying the living unit (one or two persons). According to the AAHA–Ernst and Whinney survey, the median entry fee for a one-bedroom apartment was $47,927 in 1987 dollars for one person.[9]

Communities with virtually no copayment for long-term use of nursing home beds had higher average entry fees—$62,037 in 1987 dollars for one person for a one-bedroom apartment.[10] The higher entry fees associated with these facilities reflect the greater need to prefund the long-term care services provided to their residents.

With such large entry fee requirements, the extent to which the fee is refundable is especially important to those for whom the fee represents their life savings.[11] Before 1970 communities generally charged lower entry fees that were not refundable, although this has changed over time. Lifecare communities developed during the 1970s typically charged entry fees that were 100 percent refundable during a brief trial period, after which their refundability decreased about 2 percent a month (declining refund).

Two-thirds of the communities in the 1986 AAHA–Ernst and Whinney survey provided declining refunds. About 10 percent offered fully refundable entry fees, another 10 percent nonrefundable entry fees, and another 10 percent partially refundable entry fees other than a declining refund. A minority (13 percent) offered rental units with nominal entry fees.[12] Many communities are beginning to offer a range of refundability options, charging higher entry fees for the fully refundable options.[13]

MONTHLY FEES

Besides requiring an up-front entry fee, CCRCs also charge residents a monthly fee to pay for costs of operating the facility and maintaining the apartments. Again, these fees vary by size and type of living unit and number of residents in a unit. The AAHA–Ernst and Whinney survey found median monthly fees for a one-bedroom apartment in 1987 dollars were $756 for one person. As was the case for entry fees, communities with virtually no copayment for nursing home services had higher average monthly fees—$920 in 1987 dollars for one person for a one-bedroom apartment.[14]

Financing Potential

The potential of CCRCs to finance a significant proportion of long-term care for the elderly population depends on three main factors. Program design features, such as the health care guarantee offered, the range of services covered, case management, resident selection, and third-party payment policies, are important determinants. In addition, consumer demand for retirement facilities and the availability of CCRCs strongly influence financing potential.

PROGRAM DESIGN

Health care guarantees in CCRCs are a form of risk pooling. The more long-term care services covered under the contract with little extra payment for use of these services, the greater the pooling of risks and the broader the financial protection against long-term care costs. In general, the trend in the lifecare industry is to move away from risk pooling by covering fewer services on a prepaid basis and more on a fee-for-service basis.[15] This approach clearly reduces the financial risk to the facility but puts more of a financial burden on the CCRC resident.

Some CCRCs are beginning to use a portion of their residents' entry fees to purchase insurance policies that will cover some long-term care costs. This approach benefits CCRCs because it reduces their financial risk and benefits insurance companies because they can rely on the CCRC management capabilities to control use of services.

By providing a continuum of care (for example, homemaker services and personal care), some CCRCs broaden the types of risks pooled and better protect their residents financially. Offering a variety of services may help to control use of more costly nursing home services. The 1982 Wharton survey found that communities with extensive health guarantees were more likely than those with limited guarantees to provide supportive or preventive health services that might delay or eliminate the need for nursing home care. Indeed, Bishop found that communities offering personal care and communities with full guarantees both made less use of nursing home care, other things being equal, than did communities with limited guarantees.[16]

Clearly, CCRCs with full guarantees have a strong financial incentive to monitor the amount of care provided to residents. This incentive may lead to case managers allocating nursing care only to those contract residents with more intense care needs. However, Bishop found that this careful monitoring does not translate into lower nursing home costs in full-guarantee communities, probably because the residents who do go into nursing homes incur higher nursing costs than those from limited-guarantee communities.[17]

The potential role of CCRCs in financing care for a broad population also depends on their admission policies. The percentage of applicants admitted by CCRCs is uncertain, but anecdotal evidence suggests that selection criteria typically include functional independence and mental alertness.[18] A very high proportion (91 percent) of communities in the Wharton survey required applicants to undergo physical examinations.[19] In addition, 82 percent imposed "health requirements," although these requirements were not reported in the survey. Long waiting lists also screen out seriously disabled people who cannot wait one or two years for services or who die in the interim.[20] Although these policies may help screen out those in immediate need of nursing and medical attention, it is much harder to screen people for future disability.

Some communities will accept residents with specific diseases in exchange for surcharges paid up front in addition to the entry and monthly fees. For diseases such as Alzheimer's, Parkinson's, or multiple sclerosis, these surcharges range from about $5,000 to $20,000.[21] By imposing surcharges, CCRCs can accept residents with health care risks that would drive up average expected costs.

Most CCRCs bill third parties whenever they can, thus reducing their own net costs. The Wharton survey found that most CCRCs billed medicare for covered services. Almost three-fifths (58 percent) required their residents to have medical insurance in addition to medicare. And 45 percent of the communities had medicaid-certified nursing homes, although the importance of this fact is unclear.[22] Several states require joint medicare-medicaid certification even if the facility does not bill medicaid. Nevertheless, CCRC providers often encourage their residents to apply for medicaid coverage, a practice that some states have attempted to thwart.[23]

MARKET DEMAND

Currently, demand for CCRCs is low, though probably larger than the 170,000 people in the facilities. Demand appears to be partly limited by the supply of CCRCs, as is shown by the high occupancy levels and long waiting lists for most facilities. CCRCs are seldom considered by those aged 75 or younger, and this trend toward housing an older population is increasing. The average resident is a white 81-year-old unmarried woman.[24]

According to one survey of elderly on CCRC waiting lists, the feature that most attracts people to these communities is the health guarantee, which encompasses both access to and insurance for care.[25] Relief from family burden, protection against costs of long-term care, and security and safety are other important reasons for joining. Less important reasons include protecting the family estate and the availability of social and recreational activities.

The most worrisome concerns among elderly persons waiting to enter CCRCs are financial. Potential CCRC residents are most anxious about the size of the entry and monthly fees and their ability to keep up with fee increases after joining the community. Potential residents are also concerned about changing their living environment, in particular, giving up their homes, losing their privacy, and entering highly organized living arrangements.[26] Leaving one's home is especially difficult when it requires moving into much smaller quarters—from a whole house to a one- or two-bedroom apartment. The concept of group living is foreign to many older Americans, although this may be changing. Elderly Americans are also generally unwilling to let go of their home asset, which embodies the accomplishments of a lifetime and which many wish to leave to their heirs.[27]

SUPPLY BARRIERS

Although demand for CCRCs exceeds the current enrollment rate, several related factors prevent the supply of CCRCs from fully growing to meet this demand. The most significant supply barriers are financial and organizational. Regulatory barriers are quite low.

Financial

The cost of developing and building a CCRC can be high, running to more than $20 million for some types of communities—a heavy financial burden for all but the wealthiest investors.[28] Although some of the newer proprietary sponsors may be able to finance these costs easily, the traditional nonprofit sponsors of CCRCs may have a hard time raising capital for a large number of new facilities.

Even if the obstacle of obtaining capital financing is overcome, CCRCs remain at financial risk. Although Winklevoss reports that only a few communities have gone bankrupt, other analysts have found that a substantial number of CCRCs might be facing financial problems.[29] A recent analysis of 109 CCRCs showed that 16 percent to 21 percent reported negative net incomes and negative fund balances in each of three different reporting periods.[30] The difference in findings could result from disparate methods of assessing financial position.[31]

The reported financial problems are mostly due to inadequate prefunding of costs incurred when the facility matures and the membership ages, and inefficient use of health services. Developing price schedules and, hence, adequately funding reserves for future costs requires an actuarial estimation of the resident population, their mortality and morbidity rates, and their use of health services in the future. This estimate in turn depends on accurate predictions of inflation and of the situation of a particular facility, but is often based on national rather than CCRC-specific data.[32]

According to the AAHA, although CCRC-specific data have sometimes been sparse, communities now have access to better data. The association maintains that if CCRCs periodically conduct actuarial analyses of health care use based on CCRC-specific data, price structures can be adjusted with changes in inflation, and communities should be able to avoid financial jeopardy.[33] Indeed, CCRCs may become more financially stable as they find more sophisticated methods to predict costs and start charging residents fees for use of health services.

Organizational

Financial barriers notwithstanding, CCRCs are hard to organize because they provide such varied services. Not only do operators furnish housing and related services (for example, parking and meals), but they must plan social services and activities, and either provide or contract out for health services. Thus setting up and administering a CCRC is a formidable managerial challenge.

Regulatory

Except in New York state, where they are virtually banned, current regulation of CCRCs is minimal.[34] As of May 1987 only seventeen states specifically regulated CCRCs.[35] The Federal Trade Commission (FTC) has been slightly involved in the regulation of the industry, although it has jurisdiction only over proprietary entities.[36] One form of voluntary self-regulation is the recently established Continuing Care Accreditation Commission (CCAC), which evaluates CCRCs according to guidelines prescribed by the AAHA.[37]

All states regulate CCRCs indirectly through the licensure and certification of nursing homes, and may do so as well through certificate-of-need regulation. Certificate-of-need laws, which mandate that proposed new facilities be reviewed against planning criteria and community need, could potentially limit entry, depending on the particular state's requirements.[38]

The consensus is that more regulation is needed because of the great financial risks involved for both operators and consumers. The consumer in particular is at serious risk of financial destitution, since residents of bankrupt CCRCs may lose their life savings. In this light, state consumer protection laws may not be adequate or enforced strongly enough.[39]

Model Results

CCRCs that function as comprehensive health insurance mechanisms carry the most potential for future financing of long-term care. Consequently, we modeled those communities that offer a full health care guarantee, meaning their residents pay little or nothing in additional charges for long-term care services beyond the monthly fees for their

FIGURE 5-1. **Simulation Assumptions for Continuing Care Retirement Communities**

- The simulation models CCRCs that provide a comprehensive set of benefits. CCRCs are assumed to be insurance mechanisms.
- CCRCs are assumed to bill medicare but not medicaid for nursing home and home care services. With the exception of medicare services, CCRCs are assumed to be first-dollar payers.
- CCRCs are assumed to have no effect on the use of nursing homes and home care.
- Individuals and couples are assumed to join CCRCs at age 76.
- For a two-bedroom apartment and a comprehensive set of services, CCRCs charged an average entry fee of $70,200 and an average monthly fee of $995 for one person in 1983. For two persons they charged an average entrance fee of $75,100 and a monthly fee of $1,345. Fees are indexed to inflation. Individuals and couples may pay for their entry fee with both housing and financial assets.
- People qualify financially if they have 130 percent of the income necessary for the monthly payment to cover the living costs that are not paid by the CCRC and if they have enough total assets to pay the entry fee and have at least $10,000 in assets left over.
- There is a moderate amount of health screening. All physically fit elderly and 50 percent of the disabled elderly are eligible to join CCRCs if financially qualified.
- Because of the reluctance of many elderly to move, only 50 percent of otherwise qualifying individuals and couples join CCRCs.

living units. The specific assumptions we used in the simulation of CCRCs are listed in figure 5-1.

In the simulation, people make the decision whether to join a CCRC at age 76.[40] We make this assumption because few elderly are willing to move to such an organized setting until quite late in life. Because CCRCs do not cover all living costs, applicants need income and assets considerably in excess of the entry and monthly fees to qualify financially.[41] We assume that, of those who can afford to join, all of the physically fit but only half of the disabled elderly will pass CCRC health screening tests. After applying these eligibility rules, we assume that only 50 percent would be willing to move from their homes to a CCRC.[42] This assumption also reflects the fact that the supply of CCRCs is seriously restricted by development, construction, and financial barriers.

TABLE 5-1. *Elderly Participation in CCRCs, Selected Periods, 1986–2020*[a]

Period	Number of elderly in CCRCs (millions)	Percent of elderly population
1986–90	0.399	3.21
2001–05	2.044	11.66
2016–20	3.607	18.24

SOURCE: Brookings-ICF Long-Term Care Financing Model.
a. Elderly aged 76 and older.

PARTICIPATION

There is little doubt that CCRCs are a possible alternative for many times the number of people who currently reside in them. Our model results, however, show that only 18 percent of the population aged 76 and over might be residents of CCRCs by 2016-20 (table 5-1). This amounts to only 8 percent of the population aged 65 and over.

These results are roughly consistent with those of two other studies. A 1984 study by ICF Incorporated found that 13 percent of people over 75 have sufficient income and assets to enter a lifecare center.[43] Similarly, Cohen and others found that after financing an entry fee of $35,000, about 20 percent of the elderly, devoting 10 percent of discretionary income, could afford monthly fees between $500 and $599. About half of the elderly population, devoting 25 percent of discretionary income, could afford to pay the fees.[44]

PROPORTION OF TOTAL EXPENDITURES

Assuming that 18 percent of the population aged 76 and over joined these communities, by 2016-20 CCRCs would account for 14 percent of nursing home expenditures and 8 percent of noninstitutional long-term care expenditures (table 5-2). They would be disproportionately a source of financing for those 75 and older, and for upper-income families (table 5-3).

EFFECT ON PUBLIC LONG-TERM CARE EXPENDITURES

With the availability of full-guarantee CCRCs, the model shows that medicaid expenditures for nursing homes would decline 3 percent from the base-case expenditures in 2016-20 (table 5-2). That figure is an upper-bound estimate, partly because the analysis assumes that CCRCs do not bill medicaid for long-term care services provided to residents, when in practice some CCRCs do.[45]

TABLE 5-2. *Total Expenditures for Nursing Home and Home Care, by Source of Payment, Base Case and CCRCs, 2016–20*[a]
Billions of 1987 dollars

Service and payment source	Base case	CCRCs	Percent change
Nursing homes			
Medicaid	46.192	44.993	−2.60
Medicare	1.612	1.612	0.00
CCRCs	. . .	13.478	. . .
Patients' cash income	27.889	20.419	−26.78
Patients' assets	22.423	18.017	−19.65
TOTAL	98.117	98.520	0.41
Home care			
Medicaid	2.385	2.146	−10.02
Medicare	7.699	7.700	0.01
CCRCs	. . .	1.823	. . .
Other payers	7.208	6.630	−8.02
Out-of-pocket payment	4.593	4.015	−12.58
TOTAL	21.886	22.316	1.96

SOURCE: Brookings-ICF Long-Term Care Financing Model.
a. Average annual expenditures.

TABLE 5-3. *CCRC Expenditures for Nursing Home and Home Care, by Demographic and Income Groups, 2016–20*[a]
Percentage of total payments

Category	Nursing homes	Home care
Total CRRC share	15.2	8.3
Age		
65–74	2.1	1.8
75–84	18.7	11.8
85 and over	18.0	10.4
Marital status		
Married	17.8	7.8
Unmarried	14.1	8.6
Sex		
Male	18.4	8.5
Female	13.6	8.1
Family income (dollars)[b]		
Under 7,500	0.0	0.3
7,500–14,999	3.9	2.6
15,000–19,999	7.4	6.4
20,000–29.999	28.2	7.1
30,000–39,999	40.0	24.3
40,000–49,999	30.9	21.3
50,000 and over	50.1	20.6

SOURCE: Brookings-ICF Long-Term Care Financing Model.
a. These data are based on the total payments for an admission cohort over the entire length of their stays in a nursing home or of their use of home care. For example, for a person who is admitted to a nursing home in 2016–20 for a two-year stay, we totaled two years' worth of nursing home expenditures. We then calculated the proportion of those expenditures paid by CCRCs.
b. Family income is joint income for married persons, individual income for unmarried persons.

TABLE 5-4. *Number of Elderly Medicaid Patients in Nursing Homes, Base Case and CCRCs, Selected Periods, 1986–2020*[a]
Millions of patients

Option	1986–90	2001–05	2016–20
Base case	1.334	2.006	2.343
CCRCs	1.335	1.993	2.278
Percent change	0.07	−0.65	−2.77

SOURCE: Brookings-ICF Long-Term Care Financing Model.
a. Ever in a nursing home during the course of a year.

If CCRCs were to cover the costs of home health services with no copayment by the resident, then by 2016-20 medicaid expenditures for noninstitutional services would decline 10 percent from the base case (table 5-2). Again, this is an upper-bound estimate partly because only 52 percent of the full-guarantee communities in the AAHA–Ernst and Whinney survey included home health services in their basic contract and fees.[46]

EFFECT ON PRIVATE EXPENDITURES

With the expansion of CCRCs, our model results for 2016-20 show that out-of-pocket expenditures should decrease compared with the base case as a source of funding for long-term care. Under the CCRC option, total payments to nursing homes from patients' cash income could decrease almost 27 percent (table 5-2). Similarly, total expenditures for nursing home care paid directly from patients' assets could decrease almost 20 percent. For noninstitutional long-term care expenditures, total direct out-of-pocket spending could decrease about 13 percent (table 5-2). Although direct private out-of-pocket expenditures for long-term care would be lower, those who opt for CCRCs would be indirectly paying for their long-term care through their entry and monthly fees. These fees are not reflected in the model's estimates of out-of-pocket long-term care expenditures.

As a proxy measure of the number of elderly who would avoid catastrophic long-term care costs, the number of medicaid patients in nursing homes under CCRCs would decline about 3 percent from the base case (table 5-4).

Conclusion

CCRCs offer residents housing, a variety of services, and access to nursing home care for the rest of their lives. In 1987, however, full-guarantee communities, which pool the financial risks and provide a broad range of health services in their contracts, made up only a third of all CCRCs. If CCRCs are to become a major source of long-term care financing, more communities with full health care guarantees will have to be developed.

Although risk-pooling CCRCs could solve some of the financing and delivery system problems, they would only do so for a limited number of people—at best 18 percent of the population aged 76 and over by 2016-20. These tend to be the wealthier, healthier elderly of that age group. Even if CCRC prices were to drop so that more elderly could afford them, the cultural and supply barriers might prevent CCRCs from becoming a truly widespread option. Because of limited market penetration, CCRCs will probably finance only a small proportion of nursing home and home care and have a small effect on medicaid expenditures and on the number of people who spend down to medicaid eligibility levels.

Chapter Six

Social/Health Maintenance Organizations

A social/health maintenance organization is an extension of the concept of a health maintenance organization. Enrollees in a health maintenance organization (HMO) pay a fixed fee in advance (called a capitation fee) that entitles them to a broad range of health services delivered almost entirely by physicians, hospitals, and other providers affiliated with the HMO. In contrast to the fee-for-service system, in which providers are paid separately for each service supplied, an HMO has an incentive to ensure that enrollees get appropriate care at the lowest cost and are not hospitalized when less costly home or outpatient care would be just as effective. HMOs lower health costs for their enrollees by reducing hospital use and substituting ambulatory services.[1]

A social/health maintenance organization (S/HMO) broadens this approach by covering long-term care services not normally included in health maintenance organization benefits. By consolidating acute and long-term care services and payment, S/HMOs seek to create a more efficient and coordinated system of care for the elderly. By achieving acute care savings, they can decrease the incremental cost of long-term care services; that is, reduce premiums and improve affordability for the lower-income elderly. With member use channeled to lower-cost services by cost-conscious case managers, a much richer array of home care services can be offered than in the typical long-term care insurance policy. Although discussed here as a private sector financing mechanism, S/HMOs could operate as a financing and delivery system reimbursed by a public insurance program.

The difficulty in evaluating S/HMOs is that they are more a concept than a reality. The only actual examples are from a four-site demonstration sponsored by the Health Care Financing Administration (HCFA). To date, it is unclear how well the theory of S/HMOs can work in practice. Case managers in other settings have not been able to sufficiently alter the patterns of nursing home use to generate cost savings. Although the four demonstration plans do provide more home care services than are available in conventional private long-term care insurance policies, neither the nursing home nor the home care benefits provide very deep coverage. As a result, people enrolled in the plans still risk incurring catastrophic long-term care costs and spending down to medicaid.

Obtaining adequate enrollment levels has also turned out to be a major problem for all but one of the demonstration sites. The elderly are often unwilling to give up their own doctors and other health providers and are unfamiliar with this new financing and delivery system. At most, S/HMO enrollment is likely to be a subset of the minority of the elderly who join health maintenance organizations. Moreover, even with the demonstration's fairly low premiums, the cost of membership is beyond the financial reach of a significant percentage of the elderly. Thus, as currently structured, S/HMOs are likely to have only a modest effect on medicaid.

Description of the Demonstration

Congress mandated the social/health maintenance organization demonstration as part of the Deficit Reduction Act of 1984. The four demonstration plans are Elderplan, Inc., in Brooklyn, New York; Medicare Plus II in Portland, Oregon; Seniors Plus in Minneapolis, Minnesota; and Senior Care Action Network (SCAN) in Long Beach, California. Chosen to encompass a wide variety of organizational arrangements, the principal characteristics of the four plans are presented in table 6-1.

The demonstration plans provide members a full range of acute and supplemental medical services (similar to those offered by high-option health maintenance organizations) along with a unique set of prepaid, case-managed benefits that cover chronic conditions excluded by medicare and private insurance. Frail members who meet a plan's disability qualifications can receive homemaker, personal care, respite, adult day health care, transportation, and case management services worth up to a maximum amount. Nursing home care is also covered

TABLE 6-1. *Overview of the Four Social/Health Maintenance Organization Demonstration Plans Sponsored by the Health Care Financing Administration*

Characteristics	Elderplan, Inc.	Medicare Plus II	Seniors Plus	SCAN Health Plan, Inc.
Type of sponsor	Comprehensive chronic care agency	Large established HMO	Comprehensive chronic care agency	Case management–brokerage agency
Relationship to partner(s)	Capitation contract and risk-sharing with small affiliated medical group; community hospital contracted on per diem basis	No partners; S/HMO added to existing Kaiser system	Partnership agreement with large established HMO for all acute medical; bottomline risk-sharing	Separate contracts with established medical group and medical center hospital; both on capitation-risk basis
Chief opportunity	A large untapped market	Use experience and reputation	Expertise and image of partners	A large untapped market
Chief obstacle	Creating an HMO and medical group	Creating long-term care services	A competitive HMO market	Management and incentives in the system
Long-term care benefits				
Institutional	$6,500	100 nursing home days	$6,250	$7,500
Home care	$6,500	$12,000	$6,250	$7,500
Maximum possible total annual value	$6,500	$12,000	$6,250	$7,500
Renewability of institutional benefit	Fully renewable	Only for a new "spell of illness"	$7,800 lifetime limit	Fully renewable
Benefit period				
Institutional	By benefit year	By contract year	By contract year	By benefit year
Home care	By benefit year	By month ($1,000)	By contract year	By benefit year
Cost-sharing				
Institutional	20 percent of costs to maximum of $200 a month	10 percent of costs	20 percent of costs	15 percent of costs
Home care	$10 a visit to maximum of $100 a month	10 percent of costs	20 percent of costs	$5 a visit to a maximum of $100 a month

SOURCES: Jay N. Greenberg and others, "The Social/Health Maintenance Organization and Long-Term Care," *Generations,* vol. 10 (Summer 1985), p. 53; and Walter N. Leutz and others, *Changing Health Care for an Aging Society: Planning for the Social/Health Maintenance Organization* (Lexington, Mass.: Lexington Books, 1985), p. 112.

up to the same maximum. Member out-of-pocket premiums range from $25 to $49 a month across the plans, and all have set low copayment levels for chronic care. Depending on the plan, users of expanded benefits pay $5 to $10 a visit or 10 to 20 percent of service costs.

A prime limitation of the demonstration S/HMOs is that their chronic care benefits are restricted to quite small maximum annual dollar amounts. Three of the four plans chose to serve a relatively large number of moderately impaired elderly by offering a maximum benefit of between $6,250 and $7,500 a year. The other plan offers as much as $12,000 worth of benefits a year, but coverage is available only to members who have a nursing home level of disability. Since a year in a nursing home easily costs $22,000 a year, enrollees who are confined to a nursing home for a long time face substantial personal financial liability once their S/HMO benefits are exhausted.

Financing Potential

The ability of S/HMOs to succeed financially and to play a major role in financing long-term care largely depends on how well they can control the use of services and on the market demand for managed care services. Controlling the use of the chronic care benefit is especially critical and potentially difficult because of the minimal copayments and the provision of a wide range of home care services.

CASE-MANAGED UTILIZATION CONTROL

Case managers, who are responsible for authorizing and coordinating long-term care services, are the chief means by which S/HMOs seek to control costs. Case managers assess the needs of patients and authorize the provision of specific long-term care services. They are supposed to control chronic care costs by (1) encouraging substitution of in-home care for nursing home care; (2) encouraging substitution of less expensive unskilled home help for relatively expensive skilled medical home care services; (3) helping to avoid extended hospital stays for long-term care patients who no longer have acute care needs; and (4) ensuring that the use of both nursing home and home care services is not excessive.

As mentioned earlier, case management in other settings has not altered the patterns of nursing home or hospital use or reduced the total costs of long-term care.[2] For example, the Channeling demonstration tested the ability of case management to allocate community services to frail elderly so that they could avoid institutionalization. The evaluation concluded that case management had no significant effect on the use of or expenditures on hospital, physician, and other medical services.[3] Channeling also increased total subsistence, medical, and long-term care costs per client over an eighteen-month period.[4] Providing comprehensive case management is also not cheap. The average ongoing case management cost in Channeling was $89 per client per month (in 1984 dollars), which is roughly consistent with the case management costs of other demonstrations.[5]

Based on results from most long-term care demonstrations, the likelihood that case management in S/HMOs can produce savings in total long-term care expenditures is not high. However, the earlier demonstrations had a serious limitation: they did not operate in a capitated environment in which the financial survival of the organization largely depended on the cost savings of case managers. By contrast, in the present demonstration, if the cost of providing services to enrollees exceeds revenues, the S/HMO suffers a financial loss. Incentives are thus much stronger in S/HMOs than in other case management demonstrations. In addition, none of the earlier demonstrations directly addressed the issue whether case management can limit or control the use of home care.

ADDITIONAL UTILIZATION CONTROLS

Besides case management, S/HMOs can control long-term care costs and the use of services through restrictions on service eligibility and benefit packages and through the cost-sharing and rationing of service supply. Costs can be held down by restricting eligibility for long-term care services to the severly disabled. Furthermore, the dollar limit on long-term care benefits, combined with restrictions on how often benefits can be renewed, narrows the organization's financial liability. Unlike conventional insurance, enrollee cost-sharing plays only a minor role in controlling use of expanded benefits for the demonstration.

Constraints on the supply of providers can also be used to limit the use of services in S/HMOs. Since enrollees can receive services only from specified providers, total membership use cannot exceed the capacity of those providers. As with health maintenance organizations, rationing in S/HMOs could include waits for services. Because chronic care services lack professional prestige, long-term care services in an

S/HMO may be particularly vulnerable to budget constraints, especially when they are part of a large health maintenance organization.[6]

MARKETING AND ENROLLMENT

Generating adequate enrollment has been a major problem for the current demonstration. Of the four sites, only two reached a break-even enrollment within the first two years of the demonstration.[7] Part of the problem is that potential enrollees, like most elderly, are unaware of their financial risks for long-term care expenses. Moreover, many elderly are reluctant to abandon their personal physicians and give up the freedom to choose their providers. Further, the plans with low enrollment are the same ones organized specifically for the S/HMO demonstration. The sponsors of these plans were known previously for their provision of long-term care and social services to the elderly. Thus they lack the local recognizability of an established acute health care provider.

Adverse selection is also a serious problem. Each plan must pool the financial risk of long-term care by enrolling a large majority of nondisabled persons to create a balanced membership. Adverse selection can throw an insurance pool out of balance and leave the organization with more impaired members to care for than can be financed through premiums and acute care savings. S/HMOs are especially vulnerable to adverse selection because even the limited benefit is a "bargain" to persons who must otherwise pay out-of-pocket for their nursing home or home care.

To cope with adverse selection, S/HMOs have adopted two strategies. First, in marketing their plans, they tend to portray chronic care coverage as only one of the many benefits available to members; long-term care services are not highlighted. Moreover, since the long-term care protection is limited, they can market benefits only as a partial solution to catastrophic costs. Although this strategy is a partial guard against adverse selection, it has made it difficult for social/health maintenance organizations to distinguish themselves from other health maintenance organizations and to establish a separate niche in the marketplace.

Second, to defend against adverse selection, HCFA allows the demonstration plans to limit the enrollment of the disabled elderly. Disabled persons applying after a plan's quota is reached are asked to wait until a "disabled" opening occurs. As of June 1986, if Seniors

Plus in Minneapolis allowed every disabled applicant to enroll 10.1 percent of the membership would be severely impaired rather than the current proportion of 5.7 percent.[8] The goal of the demonstration is for each site's membership to reflect the distribution of disability among the local population. Roughly halfway through the demonstration, the enrollees tend to be very much like other older people living in the community, including a 5 percent minority who have limitations in functional ability.[9]

MEDICARE, MEDICAID, AND PREMIUMS

From the perspective of social/health maintenance organizations, financing is complicated because each plan receives revenue from several sources—medicare, medicaid, private insurance premiums, and coinsurance payments.[10]

For the S/HMO demonstration, HCFA increased the regular HMO-capitated medicare payment to reflect the greater financial risks of adverse selection and the provision of long-term care services.* It also adjusted the demonstration medicare payments to reflect the higher acute care cost of caring for severely impaired medicare patients diverted from nursing homes.[11] This adjustment helped to eliminate a perverse incentive to institutionalize frail members in order to receive a higher reimbursement rate.†

For acute care, medicare payments equal what would be expected in the fee-for-service system and produce no short-term financial gains for the medicare trust fund.[12] Preliminary results show that hospital

* In HMOs (not S/HMOs), medicare pays roughly what it estimates it would pay in the fee-for-service system. The Health Care Financing Administration reimburses HMOs at 95 percent of the adjusted average per capita cost (AAPCC) of medicare services reimbursed in the enrollee's county. This payment is adjusted by enrollee age and sex and by whether or not the beneficiary is a resident of a nursing home or receiving public assistance. The AAPCC is partly based on data more than ten years old and is widely believed to be a crude predictor of acute care expenditures. Laura Himes Iversen, Charles N. Oberg, and Cynthia Polich, *Health Services Provided to Medicare Beneficiaries in HMOs: Results and Implications of a Survey of HMOs with Medicare Risk Contracts* (Excelsior, Minn.: InterStudy Center for Aging and Long-Term Care, July 1987), p. 30; and Susan Amos Kunkel and C. Keith Powell, "The Adjusted Average per Capita Cost under Risk Contracts with Providers of Health Care," *Transactions: Society of Actuaries*, vol. 33 (1981), pp. 224–26.

† The demonstration provides an AAPCC adjustment that allows a S/HMO to receive the medicare reimbursement rate calculated for beneficiaries in a nursing home for any enrollee who meets state certification requirements for nursing home placement regardless of his or her residence. Walter N. Leutz and others, *Changing Health Care for an Aging Society: Planning for the Social/Health Maintenance Organization* (Lexington, Mass.: Lexington Books, 1985), pp. 182–83.

use has been lower in the S/HMO demonstration than in the fee-for-service system, and three of the four plans are effectively controlling medicare-certified home health visits.[13]

Medicaid payments for the demonstration are also based on the idea that the state should pay roughly the same amount for medicaid-eligible members as it pays in the fee-for-service system. But state agencies have had much less experience in setting fixed, paid-in-advance rates for a representative sample of medicaid-eligible enrollees and do not know how many would qualify for long-term care services in the absence of a S/HMO program.[14]

Potential effects on medicaid include easing the problems of nursing home access for hospitalized enrollees eligible for medicaid and substituting home and community-based services for nursing home care.[15]

Perhaps medicaid's largest potential cost savings would come from substituting home care for nursing home care. If fewer elderly enter nursing homes, then fewer people are likely to use up all their income and assets and become eligible for medicaid. Moreover, by providing virtually unlimited physician and hospital services, S/HMOs should reduce the number of elderly who use up their income and assets for expenses related to acute care.

Lacking historical data on which to estimate the costs of offering long-term care benefits for the demonstration, financial planners chose to cap benefits at an annual dollar amount, thus limiting large losses from inaccurate rate setting. They derived the out-of-pocket premiums from market surveys that provided a price level elderly persons were thought willing to pay for S/HMO care.[16] They then set the long-term care benefit according to what the privately paid premium could buy, given some assumed acute care savings.*

Model Results

We used the Brookings-ICF Long-Term Care Financing Model to evaluate the potential effect of widely implementing social/health maintenance organizations similar to the ones in the current demon-

* Setting the private premium higher to cover deeper benefits could aggravate adverse selection and worsen enrollment problems. Because S/HMOs must enroll a sizable majority of "well" aged to create a broad insurance pool and because they compete with known local HMOs, the demonstration plans priced private premiums just slightly above conventional medicare supplemental care insurance premiums. Thus the premium cost for older enrollees is dramatically below that of other long-term care insurance products. Premiums, which include acute care benefits, are between $25 and $49 a month.

FIGURE 6-1. **Simulation Assumptions for Social/Health Maintenance Organizations**

- Social/health maintenance organizations are assumed to be a private insurance policy with a defined set of benefits. The simulated S/HMOs are modeled on one of the demonstration plans sponsored by the Health Care Financing Administration.
- No changes in nursing home or home care use are assumed because of case management or capitation. The results are thus more reliable for estimating the effect of non-S/HMO expenditures than of actual S/HMO reimbursements.
- The benefit covers $7,500 annually (in 1987 dollars) of long-term care services. This cap is renewable annually and may be used to cover the costs of nursing home or home care. S/HMOs are assumed to provide medicare skilled nursing facilities and home health benefits in addition to other long-term care benefits. Coinsurance is 15 percent of the cost of the nursing home and $5 a visit for home care.
- Premiums are $480 a year (in 1987 dollars) and do not vary by age. Policies are purchased if the cost is less than 5 percent of household income. Unlike the private long-term care insurance simulations, there is no asset test. Premiums are inflated by 5.8 percent a year. Disabled elderly may enroll.
- Reflecting the organizational development and enrollment barriers, only 50 percent of the elderly who can afford S/HMO premiums purchase policies.

stration. The simulation uses the assumptions described in figure 6-1, which are based on one of the current demonstration plans.

Individuals and couples who can afford the S/HMO premiums at 5 percent of income are considered financially eligible to enroll. Older persons are not required to have any specific level of assets, and disabled persons are allowed to join. Among those financially qualified, only half are assumed to enroll. We make this assumption because, as mentioned before, many elderly may be unwilling to enroll in a case-managed system of care and give up the right to choose their providers. Furthermore, even optimists do not predict that elderly enrollment in regular HMOs will exceed 50 percent.* S/HMOs will be some subset of that enrollment.

* Although the number of health maintenance organizations participating in medicare has grown rapidly, the rate of increase has recently slowed substantially. A 1987 survey of HMOs with medicare risk contracts found that 16 percent planned to terminate participation in 1988 because of inadequate capitation rates. Many of the plans remaining in the program were also unsatisfied with medicare reimbursement rates and are expecting to increase member premiums and cost-sharing and reduce or eliminate some of the current benefits provided. Such actions are likely to lessen the incentives for medicare

TABLE 6-2. *Elderly Participation in S/HMOs and Annual Premiums, Selected Periods, 1986–2020*[a]

Period	Number of elderly in S/HMOs (millions)	Percent of elderly population	Annual premium (1987 dollars)
1986–90	4.503	16.59	528
2001–05	7.361	22.32	685
2016–20	11.460	26.32	887

SOURCE: Brookings-ICF Long-Term Care Financing Model.
a. Elderly aged 67 and older.

A limitation of the simulation is that the potential saving derived from cost-conscious case management and vertical integration of services is not built into the modeling assumptions. Without evidence on the demonstration sites' effectiveness in controlling use, that omission seemed a conservative strategy. However, it is also an important caveat with regard to the following discussion.

PARTICIPATION AND PROPORTION OF EXPENDITURES

As shown in table 6-2, we found that 26 percent of the elderly aged 67 and over would be enrolled in S/HMOs by 2016–20. Each enrollee would pay an annual premium of $887 (in 1987 dollars). With this assumed widespread development, annual long-term care reimbursements by S/HMOs in 2016–20 would account for about 10 percent of total nursing home expenditures and 15 percent of all home care payments (table 6-3). Reflecting the affordability criteria, table 6-4 shows that S/HMOs would be somewhat disproportionately a source of nursing home financing for males, married persons, and upper-income elderly. The proportion of home care expenditures financed by S/HMOs would increase with income level but would be fairly uniform for other demographic characteristics.

EFFECT ON PUBLIC EXPENDITURES

The S/HMOs' long-term care benefits should reduce medicaid expenditures. By 2016–20, compared with the base case, medicaid nursing home expenditures would decline by 8 percent and medicaid home health expenditures would decline by 23 percent (table 6-3). The larger decline in expenditures on home care reflects the extensiveness

beneficiaries to enroll in HMOs. Laura Himes Iversen and Cynthia L. Polich, *Medicare Risk Contracting: What's in Store for 1988?* (Excelsior, Minn.: InterStudy Center for Aging and Long-Term Care, November 1987), pp. 1–2.

TABLE 6-3. *Total Expenditures for Nursing Home and Home Care, by Source of Payment, Base Case and S/HMOs, 2016–20*[a]
Billions of 1987 dollars

Service and payment source	Base case	S/HMOs	Percent change
Nursing homes			
Medicaid	46.192	42.603	−7.77
Medicare	1.612	1.612	0.00
S/HMOs	. . .	9.998	. . .
Patients' cash income	27.889	23.845	−14.51
Patients' assets	22.430	19.030	−15.10
TOTAL	98.117	97.090	−1.05
Home care			
Medicaid	2.385	1.827	−23.40
Medicare	7.699	7.690	−0.12
S/HMOs	. . .	3.293	. . .
Other payers	7.206	5.502	−23.65
Out-of-pocket payments	4.593	4.356	−5.16
TOTAL	21.886	22.670	3.58

SOURCE: Brookings-ICF Long-Term Care Financing Model. Figures are rounded.
a. Average annual expenditures.

TABLE 6-4. *S/HMO Expenditures for Nursing Home and Home Care, by Demographic and Income Groups, 2016–20*[a]
Percentage of total payments

Category	Nursing homes	Home care
Total S/HMO share	10.9	14.8
Age		
65–74	10.4	16.4
75–84	9.0	13.6
85 and over	12.5	14.5
Marital status		
Married	13.3	15.2
Unmarried	9.9	14.5
Sex		
Male	13.4	14.1
Female	9.6	15.1
Family income (dollars)[b]		
Under 7,500	3.8	4.2
7,500–14,999	8.3	10.8
15,000–19,999	12.9	14.9
20,000–29,999	13.8	17.4
30,000–39,999	21.2	30.0
40,000–49,999	20.8	24.9
50,000 and over	22.6	27.3

SOURCE: Brookings-ICF Long-Term Care Financing Model
a. These data are based on the total payments for an admission cohort over the entire length of their stays in a nursing home or of their use of home care. For example, for a person who is admitted to a nursing home in 2016–20 for a two-year stay, we totaled two-years worth of nursing home expenditures. We then calculated the proportion of those expenditures paid by the S/HMOs.
b. Family income is joint income for married persons, individual income for unmarried persons.

TABLE 6-5. *Number of Elderly Medicaid Patients in Nursing Homes, Base Case and S/HMOs, Selected Periods, 1986–2020*[a]
Millions of patients

Option	1986–90	2001–05	2016–20
Base case	1.334	2.006	2.343
S/HMOs	1.318	1.938	2.212
Percent change	−1.20	−3.39	−5.59

SOURCE: Brookings-ICF Long-Term Care Financing Model.
a. Ever in a nursing home during the course of a year.

of benefits provided by S/HMOs and the much higher costs associated with nursing home care.

EFFECT ON PRIVATE EXPENDITURES

The simulation shows a modest 15 percent decrease in nursing home payments from cash income and assets by 2016–20 when compared with the base-case expenditures. Reductions in out-of-pocket payments for home care are smaller, a decline of 5 percent from the base case for the same period (table 6-3). As a proxy measure of how well S/HMOs can protect people from incurring catastrophic nursing home costs, the number of medicaid nursing home patients declines by 6 percent in 2016–20 from the base case (table 6-5).

Conclusion

Social/health maintenance organizations extend the HMO concept of capitated financing to include a variety of long-term care services. The principal premises are that a case-managed continuum of care will be cost effective and that there can be enough acute care savings (along with modest premiums) to help finance expanded home care services. S/HMOs consciously link the acute and long-term care sectors, taking from acute care to give to long-term care.

Only four social/health maintenance organizations currently operate, and their existence derives directly from a congressional mandate. To increase the number of S/HMOs would require various waivers of medicare and medicaid restrictions. For example, S/HMOs would need to continue to receive higher levels of medicare payments for severely disabled elderly than HMOs receive. Otherwise, there would be an incentive to place these elderly in nursing homes so as to receive higher payments for acute care services. Given the reluctance of the Reagan administration to grant such waivers, the increase of S/HMOs in the near term is doubtful. Their future expansion probably lies in two different strategies. First, they can function as "super medigap" policies that offer short- and medium-term nursing home and home care. Second, they may develop as joint ventures between health maintenance organizations and insurance companies in which freestanding long-term care insurance policies are sold to enrollees in HMOs.[17]

Chapter Seven

Individual Medical Accounts

An individual retirement account for long-term care, often called an individual medical account (IMA), would give tax advantages to those who saved for their long-term care expenses. In contrast to an individual retirement account (IRA), which can be used for any retirement expense, the money accumulated in the individual medical account would be earmarked for long-term care services or private long-term care insurance. By encouraging private saving, an individual medical account would give people some degree of financial protection from catastrophic long-term care costs and the flexibility to construct a service package that best fit their needs.

Several proposals to establish individual medical accounts have been put forward by government agencies, Congress, and researchers.[1] At least two legislative proposals embodying this concept have been introduced in Congress.[2] Although specific features of proposed individual medical accounts vary, they have several common characteristics. Each year people could contribute up to a maximum amount to their individual medical accounts. Proposals differ on whether the contributions would be federal income tax deductions or tax credits, but in all proposals the interest earnings on deposited funds would be tax exempt. Upon reaching a certain age, people could begin withdrawing funds to pay for their long-term care needs or, in some proposals, acute care needs. Financial penalties would apply to money used for purposes other than long-term or acute care or withdrawn before the IMA owner had reached the specified age. All funds remaining at the death of the IMA owner would go to his or her designated heir.

The United States has a low savings rate, and many economists believe that prospects for economic growth would be enhanced if private saving could be increased and channeled into productive investment. It is appealing to imagine that tax incentives could be used both to expand private saving and to enable older people to finance long-term care more easily.

As part of an effort to increase saving, the Economic Recovery Tax Act of 1981 allowed individuals to contribute up to $2,000 a year to an individual retirement account. Contributions were tax deductible and interest earnings were tax deferred. Both contributions and interest earnings were taxed when withdrawn. The Tax Reform Act of 1986 eliminated the tax deductibility of contributions for upper-middle-class and wealthier taxpayers, but retained the exclusion of interest earnings for all taxpayers.*

For individual medical accounts to play a prominent role in the financing of long-term care, participation would have to be much higher than it has been in individual retirement accounts. In particular, many more young taxpayers and middle- and lower-income workers would have to participate. This greater participation seems unlikely, however, given the lack of interest in long-term care by the population aged 65 and under and the low national savings rate.

Moreover, people would have to save for many years before they could accumulate enough assets to pay for a significant proportion of their long-term care expenses. Because people who will be 85 and older in 2016–20 are currently in their fifties, IMAs could not do much for today's elderly or people approaching retirement in the near future.

It is doubtful that individual medical accounts would significantly affect medicaid expenditures or the number of people in nursing homes who spend down to medicaid, since a disproportionate share of IMA participants are likely to have fairly high incomes and substantial other assets. Most IMA assets would merely substitute for payments that the upper-income elderly could afford to make out of their annual cash income. On balance, the federal tax losses from people placing money in these accounts would far exceed the medicaid savings.

* After tax reform, the maximum deduction varies with income. Single persons with less than $25,000 in adjusted gross income (AGI) can deduct $2,000, but the deduction is phased out for persons with AGI greater than $35,000. For a two-income married couple, the maximum deduction is $4,000 if their AGI is less than $40,000 and the deduction is reduced proportionally up to $50,000 in income, where it is eliminated. Interest earnings are still tax deferred for all income levels.

Financing Potential

Although individual medical accounts do not exist today, some insights into how they would fare as a long-term care financing tool can be gained by examining the experience under the IRA savings scheme. For one thing, many of the financial incentives that induced people to contribute to individual retirement accounts would also apply to individual medical accounts. Money deposited in the account would reduce the participant's income tax for the current year, and the taxes on the interest earnings would be deferred. There could also be large tax savings when participants withdrew the money if they were in a lower tax bracket after retirement. The Tax Reform Act of 1986, by lowering the tax rates, reduced the financial value of tax deductions but did not affect the value of tax credits. With only three tax brackets, the probability that taxpayers will change brackets when they retire is smaller than before.

The participation in and effect of individual retirement accounts probably represents a best-case scenario for the operation of individual medical accounts. Indeed, it is questionable whether many people would be willing to open a separate dedicated account, such as an individual medical account, that could be used only for such a narrow purpose as long-term care. After all, to the extent that the prospect of an extended period of disability is unpleasant and undesirable, people may be reluctant to plan for it.[3]

Only a small minority of U.S. taxpayers have been willing to open and contribute to an individual retirement account. Tax returns claiming IRA deductions reached a high of 15.3 percent in 1984 (table 7-1). The total percentage of people with individual retirement accounts is probably somewhat higher, since many people do not contribute to their IRAs every year. Given the importance of the tax deduction in motivating people to contribute, participation rates may drop dramatically with the 1986 tax reform. The Brookings Tax Model estimates that only 19 percent of tax returns for households that could have been expected to contribute to an IRA will be eligible for a tax deduction in 1988.[4] Under the reformed tax law, people who want to save for retirement might be better off placing money in a tax-free municipal bond fund, since it would offer the same tax advantages as an IRA without the penalties or restrictions associated with early withdrawal.

The age groups of IRA participants cast doubt about the adequacy of the individual medical accounts to finance long-term care expenses.

TABLE 7-1. *Tax Returns Claiming IRA Contribution and Amount of Contribution, by Total Positive Income Group, 1984*[a]

Total positive income (dollars)	Total returns (thousands)	Returns with an IRA		IRA contributions	
		Number (thousands)	Percent of total	Total (millions of dollars)	Average (dollars)
Under 5,000	15,707	35	0.2	42.4	1,216
5,000–9,999	15,792	334	2.1	410.8	1,230
10,000–14,999	13,766	681	5.0	1,036.8	1,522
15,000–19,999	11,116	1,033	9.3	1,714.8	1,660
20,000–34,999	22,453	4,020	17.9	7,675.6	1,909
35,000–49,999	11,645	3,908	33.6	9,055.7	2,317
50,000–99,999	7,319	4,129	56.4	12,082.2	2,926
100,000–199,999	1,206	822	68.2	2,556.5	3,110
200,000 and over	434	268	61.9	799.3	2,982
TOTAL	99,438	15,230	15.3	35,374.1	2,322

SOURCE: U.S. Internal Revenue Service, *Statistics of Income, 1984: The Individual Tax Model File* (public use tape).
a. Total positive income is gross income before subtracting business losses, farm losses, negative capital gains, and income tax exclusions.

The standard argument is that, if people put aside money when they are young (that is, substantially under age 65), the "miracle of compound interest" acting over a long period will make the required contributions small and painless.

Workers usually delay preparing for retirement until they are middle-aged or older. As can be determined from table 7-2, 30 percent of workers aged 45 to 64 owned an IRA in 1982, while only 13 percent of workers 25 to 44 did. Starting individual medical accounts at 45 constrains the amount of money that can accumulate. The illiquidity of IRA saving is a serious deterrent to IRA participation, especially among younger persons and people with limited income and assets.

Analysis by the Social Security Administration actuaries suggests that the required IMA contributions, even if the saver is young, will have to be quite high. As shown in table 7-3, people who begin to save at age 30 must contribute at least $603 to $1,036 a year to cover only 2.2 years of nursing home care, depending on the inflation rate. Higher levels of saving would be required to cover home care benefits or longer nursing home stays.

Required contributions are large partly because individual medical accounts fail to pool the risk of institutionalization. This means that each person must save enough to cover the high costs of a long stay in a nursing home rather than take advantage of the fact that most people will not use nursing home care for long periods. For example, consider ten people of whom only four will ultimately need to be in a

TABLE 7-2. *Distribution of IRA Participation and the Total Labor Force, by Age, 1982*

Age	IRA owners		Total labor force[a]	
	Number (millions)	Distribution (percent)	Number (millions)	Distribution (percent)
25 to 34	3.1	18.6	31.8	28.7
35 to 44	4.0	23.7	22.6	20.4
45 to 54	4.5	27.1	17.1	15.4
55 to 64	4.2	24.9	12.1	10.9
Under 25 and 65 and over	0.9	5.6	27.1	24.5
TOTAL	16.7	100.0	110.6	100.0

SOURCES: Employee Benefit Research Institute, "IRAs, 401(K)s and Employer Pensions: Must There Be Tradeoffs? Retirement Income and Individual Retirement Accounts," *EBRI Issue Brief*, vol. 52 (March 1986), p. 3; and U.S. Department of Labor, Bureau of Labor Statistics, *Employment and Earnings*, vol. 29 (June 1982), pp. 25–26. Figures are rounded.

a. Noninstitutional employment, including military, May 1982.

nursing home for one and a half years at the cost of $22,000 a year. To pay for this care through individual saving will require each of the ten to save at least $33,000.* In the end, six people will deprive themselves over a lifetime in order to pay for services that they may never need. By contrast, pooling the risk requires that each person save $13,200.

Another reason the required contributions are large is that long-term care costs increase faster than the general price level. In constant dollars, the real cost of a year in a nursing home may double over the next thirty years. Thus the spread between the rate of return on the contribution and the rate of increase in nursing home costs will be small. As a result, interest earnings fail to reduce the level of required contributions dramatically.† The younger the participant, the more years the differential inflation rate will affect the savings needed.

Ownership of individual retirement accounts is strongly related to income, with little participation by low- and moderate-income families. While overall IRA participation rates have been modest, the demand for IRAs among high-earning workers has been much higher. As can be determined from table 7-1, in 1984, 58 percent of workers with total

* This figure is the minimal amount that does not include an increase in the cost of nursing home care due to inflation.

† Compared with a 4.4 percent annual nursing home inflation rate, a 5.8 percent annual nursing home inflation assumption adds 47 percent to the saving needed starting at age 50, 59 percent at age 40, and 72 percent at age 30. Technical Work Group on Private Financing of Long-Term Care for the Elderly, *Report to the Secretary on Private Financing of Long-Term Care for the Elderly* (Washington, D.C.: Department of Health and Human Services, November 1986), chap. 3, pp. 21–23 and table 5.

TABLE 7-3. *Estimated Initial Annual Savings Needed to Pay for Expected Nursing Home Use, by Age and Nursing Home Inflation Rate Assumptions*[a]
1987 dollars

Age saving begins	Annual savings at 4.4 percent nursing home inflation	Annual savings at 5.8 percent nursing home inflation
30	603	1,036
40	892	1,418
50	1,510	2,222

SOURCE: Technical Work Group on Private Financing of Long-Term Care for the Elderly, *Report to the Secretary on Private Financing of Long-Term Care for the Elderly* (Washington, D.C.: Department of Health and Human Services, November 1986), chap. 3, p. 193 and table 5. In developing their estimates, the Social Security Administration actuaries assumed the following: 1. Individuals contribute to IMAs through age 64 only. 2. Contributions must be capable of accumulating a fund at age 65 sufficient to provide the inflation-indexed coverage for a nursing home stay equal to the expected average amount of time spent in a nursing home. 3. Expected future nursing home use after the age of 65 is estimated as 2.2 years, 2.1 years, 2.0 years, and 1.9 years, on average, for people who begin contributing at ages 30, 40, 50, and 60, respectively, in 1986. These estimates are based on nursing home population counts from the 1977 National Nursing Home Survey, adjusted to reflect a 37 percent increase due to induced demand. The higher use for younger ages reflects expected increases in life span. 4. Contributions earn a 6.08 percent rate of return. 5. All unused funds are passed on to the decedent's estate at death.

a. General inflation is assumed to be 4.0 percent a year.

positive income (gross income before adjustments) of $50,000 or more contributed to an IRA. At the other end of the income distribution, only 4 percent of workers earning total positive income of less than $20,000—the majority of taxpayers—contributed to an IRA. Contributions at the legal maximum are also strongly correlated with income. Although 61 percent of IRA owners with total positive income above $50,000 contributed the maximum permissible in 1984, only 38 percent of IRA owners with incomes below $20,000 did.[5]

Moreover, IRA participation rates are also highly skewed toward taxpayers who already have substantial total assets. Within each income class, the share of eligible taxpayers who contribute to IRAs is generally greater as interest and dividend income rises.[6]

Because of the progressive rate structure, the tax advantages associated with the IRA deductions are higher at the upper end of the income scale. A $2,000 tax deduction is worth $500 in reduced taxes for earners at the 25 percent bracket but only $300 for earners at the 15 percent bracket. Clearly, low-income workers who pay no income tax cannot be motivated to save by the offer of a tax deduction. Not surprisingly, then, taxpayers with total positive income of $50,000 and more accounted for almost half of all tax losses to the Treasury from IRA deductions in 1983, despite the fact that they accounted for only 8 percent of all tax returns.[7] By limiting the tax deductibility of IRAs for upper-income taxpayers and reducing the number of tax brackets, the Tax Reform Act of 1986 attempts to redress this inequity. Tax credits, which directly reduce tax liabilities, might induce more participation by the middle- and lower-income population, but also might be far more expensive in tax losses to the Treasury.

Although one goal of individual retirement accounts is to raise the overall level of saving in the United States, it is not certain that it has had the desired effect. Taxpayers can benefit from IRAs simply by transferring their current savings from taxable accounts to tax-sheltered ones. Only if taxpayers reduce consumption in order to add to their IRAs will new savings be generated. On a macroeconomic level, personal savings as a percent of disposable personal income dropped from 7.5 percent in 1981 to 5.1 percent in 1985, despite the much wider availability of IRAs beginning in 1982.[8] Nevertheless, using individual survey data, Venti and Wise found that people reduced consumption to contribute to IRAs, thereby creating new savings.[9] Whether or not IRAs have expanded overall private savings, the portion of savings devoted to retirement purposes is likely to have increased.

Model Results

To assess the potential role of individual medical accounts in financing long-term care, we simulated three different prototypes. For the simulation we assumed the rules that were in effect before the Tax Reform Act of 1986 regarding who may deduct IRA contributions. To maximize the potential effect, contributions to individual medical accounts were assumed to be entirely new savings and not shifted from other assets. Detailed assumptions for the simulations are presented in figures 7-1, 7-2, and 7-3.

The first prototype, IMA5.8, raises the ceiling on contributions to individual retirement accounts from $2,000 for individuals and $4,000 for couples to $3,000 for individuals and $6,000 for couples. The additional $1,000 a person is treated as a dedicated individual medical account that will be used exclusively for long-term care expenditures. Because it is always more advantageous for a person to put money in an unrestricted rather than a restricted savings account, people are assumed to contribute to individual medical accounts only if they are already making maximum contributions to individual retirement accounts. Projected 1983 IRA participation rates and contribution levels are assumed. We also modeled the same prototype IMA at an annual rate of inflation for nursing home and home care of 4.4 percent (IMA4.4).

FIGURE 7-1. **Simulation Assumptions for Individual Medical Accounts at 5.8 Percent Inflation (IMA5.8)**

- Beginning in 1987, people aged 30 to 60 can start an individual medical account.
- People participate in IMAs only if they are at the maximum for IRA contributions. Ninety percent of people at the IRA maximum are assumed to contribute to an IMA.
- Participants place $1,000 a year in their IMAs. This amount is indexed to the consumer price index.
- All IMA contributions are new savings, not transfers from other assets.
- Participants stop contributing to their accounts at retirement.
- The funds in the IMA may be used only for long-term care expenses and are the first source of payment for out-of-pocket nursing home and home care expenses.
- Accumulated funds remaining in the account at the owner's death go to the spouse or the estate.

FIGURE 7-2. **Simulation Assumptions for Individual Retirement Accounts Used as a Lump Sum for Long-Term Care (LTCLUMP)**

- Individual retirement accounts are abolished and replaced by individual medical accounts. Participation rates and contribution levels for the IMAs are the same as for IRAs.
- Rules in effect before the Tax Reform Act of 1986 are assumed in terms of who may deduct IRA contributions from their income. Individuals may deduct up to $2,000, single-income couples may deduct $2,250, and dual-income couples may deduct up to $4,000.
- In the base case, IRA amounts are put into an annuity at retirement. In LTCLUMP the IRA is not put into an annuity and all funds are used solely for long-term care.
- All IRA contributions are new savings, not transfers from other assets.
- Participants stop contributing to their accounts at retirement.
- IRA funds are the first source for out-of-pocket nursing home and home care expenses.
- Accumulated funds remaining in the account at the owner's death go to the spouse or the estate.

FIGURE 7-3. **Simulation Assumptions for the Combination of Individual Medical Account and Long-Term Care Insurance (IMAINS)**

- Beginning in 1987, people aged 30 to 60 can start an individual medical account. Participation rates are the same as in the IMA5.8 simulation.
- Under this option, the participant contributes to his or her own IMA, and half of his or her interest earnings are placed in a general insurance pool to be used for nursing home care. Home care is not covered. If a person exhausts his or her IMA, he or she can draw on the insurance pool.
- The individual medical account and the insurance pool provide an inflation-indexed unlimited nursing home benefit of $50 a day (in 1986 dollars) after a 100-day deductible period. The 100-day deductible is paid out of a participant's cash income and other assets.
- The contributions needed to provide typical benefits, as estimated by Social Security Administration actuaries, vary from $824 a year for accounts begun at age 30 and rise to $1,964 for accounts begun at age 60. Participants in IMAINS contribute the full amount needed. Required annual contributions are indexed by nursing home and home care inflation rates.
- All IMA contributions are new savings, not transfers from other assets.
- Participants stop contributing to their accounts at retirement.
- Accumulated funds remaining in the account at the owner's death go to the spouse or the estate.

The second prototype, LTCLUMP, entirely eliminates individual retirement accounts and replaces them with similarly structured individual medical accounts. We assumed that participation and contribution rates for the individual medical accounts would be the same as the projected 1983 rates for individual retirement accounts. These highly optimistic assumptions about participation and contributions clearly set a very high upper-bound estimate on the potential role of individual medical accounts.

The third prototype, based on a proposal developed by the Department of Health and Human Services, combines an individual savings plan with insurance.[10] In this simulation, IMAINS, the participant contributes to an individual medical account and half of his or her interest earnings are placed in a general insurance pool to be used for nursing home care. If the person exhausts his or her individual medical account, he or she can draw on the insurance pool. Again, the simulation limits participation to those already contributing the IRA maximum.

TABLE 7-4. *Elderly Participation in IMA Savings Options, Selected Periods, 1986–2020*[a]

Option and period	Number of elderly with an IMA (millions)	Percent of elderly population	Average IMA balance (1987 dollars)
IMA5.8[b]			
1986–90	0.203	0.65	1,836
2001–05	4.033	10.91	6,371
2016–20	14.168	28.19	14,777
LTCLUMP			
1986–90	0.623	1.99	4,061
2001–05	5.681	15.37	17,063
2016–20	16.405	32.64	38,596
IMAINS			
1986–90	0.378	1.21	7,356
2001–05	4.343	11.75	22,231
2016–20	14.713	29.27	36,455

SOURCE: Brookings-ICF Long-Term Care Financing Model.
a. Elderly aged 65 and older.
b. Participation and average IMA balance in IMA4.4 is virtually the same as in IMA5.8.

PARTICIPATION

As shown in table 7-4, the Brookings-ICF Long-Term Care Financing Model projects that by 2016–20 between 28 percent and 33 percent of the elderly might have individual medical accounts. The average account balance among them varies from $14,777 (in constant 1987 dollars) for IMA5.8 to a high of $38,596 for LTCLUMP.[11] Thus, even with generous participation and contribution assumptions, the average individual medical account could finance only about six months to a year of nursing home care.[12]

PROPORTION OF TOTAL EXPENDITURES

Simulation results suggest that individual medical accounts could finance only a small part of total long-term care expenditures. By 2016–20 individual medical accounts would finance only between 3 percent and 8 percent of total U.S. nursing home expenditures (table 7-5), and between 4 percent and 5 percent of total home care expenditures (table 7-6). Under an assumption of lower nursing home inflation (4.4 percent a year), the straight IMA would finance 4 percent of total nursing home expenditures and 4 percent of total home care expenditures. Although individual medical accounts would fund only a small proportion of nursing home care for all demographic and most income categories, they disproportionately finance care for the young elderly

TABLE 7-5. *Total Expenditures for Nursing Home Care, by Source of Payment, Base Case and IMA Options, 2016–20*[a]
Billions of 1987 dollars; percent change from base case

Option	Total	Medicaid	Medicare	IMA	Patients' cash income	Patients' assets
Base case	98.117	46.192	1.612	...	27.889	22.423
IMA5.8[b]	98.352	45.616	1.612	2.925	26.372	21.826
Percent change	0.24	−1.25	0.00	...	−5.44	−2.66
LTCLUMP	98.868	44.486	1.612	8.367	23.407	20.993
Percent change	0.76	−3.69	0.00	...	−16.07	−6.38
IMAINS	98.870	44.259	1.612	8.039	24.339	20.620
Percent change	0.77	−4.18	0.00	...	−12.73	−8.04

SOURCE: Brookings-ICF Long-Term Care Financing Model.
a. Average annual expenditures.
b. Under the IMA4.4 option, total expenditures would be $66 billion (0.3 percent above the base case at 4.4 percent annual nursing home inflation), medicaid expenditures would be $23 billion (1.5 percent decrease), medicare expenditures would be $1 billion (no change), IMA expenditures would be $3 billion, and expenditures from cash income and assets would be $25 billion and $14 billion (6.6 and 2.7 percent decrease), respectively. Figures are rounded.

(aged 65 to 74), who had more time to accumulate funds (table 7-7). Reflecting the participation in IRAs, individual medical accounts are a greater source of long-term care financing for men and for wealthier people than for other groups.

EFFECT ON PUBLIC EXPENDITURES

Because IRA participants, especially those contributing the maximum, are disproportionately drawn from the higher end of the income

TABLE 7-6. *Total Expenditures for Home Care, by Source of Payment, Base Case and IMA Options, 2016–20*[a]
Billions of 1987 dollars; percent change from base case

Option	Total	Medicaid	Medicare	IMA	Other payers	Out-of-pocket payment
Base case	21.886	2.385	7.699	...	7.208	4.593
IMA5.8[b]	21.892	2.385	7.699	0.817	7.219	3.771
Percent change	0.03	0.00	0.00	...	0.15	−17.90
LTCLUMP	21.882	2.390	7.696	1.091	7.210	3.496
Percent change	−0.02	0.21	−0.04	...	0.03	−23.88

SOURCE: Brookings-ICF Long-Term Care Financing Model.
a. Average annual expenditures.
b. Under IMA4.4, total expenditures would be $14 billion (0.5 percent above the base case at 4.4 percent annual home care inflation), medicaid expenditures would be $1.5 billion (0.2 percent decrease), medicare expenditures would be $5 billion (no change), IMA expenditures would be $0.5 billion, and expenditures from other payers and out-of-pocket would be $4.5 billion and $2.6 billion (0.4 and 19 percent decrease), respectively. Figures are rounded.

TABLE 7-7. *IMA Expenditures for Nursing Home Care, by Demographic and Family Income Groups, Various Options, 2016–20*[a]
Percentage of total payments for nursing home services

Category	IMA5.8	IMA4.4	LTCLUMP	IMAINS
Total IMA share	3.1	4.4	8.9	7.4
Age				
65–74	7.0	9.7	15.7	13.3
75–84	3.5	5.1	10.0	7.9
85 and over	1.0	1.6	5.2	4.5
Martial status				
Married	3.1	4.5	10.1	9.5
Unmarried	3.1	4.4	8.4	6.5
Sex				
Male	5.3	7.4	16.1	14.2
Female	2.0	2.9	5.3	4.0
Family income (dollars)[b]				
Under 7,500	1.0	1.6	3.5	1.6
7,500–14,999	2.2	3.2	7.6	6.5
15,000–19,999	2.8	4.1	10.4	7.0
20,000–29,999	4.8	7.0	16.4	11.6
30,000–39,999	6.2	8.3	14.9	11.8
40,000–49,999	6.7	9.8	9.6	15.8
50,000 and over	5.5	7.7	13.9	15.8

SOURCE: Brookings-ICF Long-Term Care Financing Model.
a. These data are based on the total payments for an admission cohort over the entire length of their stays in a nursing home. For example, for a person who is admitted to a nursing home in 2016–20 for a two-year stay, we totaled two years' worth of nursing home expenditures. We then calculated the proportion of those expenditures paid by individual medical accounts.
b. Family income is joint income for married persons, individual income for unmarried persons.

and asset distribution, individual medical accounts are unlikely to have much effect on medicaid expenditures for nursing home and home care. Compared with the base case, by 2016–20 medicaid expenditures for nursing home care would fall 1 percent to 4 percent (table 7-5). Under IMA5.8 and LTCLUMP, the only options covering home care, medicaid spending for home care would remain virtually unchanged from the base case (table 7-6). The effect of IMA4.4 on public expenditures for nursing home care and home care is the same as that of IMA5.8.

To assess the total effect on public expenditures, the medicaid saving must be compared with the revenue loss through the granting of tax deductions to IMA participants. Given the assumed participation rates, the Brookings Tax Model was used to estimate the tax loss under IMA5.8. The result was a loss of $10 billion in 1988, far more than the offsetting annual medicaid saving of $600 million in 2016–20.[13] The

TABLE 7-8. *Number of Elderly Medicaid Patients in Nursing Homes, Base Case and IMA Options, Selected Periods 1986–2020*[a]
Millions of patients; percent change from base case

Option	1986–90	2001–05	2016–20
Base case	1.334	2.006	2.343
IMA5.8[b]	1.334	2.002	2.300
Percent change	0.00	−0.20	−1.84
LTCLUMP	1.334	1.997	2.215
Percent change	0.00	−0.45	−5.46
IMAINS	1.334	1.982	2.222
Percent change	0.00	−1.20	−5.16

SOURCE: Brookings-ICF Long-Term Care Financing Model.
a. Ever in a nursing home during the course of a year.
b. The percent decrease in medicaid patients in nursing homes under the IMA4.4 option is the same in 1986–90 and 2001–05 as under IMA5.8. In 2016–20, the percent decrease is slightly greater under IMA4.4 than IMA5.8 (2.3 percent compared with 1.8 percent). Figures are rounded.

tax losses would grow even larger over time as the exempt earnings on the accounts increased.

EFFECT ON PRIVATE EXPENDITURES

The simulations for 2016–20 show that individual medical accounts would mostly substitute for other out-of-pocket spending on long-term care. Under the range of options, cash income payments for nursing home care would fall between 5 percent and 16 percent below the base case (table 7-5). Payments for nursing home care from patients' assets would fall between 3 percent and 8 percent. Cash income payments decrease more than asset payments because IMA participants will often be able to pay for their nursing home care out of current income without resorting to use of assets.

Individual medical accounts have a larger effect on out-of-pocket payments for home care. By 2016–20 out-of-pocket spending on home care would fall 18 percent below the base case under IMA5.8 and 24 percent under LTCLUMP (table 7-6).

If nursing home inflation was only 4.4 percent a year, by 2016–20 individual medical accounts could reduce nursing home expenditures from cash income by 7 percent and from assets by 3 percent. Similarly, out-of-pocket spending on home care would fall 19 percent under those lower inflation assumptions.

The simulation results show that individual medical accounts have relatively little effect on the number of people who incur catastrophic nursing home expenses and spend down to medicaid. By 2016–20 the number of medicaid patients in nursing homes falls by only 2 percent to 5 percent (table 7-8). The decrease in medicaid nursing home residents under the straight IMA at 4.4 percent annual nursing home inflation does not differ much from the decrease at 5.8 percent inflation.

Conclusion

The problem with an individual savings strategy is that everyone must save quite a lot each year to accumulate enough to pay for the catastrophic long-term care expenses that only a minority will incur. On the one hand, because risk is not pooled and nursing home and home care cost increases erode the purchasing power of contributed savings, the savings that people must put aside each year are by no means trivial.[14] On the other hand, perhaps only one in four of the elderly will spend a year or more in a nursing home. Thus under the IMA savings scheme as many as three-quarters of the participants will vastly oversave for catastrophic expenses they will never incur. Moreover, because most tax deductions and interest income exclusions for individual medical accounts would accrue to persons who typically would pay for their long-term care expenses from private funds, the revenue loss to the U.S. government could be large, even though the effect on medicaid would be small. The irony is that a program promoted as a way of reducing public costs could result in a large increase in the federal deficit.

Chapter Eight

Home Equity Conversions

The vast majority of the elderly, including the poor, have substantial assets in their homes. Approximately three-quarters of all elderly households own their own homes in 1986–90, with an average net home equity value of $54,000 in 1987 dollars.[1] This asset, however, is illiquid and cannot readily be used without sale of the house and relocation by the homeowner. As a result, the elderly live too poor and die too rich.

Home equity conversions allow elderly homeowners to transform this illiquid asset into a stream of income or readily available cash, which could help them to purchase long-term care services or insurance policies. Although home equity conversion plans can take various forms, the basic concept explored in this chapter is the reverse mortgage, in which the bank gives the homeowner a loan, usually in the form of monthly installments. At some time in the future, preferably after his or her death, the homeowner or heirs repay the loan and its interest, using the proceeds from the sale of the home.

There are few existing reverse mortgages—perhaps 2,000 transactions had been closed as of 1987.* Although the number of elderly home-

* As of September 1987 the two programs drawing the most attention—the reverse annuity mortgage (RAM) program and the American Homestead Mortgage Corporation (AHMC) individual retirement mortgage account (IRMA)—had completed about 400 and 1,200 transactions, respectively. (The IRMA was previously called the Century Plan.) Among the quasi-public programs are the Connecticut Housing Finance Authority reverse mortgage program (191 loans), the Buffalo HELP program (65 transactions), and the elderly home equity program sponsored jointly by the Rhode Island Housing and Mortgage Finance Authority Corporation and the Rhode Island Department of Elderly Affairs (60 loans). The number of transactions taking place outside of these programs has not been substantial. Maurice D. Weinrobe, Clark University, personal communication, October 6, 1987; Frank Engel, financial planner, American Homestead Mortgage

owners is large, the growth of the reverse mortgage market is expected to be quite slow, partly because home equity conversions are complex and unconventional. They deplete an asset that many Americans hold nearly sacred and have worked their entire lives to obtain. Moreover, the home is largely a protected asset under medicaid, except that in some states elderly medicaid recipients can be required to sell their houses after it has been determined that they will not return home. Elderly people may not be willing to consume the home asset to prevent the use of usually smaller liquid assets that medicaid does not protect.

Not only are homeowners uncomfortable with the concept of liquidating their homes, but the mortgage industry is also leery of reverse mortgages for the elderly. If an elderly homeowner lives longer than expected, the financial institution may have to foreclose or postpone claiming its asset. Banks could incur large financial losses even if only a few elderly live longer than expected or if houses depreciate in value. Moreover, lending institutions would have to develop and implement new procedures and systems to accommodate reverse mortgage transactions and to counsel elderly borrowers.

As a mechanism for financing long-term care, home equity conversions have two main advantages. First, they are the only private sector option in which many low-income elderly could realistically participate, since about a quarter of low-income elderly have homes valued at more than $50,000.[2] Second, home equity conversions potentially alleviate the problem of institutional bias in the current delivery system. Although the funds from a reverse mortgage may not be enough to cover the costs of nursing home care, such funds could be adequate to purchase home care directly.[3]

Having the additional income from home equity conversions, the elderly would also be in a stronger position to pay for long-term care services out-of-pocket or to purchase insurance, and thus might delay or prevent spending all their income and assets down to the medicaid eligibility level. The reverse mortgage instrument that we modeled,

Corporation, Mount Laurel, N.J., personal communication, October 6, 1987; and Sandra Sullivan, formerly of the Rhode Island Housing and Mortgage Finance Authority Corporation, personal communication, October 23, 1987. The approximately 2,000 transactions do not include more than 12,000 property tax deferrals. As of early 1986 seventeen states allowed elderly homeowners to defer paying property taxes until death, sale, or transfer of the home. Ken Scholen and others, *The Role of Home Equity in Financing Long-Term Care: A Preliminary Exploration,* report submitted to the Minnesota Housing Finance Agency (Madison, Wis.: National Center for Home Equity Conversion, February 28, 1986), p. 30.

however, is unlikely by itself to have much effect on medicaid nursing home expenditures. The loss in the home equity that would otherwise be used to help pay for nursing home care for patients not expected to return home offsets the gain in reverse mortgage income.

Nevertheless, if combined with long-term care insurance, the reverse mortgage that we modeled could achieve significant medicaid savings. Achieving those savings, however, would require widespread use of home equity conversions specifically to finance long-term care insurance. Though technically possible, this combination of financing might be difficult to realize. Unless home equity conversions can be successfully marketed as a means of purchasing long-term care insurance, such conversions are likely to play a more important role in supplementing the income of low-income elderly than in financing long-term care.

How Do Home Equity Conversions Work?

Of the various home equity conversion instruments, the kinds most appropriate for financing long-term care are reverse mortgages and home equity lines of credit. These loans last for a period of five to fifteen years or even longer and do not have to be repaid until at least the end of the loan term. Standard home equity loans or second mortgages are available through many banks, but these are not included in our analysis because repayment is expected to begin immediately. Sale-leaseback arrangements are also excluded from our analysis because tax barriers to formal sale-leasebacks limit the attractiveness of this type of residential transaction.*

* Under a sale-leaseback (SLB) arrangement, the homeowner sells the home to an investor who leases the property back to the seller for life. The seller usually continues to live in the house. The seller receives a lump-sum payment for the home and an annuity for life from which rent payments are subtracted. The buyer is obligated to pay the seller this monthly payment and to cover all house expenses, including property taxes, repairs, and homeowner's insurance. Ken Scholen, "An Overview of Home Equity Conversion Plans," in *Home Equity Conversion: Issues and Options for the Elderly Homeowner,* Committee Print, Joint Briefing by the Subcommittee on Housing and Consumer Interests, House Select Committee on Aging, and the Senate Special Committee on Aging, 99 Cong. 1 sess. (Washington, D.C., 1985), p. 12. Although undoubtedly more transactions have been arranged among relatives and by accountants, lawyers, and other professionals, as of 1986 probably fewer than 100 loans were closed through copyrighted SLB programs by real estate companies. Scholen and others, *Role of Home Equity in Financing Long-Term Care,* p. 30.

A publicly subsidized variation of a sale-leaseback program is the home equity living plan (HELP) in Buffalo, New York. As of September 1987 the program had completed 65 transactions and expects to maintain that steady-state number of loans. Maurice D. Weinrobe, personal communication, October 6, 1987. In this program the elderly

REVERSE MORTGAGES

With a reverse mortgage, the homeowner receives a series of monthly loan advances determined by the value of the home, the length of the loan term, and the interest rate. Repayment of the principal and interest is deferred until the end of the loan term, at which time the borrower usually sells the home to repay the lender in a lump sum. There are two basic kinds of reverse mortgages—those with fixed loan periods (for example, five to ten years) and those with open-ended loan terms that terminate when the borrower dies, moves, or sells the home.*

---

homeowner sells his or her home to HELP, a public entity, but retains occupancy rights until death. When the elderly person dies, the home becomes the property of HELP, which receives the residual equity from the previous owner. The program was created from a combination of HUD block grants and City of Buffalo general revenue funds totaling $1.3 million. Robert Garnett and Jack M. Guttentag, "HELP in Buffalo," *Housing Finance Review,* vol. 1 (October 1982), pp. 387–406.

Tax barriers could seriously limit the future of SLB plans. According to current tax law, the purchaser of income-generating property is entitled to deduct the costs of property maintenance, depreciation, and improvements in calculating taxable income. For the buyer to qualify for this deduction, however, the SLB transaction must be considered a bona fide commercial real estate sale. "There are two principle indicators of whether or not a sale-leaseback transaction is a bona fide sale for tax purposes. The first is the extent to which the seller retains the future right to use of the property. The second is the extent to which investment risk is transferred to the buyer." Jack M. Guttentag, "Some Perspectives on Sale-Leaseback Transactions Used for Home Equity Conversion," in *Home Equity Conversion,* Committee Print, p. 82. The more the occupancy rights of the seller are protected, the less likely the investor is to qualify for the tax deduction. Richard Daniel, "Role of the Secondary Market," in *Home Equity Conversion,* Committee Print, p. 66. Under the new tax law of 1986, investors should be even less eager to engage in SLBs because of four new provisions that (1) lower the after-tax value of current real estate deductions for maintenance, depreciation, and property improvements; (2) increase the tax on capital gains; (3) extend the depreciation schedule; and (4) lower the marginal tax rate. Abbott A. Leban, former vice president, American Homestead Mortgage Corporation, personal communication, March 1986; and Ken Scholen, "An Analysis of the HUD Report on Reverse Mortgage Insurance," NCHEC, undated.

* A fixed-term loan that allows elderly persons to remain in their homes is offered by the Connecticut Housing Finance Authority (CHFA) in conjunction with the Connecticut Department on Aging. The CHFA Reverse Mortgage Program offers a ten-year fixed-term loan (which may be extended longer than the ten years if the house has appreciated in value). The loan can be repaid up to forty years later, although interest on the loan will continue to accrue at a rate of 7 percent to 8 percent a year. The CHFA reverse mortgage is available only to those persons whose incomes are lower than 50 percent of the median income of the entire population of a county. Moreover, initial monthly payments can go no higher than $402 but are increased 3 percent a year. Connecticut Housing Finance Authority, "Pilot Reverse Annuity Mortgage Loan Program for Connecticut Elderly Homeowners," undated information pamphlet; and Arnold Pritchard, planning analyst, Connecticut Department on Aging, Hartford, Conn., personal communication, September 22, 1986.

Fixed-Term Loan

A fixed-term loan poses some risk for those wishing to stay in their homes indefinitely, because the borrower may outlive the loan term and have to sell the home to pay off the loan. If there is adequate remaining equity in the home when the term ends, the homeowner may be able to postpone repayment or to repay the first loan by taking out a second loan.[4] Recipients of fixed-term loans are betting that at the end of the loan period they will be dead, in a nursing home, or living with relatives. Because of the risk, fixed-term programs usually include extensive counseling services to determine whether the fixed-term limit is appropriate for the borrower. In fact, more people are advised not to take out this type of loan than are encouraged to participate in such a program.[5]

The amount of money generated from a fixed-term loan could be substantial. For example, a person who has a house worth $100,000 (final outstanding loan balance is 80 percent of equity, or $80,000) and a five-year loan term at 10 percent annual interest would receive $1,033 a month from a fixed-term reverse mortgage (table 8-1).* Because of such large potential payments, this type of reverse mortgage could be particularly useful for directly purchasing long-term care services.

In general, a higher interest rate, a longer loan term, or a lower house value means a lower monthly payment (table 8-1). Holding all other variables equal, reverse mortgage monthly payments are very sensitive to the length of the loan and somewhat sensitive to interest rates.† As with all loans, a substantial amount of the repayment is

* Most instruments usually limit the loan to 80 percent of the home value to allow the owner to use the proceeds from the home sale to pay for closing costs and real estate commissions as well as the loan balance. In addition, the 80 percent ensures that even if the house value depreciates somewhat, there will be enough money to pay off the loan. Monthly payments (*MP*) for the typical reverse mortgage are calculated by the following formula:

$$MP = \frac{rL}{(1 + r)^n - 1}$$

where r = monthly interest rate; L = maximum loan balance; and n = number of months in loan term. ICF Inc., *Private Financing of Long-Term Care: Current Methods and Resources, Phase II,* report prepared for the Assistant Secretary for Planning and Evaluation, Department of Health and Human Services (Washington, D.C., January 1985), pp. 17–18.

† For example, for a five-year loan term on 80 percent of a house valued at $50,000 and a 10 percent annual interest rate, monthly payments are $517. For a ten-year loan

TABLE 8-1. *Monthly Payments for Reverse Annuity Mortgages and Individual Retirement Mortgage Accounts, by House Value, Interest Rate, Age, Marital Status, and Shared-Appreciation Rates*
1987 dollars

Property value	Reverse annuity mortgage (RAM)			
	Maximum loan	Annual interest rate (percent)	Monthly payment	
			5 years	10 years
50,000	40,000	10.0	517	195
	40,000	11.0	503	184
	40,000	11.5	496	179
	40,000	12.0	490	174
100,000	80,000	10.0	1,033	391
	80,000	11.0	1,006	369
	80,000	11.5	993	358
	80,000	12.0	980	348

Property value	Individual retirement mortgage account (IRMA)[a]					
	Annual interest rate (percent)	Age	Monthly payment			
			100% shared appreciation		75% shared appreciation	
			Single	Married	Single	Married
50,000	11.5	70	185	112	139	84
	11.5	75	233	152	175	114
	11.5	80	336	212	252	159
	11.5	85	440	262	330	197
100,000	11.5	70	399	245	292	178
	11.5	75	496	332	365	243
	11.5	80	710	472	523	347
	11.5	85	924	679	682	501

SOURCES: IRMA monthly payments data from James Burke, chairman, and Frank Engel, financial planner, American Homestead Mortgage Corporation. Formula for RAM payments from ICF Inc., *Private Financing of Long-Term Care: Current Methods and Resources, Phase II,* report prepared for the Assistant Secretary for Planning and Evaluation, Department of Health and Human Services (Washington, D.C., January 1985).

a. IRMA payments are all at 11.5 percent interest; they vary with the age of the borrower.

interest. For example, in the $80,000 loan described earlier, the homeowner receives only $61,980 in total monthly payments; the rest is interest paid to the bank. In this type of reverse mortgage, the homeowner keeps all of the home's appreciation.

An example of a fixed-term reverse mortgage instrument is the reverse annuity mortgage (RAM) used by the San Francisco Development Fund (SFDF). The RAM program, which has been in operation in California since 1981, has expanded to include seven other sites that operate and use instruments based on the RAM model. As of September

term at the same interest rate, monthly payments drop to $195. A five-year loan at 12 percent interest drops only to $490. See table 8-1.

1987, 253 loans had been closed in California under the SFDF RAM program and about 125 in other RAM sites throughout the country.

The program is not entirely self-financing, since grant-funded nonprofit organizations act as intermediaries between aged homeowners and lending institutions. Although the RAM instruments are offered through commercial financial institutions, it is uncertain whether the market could successfully copy a RAM-type program without the nonprofit intermediary. The intermediary performs many support functions that commercial financial institutions may not be familiar with and may deem too costly to provide.*

Open-Term Loan

By comparison, a pure open-term reverse mortgage is a long-term loan paid to the borrower in monthly advances until the borrower dies, moves, or sells the home. The best known open-term reverse mortgage is the American Homestead Mortgage Corporation (AHMC) individual retirement mortgage account, or IRMA (formerly called the Century Plan). The IRMA accounted for about 1,200 of the 2,000 reverse mortgage transactions closed as of September 1987. It is the only financially self-supporting or market-based plan. No public or nonprofit subsidy is involved. Under the plan homeowners receive monthly tax-free loan advances (usually no higher than $700 a month) that continue as long as the owner lives in the home.[6] Borrowers are charged interest on the sums advanced at a fixed interest rate, and the principal and interest are repaid when the homeowner dies, moves, or sells the home.

In the IRMA, homeowners pledge a certain percentage of their future home appreciation to the lender. This system can be advantageous to the borrower because the higher the percentage of appreciation owed to the lender, the higher the monthly loan advance. It can be advantageous to the lender if the home appreciates as fast as expected or faster. The catch is that upon repayment of the loan the homeowner must pay back the principal plus compounded interest in addition to the pledged appreciation, which can result in a high effective interest

* The SFDF RAM program and the expansion sites—acting as intermediaries—are all nonprofit or public entities that receive administrative funds from various foundations and public agencies. In addition, the RAM sites initially benefited from SFDF assistance in many functions such as information referral, data collection, and lender liaison. Maurice D. Weinrobe, *Home Equity Conversion for the Elderly in the United States: An Examination of the Initial Experience* (Madison, Wis.: NCHEC, September 1986), pp. 5–7; and Kathleen Kenny, assistant director, San Francisco Development Fund, personal communication, September 23, 1986.

rate.* Hence the IRMA can consume more home equity in interest charges at a faster rate than other reverse mortgage plans. Given this trade-off between the size of the monthly payment and the residual equity upon death, the IRMA may be best suited to those who care little about leaving money to their heirs and want as high a monthly payment as possible for an indefinite period.

IRMA monthly payments vary according to marital status, age, house value, and percentage of appreciation shared. As shown in table 8-1, IRMA payments tend to be smaller than for the five-year fixed-term reverse mortgage and larger than for the ten-year fixed-term reverse mortgage. Thus the IRMA is most appropriate for persons who do not expect to leave their homes.†

LINE OF CREDIT

A new approach to home equity conversions is a home equity payment account or line of credit. With minor restrictions, this instrument allows the homeowner to borrow funds at any time and amount, up to a credit limit that is secured by the equity in the house.[7] Ideally, the homeowner would be guaranteed life tenure. This instrument may be more appropriate for long-term care than other instruments, especially for home care, because of the instrument's flexibility in allowing borrowers to draw from the account as needed, rather than receive a fixed amount every month as from reverse mortgages or sale-leasebacks. Although no such program is now in operation, both the Virginia Housing Development Authority and the Maryland Department of Housing and Community Development are planning to make home equity line-of-credit programs available to lower- to middle-income elderly in those states.‡

* All else being equal, for those who remain in their homes for relatively short periods, interest costs can be very high; for those who stay in their homes for long periods, interest costs can be very low. Ken Scholen, Maurice Weinrobe, and William Perkins, *A Financial Guide to the Century Plan,* 4th ed. (Madison, Wis.: NCHEC, April 1986), p. 12.

† A disadvantage of the IRMA is its provision that the borrower must repay the loan if he or she does not live and sleep in the home for one year. Because of this shortcoming, the IRMA may not be the most efficient or flexible home equity conversion instrument for financing a long nursing home stay.

‡ The basic model proposed by Virginia and Maryland is an open-term line of credit that does not have to be repaid until the homeowner moves or dies. Interest begins at loan closing and continues to accrue until loan repayment. Robert Adams, program development director, Virginia Housing Development Authority, personal communication, December 10, 1987; and Kenneth R. Harney, "Maryland Leads the Nation in New Elderly Credit Line," *Baltimore Record,* September 18, 1987.

Market Potential

The ability of home equity conversions to finance long-term care largely depends on the market for this financing mechanism. Both demand for and supply of home equity conversion instruments are currently very low. Some analysts argue that home equity conversions are in their early stages of development and that progress has been made with innovations in instrument design, consumer education, and a public demonstration program to insure both borrowers and lenders.*

MARKET DEMAND

Consumer demand for reverse mortgages is currently much lower than the demand for most other private sector options. The market has the potential to grow, however, because of the high rates of homeownership and the amount of equity tied up in the homes of the aged. Approximately 80 percent of the 17.8 million elderly homeowners that lived in their homes in 1983 had paid off their mortgages.[8] Moreover, net home equity accounts for the bulk of assets held by the elderly.[9] Expressed in 1987 dollars, about 72 percent of all elderly homeowners have more than $25,000 in net home equity and 24 percent have more than $75,000. In aggregate terms, the elderly hold close to $800 billion in home equity.[10] Even more important, about 50 percent of all elderly poor were homeowners in 1980, and many of these homeowners possessed substantial wealth in their homes.[11] Almost one-fourth of all aged homeowners below the poverty line and 32 percent of those near poverty (100 percent to 124 percent of the federal poverty level) have more than $50,000 in net home equity.[12]

The initial experience of the California RAM program indicates that participants were more likely to be somewhat older, to have fewer children, and to be widowed than those who applied but chose not to participate. Participants also had higher property values and lower income relative to net home equity. Reflecting the high housing costs of the San Francisco area, the median property value for RAM applicants

* New line-of-credit programs in both Maryland and Virginia are scheduled to begin in 1988. The American Association of Retired Persons has opened a Home Equity Information Center to collect and distribute information to its members. Legislation enacting a Federal Housing Authority reverse mortgage insurance demonstration program was passed by Congress in December 1987. Letter to the authors from Ken Scholen, November 11, 1987; and Housing and Community Development Act of 1987, P.L. 100-242.

was $125,000 to $150,000, but their median annual income was only $9,600.*

In state surveys of older homeowners conducted in the 1970s and early 1980s, between 9 percent and 48 percent of elderly homeowners expressed interest in some form of home equity conversion.[13] Two national surveys in 1986 indicated that 15 percent of elderly people might be interested in a home equity conversion and that 24 percent of elderly homeowners were specifically interested in a reverse mortgage.[14]

There are, however, significant barriers to the development of an adequate market for home equity conversions. Home equity conversions may not be necessary for higher-income elderly who have adequate income and substantial liquid assets. Nor may they be feasible for persons with low property values for whom the monthly payments would be too small to be worth the conversion costs to lenders.†

Even if their characteristics are suitable for a home equity conversion, many elderly are still unwilling to "let go" of their home assets.‡ Although in most current loans home ownership rights are not lost until death or sale of the home, all reverse mortgages deplete home equity. A large research literature suggests that the elderly are extremely

* Weinrobe, *Home Equity Conversion for the Elderly,* pp. 32, 40–47. Also, most of these characteristics are similar to those of participants in the Buffalo HELP program. HELP participants tended to be single and women; the average age was 73 for single women and 76 for single men. HELP participants tended to have properties of lower value (average for a single family home was about $22,000) and lower incomes (average for a single person was about $7,000). The HELP program, a publicly subsidized program, has income limits on eligibility and was initially intended to preserve a particular low-income neighborhood in Buffalo. Maurice Weinrobe, "HELP Comes to Buffalo: A Review and Analysis of the Initial Equity Conversion Experience," *Housing Finance Review,* vol. 4 (January 1985), p. 539, 544. Consequently, these characteristics may not be representative of the typical reverse mortgage participant. Moreover, the difference in house values also reflects location. San Francisco has experienced very high real estate inflation, whereas Buffalo is a less economically successful city, where homes have appreciated relatively little.

† A Department of Housing and Urban Development report on home equity conversions suggested that homeowners who receive at least $20,000 in yearly money income and elderly homeowners who have home equity of less than $50,000 would not be likely to be part of the reverse mortgage market. The study concluded that excluding these groups of elderly reduced the market potential from 9.35 million elderly homeowners with no mortgage debt whose total home equity was $548 billion in 1983, to as few as 2.6 million elderly households whose total equity was $206 billion. Department of Housing and Urban Development, Office of Policy Development and Research, *Home Equity Conversion Mechanisms* (Washington, D.C., December 1985), p. 57.

‡ An AARP survey of people aged 60 and over found that 70 percent agreed with the statement "What I'd really like to do is stay in my home and never move." Eighty-five percent disagreed with the statement "What I'd really like to do is move from here." AARP, *Understanding Senior Housing: An American Association of Retired Persons Survey of Consumers' Preferences, Concerns, and Needs* (Washington, D.C., undated), p. 22.

averse to risk and do not use up assets at anywhere near the rates predicted by the "life-cycle hypothesis".[15] A person who behaves according to the life-cycle hypothesis maintains a "smooth" consumption pattern, borrowing at a younger age, saving during middle age, and using savings during old age. To the extent that the elderly do dissave, they spend more from their nonhousing assets than from savings locked up in the home.* Indeed, Venti and Wise argue that the elderly typically do not wish to reduce housing wealth to increase current consumption.[16] Moreover, some elderly want to leave their homes to their heirs.

Financial risks may also limit demand. The costs of the plan to the borrower are not easy to predict, especially for open-term reverse mortgages that have unknown loan periods and therefore unknown total interest.[17] Other financial drawbacks relate to the amount of the monthly payment. For example, in times of high inflation the buying power of the cash advances will be diminished. In particular, many elderly may see reverse mortgages as costly if at the end of the loan term they must sell their homes and pay rent that rises with inflation.[18]

A key barrier to the spread of home equity conversions is the lack of knowledge about home equity conversion instruments. This ignorance is a result of the tiny current market and the complexity of the instruments. Hence financial institutions must commit a substantial amount of resources to counseling and educating clients about the concept.

From the perspective of financing long-term care, it is uncertain whether the elderly will be willing to engage in home equity conversions in order to pay for nursing home care, home care, or private insurance. People can use their loan payments for vacations as well as for long-term care. The preliminary evidence from the reverse mortgage experience is that 8 percent to 33 percent of participants take out the loans to help pay for health care costs.†

* King and Dicks-Mireaux found that the rate of dissaving (percent reduction in total net worth excluding pension and social security wealth) between ages 60-64 and 75 and over was 26 percent. Excluding the equity in owner-occupied housing from net worth, the rate of dissaving was 39 percent. The difference in these percentages indicates that the elderly tend to spend less from their home assets than from their more liquid assets. M. A. King and L.-D. L. Dicks-Mireaux, "Asset Holdings and the Life Cycle," *Economic Journal*, vol. 92 (June 1982), p. 258.

† An early survey of fifty-nine applicants to the Connecticut program found that only five persons listed health costs as the most important reason for entering the program. "The CHFA/Aging Reverse Mortgage Program: Some Early Data and Reactions," unpublished survey results provided to the authors by Arnold Pritchard of the Connecticut

Reverse mortgage payments could also be used to purchase private long-term care insurance, but such an approach faces some obstacles.* First, given the mythic quality of the home in American society, is it likely that people will be willing to use that asset to buy something as mundane as insurance? Second, in determining medicaid eligibility for nursing home care, the home is usually not counted toward the asset limits. Since many people purchase insurance to protect their assets, why would they want to deplete their major asset to guard others?

MARKET SUPPLY

Even if the elderly show a greater interest in home equity conversions, the supply of these instruments may remain limited. In the case of fixed-term reverse mortgages, lending institutions are reluctant to enter into nontraditional relationships under circumstances in which the elderly might live longer than expected, forcing financial institutions to foreclose or postpone claiming their assets. Banks do not like waiting to be repaid, and foreclosing on elderly widows conjures up the worst image of bankers. Neither option is attractive to the financial community.

More generally, the relatively small markets of local lending institutions also act as a financial barrier. If lenders have a small number of borrowers, they could incur large financial losses with open-term loans even if only a few elderly live longer than expected.[19] Their pool of mortgages is not large enough to ensure that the loan terms will average out to the actuarial estimates. Furthermore, in shared-appreciation loans mortgage lenders are tying their investments to future

---

Department on Aging, 1986. Information on the reasons for securing a reverse mortgage loan was collected for forty-eight cases in two specific RAM sites (Nassau County, New York, and Tucson, Arizona). Only fifteen cases (31 percent) cited health and medical reasons, seventeen cases (35 percent) cited rehabilitative work on the home, and thirty-five cases (73 percent) cited assistance in meeting daily living expenses. Technical Work Group on Private Financing of Long-Term Care for the Elderly, *Report to the Secretary on Private Financing of Long-Term Care for the Elderly* (Washington, D.C.: DHHS, November 1986), chap. 3, p. 122. Weinrobe analyzed applicants of the California RAM program. Of the 345 applicants listing the most difficult expenses during the last year, the largest proportion (about 33 percent) responded that nonreimbursed health care was the greatest problem. Weinrobe, *Home Equity Conversion for the Elderly,* p. 28. According to Scholen, participants in fixed-term reverse mortgage programs that include counseling are more likely to use the payments for long-term care services than participants of other reverse mortgage programs. Letter to the authors from Ken Scholen, November 11, 1987.

* This general approach has been analyzed by Jacobs and Weissert, and Scholen and others. Bruce Jacobs and William Weissert, "Using Home Equity to Finance Long-Term Care," *Journal of Health Politics, Policy and Law,* vol. 12 (Spring 1987), pp. 86–90; and Scholen and others, *Role of Home Equity in Financing Long-Term Care,* pp. 79–80.

housing values. If poor home maintenance results in houses depreciating in value, the lender could suffer a financial loss. The ability of elderly homeowners to maintain their homes may decrease as they age, especially if they are participating in reverse mortgages because of their need for long-term care.

Because of these economic risks to financial institutions and to the elderly, the evolving consensus is that public reverse mortgage insurance or some sort of secondary market is needed to expand participation significantly.[20] Without some form of reinsurance, lenders might not enter the market or might try to protect themselves from large losses in other ways. For example, lenders might offer only fixed-term loans, demanding repayment at the end of the term regardless of the borrower's desire to stay in his or her house. Alternatively, lenders might try to ensure adequate resale of the house by undervaluing the homes of elderly clients, which would result in lower monthly payments.[21]

Congress recently passed legislation to publicly insure 2,500 home equity conversion mortgages in a four-year demonstration project. The insurance will protect qualifying elderly homeowners and lenders from financial losses associated with home equity conversion mortgages. It will prevent elderly homeowners from being displaced from their homes and will place limits on the interest rates charged by lenders insured under the demonstration.[22]

Model Results

To assess the potential role of home equity conversions in financing long-term care, we simulated the IRMA of the American Homestead Mortgage Corporation. As described earlier, this home equity loan is a shared-appreciation mortgage in which the borrower pledges a portion of the home's appreciation to the lender. In the simulations the borrower pledges 100 percent of the appreciation. All individuals and couples who have $25,000 or more in home equity are assumed to take out this reverse mortgage at age 75.*

* In the simulations, all qualifying elderly participate in home equity conversions regardless of their need for long-term care. The reasons for choosing a blanket participation assumption are threefold. First, it is not clear why people take out home equity loans. One of the advantages of home equity conversions for the elderly is that the cash can be used for a variety of purposes. Second, if only those in need of long-term care had participated, then they would not have been able to purchase long-term care insurance with their reverse mortgage payments, because insurers do not sell policies to the disabled. Joshua M. Wiener, Deborah A. Ehrenworth, and Denise A. Spence, "Private

There are several reasons for modeling this type of reverse mortgage.* First, the IRMA accounts for the greatest number of reverse mortgages written to date. Second, as an open-term loan it allows elderly homeowners to remain in their homes until they die or sell the property. Third, relative to other longer fixed-term loans, it provides a larger monthly payment to borrowers with similar demographic characteristics (table 8-1). And finally, as a private sector option, this program is the only major one that does not depend on either government or philanthropic subsidy. Because lenders keep at least part of the home appreciation, this type of home equity conversion could act as an incentive for lenders to enter the business.

Home equity values are assigned in the model at age 65 according to income, marital status, and pension receipt. Once home equity values are assigned, they increase each year at a level consistent with the increase in the consumer price index (CPI)—4.0 percent a year over the long run. Although home prices in some U.S. cities in the late 1970s increased at a much faster rate than the CPI, the superinflation of home prices is not likely to continue through the next thirty-four years. From 1981 to 1986 the average annual rise in the CPI was 3.8 percent.[23] Roughly consistent with the CPI, the average annual increase in the median price of existing single family homes was 3.9 percent.†

Long-Term Care Insurance: Cost, Coverage and Restrictions," *Gerontologist,* vol. 27 (August 1987), p. 488. Third, although we did not specifically target those needing long-term care, people at age 75 face a high lifetime risk of using long-term care services. Younger elderly are excluded from participation in home equity conversion because the monthly payments would be too low for the elderly to consider dissaving worthwhile.

* There are arguments for other types of financial instruments. A five-year fixed-term reverse mortgage could provide higher monthly payments than the IRMA, but a fixed-term reverse mortgage does not usually guarantee home occupancy until death. It is an open question whether significant numbers of elderly would be willing to take the risk of outliving the loan terms and selling their homes to pay back the loans. Similarly, a line-of-credit loan might cost less and could be a more flexible instrument for financing long-term care, but its feasibility has not been tested.

† Over a longer time period, 1970 to 1985, the average annual increase in the median price of existing-single family homes was 8.2 percent, compared with the average increase in the consumer price index of 7.0 percent. U.S. Bureau of the Census, *Statistical Abstract of the United States, 1987* (Washington, D.C.: Department of Commerce, 1987), p. 707; data supplied by the National Association of Realtors (NAR), Washington, D.C.; and *Economic Report of the President, January 1987,* p. 310. The 8.2 increase is not strictly a measure of home appreciation because it does not measure the same houses at two different points in time. Using the weighted repeat sales (WRS) index of housing prices, Case and Shiller reported that from 1981 to 1986 the NAR report of median existing home sales data increased significantly faster than the WRS index in three of the four cities analyzed. Using the WRS index, they found that in one of the four cities real home values actually declined during that period. Karl E. Case and Robert J. Shiller, "Prices of Single Family Homes since 1970: New Indexes for Four Cities," Working

FIGURE 8-1. **Simulation Assumptions for Home Equity Conversion (HEC)**

- Home equity is assigned at age 65 and varies by income, marital status, and receipt of pension. After age 65, home values increase by the consumer price index (CPI)—4.0 percent a year over the long run.
- All individuals and married couples who have $25,000 or more in home equity take out a home equity loan at age 75.
- The loan is generally based on the individual retirement mortgage account (IRMA) offered by the American Homestead Mortgage Company. Monthly payments vary by whether the borrower is married or single; payments are higher for single persons. Payments continue while patients are in the nursing home. Repayment of the loan is postponed until after death, and all home appreciation accrues to the mortgage company.
- HEC payments are added to family income and are available to pay for long-term care expenses.
- For those who have a long-term care expenditure in a given year, the income from HEC is used before any other cash income or assets are used. Assets are used only when cash income is inadequate to pay for long-term care. If there are no long-term care expenditures in a given year, the HEC income is assumed to be used on some other immediate expense and not saved from year to year.
- As with the base case, 10 percent of all long-stay nursing home patients sell their homes after one year of institutionalization.

While the model does not explicitly assume that home values increase in real terms, this in fact happens in the model because of the improved financial position of the elderly. From 1986–90 to 2016–20 the mean home equity of those between ages 73 and 77 increases 27 percent.[24]

In the simple home equity conversion simulation, HEC, the loan advance to the elderly is added to the individual's or couple's cash income. This income is used to pay for out-of-pocket long-term care expenses incurred during the year. If the elderly person or couple do not incur out-of-pocket long-term care expenses in the year, then they spend the loan on other goods and services. Assumptions used in this simulation are shown in figure 8-1.

Since combining insurance and home equity conversions has the largest potential effect on long-term care financing, we simulated four different approaches. The assumptions used in these simulations are shown in figure 8-2.

Paper 2393 (Cambridge, Mass.: National Bureau of Economic Research, September 1987), pp. 23, 31.

FIGURE 8-2. **Simulation Assumptions for Home Equity Conversions and Long-Term Care Insurance (HECIN1, HECIN2, HECIN3, HECIN4)**

- In these simulations, the same assumptions of the simple HEC simulation are used to generate a stream of income. HECIN3 and HECIN4 assume higher housing appreciation than do HECIN1 and HECIN2.
- In all the HEC-insurance combinations, nondisabled elderly at age 67 buy a currently marketed private long-term care insurance policy if they can afford it for 5 percent of their income and have $10,000 in nonhousing assets. (See the description of the LOWBEN insurance policy in chapter 4.) At age 75, after the home equity conversions, nondisabled elderly are allowed to purchase insurance again if they meet the financial criteria.
- In the first home equity conversion–insurance simulation, HECIN1, the payment from the HEC at age 75 is added to the individual's or couple's income. Then the individual or couple purchase insurance if the insurance premium is less than or equal to 5 percent of their income and they have $10,000 in nonhousing assets. Houses appreciate by the CPI (4.0 percent a year).
- In the second simulation, HECIN2, insurance is purchased at age 75 if the HEC generates enough income alone to cover the costs of the insurance and the individual or couple have $10,000 in nonhousing assets. Houses appreciate by the CPI.
- The third simulation, HECIN3, is the same as HECIN2, except that aggregate home appreciation equals the nursing home and home care inflation rate of 5.8 percent a year.
- The fourth simulation, HECIN4, is identical to HECIN3, except that the elderly HEC participant does not need to have $10,000 in nonhousing assets to purchase insurance at age 75.

In the first approach, HECIN1, nondisabled elderly at age 67 buy a currently marketed private long-term care insurance policy if they can afford it for 5 percent of their income and have $10,000 in nonhousing assets. This is the LOWBEN insurance policy described in chapter 4. At age 75, after the home equity conversions, the nondisabled elderly purchase insurance if they can afford a policy for 5 percent of their combined income and home equity conversion payment and if they have $10,000 in nonhousing assets.* In HECIN2, the elderly purchase insurance at age 67 if they meet the criteria for HECIN1, or at age 75 if the home equity payment by itself is adequate to cover the cost of insurance and they have $10,000 in nonhousing assets. This approach

* The nonhousing asset requirement is based on the concept that people would not buy insurance unless they had substantial assets to protect.

TABLE 8-2. *Home Equity Conversion (HEC) Participation Rates for Heads of Households Aged 75 and Over, by Marital Status and Appreciation Rate, Selected Periods, 1986–2020*
Percent

Period	Single	Married	All
	Consumer price index home appreciation		
1986–90	26.1	63.9	40.8
2001–05	51.1	79.7	62.5
2016–20	55.2	83.3	66.6
	Nursing home and home care inflation rate of appreciation		
1986–90	26.1	64.4	41.0
2001–05	53.7	85.9	66.5
2016–20	60.0	92.1	73.0

SOURCE: Brookings-ICF Long-Term Care Financing Model.

assumes that the elderly would enter into reverse mortgages specifically to pay for long-term care insurance.

The last two simulations, HECIN3 and HECIN4, test the sensitivity of the results to a more rapid home appreciation assumption. In these last two simulations, home equity values (including the effect of higher incomes) increase at the same rate as nursing home and home care inflation. HECIN3 is the same as HECIN2 except for the higher home appreciation rate. HECIN4 is the same as HECIN3 except that persons may purchase insurance at age 75 even if they do not have $10,000 in nonhousing assets.

PARTICIPATION RATES

A higher proportion of the elderly could participate in home equity conversions than in other private sector options. For HEC, HECIN1, and HECIN2, the model results indicate that 41 percent of the population aged 75 and over would participate in this type of reverse mortgage program in 1986–90 (table 8-2). By 2016–20 the participation rate would increase to 67 percent of the population 75 and over. Married couples would be more likely to participate (83 percent) than single persons (55 percent) in 2016–20, probably because married couples are more likely to have higher incomes and thus higher house values. Under a more generous home appreciation assumption, participation rates are somewhat higher in future years. For HECIN3 and HECIN4, 73 percent of the elderly aged 75 and over could take out this type of reverse mortgage by 2016–20.

AVERAGE ANNUAL PAYMENTS

The model results show that the average yearly income from a shared-appreciation home equity loan in 1986-90 is $1,614, increasing to $2,182 by 2016–20.* Under a higher home equity appreciation assumption, the yearly income is $1,697 in 1986–90, rising to $2,931 by 2016–20† In both years the average payment to single persons is over twice that to married couples. Home equity conversion payments of this average size would not cover nursing home care for long but would be useful in purchasing home care.‡

PURCHASE OF INSURANCE

Home equity conversions appear to increase substantially the proportion of the elderly who have private long-term care insurance, but only if they take out the loan specifically to pay for the insurance.§

* This average annual payment in 1986–90 is much lower than that experienced by current programs because we allow persons who have relatively low home equity to participate. In current programs such persons either would not be allowed to participate or would be counseled away from it.

† Using data from the 1983 Annual Housing Survey (AHS) and the American Homestead Corporation IRMA, Jacobs also projected potential yearly reverse mortgage payments. He found that almost one-half of all single homeowners and couples aged 75 or over could receive at least $2,000 a year from the IRMA. When analyzed by income, the proportion of homeowners who could receive at least $2,000 a year from the IRMA is not drastically lower for the poor elderly than for those where income is twice the poverty level or more (39 percent and 48 percent respectively). Other high-risk groups could also benefit from this type of reverse mortgage. Jacobs found that a higher proportion of elderly aged 80 and over could receive $2,000 a year from IRMA payments than younger elderly (aged 65 to 79) could. Analyzing payments from a five-year fixed-term reverse mortgage, he found that a particularly vulnerable group—low-income singles aged 75 and over—could receive a median annual payment of $3,900. Bruce Jacobs, "The National Potential of Home Equity Conversion," *Gerontologist,* vol. 26 (October 1986), pp. 498, 502.

‡ The expected average income generated from a shared-appreciation loan would not cover much nursing home care. With an average annual payment of $1,536 in 1986–90 and nursing home charges of $60 a day, this type of loan would pay for about one month of nursing home care a year. In contrast, the home equity conversion payment would cover about sixty-five home health visits a year, or about five a month (assuming $30 a visit). Consistent with this analysis, Jacobs and Weissert estimated that 63 percent of all "high-risk" single homeowners could afford a "comprehensive" package of home care services using payments from an open term reverse mortgage and one-half of discretionary income. The authors do not, however, estimate how many such homeowners could purchase the package without a reverse mortgage. Jacobs and Weissert, "Using Home Equity to Finance Long-Term Care," p. 85. Firman estimated that "at least one million older home owners currently in need of long term care would be able to pay for the homecare they need if home equity conversion programs were available to them." James Firman, "Implications of Home Equity Conversion for Financing Health Care Needs of Older Americans," in *Home Equity Conversion,* Committee Print, p. 29.

§ The effect of two different reverse mortgage instruments on the affordability of

TABLE 8-3. *Elderly Participation in Private Long-Term Care Insurance, LOWBEN and HEC-Insurance Options, Selected Periods, 1986–2020*[a]
Percentage of elderly population

Period	LOWBEN[b]	HECIN1	HECIN2	HECIN3	HECIN4
1986–90	20.6	21.3	28.7	28.7	34.2
2001–05	37.9	38.8	47.0	47.7	57.7
2016–20	45.0	45.8	52.0	52.8	60.7

SOURCE: Brookings-ICF Long-Term Care Financing Model.
a. Elderly aged 67 and older.
b. Insurance only (no HEC). See chapter 4.

Significant proportions of the elderly remain unable to purchase insurance even with the help of home equity loans. When the home equity loan is simply added to current income and not earmarked specifically for insurance (as in HECIN1), the proportion of elderly with insurance does not materially increase. If no home equity loans were available, 45 percent of the elderly would have private insurance by 2016–20; if home equity loans were available, 46 percent of the elderly would have insurance by 2016–20 (table 8-3).*

Having people use their home equity loans directly for insurance (HECIN2) increases the proportion of elderly with insurance to 52 percent (table 8-3). Surprisingly, the higher home appreciation assumption (HECIN3) does little to increase the insurance coverage of the elderly (53 percent) when compared with a lower home appreciation assumption (HECIN2) or for insurance coverage without home equity conversion (LOWBEN). This result suggests that most elderly with enough home equity to purchase an insurance policy already have enough income without the reverse mortgage funds to purchase a policy. Dropping the requirement that reverse mortgage participants purchase insurance only if they have $10,000 in nonhousing assets

private insurance has also been estimated by Jacobs and Weissert. Their calculations suggest that about 50 percent of homeowners aged 65 and over could currently afford insurance if they used one-quarter of their discretionary income and payments from the IRMA reverse mortgage. Their study is difficult to compare with ours because of the differences in methodologies, assumptions, and data sources. Analyzing payments from a different reverse annuity mortgage (and in some cases, one-quarter of discretionary income) and two different insurance policies, they found that from about 50 percent to as many as 72 percent of elderly homeowners could be covered by insurance. Jacobs and Weissert, "Using Home Equity To Finance Long-Term Care," pp. 88–90.

* Lower assumptions on the percentage of income that people are willing to spend on insurance (for example, 2 percent rather than 5 percent) will increase the relative importance of home equity conversions in making insurance affordable (that is, increase the percentage change in the number of people who have insurance). However, that will also lower the total proportion of the elderly who have insurance.

TABLE 8-4. *Total Expenditures for Nursing Home Care, by Source of Payment, Base Case, LOWBEN, HEC, and HEC-Insurance Options, 2016–20*[a]
Billions of 1987 dollars; percent change from base case

Option	Total	Medicaid	Medicare	Insurance	Paients' cash income	Patients' assets
Base case	98.117	46.192	1.612	0.000	27.888	22.423
LOWBEN[b]	100.107	43.903	1.612	11.699	24.745	18.145
Percent change	2.03	−4.95	0.00	...	−11.27	−19.08
HEC	97.518	47.123	1.612	0.000	29.229	19.552
Percent change	−0.61	2.02	0.00	...	4.81	−12.80
HECIN1	99.935	44.000	1.612	12.145	27.037	15.140
Percent change	1.85	−4.75	0.00	...	−3.05	−32.48
HECIN2	101.576	41.055	1.612	17.073	27.109	14.725
Percent change	3.53	−11.12	0.00	...	−2.79	−34.33
HECIN3	101.869	39.511	1.612	17.682	28.137	14.925
Percent change	3.82	−14.46	0.00	...	0.89	−33.44
HECIN4	104.298	37.009	1.612	22.777	28.118	14.780
Percent change	6.30	−19.88	0.00	...	0.82	−34.09

SOURCE: Brookings-ICF Long-Term Care Financing Model.
a. Average annual expenditures.
b. Insurance only (no HEC).

(HECIN4) increases the proportion of the elderly with insurance in 2016-20 to nearly 61 percent.

PROPORTION OF TOTAL EXPENDITURES

Using this kind of reverse mortgage alone to pay for long-term care has a small effect on the proportion of nursing home expenditures (HEC), but the effect becomes larger if the reverse mortgage income is used to purchase insurance. As opposed to the 12 percent of nursing home expenditures paid by insurance alone, the reverse mortgage–insurance combinations pay for 12 percent to 22 percent of nursing home expenditures (table 8-4).

Altogether, HEC-insurance options are a more important source of financing for the young old (aged 65 to 74), men, married couples, and higher-income persons than for others (table 8-5). It appears that the most generous option, HECIN4, allows more women, older, single, and poorer people to benefit from this source of payment. Since the HECIN4 option drops the requirement that the elderly have at least $10,000 in nonhousing assets, its wider coverage suggests that many elderly with substantial home equity have only a modest amount of nonhousing assets.

TABLE 8-5. *Insurance Expenditures for Nursing Home Care, by Demographic and Income Groups, LOWBEN and HEC-Insurance Options, 2016–20*[a]

Percentage of total payments for nursing home services

Category	LOWBEN[b]	HECIN1	HECIN2	HECIN3	HECIN4
Total insurance share	11.3	11.8	16.0	16.4	20.8
Age					
65–74	19.0	19.0	19.8	19.8	20.4
75–84	13.0	13.4	18.2	18.9	24.6
85 and over	6.8	7.5	12.7	13.1	18.1
Marital status					
Married	17.2	17.4	21.0	21.5	25.2
Unmarried	8.9	9.4	13.9	14.3	19.0
Sex					
Male	14.7	15.0	18.1	18.6	21.8
Female	9.6	10.1	14.9	15.3	20.3
Family income (dollars)[c]					
Under 7,500	0.8	0.5	5.0	4.4	9.6
7,500–14,999	4.9	5.0	13.0	13.5	22.1
15,000–19,999	13.1	12.0	16.1	17.5	20.3
20,000–29,999	20.8	20.3	23.0	22.7	27.0
30,000–39,999	25.1	22.9	24.9	25.3	25.7
40,000–49,999	29.0	31.2	31.2	32.2	32.2
50,000 and over	27.4	26.9	26.9	26.5	26.5

SOURCE: Brookings-ICF Long-Term Care Financing Model.

a. These data are based on the total payments for an admission cohort over the entire length of their stays in a nursing home. For example, for a person who is admitted to a nursing home in 2016–20 for a two-year stay, we totaled two years' worth of nursing home expenditures. We then calculated the proportion of those expenditures paid by the options.

b. Insurance only (no HEC).

c. Family income is joint income for married persons, individual income for unmarried persons.

EFFECT ON PUBLIC LONG-TERM CARE EXPENDITURES

Simulation results suggest that using home equity conversions to pay for nursing home services directly will not reduce medicaid expenditures. Under HEC, medicaid nursing home expenditures would increase 2 percent by 2016–20 above the base case (table 8-4). This result was surprising, since the additional income from HEC was expected to reduce the rate of medicaid spend-down and public long-term care expenditures.

The reasons for the increase in medicaid expenditures are twofold. First, by 2016–20 the actual income generated (average about $2,182 a year) is not substantial compared with the potential magnitude of nursing home expenditures in that period ($44,000 a year). If a five-year fixed-term RAM had been simulated instead, it might have resulted in medicaid savings because the payments would have been higher.

And if some younger elderly (under age 75) with very high house values had taken out loans, medicaid expenditures might have been reduced slightly.

Second, we assume that 10 percent of nursing home patients sell their homes after one year in institutions. For those reverse mortgage participants who must sell their homes, the home equity remaining after their loans are repaid is too low to keep them off medicaid for long. If those persons had not taken out home equity loans, their home equity would have been greater. Thus medicaid loses some of the savings it might have achieved if the nursing home patients had sold their homes at full value to finance their care.

In combination with private insurance, this kind of open-term, shared-appreciation reverse mortgage could have a moderate effect on medicaid expenditures. Assuming that elderly borrowers purchase long-term care insurance if they meet the insurance affordability tests with the additional income from their home equity payments, then medicaid nursing home expenditures are reduced. Medicaid expenditures in 2016–20 would be reduced from the base case by a low of 5 percent under HECIN1 to a high of 20 percent under HECIN4 (table 8-4). In the pure private long-term care insurance simulation (with no home equity conversions), LOWBEN, medicaid expenditures would be reduced by 5 percent.

EFFECT ON PRIVATE LONG-TERM CARE EXPENDITURES

By 2016–20 out-of-pocket expenditures for nursing home care should increase if many older people participate in a shared-appreciation reverse mortgage program. If the home equity income is used to purchase long-term care directly, cash income as a source of nursing home payment rises almost 5 percent, reflecting the increase in income from HEC (table 8-4). However, assets as a source of payment fall almost 13 percent.

The four combined HEC-insurance simulations show a larger effect on nursing home expenditures from assets than the HEC alone and a smaller effect on nursing home expenditures from cash income (table 8-4). Nursing home expenditures from assets decline by approximately one-third. Since the loan advances are added to cash income, it is not surprising that total nursing home expenditures from that source are almost unchanged. However, between the insurance payments and the additional cash income, fewer people are required to make large contributions from other assets.

TABLE 8-6. *Number of Elderly Medicaid Patients in Nursing Homes, Base Case, LOWBEN, HEC, and HEC-Insurance Options, Selected Periods, 1986–2020*[a]
Millions of patients; percent change from base case

Option	1986–90	2001–05	2016–20
Base case	1.334	2.006	2.343
LOWBEN[b]	1.333	1.952	2.237
Percent change	−0.07	−2.69	−4.52
HEC	1.337	2.036	2.399
Percent change	0.22	1.50	2.39
HECIN1	1.335	1.968	2.276
Percent change	0.07	−1.89	−2.86
HECIN2	1.328	1.891	2.199
Percent change	−0.45	−5.73	−6.15
HECIN3	1.322	1.869	2.149
Percent change	−0.90	−6.83	−8.28
HECIN4	1.311	1.846	2.134
Percent change	−1.72	−7.98	−8.92

SOURCE: Brookings-ICF Long-Term Care Financing Model.
a. Ever in a nursing home during the course of a year.
b. Insurance only (no HEC).

By 2016–20 under HEC the number of medicaid patients in nursing homes increases by more than 2 percent over the base case (table 8-6). If the reverse mortgage income is used to purchase long-term care insurance, however, fewer people would have to depend on medicaid. By 2016–20 the reduction from the base case in the number of medicaid nursing home patients ranges from roughly 3 percent under HECIN1 to 9 percent under HECIN4 (table 8-6).

Conclusion

Home equity conversions allow people to use the assets tied up in their homes to pay for a variety of goods and services, including long-term care. Through monthly loan payments or a line of credit from a lending institution, elderly borrowers can use the income or credit to buy a long-term care insurance policy or to purchase services directly. Although only about 2,000 of these types of transactions have been closed, home equity conversions are appealing in that they allow even the low-income elderly to participate and could improve the affordability of both home care and long-term care insurance. If a way was found to ensure that home equity conversion payments were used specifically to purchase long-term care insurance, the approach could broaden the potential insurance market appreciably.

Chapter Nine

Private Sector Approaches and Delivery System Reform

Private sector approaches for financing long-term care will vary in their effect on quality of care, the balance of nursing home and home care services, access to care, family caregiving burdens, and government administrative burdens and in their flexibility to meet the demands of individuals and local conditions. Although most private long-term care insurance now available merely reimburses people for services used, insurers are becoming more interesed in actively shaping the delivery system. Continuing care retirement communities (CCRCs) and social/health maintenance organizations (S/HMOs) deliberately try to change the way long-term care services are provided by creating their own service systems. In contrast, individual medical accounts (IMAs) and home equity conversions (HECs) provide elderly consumers with more cash but do not directly change the way services are organized. Thus the effect of IMAs and HECs depends on how consumers decide to spend the additional money available to them.

Quality of Care

If the expansion of private sector financing mechanisms leads to an increase in the number of private pay patients relative to medicaid patients, nursing home providers may improve quality in order to compete in the much more profitable private pay market.[1] Families paying privately may feel that they have the right to demand more from nursing homes than medicaid patients do;[2] they also have the resources to go elsewhere if they are not satisfied. Since prices charged to private pay patients are much higher than medicaid reimbursement rates, more private pay patients could provide additional revenues to better the quality of nursing home care. Improvements in quality of care directed to private pay patients could spill over to medicaid patients.[3]

It is also possible that an increase in the number of private pay patients would lead to reduced quality. If more privately financed nursing home coverage results in a large increase in demand, bed shortages may occur, reducing quality at least temporarily.[4] When there is excess demand, a consumer has more trouble selecting a good home because there are fewer empty beds and less incentive for providers to improve the quality of care.[5] Excess demand also limits the ability of regulators to discipline poor quality providers.[6] However, if private sector financing approaches were able to reduce medicaid nursing home expenditures, then state governments might relax controls on nursing home supply.[7]

Private long-term care insurance, IMAs, and HECs do not directly try to affect quality, relying instead on federal and state mechanisms and consumer choice. Some private long-term care insurance policies will cover only services provided by medicare-certified facilities, and all require that nursing homes be licensed by the state. But even facilities meeting those standards may not provide good quality care.[8]

The alternative delivery systems found in CCRCs and S/HMOs should advance the quality of patient care. Providing a single point of entry to receive services should offer the elderly a more coordinated delivery system. Residents of expensive CCRCs can be expected to demand high-quality care when using the facility's long-term care services. If S/HMO case managers are charged with more than controlling costs, they should improve the quality of home care by ensuring appropriate use of long-term care services.*

* Typically, a case manager does a comprehensive assessment of a patient's strengths and weaknesses for independent living and then attempts to coordinate family care with any paid home care prescribed. In addition, persons under case management will usually be monitored to ensure that the services ordered continue to be appropriate. Carol D. Austin and others, "Case Management Goals," in Mark R. Todd, ed., *Case Management: A Critical Review* (University of Washington, Institute on Aging, September 29, 1985), pp. 18–33. For example, the disabled elderly using case managers in the Channeling demonstration reported more satisfaction with in-home service arrangements, more confidence about receiving needed care, and fewer demands for additional help than a randomized control group. Robert A. Applebaum and Margaret Harrigan, *Channeling Effects on the Quality of Clients' Lives,* report prepared for the Department of Health and Human Services (Princeton, N.J.: Mathematica Policy Research, April 1986), p. i.

The main threat to quality of care in CCRCs with health care guarantees and S/HMOs is that people must pay a fixed fee in advance for long-term care benefits. As with any prepaid health care arrangement, this type of financing provides incentives for the underprovision of services, since the organization can maximize its profits by providing fewer services. If services cost more than planned, CCRCs and S/HMOs may cut back on quality. The potential for underuse of services can be aggravated by the requirement that members use only certain providers. If dissatisfied, the disabled elderly have less recourse to other providers than in the fee-for-service system.

The Balance of Nursing Home and Home Care Services

Almost all disabled elderly persons prefer home care to any form of institutional care.[9] The medicaid program provides the vast bulk of public long-term care expenditures for the elderly; yet less than 4 percent of its long-term care expenditures for the elderly went for home care in 1984.[10] These limited financing arrangements provide weak financial incentives for the present delivery system to devote resources to home care.[11]

Current private insurance policies may exacerbate this weak point in the delivery system by covering nursing home services more extensively than home care services. To date, long-term care insurance policies cover only a small amount of home care. In response to consumer preference for home care, some companies are beginning to offer more coverage of those benefits.[12] Some newer insurance policies are also starting to experiment with case management instead of more restrictive cost-control measures.* As of now, however, insurers have not made much use of case management, partly because of the limited number of policies and the geographic dispersion of policyholders.

Both IMAs and HECs could broaden the use of home care services. Since these approaches increase the discretionary income of disabled elderly in the community, the money is more likely to be used to pay

* Blue Cross of Washington and Alaska plans to use case management to control use in its long-term care policy. Paddy Cottrell, Blue Cross of Washington and Alaska, personal communication. Other insurance companies that have arrangements with health maintenance organizations or CCRCs to insure their member populations count on the organizations to control use through case management. For example, Group Health Cooperative of Puget Sound, a large health maintenance organization in Seattle, will provide case management services for their members who have long-term care insurance with Metropolitan Life. Lynn Wagner, "Seattle HMO, Insurer Offer Long-Term Care Option," *Modern Healthcare*, April 10, 1987, p. 92.

for home care than for nursing home care.* The average IMA balance or HEC monthly payment is not sufficient to pay for very much nursing home care but might be adequate to finance a greater amount of home care.[13]

As for S/HMOs and CCRCs, their expansion could help redirect more long-term care resources toward in-home care for the disabled elderly. Besides offering more extensive home care benefits than generally available, these two options are philosophically committed to keeping people out of nursing homes. They also have financial incentives to substitute home care for nursing home services whenever home care is cheaper.

Access to Care

Under the current delivery system, access to care is especially limited for both low-income and severely disabled nursing home patients.[14] Nursing homes admit as many private patients as they can, filling any remaining beds with medicaid patients.[15] Expanding private sector coverage to finance nursing home care should therefore improve access for persons with such coverage, but access for medicaid patients may decrease. Moreover, if more nursing home residents have private insurance, nursing homes may substantially raise their private pay rates. If medicaid reimbursement rates do not keep pace with higher private charges, medicaid patients will become even less financially desirable. Increases in demand for nursing home beds that are not met by an increase in supply could further diminish access by medicaid patients. Although this analysis holds generally for private sector options, CCRCs and S/HMOs may pose an additional barrier because they usually restrict the access of nonmembers to their providers. Thus, unless the government heavily subsidizes their entry to these closed delivery systems, lower-income patients will be largely shut out.

Access to nursing homes by patients with extensive disabilities is also a problem in the current delivery system because their care is so expensive.[16] If insurance coverage increases, it may be even harder to place the severely disabled, since they require more care and will be less likely to have insurance. Unlike private insurance policies, demonstration S/HMOs allow a limited number of disabled elderly to

* This result assumes that people use the funds for the direct purchase of services. If people use the money from IMAs or HECs to purchase insurance, then the institutional bias of the current system might be reinforced.

enroll. But since that is a condition of the demonstration imposed by the Health Care Financing Administration and not a market response, its importance is difficult to evaluate. As for CCRCs, though health screening plays a role in restricting entrance to them, some communities will admit persons with a disability if they pay an additional charge.

Family Care Burdens

Adult children and spouses of long-term care recipients often face heavy physical, emotional, and sometimes financial stress in providing care.[17] Indeed, the elderly's desire to avoid this situation is a prime motive for people to participate in private sector options. In a survey of elderly persons on CCRC waiting lists, about three-quarters of the respondents reported "fear of being a burden on other family members" as a very important reason for wanting to enter a facility.[18] By providing financial help in purchasing services, all the private sector financing options would help somewhat in relieving family burdens. But those approaches that provide for greater home care benefits would do a better job of easing caregiver burdens.

Flexibility to Adapt to Local Conditions and Individual Needs

Each disabled elderly person is unique in the combination of services that will best help him or her cope. The range of available services and the style of practice also vary across the country. So flexibility is an important goal in any financing mechanism.

Since current insurance covers only a small range of services under a limited set of circumstances, its flexibility to adapt to individual needs is rather restricted. With a broader range of services and more reliance on case management, it may become more flexible. In any event, long-term care insurance is a versatile financing option because it can be combined with other options. For example, it can provide supplemental coverage for persons in CCRCs or in health maintenance organizations.

CCRCs can be very flexible. They are often designed to satisfy the preferences of a local elderly market. Once built and operating, residents often participate in decisionmaking through resident boards. However, CCRCs are usually difficult to get started. Financial and organizational barriers have limited the availability of such facilities to date.

S/HMOs have the ability to meet individual needs through case management and by control over a delivery system with a wide variety of long-term care services. Like CCRCs, S/HMOs must also be responsive to local conditions to attract and maintain enrollees. But the problems in rural areas of a geographically dispersed membership, lack of providers, and a small population could limit S/HMOs to urban settings.

One of the strongest arguments in favor of IMAs and HECs is that the cash would enable people to assemble the best service package possible to meet their individual preferences. Several factors, however, may prevent that from happening. The disabled elderly may not have the ability or access to information to make the best choice in nursing home or home care alternatives. Elderly in need of long-term care may be too ill and feeble to shop actively for services. The decisions about long-term care are often made by harried hospital discharge planners or families unable to wait to obtain the desired services.

Administrative Activity of Government

All the private sector financing options are likely to enlarge government's administrative activities, principally in the areas of public education and regulation. Consumers need to better understand these new financing mechanisms and to be assured that they are financially sound and provide a reasonable return of benefits for the money.

Since long-term care insurance is administered privately through existing insurance companies, it is not complicated or expensive to administer from a public perspective. The degree of administrative complexity depends on the level of regulation imposed. The principal areas of regulatory concern are benefit levels, policy restrictions and exclusions, loss ratios, and policy renewability.* Overall, however, the government's regulatory burden would seem to be small.

The incentives in CCRCs with health care guarantees and S/HMOs to underprovide services will probably require vigorous oversight of the quality of care in these two options. In addition, the risk that the elderly could lose their entire life savings in their entry-fee payment to CCRCs suggests a strong consumer protection role for government. Regulating the financial relationship between CCRCs and the residents could require more government oversight.[19]

IMAs, unlike individual retirement accounts (IRAs), which can be

* For a discussion of insurance regulation, see chapter 4.

spent on anything, would require some additional government oversight to ensure that the funds were spent only on long-term care. Monitoring the accuracy of claims would fall on the Internal Revenue Service, which already has some experience administering a similar IRA provision and could use the general audit process to determine inappropriate taxpayer expenditures. If the government provided some type of reinsurance for elderly HEC borrowers or mortgage companies, HECs would also increase government's administrative burdens.

Conclusion

By expanding the private sector's participation in financing long-term care, the current delivery system for services could change. Approaches that rely on people to use their home assets or savings to purchase more services privately have the least predictable systemwide effects because of the many things on which each person could spend the money. Approaches that pool individual funds and seek to manipulate the service delivery system have the potential to improve the present arrangement for participants, providing that the insurers or the organizations do not undersupply services. For the remaining patients under medicaid, current problems with nursing home access would worsen. However, since our simulations suggest that all of these private sector options will finance only a modest proportion of nursing home and home care, their actual effect on the delivery system will be relatively small.

PART 3
Public Sector Strategies for Reform

Chapter Ten

Introduction to Public Sector Strategies

The role of the public sector in financing long-term care in the United States urgently needs reexamination. One reason is that public sector spending for long-term care is already large and likely to expand rapidly as the population demanding long-term care and eligible for medicaid increases. According to our model projections, if no substantial changes are made in current policies, medicaid spending will triple in real terms by 2016–20.

While the income and assets of the elderly will grow over the next several decades, the cost of long-term care is expected to grow even faster. Hence the proportion of bills paid by medicaid is projected to increase. The percent of nursing home expenses paid by medicaid is estimated to rise in the base case from about 43 percent in 1986–90 to 47 percent by 2016–20.[1]

Although a substantial potential market exists for private financing mechanisms, especially private long-term care insurance, the growth of private financing is unlikely to reduce the growth of public spending appreciably. Even with favorable assumptions about who would buy insurance or participate in other private financing schemes, medicaid spending will continue to grow rapidly. Lower- and lower-middle-income people simply cannot afford to finance long-term care without some public contribution.

Moreover, more direct methods of holding down medicaid spending—putting a cap on medicaid, converting the program to block grants to contain future spending, or increasing the legal responsibilities of families for long-term care of their relatives—seem unlikely to reduce total public spending without risking both the quality and availability of care to needy people. Medicaid expenditures probably cannot be held down painlessly.

A second reason for reexamining the role of the public sector is that the current structure of public programs for financing long-term care is the haphazard result of a series of efforts to limit total public spending. It does not reflect a deliberate public choice about the appropriate role of government.

Long-term care was not included in medicare, passed in 1965, for fear that the program would become too expensive.[2] The limited nursing home benefits covered by medicare were designed for convalescence from a hospital episode, not for chronic disability. Medicaid, passed at the same time, did include long-term care benefits for the poor, but few expected it to become an important safety net for the middle class as well. More recently, long-term care benefits have been excluded (to control costs) from the catastrophic health care amendments to medicare proposed in 1987, even though long-term care is the main reason that older people incur catastrophic health expenses.[3]

The result of this series of decisions is an anomalous situation with no cogent rationale. Social insurance covers acute care expenditures, whereas long-term care expenditures are paid by a means-tested program that is intended for the poor but that actually serves a large portion of the population. An increasingly affluent society depends on a program for long-term care financing that continues to require a majority of elderly nursing home patients to prove themselves needy in order to qualify for public charity.

Before pouring increasing resources into these programs, Americans should take stock of the situation and decide whether there is a better way to spend public money on long-term care. In particular, is it desirable to allow the gulf between the public and private systems to widen as upper-income people acquire long-term care insurance in the private sector and the less affluent half of the population increasingly depends on a welfare program?

Public Responsibility for Long-Term Care

Almost no one would dispute that there should be *some* public responsibility for long-term care for older people. A civilized society does not abandon its disabled elderly. The important question is how the responsibility should be divided between families and the government, a question resolved in different ways in different cultures.

Some people believe the primary responsibility for care of the elderly—whether acute or long term—should fall on the patients themselves and on their families. In their view, the role of the government is to act as a safety net or payer of last resort for those who are unable to provide for themselves.

Others believe the government should take the lead in ensuring care for all older people, regardless of their financial condition, either by providing such care directly or by mandating comprehensive social insurance to enable everyone to pay for needed care. Here the role of private financing is residual, limited to providing nonessential services or a more luxurious standard of care.

Those are the two extreme positions. In between can be found many views about how to combine public and private responsibility in varying degrees.

Methods of Government Involvement

Government could, of course, provide long-term care services directly, using publicly owned facilities and health professionals who work for a local, state, or federal health service. But with a few exceptions (such as veterans' services), direct government provision of health services has been much less important in the United States than in many other countries and is not an option being seriously considered in the current debate over long-term care. Rather, attention centers on ways in which the government should help finance services to be provided by the private sectors of the economy.

Discussion of government financing of long-term care, in turn, focuses on two distinct approaches: welfare programs and social insurance. Welfare programs, such as medicaid, involve government subsidies usually paid out of general revenues and are specifically directed to the poor or some subgroup of the poor. The hallmark of the welfare program is the means test, in which the potential beneficiary has to prove both low income and meager assets to qualify for benefits.

An argument for the welfare approach is that government funds can be used with maximum efficiency, since programs are targeted on those demonstrably most in need of assistance. Counterarguments are that means-tested benefits discourage work and saving, that the means test is demeaning and stigmatizes recipients, and that programs directed only at the poor often offer a lower quality of service than programs directed at the general population. All these arguments have been applied to medicaid long-term care benefits.

Social insurance uses the auspices of the government to enable or require citizens to pool their risks. Citizens contribute to a fund from which they are entitled to receive benefits under specified conditions without regard to financial need. Contributions usually take the form of a premium or an earmarked tax, such as the payroll tax paid into the social security and medicare trust funds.

The argument for social insurance is that beneficiaries feel they have earned their benefits by paying their contributions. There is no welfare stigma, even though the poor may, in fact, receive higher benefits relative to their contributions than those who are better off. Moreover, the political power of the middle- and upper-income beneficiaries helps ensure adequate levels of payments or quality of services for everyone. The disadvantage is that the benefits are not targeted on those most in need, but go to many who could rely on their own resources.

Social insurance in its pure form is self-financing. Payments into the fund are set to cover anticipated outflow. A broader definition of social insurance, however, encompasses programs that may be partly subsidized from general tax revenues. Indeed, in practice, this broader definition is a flexible concept that can be adapted to reflect gradations of public and private responsibility and can be used to accomplish considerable redistribution of resources from higher- to lower-income groups without the stigma of means-testing. Social insurance can be mandatory or voluntary. It can cover full costs or involve cost-sharing. It can be financed by a payroll tax, a premium, or some other form of contribution from beneficiaries, and can be subsidized out of other sources of revenue.

Medicare part A, covering acute care hospital expenses, is an example of a relatively pure form of social insurance. Financed by a payroll tax, it provides broad benefits to all those who have established eligibility, regardless of financial need or amount of prior contribution. Because people with high lifetime earnings contribute more than those with low lifetime earnings, the program effectively taxes the better off to pay part of the cost of acute health care benefits for low wage earners.

Medicare part A, however, does not provide complete coverage of acute care costs; substantial coinsurance and deductibles are required and benefits are not unlimited. Many elderly people purchase private supplemental policies (medigap insurance) to cover hospital costs not covered by medicare. Those who cannot afford medigap or whose resources have been exhausted must turn to medicaid for assistance.

Medicare part B, which covers physicians' services, is a variant of the social insurance approach. Participation is voluntary rather than mandatory. The contribution is in the form of a premium paid by elderly participants rather than a payroll tax paid during working years. To cover the full cost of the program, the premium would have to be higher than many elderly could afford. But the premium has been kept low. At present it contributes approximately 25 percent to the financing of the program, and the government makes up the difference out of general revenues.[4] Hence medicare part B is actually a mixture of social insurance and a government subsidy.

What Level of Government?

The Constitution does not clearly define the roles of federal and state governments in social policy. As a result, especially in the last several decades, social programs have grown at the federal and state levels in ways that are sometimes parallel, sometimes overlapping, and sometimes closely intertwined.

If it were possible to roll back the history of social policy and consider anew the appropriate division of responsibility between federal and state governments, one might handle programs for the elderly differently. Older people are less mobile than younger people and often have strong ties to a local community. Views about the responsibility of families and the role of older people in society differ sharply among ethnic and religious groups. Hence one might argue for a strong state and local involvement in programs for the elderly and a federal role limited to equalizing state resources in relation to need. This line of reasoning suggests a federal block grant program to help the states finance different mixes of income support and service programs for the elderly.

In fact, however, the federal government has predominated in programs for the elderly since the establishment of the social security system in the 1930s and the addition of medicare and medicaid in the 1960s. The United States already has a functioning, mature system of social insurance that provides income and acute care protection for the elderly and to which it can logically add long-term care coverage. Using a block grant approach to long-term care, while retaining a federal social insurance program for retirement income and acute care, would perpetuate the anomaly of treating long-term care needs separately from other normal aspects of growing old. Therefore, a strong case can be made that the federal government should take primary responsibility for developing a social insurance approach to long-term care.

Options

There are three alternative public sector strategies to reforming long-term care financing. One is to hold down medicaid expenditures in the future by shifting the burden to the states, localities, and families. Another is to enhance the public role in financing long-term care by incremental reform of medicaid, medicare, or the tax system. The final approach is to implement a social insurance program.

Chapter Eleven

Block Grants

Frustrated by the restrictions of multiple federal funding programs or worried about the fiscal implications of an increasing elderly population, some observers have proposed consolidating federal long-term care expenditures into a block grant to the states. Such a strategy would clearly place primary responsibility for determining and fulfilling the long-term care needs of the elderly with the states. Thus a long-term care block grant reflects the view that the problems of long-term care are most appropriately addressed by state and local governments, not by national policies and programs.

Advocates of a long-term care block grant contend that it will restrain the rapid growth of federal spending, increase support for home care services, overcome fragmentation of the financing and delivery system, and foster flexibility to adapt to local conditions and individual needs.[1] Opponents fear that a block grant will shift the financial burden of long-term care to the states because federal funds will become increasingly inadequate, forcing service levels to be reduced, eligibility to be tightened, and quality of care to erode.[2] Because of differences in the fiscal capacities and political wills of the states, critics also fear that a block grant will perpetuate inequities in long-term care programs.

Every president since Nixon has proposed block grant funding to consolidate certain health and welfare programs, both to slow the growth in the number of categorical programs, which define in detail how the money should be spent, and to shift funding emphasis to general purpose grants.[3] The Reagan administration accelerated the shift from categorical to block grant funding. The Omnibus Budget Reconciliation Act of 1981 (OBRA) consolidated more than fifty categorical and two existing block grants into nine new block grants.[4]

The OBRA block grants sparked interest in a federal block grant to the states for long-term care. In 1983 the Reagan administration proposed such a long-term care block grant as part of an initiative to federalize medicaid. The administration also gave serious consideration to a block grant in 1984 and 1985. Both the Heritage Foundation and a recent task force on federalism recommended a long-term care block grant, and a Robert Wood Johnson Foundation–sponsored study group on state medicaid strategies recommended a long-term care block grant to replace current medicaid funding of long-term care.[5]

The basic elements of a block grant policy for long-term care can be quickly outlined. Long-term care funds from medicaid, the social services block grant, and Title III of the Older Americans Act would be merged and distributed to states on a fixed-formula basis. States would not be required to match the federal funds, but could augment them. Medicaid long-term care funding would no longer be an open-ended entitlement. Money going to the states would be fixed, directly controllable through the federal budget appropriations process. To anticipate future funding needs, policymakers could index a block grant to a measure of long-term care inflation and the growth of the elderly population.

Under a block grant, long-term care programs would be administered almost entirely by the states. The federal government's role would be reduced and confined to providing money and enforcing general federal legislation, such as civil rights statutes, and perhaps overseeing quality. States would have wide latitude in setting financial and disability eligibility criteria and deciding what services to cover. A key feature of a long-term care block grant is that it could provide both medical and social services within a single program.

In the United States block grants have been discussed primarily as a way of financing a state means-tested program. However, block grants could be used for broader purposes. In Canada, for example, each province that agrees to meet minimum standards receives a block grant from the central government to finance a universal entitlement to long-term care services.[6]

Funding Levels

In a time of large budget deficits, some argue that the federal government can no longer afford to provide long-term care services through an open-ended entitlement program such as medicaid. They see a block grant as a way to reduce the growth in federal medicaid expenditures and to make them more predictable.

Medicaid expenditures are hard to control.[7] As an entitlement program, medicaid is obligated to pay for certain services to all people who meet the eligibility standards and manage to obtain services. The federal government shares this fiscal burden on at least a fifty-fifty basis with the states. Because medicaid is administered by the states within broad general guidelines, the financial burden on the federal government is largely the result of state decisions. Neither the federal nor state governments can control medicaid expenditures by simply setting appropriations at the desired level. They must resort to more indirect means, such as making the eligibility standards more stringent, slowing the growth in the supply of services, or restricting reimbursement levels.[8]

All of the standard cost-controlling strategies have undesirable consequences. For example, the levels of medicaid financial eligibility are already low. Few states have been willing to reduce them further, especially for the elderly. While several states have curbed the growth in the supply of nursing homes by imposing moratoriums on new beds, the expected large increases in the elderly population make this an unrealistic permanent strategy. The most common approach, reducing the reimbursement rate to service providers, is also not sustainable. States cannot continuously reduce reimbursement and still ensure that care meets minimum standards. Such efforts to control public costs may simply shift costs from the government to the private sector as the elderly are forced to pay more of the bill for long-term care services.[9]

It is theoretically possible to construct a block grant with funding at the same level as that of the existing system. But given the current fiscal standing of most states and the federal government, a long-term care block grant would probably be used to reduce expenditures. Once entitlement is eliminated, it is technically simple to set funding at whatever level is desired. Congress could easily reduce the indexing rate without having to think through how the cuts would actually be made at the state, local, or facility level.[10] One illustration of how vulnerable a long-term care block grant could be to federal budget pressures is that the first point of agreement during the fiscal year 1986 federal deficit reduction negotiations was to freeze appropriated accounts.

Recent experience suggests that changing categorical grants to block

TABLE II-1. *Federal Entitlement and Nonentitlement Domestic Spending, Fiscal Years 1967–84*
Millions of dollars

Year	Entitlement spending[a]	Nonentitlement spending
1967	40,243	19,476
1968	46,500	18,252
1969	53,639	14,009
1970	60,687	19,475
1971	75,173	26,297
1972	85,823	34,628
1973	96,232	35,655
1974	111,430	37,129
1975	144,051	53,187
1976	168,523	66,513
Transitional quarter[b]	42,567	15,804
1977	183,275	75,549
1978	196,111	85,528
1979	216,277	91,224
1980	255,719	101,931
1981	298,837	96,986
1982	331,146	74,965
1983	365,660	64,554
1984	368,995	69,766
Addendum	*Growth rate (percent)*	
1968–72	16.6	17.4
1972–76	18.4	17.7
1976–80	10.5	10.5
1980–84	9.6	−9.0

SOURCE: *Budget of the United States Government, Fiscal Year 1986: Historical Tables,* tables 8.1 and 11.3.
a. Includes food stamps.
b. The beginning of the fiscal year was changed from July 1 to October 1 starting in fiscal year 1977.

grants tends to reduce funding. Appropriations for seven of the nine block grants created by OBRA averaged 15 percent below the level provided under the prior categorical programs.[11] Although some of the fiscal year 1982 cuts were restored through increased appropriations in 1983 through 1985, fiscal 1985 appropriations for five of the seven block grants were still from 1 percent to 29 percent below their fiscal 1981 categorical levels.[12]

A comparison of federal entitlement and nonentitlement spending over the past two decades also shows how likely nonentitlement programs are to be cut. From 1968 through 1980, expenditures for both types of programs grew at similar rates (table 11-1). From 1980 through 1984, despite large federal deficits and widespread program retrenchment, entitlement spending rose an average 9.6 percent a year. At the same time, spending for nondefense appropriated programs declined substantially, dropping from a 10.5 percent average annual rate of *increase* during 1976–80 to a 9.0 percent average annual rate of *decrease*.

Delivery System Reform

One of the strongest points in the case for a long-term care block grant is that it offers states the freedom to develop a variety of services to meet the needs of the elderly. Without substantial increases in funding, however, states may have a hard time reallocating money to home care and guaranteeing that adequate quality care is provided.

BALANCE OF NURSING HOME AND HOME CARE SERVICES

By grouping existing long-term care programs under a single administrative structure and by removing the federal requirements that encouraged the dominance of nursing homes in the delivery system, a block grant could eliminate artificial distinctions between health and social services.[13] A block grant would allow states to offer a wide mix of community services and to place greater emphasis on nonmedical home care services as a substitute for nursing home care. The result could be a better delivery system at less cost.

Currently, federal and state policymakers are reluctant to offer home care services on an entitlement basis because the large majority of disabled elderly who medically qualify for services do not receive any. If they did, expenditures would rise significantly. Under a block grant, the states' financial risk in offering these services would be reduced; people would not be automatically entitled to services, and states would have to spend no more than appropriated amounts.

Although removal of restrictive provisions would theoretically make it easier for states to move toward such noninstitutional services as home health care, personal care, adult day care, and homemaker services, provision of those services will partly depend on how much money is available. Early evaluations by the General Accounting Office of the OBRA block grants show that states did not substantially reallocate resources when given the freedom to do so.[14] Faced with reduced funds, most states used the new block grants to support the same programs funded under the prior categorical grants, citing a continued need for the services and a desire to minimize the disruption of existing services.

The "political market" at the state level might also prevent expansion of noninstitutional services.[15] Highly organized nursing home providers make political contributions to state legislators and have long-standing access to public officials. As a result, nursing homes are better situated politically to press their need for funding than are less numerous, less organized home care providers.

Further, there is little reason to believe that even a substantially more efficient delivery system could compensate for reduced federal funding. In particular, there is little evidence that expanded home care services will result in lower, or even the same, aggregate long-term care expenditures (see chapter 14). Expanding home care services raises total long-term care costs because most home care is provided to people who would not otherwise enter nursing homes. Thus the small decrease in nursing home use will probably be more than offset by the increase in home care use.

GOVERNMENTAL ADMINISTRATIVE SIMPLICITY AND COSTS

Another advantage frequently cited by advocates of a block grant is that the reduction of federal directives and reporting requirements could cut administrative costs, thereby offsetting and partly justifying a reduction in funding. The General Accounting Office's overview of pre-1981 block grants showed that consolidating the categorical programs into block grants had mixed effects on administrative costs.[16] In a more recent GAO study of the implementation of the OBRA block grants in thirteen states, all thirteen claimed widespread management improvements. Because of measurement problems, however, the GAO could not determine whether administrative costs were cut.[17]

In any case, administrative savings could not offset any major reduction in funding. Administrative costs make up only 5 percent of total medicaid payments to the states.[18] Administrative costs for long-term care are probably lower than those for acute care, as a percentage of total expenditures, because few people receive long-term services and hence fewer bills are processed. Thus even if all long-term care administrative costs were eliminated, the savings would be small.

FLEXIBILITY TO ADAPT TO LOCAL CONDITIONS AND INDIVIDUAL NEEDS

Proponents argue that a block grant would enable states to organize programs and establish priorities to suit local conditions and preferences.[19] Existing federal requirements for long-term care programs, however, are not cumbersome or difficult. While supporters of block grants proclaim the merits of reducing federal requirements, they tend not to specify which requirements they wish to eliminate. Indeed, aside from easing the requirements that make it difficult to provide nonmedical home care services, many of the requirements that advocates of a block grant wish to eliminate provide beneficiary protections.[20]

Some observers have also argued that state and local governments will be less protective of the poor and disabled than the federal government is.[21] Physical and mental impairments and the long-standing social isolation of the disabled make it difficult for them to press their case politically. A GAO study of the community services block grant (CSBG) showed that the majority of interest groups believed that "the changes made by the state to programs supported with CSBG funds have adversely affected the individuals or groups they represented."[22]

QUALITY OF CARE

Under the current system of quality assurance, long-term care facilities that do not meet federal quality-of-care standards are not eligible to receive reimbursement under medicaid or medicare. The threat of payment termination is the core of the current quality enforcement system, providing an incentive for compliance with the standards, which in fact are minimal.[23] Few facilities can survive without medicaid reimbursement.

Nursing homes have improved since 1950 because of federal involvement in standard setting and enforcement.[24] States may not necessarily do an adequate job of inspecting nursing homes and other long-term care providers if left to themselves. Few people want to turn the assurance of nursing home quality entirely back to the states. Indeed, the recent report by the Institute of Medicine on quality of care in nursing homes called for more, not less, federal involvement.[25]

A principal argument against a block grant is that quality of care in long-term care facilities, already variable, may decline if the federal quality enforcement role is restricted. Federal authority to ensure quality of care might diminish even if standards are retained. Because the financing structure of a block grant would not be a federal-state match, the link between eligibility for medicaid funding and adherence to quality standards would be weakened. If state dollars were used to supplement the grant, the federal government could not prevent the state from directing its money to substandard facilities. Indeed, all federal money could be spent in a few high-quality nursing homes rather than distributed to all facilities—effectively restricting the reach of federal quality enforcement.

The increased range of services made possible by a block grant presents a similar quality-control problem. A wide range of residential services beyond skilled nursing and intermediate care facilities would make it difficult to differentiate between poor-quality intermediate care facilities and adequate-quality, less medically intense domiciliary or board and care facilities. For example, four hours of nursing care a month may be adequate for a domiciliary care facility but would be considered substandard for an intermediate care facility. Under a block grant, poor-quality intermediate care facilities could merely be reclassified as domiciliary care facilities.[26] Because funding of domiciliary care facilities under a block grant would not be precluded, residential facilities would have little incentive to meet the skilled nursing or intermediate care facility standards.

FAMILY BURDEN

The effect of a long-term care block grant on the financial and caregiving burden on families depends on the design and funding of a state's program. The block grant's emphasis on home care services could ease the burden on families. However, the flexibility in regulation given to states would allow them to require mandatory family contributions by adult children toward the cost of care of medicaid nursing home patients (see chapter 12). If funding does not keep up with the demand for long-term care and if service availability is restricted, individuals and their families may have to provide more care themselves.

Conclusion

Although a block grant could be devised that would not cut federal funding, Reagan administration proposals for block grants have generally been coupled with budget savings. Moreover, recent experience with block grants suggests that funding would be lower than it would be under the current set of programs.

Supporters of a long-term care block grant propose to curtail the growth in public costs and reorganize the delivery system by giving states the responsibility for long-term care. They argue that reductions in funding can be at least partially offset by savings from cost-effective home care services and lower administrative costs. In fact, there is little evidence that expanded home and community-based services will lower long-term care costs. And administrative costs are such a small part of current medicaid expenditures that reducing them will save little.

Chapter Twelve

Family Responsibility

A family responsibility policy would require adult children, spouses, and parents to contribute to the cost of nursing home care for relatives who are medicaid-eligible.* In essence, state-administered family responsibility programs would hold designated kin legally responsible for making cash payments, either to the state or directly to the nursing home, to offset the medicaid costs of their relative's nursing home care. Such a program could reduce net federal costs both by collecting money to be applied to the cost of care and by discouraging nursing home placement.

Precedent for family responsibility legislation dates back at least as far as the Elizabethan Poor Laws of 1601.[1] Under the old age assistance (OAA) program, which was replaced by the supplemental security income (SSI) program in 1974, most states required financially capable children to help support their parents.[2] Although rarely enforced, family responsibility laws remain on the books in about half the states.[3]

Since 1965 federal law has not allowed states through their medicaid state plan to hold adult children financially responsible for their parents.[4] The prohibition was a congressional response to testimony on the harmful effects on family relationships of holding adult children financially responsible for parents receiving OAA support. Section 1902(a)(17)(D) of the Social Security Act prohibits a state medicaid plan from "taking into account the financial responsibility of any

* The following discussion will focus on policies seeking contributions from spouses and offspring for their institutionalized aged kin on medicaid, but family responsibility policies may also require payments by parents of children receiving medicaid in institutional settings, mostly intermediate care facilities for the mentally retarded.

individual for any applicant or recipient of assistance under the plan unless such applicant or recipient is such individual's spouse or such individual's child who is under age 21."[5] The supplemental security income program also follows this rule.

Under medicaid, even a husband or wife is usually financially responsible for an institutionalized spouse for only one month after nursing home placement. After the one month of separation, most states consider only the income and assets of the institutionalized spouse in determining medicaid eligibility.[6]

In the early 1980s the federal position was partially reversed. The Health Care Financing Administration (HCFA) announced that a state's medicaid program was not in conflict with the Social Security Act restrictions when family contributions are enforced under a state statute of general applicability (that is, not applied only to medicaid patients) and when all family contributions are counted as additional patient income.*

Despite a flurry of initial interest, only Idaho implemented a family responsibility policy. Idaho stopped its program after only six months because the state attorney general ruled that it did not comply with HCFA requirements. No state is currently operating a family responsibility program.

The issue of family responsibility under means-tested programs raises basic questions about which Americans have conflicting views and strong emotions. As a society, Americans value family solidarity and admire families whose members help each other. The sacrifices that adult children and other relatives make to care for disabled elderly family members, both at home and in institutions, reflect widely shared values of family responsibility. At the same time, society encourages individual self-reliance and generally holds that adults are legally, financially, and socially independent unless voluntarily joined together by marriage or responsibility for minor children. The issue of extending

* *Medicaid and Family Responsibility: Who Pays?* Committee Print, Briefing by the Subcommittee on Human Services, House Select Committee on Aging, 98 Cong. 1 sess. (Washington, D.C., 1983), pp. 5, 6, 9. HCFA's rationale was that a person's eligibility for medicaid should not be affected by whether a relative could contribute, only when he or she did contribute. Further, because a state law of general applicability is not part of a state's medicaid plan, such laws are not subject to federal regulation. Finally, by treating a relative's contribution as the medicaid patient's income, the policy would be entirely consistent with the Social Security Act, which requires the counting of all available income except that which is specifically excluded by law and regulation.

family responsibility under medicaid brings the norm of family sacrifice into conflict with the norm of adult independence.

A second source of conflict is the question that underlies all arguments about means testing: does the responsibility for solving the problem belong to individuals or to society at large? People who believe strongly in personal responsibility tend to favor severe means testing to ensure that public funds go only to the genuinely needy. They tend to favor requiring children to contribute to the cost of their parents' long-term care on the grounds that a parent whose children can afford to contribute is not really poor and should not be supported by the tax-paying public. People who put more stress on community responsibility for long-term care and other hazards of growing old favor relaxing or eliminating means tests. They believe that the cost of long-term care should be widely shared, not imposed on those unlucky enough to need it, or on their families. They tend to favor either replacing medicaid with a non-means-tested program or liberalizing the means test so that medicaid benefits can flow to a larger portion of the population than the very poor. Those who favor liberalizing medicaid generally do not favor increased family responsibility.

Rationale

Advocates of family responsibility programs see them as a way to promote equity, reduce costs, and encourage family care.[7] Some policymakers argue that it is inequitable to tax lower- or moderate-income people to pay for care for the parent of an affluent adult child. Raising taxes as an alternative to family responsibility forces everyone to share the burden of supporting elderly medicaid nursing home patients from well-to-do families. Moreover, advocates would like to see some middle ground for families who are able, and may want, to contribute to the cost of care, but currently have to choose between paying the whole cost of private care (something financially prohibitive) or relying solely on the medicaid program.

Fiscal justification for family responsibility stems from a general perception that the public costs of long-term care, primarily through medicaid, are too high. The family responsibility strategy seeks to reduce medicaid nursing home expenditures by increasing the medicaid patient's contribution toward his or her cost of care. Medicaid rules require that recipients contribute all of their income, except for a small personal needs allowance, to the cost of care. Family responsibility is seen by its proponents as a way to achieve government savings preferable to cutbacks in other public assistance programs like aid to families with dependent children, food stamps, or medicaid for children.

Last, a family responsibility program could encourage informal caregiving by delaying the point at which families seek institutional placement for their elderly kin. It would thereby generate further medicaid savings. Advocates contend that family members who know that they would be held financially responsible for part of the cost of institutional care might be more inclined to seek noninstitutional alternatives or to purchase long-term care insurance. By the same token, the elderly nursing home candidates themselves might be more resistant to placement that could lead to a financial burden for their children.

Critics of family responsibility programs question the wisdom of discouraging people who need institutional care from seeking it because they are dead set against burdening their kin. Critics also point to limited family means for contribution and to the high administrative costs of the program. In short, detractors contend that the approach would produce both undesirable consequences and little additional money.

Opponents also argue that adult children should not be "punished" because they happen to have a parent who needs expensive nursing home care. The need for long-term care is not the result of any moral failing on the part of the parent or the adult children. Indeed, the need for nursing home care usually arises only after a long, difficult effort to keep the disabled relative at home. As a result, public opinion polls find little support for this kind of policy.[8]

Potential Cost Savings

Available data offer little hope that a family responsibility program will significantly lower medicaid nursing home expenditures. In 1983 HCFA estimated a net saving of only $25 million a year for a national family responsibility initiative.[9] Similarly, the Idaho program had a projected goal of $1.5 million in annual collections from relatives but succeeded in collecting less than $32,000 in its six months of operation.[10]

Many medicaid nursing home patients have children, but few have spouses. Almost nothing is known about the wealth of relatives of such patients or the dollar amounts that families currently contribute. But for the entire elderly nursing home population, both children and spouses appear to have modest incomes, and a substantial minority are already making contributions toward the cost of nursing home care. Spouses, in particular, already make heavy contributions, given their income levels. Although it is difficult to project the savings from deterring the disabled elderly from seeking nursing home care, it is likely that the administrative costs of a family responsibility program will be high.

ADULT CHILDREN

The exact proportion of aged medicaid patients in nursing homes who are parents is uncertain, but could be substantial. Using data from three large nationally representative surveys, Burwell estimated the proportion to be between 55 percent and 75 percent; Koskela estimated a somewhat lower range for Wisconsin.[11] The state of Idaho estimated that about 60 percent of the elderly medicaid recipients in nursing homes had a living spouse or adult child. However, in Idaho fully 48 percent of all identified responsible relatives lived out of state, and only about 10 percent of such relatives complied with the first assessment notice.[12]

Adjusted for inflation and real wage growth, data from the 1976 Survey of Institutionalized Persons suggest that the median income of an adult child whose parent was institutionalized was moderate, just over $28,000 in 1986 dollars. About one-fifth of the offspring were already making some contribution to the cost of care.[13]

State data tend to show that relatives' means are more limited. The Idaho program found that 63 percent of the responsible relatives of medicaid nursing home patients had incomes under $20,000; 81 percent had incomes under $30,000.[14] In Wisconsin only 4 percent of the adult offspring with a parent in a nursing home had adjusted gross incomes of $30,000 or more.[15]

SPOUSES

Spouses of institutionalized medicaid recipients appear to be an even more restricted source for additional funds. First, only 8 percent to 17 percent of medicaid nursing home patients are currently married.[16] Second, according to the 1976 Survey of Institutionalized Persons, the residents' spouses also tend to have modest annual incomes and are already contributing substantially to the costs of nursing home care. Median annual family income reported by spouses with an institutionalized mate was about $15,000 in 1986 dollars. Among the 29 percent who contributed to their spouse's cost of care in 1975, the average contribution was just over 25 percent of median income.[17]

DETERRENCE

Savings that could accrue indirectly from the deterrent effect on a family's or a patient's decision to seek nursing home admission could exceed direct savings of actual dollars collected from relatives by the program.[18] During the 1960s the OAA program's family requirements resulted in many elderly parents choosing not to apply for assistance rather than force their children to contribute.[19] Some who did seek public assistance chose to survive on less income rather than to sue their own children if they did not contribute. For understandable reasons, prosecutors and judges were reluctant to bring such cases to trial.

The size of the deterrent effect is unclear. On the one hand, repeal of relative responsibility requirements for OAA in Washington and Texas was followed by large increases in caseloads.[20] Likewise, Idaho's short-lived family responsibility program reported that applications for medicaid nursing home coverage dropped 8 percent after enactment of the law and rose 8 percent after program termination.[21] On the other hand, few studies have found financial cost to be an important determinant of nursing home placement.[22]

ADMINISTRATIVE COSTS

The administrative costs of a family responsibility policy may be substantial. Responsible relatives must be identified, their incomes evaluated, assessments distributed to relatives, and collections enforced. Compliance with the state's assessment cannot be assumed, especially if the relative lives in another state. In developing its estimates of savings from implementing such a policy, HCFA concluded that almost 75 percent of the reductions in medicaid expenditures would be offset by administrative costs.[23]

Delivery System Goals

A family responsibility policy would change only slightly the service delivery system. Such a policy is primarily a shift in financial responsibility from the government to families of the disabled elderly.

FAMILY BURDEN

Family responsibility initiatives start with the premise that family members of some disabled elderly do not do enough to help their disabled older relatives. But virtually all studies demonstrate that relatives make significant commitments to provide informal home care based on their own sense of family responsibility.[24] The evidence is that families do not "dump" aged kin into nursing homes.

Some supporters of family responsibility programs note the anomaly in public policy between what is expected of families when relatives are at home and what is expected when they are in a nursing home. Families are expected to make large personal and financial sacrifices as long as an elderly relative remains at home. Once the patient enters a nursing home and establishes medicaid eligibility, however, the family's formal financial commitment often ends.

Continuing a family's financial responsibility after nursing home placement would make the long-term care system more consistent across settings but at the cost of making the individual family worse off. A family responsibility policy does not spread the risk of long-term care costs; it merely extends the family's commitment to an elderly relative into the nursing home. Although a family responsibility requirement will always increase family burden, at least somewhat, the increase may be more psychological than financial. In the Idaho program the median assessment was only $40 a month, and one-third of the relatives had an income low enough to require no contribution.[25] By contrast, the additional family strain of caring for an elderly relative who chooses to postpone placement could be substantial. The family support system would be strained by the additional care required by this kind of policy.[26]

Some nursing home patients' adult children are themselves elderly and facing reduced and fixed incomes because of retirement. In 1977, 11 percent to 18 percent of elderly medicaid nursing home residents were aged 90 or older.[27] Their children, probably retirees, would be the candidates for absorbing medicaid's reduced role in financing their parents' nursing home costs.

QUALITY OF CARE

Family responsibility requirements will have little effect on quality of care. The policy merely substitutes private monies for medicaid dollars without any net increase in total or per patient expenditures for long-term care. It offers no incentives for nursing homes to change present care practices.

FLEXIBILITY TO MEET LOCAL CONDITIONS AND INDIVIDUAL NEEDS

By relying on states to enact the enabling legislation and to enforce family financial responsibility, the policy should provide sufficient latitude for flexibility to meet local conditions. For example, states like Idaho, which appear to have a significant number of out-of-state responsible relatives, might focus on establishing interstate reciprocity agreements to increase their contribution base. Other states with fewer out-of-state responsible relatives might concentrate on expediting the initial identification and assessment process, since compliance for in-state relatives would be more within the state's control.

ADMINISTRATIVE SIMPLICITY

Family responsibility programs are not administratively simple. The first administrative hurdle is to identify responsible relatives and secure their compliance with the assessment. This task begins with obtaining the names of designated nursing home residents and then checking the actual eligibility determination case files to link them to kin. This check will work for parents of institutionalized children receiving medicaid and for those few elderly residents with a living spouse, but it will not identify older patients' adult children. This information must be requested directly from the nursing home. In all likelihood, such next-of-kin data would be incomplete, and the patient would have to be consulted. In Idaho, the state also had to rely on telephone directory assistance to locate many relatives.

If this process netted current information on the location of relatives, an assessment notice would be sent. The notice in Idaho required information on income and allowable deductions or a copy of relatives' latest federal tax returns. Tax returns could not be directly requested from the Internal Revenue Service because filing confidentially is protected by federal law. If no response was received within some period after the first assessment notice had been sent, the notice process would be repeated, with another delay to await reply to a second letter.

Meanwhile, the state officials would have to decide on appropriate measures to secure compliance. For in-state residents, they could garnish or attach wages or put a lien on property holdings. Such measures are not easy to set up or implement and probably will not be politically popular. Identifying out-of-state relatives who own property in the state so that liens might be put against their holdings and attempting to negotiate agreements with other states to help increase the collection rate for out-of-state residents would add to the administrative burden.

For all this effort a state could keep less than half of all the collections—the rest to be returned to HCFA because of the federal medicaid match. A Wisconsin study pointed out that, because of federal financial participation rates, for every $1.00 saved by the state through a family responsibility policy some family member would be required to contribute $2.22.[28]

Conclusion

A family responsibility policy under medicaid is not a basic reform of the long-term care system. It is a relatively small change in the medicaid rules that offers a chance for substituting private money for government money by shifting some of the cost of long-term care from medicaid onto the families of medicaid patients. The proposal is controversial and arouses deep-seated emotions about the obligations of families and the fairness of distributing the long-term care burden. As a practical matter, increased family responsibility under medicaid appears likely to reduce medicaid expenditures only slightly, at considerable administrative and political cost.

Family responsibility policies for aged nursing home medicaid recipients rest on the assumption that spouses and adult children shirk their obligations to disabled relatives in the community. But national data show that family care is flourishing. Four out of five elderly with long-term care needs are not in nursing homes. Almost all depend on family and friends to provide the services they require.[29] The more practical approach to family responsibility may be to encourage the high level of care now borne by families, not to increase their burden with the threat of additional expenditures.

Chapter Thirteen

Support for Unpaid Caregivers

Family-provided help is the backbone of in-home care for the elderly. In 1982 roughly 90 percent of the 4.65 million older persons in the community who had a chronic disability depended on family or friends to remain at home.[1] Fully 78 percent of this group reported no other caregivers. Moreover, these informal arrangements are not temporary. In most cases disabled older persons had received informal, unpaid care for more than one year, and a large minority for more than five years.[2] Family caregivers themselves say they have a permanent commitment to this role.[3] One can argue that without their help in providing home care for the elderly, public expenditures would be several times what they are today. Thus it is not surprising that policymakers are examining ways to maintain and even increase unpaid care.[4]

Two approaches to strengthening elderly informal care networks are special income tax credits or deductions and direct payments to family providers.* Proponents of support for informal care contend that government policies to promote their efforts could moderate future medicaid costs by deterring or postponing nursing home placement. Such policies could also moderate public outlays for in-home services, since informal caregivers' time costs less than payments to formal agency-employed care providers. Finally, the quality of in-home assis-

* Another support approach is to direct services toward the unpaid provider. In general, programs that provide such services are more of a tribute to the organized efforts of dedicated volunteers than to government initiatives. These programs tend to provide education and training to enhance caregiving skills and understanding. Some also offer emotional support, generally in the form of self-help groups, along with some arrangement for respite to give short-term relief to the unpaid provider.

tance is high because of the emotional attachment of family providers, less job turnover, flexibility of hours, and access in remote areas.

The case for supporting family care is made more urgent by demographic changes. Families may not be able to provide as much care in the future as they do now. More working women, fewer children, and more divorce may lessen the future availability of informal care.[5] Yet longer life spans will continue to put more family members in the position of providing care to elderly relatives. By 2015 a retiree's chance of having a parent alive may have increased nearly fourfold—from 7 percent to 28 percent.[6] Hence care for the disabled elderly may increasingly fall on those who are old themselves.

Although providing financial support for informal caregivers would offer more societal recognition for their contributions, there is no evidence that additional monies would encourage more care or reduce nursing home expenditures. The main problem with using tax incentives is the difficulty of targeting the tax so that it will actually increase informal caregiving. Because of the way the tax system operates, tax incentives are also more likely to benefit affluent families who can afford to purchase care. And because of the vast amount of informal care, tax incentives are a potentially expensive approach. By contrast, a small direct payment to caregivers in low-income families would allow more precise targeting than a tax benefit and could possibly help the poor cope with the added expense of care.

Financial Incentives

Informal caregivers seldom identify financial hardship as a major problem in providing care or as an important reason for deciding on nursing home placement.[7] In fact, some caregivers become upset when asked to even consider financial support in return for their help.[8] But what is seen as socially undesirable to some can be a financial necessity to others. For low-income families, the subsidy might enable the caregiver to purchase adult disposable diapers or respite services. Financial support can help to reduce unmet needs of both informal providers and care recipients. Money can be either an incentive to encourage more families to provide care or compensation to help families deal with stress and expenses to maintain already voluntarily initiated care.

TAX SYSTEM APPROACHES

Tax incentives—either tax deductions or tax credits—can offer some economic help to family care providers while not directly expanding the role of government in providing home care. Tax incentives promote consumer choice by allowing the elderly and their families to decide how best to use home care resources. Tax incentives are quite easy to administer, requiring little new program development.

Tax incentives do involve some cost-sharing for caregivers. Since families must first contribute to the cost of care to receive a subsidy after filing, some people view tax incentives as an effective method for increasing privately purchased home care services for the elderly. Most proposed tax subsidies fall in the range of 20 percent to 30 percent of expenses, which means that the total value of such privately purchased care would exceed public costs three- to fivefold.

The principal drawback to this approach is the difficulty of using the tax system to target resources effectively. The mechanisms available to target—age, income, diagnosis, and living arrangement—are poor proxies for unmet need. For instance, although age is a straightforward, easily verified, and unambiguous targeting device, most people aged 75 and over are not seriously functionally impaired.[9] Moreover, as discussed later, more sophisticated targeting mechanisms are expensive, cumbersome, and difficult to monitor. Consequently, tax proposals for family care run the risk of covering many taxpayers who would provide care without the incentive, thus causing a large tax loss with little or no change in family behavior. National estimates of the market value of present informal arrangements for care of the aged are in the billions of dollars.[10]

The other weak point in using tax subsidies is that the distribution of financial benefits is restricted by income. The itemized deduction misses households that do not itemize; adjustment to gross income allows a subsidy proportionate to tax liability, but there is no subsidy if there is no tax liability. Also, in a low tax bracket the subsidy for the deduction is low. Tax credits, especially when refundable, more equally support caregiving activities regardless of income. However, under the tax credit approach, low-income households are unlikely to be able to come up with the money to purchase services during the year to claim a tax credit at the end of the year. Further, because both federal and state tax systems are structured so that it is easier to provide a subsidy for purchased care than informal care, tax incentives will always direct subsidies to families who can better afford to purchase care.

Child and Dependent Care Credit

Most of the proposed tax initiatives to subsidize informal care have attempted to expand the credit for child and dependent care in federal tax law. This credit is now the only federal tax incentive available for family care of the aged. Over the years many proposals have been introduced in Congress to expand coverage to more caregivers.[11] The credit was originally enacted to help offset some of the employment-related expenses of child care and was not intended to help with family care of a disabled elderly relative.[12] It was not changed by the Tax Reform Act of 1986.

To claim the credit, a taxpayer must incur the expenses for care in conjunction with his or her need for gainful employment. In addition, the dependent must be mentally or physically unable to care for himself or herself, must regularly spend at least eight hours a day in the taxpayer's home, and must receive more than half of his or her financial support from the taxpayer. Qualified expenses can include household services necessary for care, day care, and medical expenses not claimed as itemized deductions.

Total tax expenditures for the current federal child and dependent care credit exceeded $2.6 billion in 1984, but only roughly 10 percent went for the care of disabled dependents, only some of whom were elderly.[13] Because no data on age are collected, the elderly's share of this small proportion is unknown, but the restrictions placed on the credit exclude the vast majority of the disabled aged.[14]

State Tax Incentives for Family Care

Oregon, Arizona, Idaho, Iowa, and North Carolina currently encourage family care through their income tax codes, but few taxpayers make use of the benefit. It is unclear how much of this low response can be attributed to the newness of the tax changes (none before 1979), to the relatively low level of the subsidy (none more than $55 a month), or to the types of restrictions placed on dependents or taxpayers to qualify.[15] Table 13-1 compares the characteristics of each state tax program with the federal dependent care credit.

Direct Payment Approaches

To meet the growing demand for in-home services, at least thirteen states have implemented programs that pay family caregivers.[16] Some programs receive funding from medicaid, some use social services block grant monies, others use state-only funds, and still others rely on a combination of funding sources.[17]

Like tax incentives, a cash subsidy paid directly to the informal provider is attractive because of its positive effect on consumer choice. According to a survey of administrators of programs that provide cash subsidies for family care, the benefits of this approach include provider flexibility, low per unit cost, and high-quality care.[18] Some officials believe elderly users of home care services should be able to choose their providers and, when given the option, commonly want kin. Some administrators contend that family care tends to foster high-quality services because of the blood bond between caregiver and recipient. Other officials argue that families are more motivated by the formal recognition of their efforts than by the actual dollar value of the program subsidy.

Because families would probably provide most of the help without payment, these subsidies are open to the criticism of using public funds to pay for care that was previously delivered free.[19] States have attempted to address this problem by only paying family members under highly controlled circumstances. Evidence of financial hardship, special approval procedures, exclusion of some family members (namely, spouses) as eligible providers, and very low subsidy levels are the chief mechanisms used to limit the use of the cash subsidies.[20]

Effect on Public Expenditures

Ideally, the net effect of financially supporting informal care would be to sustain or increase the level of family care so that people do not have to enter nursing homes. The tax incentive approach tries to leverage private resources for the purchase of formal care; the direct payment approach provides a low-cost, flexible alternative to agency-provided services. Both rely on spending more for home care to guard against the larger potential cost of medicaid paying for institutional care.

Unfortunately, incentives to support family care will probably not

TABLE 13-1. *Design Characteristics of Federal and State Tax Incentive Programs*

Item	Federal dependent care credit	Oregon, 1979	Arizona, 1981	Idaho, 1981	Iowa, 1983	North Carolina, 1986
Tax vehicle	Nonrefundable tax credit	Nonrefundable tax credit	Exemption and itemized deductions	Deduction or refundable credit	Deduction	Deduction
Value of subsidy	20–30 percent of eligible expenses per elderly dependent	8 percent of eligible expenses	Unlimited medical deductions; additional $600 exemption if deductions exceed $800	Standard $1,000 deduction or $100 tax credit	Up to $5,000 deductions	Up to $3,000 deduction
Maximum subsidy	$720 per dependent for lowest income group; $480 per dependent for highest income group	$250	Value of exemption is $48; no limit on itemized deductions	$75 for deduction; $100 for credit	$650 for taxpayer in highest tax bracket; $312 for taxpayer with median income	$210
Recipient qualifications						
Age requirement	No	65 and over	65 and over	65 and over	No	65 and over
Income limit	No	No	No	No	Yes	Yes
Disability requirement	Yes	Yes	No	No	Yes	No
"Shared household" requirement	Yes	Yes	No	Yes	Yes	No
Relationship test	Yes	No	No	Yes	Yes	Yes

Household qualifications						
Income limit	No	Yes	No	No	No	No
Employment requirement	Yes	No	No	No	No	No
Support test	Yes	Not specified	Yes for exemption; no for deductions	Yes	Not specified	No
Maximum elderly dependents per household	Two	Not specified	Not specified	Three	Not specified	Four
Eligible expenses	Work-related expenses for dependent care providers	Food, clothing, housekeeping, transportation, medical care	Medical expenses as defined under federal code; expenses must exceed $800 annually to claim exemption	No expenses required to be eligible for deduction; only support test	Any expense directly attributable to care of relative (food, clothing, medical expenses, transportation)	Any expense

SOURCES: Brian O. Burwell, "Shared Obligations: Public Policy Influences on Family Care for the Elderly," Medicaid Program Evaluation Working Paper 2.1 (Baltimore, Md.: Health Care Financing Administration, Office of Research and Demonstrations, May 1986), p. 94; National Association of State Units on Aging, "State Strategies for Enhancement: Family Supports" (Washington, D.C., 1987), p. 53; and information from the North Carolina Department of Revenue.

greatly reduce institutional costs.[21] First, there is little evidence that families place relatives in a nursing home except as a last resort.[22] Second, although the reasons that lead to a family's "breaking point" and subsequent decision on nursing home placement are only poorly understood, financial considerations seem to play only a very small role.[23] Third, most in-home care demonstration programs have had difficulty identifying and serving only persons at risk for nursing home placement.[24] Among paid family caregivers in Florida's home care for the elderly program, 58 percent said they "definitely or probably" would not have been able to provide care without the subsidy.[25] But this means that the remaining 42 percent felt they would provide care without the subsidy.[26]

The estimated cost of tax incentives and direct reimbursements depends on how they are targeted. The Congressional Budget Office estimated that projected revenue losses from Senator Orrin Hatch's Community Home Health Services Act (S.234) would be $300 million a year.[27] The Maryland State Office of Aging speculated that a tax credit program covering 50 percent of personal care expenses totaling $2,060 for each person would cost the state $8 million in lost revenue and would benefit just over 12,000 people.[28] Similarly, a very limited program of paying family members could require public outlays of approximately $300 million a year.[29]

Delivery System Effects

Financial support for informal caregivers is a deliberate policy to change the delivery system so that more family care will be provided or at least current levels are maintained. The effectiveness of this approach depends on the relative importance of financial considerations in providing help to disabled relatives.

QUALITY OF CARE

Public support for informal care rests partly on the judgment that the love and care provided by family and friends is superior to any formal system of care.[30] Although tax credits or cash transfers run the risk of damaging caregiving efforts by adding a profit motive, there is not much evidence that this occurs.[31] For example, the evaluation of the Maryland caregiver cash grant program suggests that the quality of care improved with the purchase of more medical items such as bedpans, thermometers, and diapers not covered under existing insurance programs.[32]

One way to help ensure quality is to direct the cash grant to the disabled person, who can then choose a family or nonfamily provider. These cash disability grants for long-term care, often called attendance or attendant care allowances, in recognition of the need for assistance by another person, are used in several European countries and for the last thirty-five years by the Veterans Administration.[33] The VA's program is part of the larger pension benefits program, is means-tested for nonservice-connected disabilities, and provides cash grants to more than 220,000 disabled veterans of all ages. Although there are no separate estimates for attendants, expenditures for the entire pension aid and attendance program were about $452 million in fiscal 1985, or only about $2,000 per person.[34]

While the idea of a cash grant is appealing, such unrestricted transfers have certain drawbacks. One problem is that the elder recipient may be confused or incapable of making an informed choice of a provider. Another problem is that an unrestricted cash payment can push an aged person's income over eligibility requirements for supplemental security income, which in most states affects his or her medicaid eligibility. Further, having the care recipient disperse provider payments can require the disabled older person to pay for social security, unemployment and workmen's compensation, and other employee benefits normally required of employers.

INSTITUTIONAL BIAS

The main reasons that families seek nursing home placement are the declining health of the patient or changes in the availability of family caregivers, not the monetary cost of home care. Not surprisingly, evaluations show that institutional use has not been significantly reduced by projects that offer financial or service support to families involved in caregiving. The state of Maryland's family support demonstration found that after twenty-two months nursing home admission rates were the same for caregivers receiving a modest cash grant as for nonsubsidized families.[35]

Tax incentives for family care have not been evaluated for reducing institutionalization. But, as discussed earlier, the difficulties of targeting a tax subsidy to an at-risk population through the tax code offers little hope of substituting community services for nursing home care to any great extent. Moreover, the tax-targeting problems necessitate a small subsidy level in order to keep total tax expenditures within bounds, an approach that is unlikely to produce much behavioral change.

ACCESS

Programs to support informal caregivers seek to improve access to formal home care services by making them more affordable (through tax incentives) or by extending the ability of family members to provide services (through payments to family members). However, assuming financial support has only a minor effect on total caregiving behavior, access to informal care will probably not change noticeably.

FAMILY BURDEN

A number of state programs that directly pay family members offer some evidence of a positive effect on family burden. The Maryland subsidized family care demonstration reported that after seventeen months of participation nearly half the families said that the money enabled them to purchase nursing and respite services and that they felt emotionally relieved and less confined as a result. Other participants reported better caregiving skills and a general improvement in their home care situation.[36]

FLEXIBILITY TO MEET LOCAL CONDITIONS

Providing support to informal providers offers a great deal of flexibility to meet local conditions. Tax incentives, at a national level, would give flexibility by vesting the service brokering with a taxpayer. But since most such proposals tend to provide money for the purchase of paid care, tax incentives will be of little benefit to people in areas that have few services. Cash transfers to families that provide care are probably a bit more flexible in areas that are service poor.

ADMINISTRATIVE SIMPLICITY

Policies to support informal caregivers must trade off administrative simplicity in targeting the people most in need of support against limiting expenditures. For example, tax credits that depend on simple self-reported disability and demographic characteristics, such as age, income, and living arrangement, are administratively easy to implement but are poor proxies for long-term care need. Thus tax credits would be available to persons whose needs are low and arbitrarily exclude some persons worthy of support who do not happen to fit the established categories. At the other extreme, having eligibility determined by an independent assessment authority could be extremely expensive, administratively complex, and likely to deter some people who cannot or do not wish to undergo the necessary review.

Programs that pay family members face the difficult administrative problem of how to minimize the substitution of paid for unpaid help. To date, state administrative guidelines to reduce this problem remain poorly specified. Most jurisdictions have added a new administrative layer for oversight that must rely on subjective judgments. As states have wrestled with supporting some family caregivers while attempting to control expenditures, their administrative burden has increased.

Conclusion

Proposals to provide tax credits and pay caregivers epitomize the classic conflict between equity and efficiency.[37] On the one hand, these policies are inefficient uses of public resources because they are unlikely to result in increased informal care or fewer nursing home placements. There is no evidence either that families are abandoning their disabled aged relatives by placing them in nursing homes or that they would be willing to keep them at home for a relatively small tax credit or payment. Thus these financial approaches would not change behavior much, but could be very costly because government would end up paying for the vast quantities of informal care that are already supplied at no public cost.

On the other hand, the proposals are appealing from an equity perspective. Families and friends are making enormous personal sacrifices to care for their relatives. It seems unfair that they are worse off financially than persons who choose not to care for their elderly relatives. Moreover, as recognition for performing a valued social activity, it would be good to provide some tangible reward to caregivers or to otherwise help them cope with the demands placed on them.

Expanded Home Care

Most disabled elderly are at home and want to stay there. Home care services, such as home health care, homemaker help, personal care, meals-on-wheels, respite care, and adult day care, enable them to do so. Only a small minority of the chronically disabled elderly, however, receive any paid home care services. In 1982 only 25 percent of the 4.65 million disabled elderly living at home used any paid in-home care.[1] Public expenditures for long-term care are overwhelmingly for nursing home rather than home care. Less than 5 percent of medicaid long-term care expenditures for the elderly in 1984 went for home care.[2] An obvious approach to reforming long-term care is to increase public funding for home care.

Supporters often justify expanded home care services by arguing that these will substitute for nursing home care and thus actually reduce public long-term care expenditures. Evaluations of community care programs, however, tend to show not only that expansion of community care has little effect on nursing home use, but that it raises, rather than lowers, total expenditures.[3] One reason for the cost increase is that the expanded home care goes primarily to people who were not receiving paid services. Another is that home care services do not keep disabled people out of nursing homes. They are almost always a complement to, not a substitute for, nursing home care in the overall system of long-term care.

Saving public money may be the most popular way to justify an expansion of home care, but there are other reasons to expand home care. One is that the elderly strongly prefer home care and that their demands for that care are unmet. Others are to establish a more balanced delivery system and to relieve the financial burdens of extended disability on the elderly.[4]

Public expenditures for home care services are low because policymakers fear the costs of more extensive programs. One fear is that many people who are not receiving paid home care would medically qualify for it. Another is that paid home care would substitute for unpaid home care provided by family and friends. But while expanded home care services would surely increase public expenditures, carefully designed programs need not be uncontrollably expensive. Because home care expenditures are currently so small, they could be substantially increased without significantly affecting total long-term care expenditures.

The Cost Saving Issue

Finding the conditions under which expanding home care would not increase public costs has become the dominant issue in home care.* For example, section 2176 of the Omnibus Budget Reconciliation Act of 1981 allows a state to offer certain nonmedical home and community-based services through its medicaid program, but only when they do not increase medicaid costs.[5]

* The wide variation of costs that can be counted or omitted from a cost analysis makes comparisons between program findings difficult. Generally, the broader the costs included in the comparison, the less likely it is that home care services will reduce costs. Pamela Doty, "Can Home and Community-Based Services Provide Lower Cost Alternatives to Nursing Homes?" Working Paper (Washington, D.C.: Health Care Financing Administration, Office of Policy Analysis, May 1984), pp. 29–30. Four sets of care costs are associated with supporting an elderly person in the community: (1) the direct costs of providing health-related services to the patient (for example, skilled nursing care and physical therapy) combined with administrative costs for the program arranging the care; (2) the private health-related expenditures that are paid by the patients, families, or friends (for example, pharmaceuticals); (3) the personal living expenditures of the patient and family, especially important when comparing home care with nursing homes, in which room and board are part of the total cost; and (4) the indirect family costs associated with home care, including family caregivers' forgone earnings and emotional stress, neither of which is normally included in cost estimates. Neville Doherty and Barbara Hicks, "Cost-Effectiveness Analysis and Alternative Health Care Programs for the Elderly," *Health Services Research,* vol. 12 (Summer 1977), pp. 190–203; Hans C. Palmer, "Home Care," in Ronald J. Vogel and Hans C. Palmer, eds., *Long-Term Care: Perspectives from Research and Demonstrations* (Washington, D.C.: HCFA, 1983), pp. 337–90. Total or aggregate costs, including individual out-of-pocket expenditures and public income subsidies (that is, food stamps, supplemental security income, and state supplementation payments), will also differ from government health costs (that is, medicaid and medicare), and federal and state government costs will depend on whether the services are financed through medicaid or medicare.

Whether expanding home care services will save money depends on the answers to several questions. First, can home care services actually reduce the use of expensive nursing home and hospital care? Second, can home care be targeted to those elderly who would most likely be placed in nursing homes in the absence of the services? Third, will expanded paid home care simply substitute for unpaid care? And finally, can services be delivered for less per client than nursing home care? The final test of whether home care saves money is whether total long-term care costs are higher or lower when home care services are provided.[6]

Over the course of the last fifteen years, a number of large-scale demonstration projects that expanded home care services have been conducted with the goal of reducing long-term care costs and improving the lives of disabled participants. A list of these projects, and their expanded publicly financed home care services, is shown in table 14-1. In general, the demonstrations expanded home care by covering persons or services not normally covered under medicare or medicaid. Although services varied among projects, all the demonstrations offered nonmedical services, such as homemaker and personal care, and all used case management to arrange expanded home care services for each participant. Most projects focused on the elderly, and all shared the common objective of substituting the expanded home care service package for nursing home care when appropriate.

EFFECTS ON NURSING HOME AND HOSPITAL USE

Most of the demonstration studies showed a slight, but statistically insignificant, reduction in nursing home use associated with the expansion of home care services. Projects with these results were Channeling (both case management models),[7] Wisconsin's Community Care Organization, New York's ACCESS program, the National Center for Health Services Research Section 222 homemaker and adult day care services experiment, Georgia's Alternative Health Services program, San Diego's Long-Term Care program, and San Francisco's Project OPEN.[8]

Four demonstration projects found statistically significant reductions in nursing home use, but of the four, all but one relied on weaker research designs to draw conclusions, using comparison groups rather than randomly assigned control groups. San Francisco's On Lok, Chicago's Five Hospital Homebound Elderly Program, and New York's Nursing Home Without Walls reported significantly less nursing home use for alternative community service clients than for comparison group members.[9]

The lone exception to the charge of potentially deficient comparison methods is the study by South Carolina's Community Long Term Care project, which did use a randomized research design. It concluded that significantly fewer people entered nursing homes among those receiving the expanded community services than among the control group (43 percent, as against 59 percent), and that participants spent significantly less time in nursing homes than controls (an average of forty days difference).[10] The South Carolina project is probably successful in identifying people with a high risk of institutionalization because it targets services to medicaid-eligible persons actually applying for nursing home care. No other randomized expanded home care study has replicated its finding.

There is no strong reason to presume that expansion of home and community-based services for the disabled elderly will produce either a net increase or a net decrease in the use of hospital services.[11] However, because hospital services are so expensive, even small reductions in hospital use can decrease costs significantly.

Most demonstration studies have not resulted in less hospital use. Preliminary findings from the On Lok study showed that hospitalization rates were lower for program participants than for a nursing home-eligible population, but later comparisons failed to show similar differences.[12] Six other expanded community-based care studies also found no difference in hospital use. In the Channeling demonstration, the Five Hospital Homebound Elderly Program in Chicago, the South Carolina Community Long Term Care project, the San Diego Long-Term Care program, San Francisco's Project OPEN, and Georgia's Alternative Health Services program, the participant hospital admissions rates or expenditures were not statistically different from the control or comparison group.[13] Channeling also found no effect on physician use or acute care lengths of stay.[14] A few projects that expanded community-based care reported lower hospital costs for participants. In all cases these findings were significant for only a subgroup of service users or could be attributed to more demonstration participants dying at home than in a hospital.[15]

In contrast, a few studies found increases in hospital inpatient service use among the alternative community service users.[16] The New York ACCESS demonstration and the Section 222 homemaker services program reported that acute hospital use rates and lengths

TABLE 14-1. *Publicly Financed Home Care Demonstration Projects, 1975–84*

Demonstration project (evaluation period)	Type of services			
	Home health care	Other in-home care	Transportation and meals	Other
National Center for Health Services Research Section 222 Experiment (1975–77)				
Day care	. . .	. . .	Transportation[a]	Day care
Homemaker	. . .	Homemaker; personal care; escort; help with shopping	Transportation[a]	. . .
Combined day care and home care	. . .	Homemaker; personal care; escort; help with shopping	Transportation[a]	Day care
Connecticut Triage (1976–79)	Skilled nursing; therapies; home health aide	Homemaker	Home-delivered meals	Dental care; glasses; hearing aids
Chicago Five Hospital Homebound Elderly Program (FHHEP) (1977–80)	Skilled nursing; therapies; home health aide	Homemaker; chore; friendly visiting; telephone reassurance	. . .	. . .
Georgia Alternative Health Services (AHS) (1977–80)	Skilled nursing; therapies; home health aide	Homemaker; personal care	Home-delivered meals	Day care
Monroe County, New York, ACCESS (1977–80)	. . .	Homemaker; chore; friendly visiting	Transportation	Respite care; foster care; housing improvements
San Francisco On Lok (1979–83)[b]	Skilled nursing; therapies; home health aide	Homemaker; personal care	Transportation; home-delivered meals	Day care; hospice; nutrition; group exercise;

Wisconsin Community Care Organization (CCO) (1978–80)	Skilled nursing; therapies; home health aide	Personal care; companion	Transportation; home-delivered meals	Day care; respite care
New York City Home Care (1980–83)	. . .	Homemaker; personal care	Transportation	Prescription drugs
New York Nursing Home Without Walls (1980–83)	Skilled nursing; therapies; home health aide; medical social services	Homemaker	Transportation; home-delivered meals; congregate meals	Respite care; moving assistance; housing improvements; nutrition counseling
San Francisco Organizations Providing for Elderly Needs (OPEN) (1980–83)	Skilled nursing; therapies; home health aide	Homemaker; chore	Transportation; home-delivered meals	Day care; mental health counseling; respite care; interpreter
South Carolina Community Long-Term Care (1980–84)	Therapies; medical social services	Personal care	Home-delivered meals	Day care; respite care
San Diego Long-Term Care (1981–83)	Skilled nursing; home health aide	Homemaker	Transportation; home-delivered meals	Day care; health education
DHHS Channeling (1982–84)	Skilled nursing; therapies; home health aide	Homemaker; personal care; chore; companion	Transportation; home-delivered meals	Day care; respite care; foster care; mental health services; medical supplies and equipment; housing assistance; discretionary[c]

SOURCES: Peter Kemper, Robert Applebaum, and Margaret Harrigan, "A Systematic Comparison of Community Care Demonstrations," National Center for Health Services Research, Rockville, Md., March 1987, table 1; and Susan L. Hughes, David S. Corday, and V. Alan Spiker, "Evaluation of a Long-Term Home Care Program," *Medical Care*, vol. 22 (May 1984), p. 462.

a. NCHSR day care/homemaker experiment provided transportation to day care or with escort depending on the model.

b. On Lok also expanded coverage for physician, hospital, and nursing home services.

c. Basic model Channeling had limited funds to purchase services to fill in gaps in the existing system without restrictions to the other service categories listed; financial model Channeling was restricted to the defined categories.

of stay rose for program participants, but the increases were not significant.[17]

TARGETING

Identifying persons who would be admitted to nursing homes unless they received home care services has proved to be extremely difficult. Few demonstration projects have managed to target a population in which a high proportion of the control group was subsequently admitted to a nursing home.[18] Most projects thus find that most people receiving home care would not enter nursing homes even if home services were not available.

Participants in the Channeling demonstration were frail, but only 19 percent of the control group were in nursing homes at the end of eighteen months.[19] Similar low rates of nursing home use have been noted in the control groups of most other demonstration programs.[20] In the South Carolina project, one of the few to identify a population with a relatively high risk of being institutionalized, fully 49 percent of the control group entered a nursing home.[21] Even so, half of the control group did not.

To identify persons with a high risk of nursing home placement, it is necessary to take into account not only functional status and medical diagnoses, but also social and environmental factors, including marital status, living situation, availability of nursing homes and home care, availability of unpaid care, earlier hospitalization, income, education, and the person's commitment or "will" to stay in the community. At present, no reliable way has been found to use these characteristics to predict nursing home entry.[22]

Even if the characteristics of people with a high risk of institutionalization could be identified, difficult public policy questions would arise. For example, it is not clear that home care service programs should be available only to the most severely impaired. Although severely impaired elderly are far more likely to enter a nursing home than are the less impaired, some moderately and mildly impaired people will also enter nursing homes, primarily because of lack of family or social service supports. Thus, while targeting services to the most impaired may do little more than delay nursing home admission for a short time, targeting the less impaired groups might delay institutionalization longer or perhaps prevent it altogether. Home care may not substantially reduce nursing home use for the relatively few severely impaired elderly in the community, but may do more for the less severely impaired, relatively few of whom will ever enter a nursing home.

Equally problematic is whether home care services should be targeted only to people without family support. Doing so would minimize the substitution of paid public service for existing unpaid care and would target people with a higher risk of institutionalization. However, the strain of family caregiving is often considerable, and the argument can be made that family care should be supplemented through public programs. Further, providing services only to people without family supports creates an incentive for families to withdraw support.

EFFECT OF EXPANDED HOME CARE ON UNPAID CARE

Most of the care for the functionally impaired elderly is provided by family and friends.[23] To the extent that expanded paid services substitute for this unpaid assistance, the public pays for care already being given at virtually no public cost. The substitution of paid for unpaid services has not been extensively studied in most demonstration programs that expand home care services.[24] In the Channeling demonstration, the case management model that provided a rich array of services found a small reduction in unpaid care, more by nonfamily than family caregivers. The small reductions in unpaid care were associated with much larger increases in paid care. For meal preparation, housework, laundry, and shopping, for example, a 4 percent to 5 percent increase in the number of clients receiving services from paid providers was associated with a 1 percent decrease in the number of clients receiving the same services informally.[25] Channeling results suggest that the primary effect of the paid services was to reduce the unmet demand for additional assistance rather than to reduce the amount of unpaid care.[26]

ESTIMATING PROGRAM COSTS

To estimate whether expanding home care saves money, evaluators have taken two different strategies. One strategy, to compare average home care users' daily costs with nursing home per diem rates, generally produces findings favorable to the community-based program. For example, average medicaid daily costs for all home care services provided to ACCESS participants were estimated to be 52 percent of the comparable medicaid nursing home per diem.[27] Similarly, On Lok showed that average daily home care charges per client were about 80 percent of the daily rate for skilled nursing facility care in San Francisco.[28]

Other studies using comparisons with hypothetical nursing home residents have produced similar results.[29]

The problem is that this strategy assumes that users of services would be institutionalized without the demonstration services. As indicated above, this assumption is wrong. The costs associated with increased home care use more than offset the nursing home per diem savings.

A preferable evaluation strategy, which compares public expenditures for a group of people eligible for expanded home care with public expenditures for people eligible only for those services regularly available in the community, usually finds that expansion of home care services increases costs.[30] The most recent example is the Channeling demonstration, which found that the basic case management model that coordinated available services increased total costs about 6 percent per client. The financial-control case management model, which provided a wide range of home care services, increased costs about 18 percent compared with randomized controls.[31]

Other Reasons to Expand Home Care

Although the recent public debate about expanding home care has tended to focus only on cost savings, there are quite independent reasons for a public investment in increased home care. Probably the most important is that the elderly strongly prefer home care to nursing home care.[32] Fully 95 percent of the chronically disabled elderly in the community in 1982 said they would prefer to stay out of a nursing home as long as possible.[33] Community-based long-term care preserves the elderly's independence, autonomy, and choice.[34]

Recipients of home care services also tend to report higher morale, well-being, and life satisfaction than nonrecipients in demonstration projects.* There are limits, however, to what home care can accomplish.

* Although the differences are not statistically significant, life satisfaction and morale self-assessments tend to be more consistently positive for expanded home care service recipients in community care demonstration projects. Margaret Stassen and John Holahan, "A Comparative Analysis of Long-Term Care Demonstrations and Evaluations," Working Paper 1227-2 (Washington, D.C.: Urban Institute, September 1980), p. 197; Robert A. Applebaum and Margaret Harrigan, *Channeling Effects on the Quality of Clients' Lives,* report prepared for the Department of Health and Human Services (Princeton, N.J.: Mathematica Policy Research, April 1986), pp. 58–61; and Brenda Haskins and others, *Evaluation of Coordinated Community-Oriented Long-Term Care Demonstration Projects,* report prepared for HCFA (Berkeley, Calif.: Berkeley Planning Associates, May 1985), pp. 154–55. The Channeling project, for example, found a slightly higher rating of well-being for expanded community care recipients on some measures, but no consistently

There is only weak evidence that it lowers mortality rates.* Nor does it significantly improve physical and mental functioning, although several studies suggest that home care services prevent or postpone further deterioration of a person's functional abilities.†

Another reason for expanding home and community-based services is to reduce unmet demands for care among disabled elderly in the community.[35] Disabled older people often report that they need additional help with their daily activities.[36] Approximately 70 percent of disabled elderly in the community in 1982 were receiving help solely from their family and friends, often at great personal sacrifice in terms of time, effort, emotional strain, and sometimes financial expense.[37] While community care users may not be at high risk of having to enter nursing homes, they still require help. Home care programs could help reduce the burden on caregivers by offering respite from their daily responsibilities, and could supply services that disabled older people reportedly desire.

Unpaid caregivers prefer wider availability of home care services to tax deductions or cash payments.[38] Although the Channeling demonstration did not find that expanded home care reduced emotional, physical, or financial strain among unpaid providers, it did find significant short-term (six-month) improvement in their ratings of overall life satisfaction.[39] This finding of limited beneficial effects for primary unpaid caregivers is consistent with the reported small reduction in unpaid caregiving in the demonstration.

A final reason to expand home and community-based services is to reduce financial burdens on the elderly and their families. Base case estimates from the Brookings-ICF Long-Term Care Financing Model for 1986–90 show that almost 20 percent of the $8.7 billion spent annually on home care will be financed by out-of-pocket expenditures.

---

large differences. Peter Kemper and others, *The Evaluation of the National Long Term Care Demonstration: Final Report,* report prepared for DHHS (Princeton, N.J.: Mathematica Policy Research, May 1986), pp. 157–63.

* Most studies found reductions in mortality as a result of the receipt of expanded home care services, but they were not statistically significant. Peter Kemper, Robert Applebaum, and Margaret Harrigan, "Community Care Demonstrations: What Have We Learned?" *Health Care Financing Review,* vol. 8 (Summer 1987), p. 96; Haskins and others, *Coordinated Community-Oriented Long-Term Care,* pp. 160–61; and Stassen and Holahan, "Comparative Analysis of Long-Term Care Demonstrations," p. 196.

† Several studies found that alternative home care services can at least slow the deterioration of functional ability. Kemper and others, "Community Care Demonstrations," p. 95; Haskins and others, *Coordinated Community-Oriented Long-Term Care,* pp. 155–57; and Stassen and Holahan, "Comparative Analysis of Long-Term Care Demonstrations," p. 197.

FIGURE 14-1. **Simulation Assumptions for the Expanded Medicare Home Care Benefit (MEDHC)**

- Skilled as well as unskilled home care is provided. The current medicare benefit would be retained.
- Only persons with three or more limitations in activities of daily living would be eligible for the expanded benefit.
- The expanded benefit has a one-month deductible and 20 percent coinsurance. Medicaid pays for cost-sharing for all elderly below poverty level.
- Payment rates for the expanded benefit are 115 percent of the weighted average cost per visit of all noninstitutional services.

Expanded public financing of home care services could help relieve the financial demands of extended disability on older people.

Model Results

Expanded home care services could be funded through a variety of programs, including medicare, medicaid, the Older Americans Act programs, and the social services block grant. One possible avenue is to liberalize the medicare home health benefit, which at present is highly restricted and provides primarily skilled nursing care on a part-time and intermittent basis to homebound persons.

We simulated a liberalized medicare home care benefit, MEDHC, which provides a broad range of both skilled and unskilled services with a fairly low level of cost-sharing. To control use and costs, we limited eligibility for the expanded benefit to severely disabled persons—elderly with three or more deficiencies in the activities of daily living.* Because services for the expanded benefit would probably cost more than existing services, we set payment rates at 115 percent of the weighted average of all home care services. The assumptions of MEDHC are described in figure 14-1.

* In 1982, 33.2 percent of the 4.65 million chronically disabled elderly reported three or more limitations in activities of daily living. The six activities of daily living are eating, dressing, bathing, getting to bathroom or using toilet, transferring from or getting in or out of bed or chair, and getting around inside. Among persons with three or more functional limitations, 33.6 percent received paid home care. DHHS, 1982 National Long-Term Care Survey, available from the National Technical Information Service, accession nos. PB-86-161775 and PB-86-161783.

TABLE 14-2. *Total Expenditures for Home Care, by Source of Payment, Base Case and MEDHC, 2016–20*[a]
Billions of 1987 dollars

Payment source	Base case	MEDHC	Percent change
Medicaid	2.385	1.956	−17.99
Medicare	7.699	7.721	0.29
MEDHC	. . .	8.108	. . .
Other payers	7.208	3.294	−54.30
Out-of-pocket	4.593	4.844	5.46
TOTAL	21.886	25.925	18.45

SOURCE: Brookings-ICF Long-Term Care Financing Model.
a. Average annual expenditures. Assumes no increase in use rates.

In 2016–20 total home care expenditures including MEDHC would be $25.9 billion, an increase of 18 percent over the base case of $21.9 billion (table 14-2). If there was no change in use rates, expenditures for the additional medicare home care benefit would be $8.1 billion, or 31 percent of total home care expenditures. In 1986–90 new program outlays would be roughly $3.1 billion.

The importance of the new program in financing home care services varies little by demographic and income categories. In 2016–20 medicaid and other-payer expenditures would decline 18 percent and 54 percent, respectively. Total out-of-pocket costs would actually increase, reflecting the fact that the new benefit replaces some programs that currently do not impose any cost-sharing. However, while more people pay something, the average out-of-pocket expense declines 13 percent.*

Given the likely popularity of home care and the unmet demand for additional help among disabled elderly in the community, it would be difficult, perhaps undesirable, to hold use constant. Spending for the benefit is relatively small, especially compared with nursing home expenditures. Even if use doubled or tripled, spending would still remain a small part of total long-term care expenditures.

Conclusion

Fears of uncontrollable public costs have blocked past federal initiatives to expand home care. Thus a key policy issue is whether use and expenditures can be controlled. There are several ways to do so.

* In 2016–20 out-of-pocket home care expenditures for the base case averaged $2,278, compared with $1,986 for MEDHC. Brookings-ICF Long-Term Care Financing Model.

Cost-sharing and case management can help to avoid excessive use and to coordinate services (including those of unpaid helpers). Restricting in-home benefit eligibility to severely disabled people, limiting the type of services offered, and regulating the total number or frequency of visits can also help to control use. Other alternatives include financing expanded home care as an indemnity benefit (as do most private insurance policies) or as a benefit limited to an annual dollar maximum (as does the social/health maintenance organization demonstration). Nonetheless, while by no means trivial, expanded home care costs are unlikely to be large compared with nursing home expenditures, even assuming a large increase in use.

Although expanding home-based long-term care services is likely to increase public costs, it is also likely to improve the quality of life for program participants. Moreover, expanded home care services are not likely to lead to a wholesale substitution of paid services for unpaid care. The policy issue should not be whether expanded public financing of community care will reduce costs. The real issues are how much community care society is willing to pay for, who should receive it, and how it can be efficiently delivered.[40]

Chapter Fifteen

Liberalized Medicaid

At present the main source of public financing for long-term care is medicaid, the joint federal-state program intended to finance medical care for the poor. To become eligible for medicaid, an elderly disabled person must prove both low income and low assets. Nursing home residents must turn over their social security checks and other income, except for a personal needs allowance of $30 a month. In some circumstances the spouse of a medicaid patient in a nursing home will be left with only minimal amounts of the couple's income and assets. Although the home is normally a protected asset, some states will force the sale of a house if it is unlikely the patient will be able to return to it and there is no spouse or minor child living in it.

Dissatisfaction with the current medicaid program is high. Not only does the demeaning means test often imply hardship for patients and their spouses, but low reimbursement rates mean that nursing homes frequently resist taking medicaid patients or provide poor care.

Despite these inadequacies, however, medicaid has come to serve as a last resort, not just for the poor, but for much of the middle class as well. After being in a nursing home for a while, many private patients use up their assets (spend down) and become eligible for medicaid. The Brookings-ICF Long-Term Care Model estimates that for the period 1986–90, 58 percent of all nursing home patients—and a higher percentage of long-stay patients—are or will be dependent on medicaid to help pay for their care, even though many were not poor when they entered the nursing home. Although the income of the elderly is projected to increase over time, the income for the population aged 85 and over will probably not rise as fast as the cost of nursing home and home care. Indeed, the Brookings-ICF model suggests that the elderly at the highest risk of institutionalization will be less able to afford long-term care in 2016–20 than they are today. Hence the prospects are for greater reliance on medicaid in the future.

There are two major alternatives to continuing reliance on an unpopular means-tested program to finance long-term care for a large fraction of the population. One is to find new ways for most people to finance long-term care so that many fewer patients are forced to rely on medicaid. This approach would relegate medicaid to its original role of protecting the very poor. Since expansion of private sector initiatives is unlikely to reduce dependence on medicaid appreciably (see chapters 3–9), this approach implies enactment of some kind of public insurance covering long-term care.

The second alternative, discussed in this chapter, is simply to liberalize medicaid, retaining a less severe means test but making the program more attractive both to patients and providers. Such an approach could also be an adjunct to a social insurance program. This, of course, entails making the program more expensive for the taxpayer.

Rationale

A major justification for improving rather than abandoning the medicaid program is that the status quo is not so bad as often alleged. The current system meets the needs, albeit crudely, of many of its participants. For example, the entitlement character of medicaid means that expenditures tend to rise with need and are not arbitrarily limited by the appropriation process. Though medicaid is targeted on the poor, it also provides a useful safety net for the middle class. The medicaid spend-down requirements mean that medicaid finances only the care that the income and the assets of the elderly cannot, thus keeping public expenditures down. The institutional bias ensures that persons receiving publicly financed care are predominantly the severely disabled and those without family support. And, finally, home care services, though not as widespread as many would like, are moderately available. If one accepts this argument, then it seems attractive to build on the strengths of medicaid but to make it less onerous for patients and providers.

There are also equity arguments for retaining means testing rather than moving to a public insurance program that pays benefits regardless of need. Under such a public insurance program low- and moderate-income people could end up paying taxes that would go in part to finance long-term care for the well-to-do, allowing them to pass their savings on to their heirs.

Those who defend retention of some means testing argue that it is appropriate for nursing home patients to spend most of their income and assets for their care. Given their disabilities, nursing home patients may not have much else on which to spend their money. There is no public purpose in allowing people at the end of their lives to retain a large amount of income and assets to leave to their heirs. Moreover, assuming that there is some upper limit to which Americans will allow themselves to be taxed, programs for lower-income groups should be expanded before programs that benefit the middle class.[1]

Finally, modifying the current system has the political advantage that it can be accomplished incrementally. Thus it is consistent with how social policy tends to be developed in the United States.[2] As evidenced by recent legislation to allow spouses of medicaid patients in nursing homes to retain more of the couple's income and assets, Congress appears willing to make modest liberalizations in the medicaid program even if it is currently unwilling to add long-term care to the medicare program. One lesson from the effort to enact a national health insurance program in the 1970s was that the emphasis on comprehensive reform precluded serious consideration of many desirable medicaid reforms that would have substantially improved the lot of the poor. Something similar could happen with efforts to enact highly ambitious programs for reforming long-term care.

This line of argument is rejected by those who believe means testing is inherently undesirable and should be used sparingly, if at all, not extended to a larger portion of the population under a liberalized medicaid program for long-term care. First, "services specially designed for poor people are poor services,"[3] typically underfunded and vulnerable to budget cuts.[4] Second, it is stigmatizing and degrading to have to prove oneself "poor" before obtaining the benefits that one desperately needs. One reason for the relatively low participation by the elderly in the supplemental security income program is their unwillingness to submit to what is perceived as the indignity of the means test.[5] Moreover, means-tested programs require extensive administrative mechanisms designed to prevent unqualified people from obtaining benefits.[6] Third, because the benefits of means-tested programs hinge on proving oneself poor, there is an incentive to hide income and assets. Currently, some elderly transfer their assets to relatives in ways that allow them to qualify for medicaid nursing home benefits.[7]

FIGURE 15-1. **Simulation Assumptions for Liberalized Medicaid Program**

- The basic structure of the medicaid program is retained.
- The personal needs allowance is increased to $200 a month.
- The level of protected assets is increased to $15,000.
- The home is always a protected asset.
- In circumstances where the institutionalized spouse has the bulk of the income, the community-based spouse may retain up to two times the poverty level in income.
- The new medicaid reimbursement rate is raised to 115 percent of the current medicaid program's rate.

Those who reject means tests argue that the appropriate vehicle for income and wealth redistribution is tax policy, not forcing the disabled into poverty. Allowing people to incur catastrophic health care costs essentially forces the sick to pay a very large "tax," while people lucky enough to be well pay taxes only for the means-tested program. Since society will incur most of these costs under any financing system, the key question is whether the costs will be spread over a large number of people or concentrated on the relatively few people who need nursing home or extended home care.

They would also argue that social policy is not always made best when it is made incrementally. The enactment of social security, unemployment compensation, disability insurance, and medicare cannot be considered incremental changes. Although Congress and the executive branch are currently reluctant to sponsor comprehensive reform, there is considerable public support for such a move. In a recent survey of registered voters sponsored by the American Association of Retired Persons and the Villers Foundation, a large majority believed that public financing for long-term care should not be means-tested.[8]

Model Results

Many incremental medicaid improvements would make the program less onerous, yet retain its fundamentally means-tested character. To establish an outer-bound estimate of these possible changes, we simulated a very substantially liberalized medicaid program. Figure 15-1

TABLE 15-1. *Total Expenditures for Nursing Home Care, by Source of Payment, Base Case and Liberalized Medicaid, 2016–20*[a]
Billions of 1987 dollars

Payment source	Base case	Liberalized medicaid	Percent change
Medicaid	46.192	73.743	59.64
Medicare	1.612	1.773	10.00
Patients' cash income	27.889	23.188	−16.86
Patients' assets	22.423	16.122	−28.10
TOTAL	98.117	114.827	17.03

SOURCE: Brookings-ICF Long-Term Care Financing Model.
a. Average annual expenditures. Assumes a 10 percent increase in nursing home use under liberalized medicaid.

presents the detailed assumptions for this option. In this new program the basic structure of the medicaid program would be retained with several modifications. First, the personal needs allowance would be increased from $30 to $200 a month. Second, the level of protected assets would be increased from $1,800 to $15,000. Third, the home would always be a protected asset; people would not be forced to sell a home under any circumstances. And fourth, when the institutionalized spouse received the bulk of the income, the spouse left at home would be able to retain income of up to 200 percent of the poverty level. To make patients more attractive to nursing homes, the payment rate for the liberalized program would be raised to 115 percent of the current medicaid program's rate. Since liberalized medicaid would be less severe than the current program, it would probably attract persons who were previously deterred by the strict means test. A 10 percent across-the-board rise in nursing home use is therefore assumed.

EFFECT ON PUBLIC EXPENDITURES

Table 15-1 compares total spending for nursing home care under liberalized medicaid with the base case for the years 2016–20. Liberalizing the program would increase medicaid payments to nursing homes to more than $70 billion, or 60 percent higher than under the base-case option. Thus medicaid, already the dominant source of financing for nursing home care, would play an even larger role, accounting for almost two-thirds of the total expenditures.

Table 15-2 shows that medicaid would increase significantly as a source of payment for all demographic and most income groups. It would increase disproportionately for married couples, reflecting the higher level of financial protection offered spouses of nursing home

TABLE 15-2. *Medicaid Expenditures for Nursing Home Care, by Demographic and Income Groups, Base Case and Liberalized Program, 2016–20*[a]
Percentage of total payments for nursing home services

Category	Base case	Liberalized medicaid
Total medicaid share	47.4	63.3
Age		
65–74	29.5	44.7
75–84	44.7	62.3
85 and over	57.2	71.7
Marital status		
Married	35.3	56.6
Unmarried	52.5	66.0
Sex		
Male	33.1	50.6
Female	54.6	69.5
Family income (dollars)[b]		
Under 7,500	82.8	93.8
7,500–14,999	57.0	75.6
15,000–19,999	36.2	59.0
20,000–29,999	25.2	45.8
30,000–39,999	9.9	23.6
40,000–49,999	4.0	10.4
50,000 and over	1.8	3.3

SOURCE: Brookings-ICF Long-Term Care Financing Model.

a. These data are based on the total payments for an admission cohort over the entire length of their stays in a nursing home. For example, for a person who is admitted to a nursing home in 2016–20 for a two-year stay, we totaled two years' worth of nursing home expenditures. We then calculated the proportion of those expenditures paid by a liberalized medicaid program.

b. Family income is joint income for married persons, individual income for unmarried persons.

patients. It would also increase disproportionately for middle-income people ($15,000 to $29,999), reflecting the higher levels of protected income and assets.

EFFECT ON PRIVATE EXPENDITURES

Compared with the base case, the liberalized program by 2016–20 would reduce payments by patients from cash income 17 percent and from assets 28 percent (table 15-1). Finally, if financial eligibility standards were liberalized, the model shows that the number of medicaid patients in nursing homes would increase 31 percent by 2016–20 (table 15-3). Note that the percentage increase in medicaid expenditures for nursing home care considerably exceeds the increase in the number of medicaid patients in nursing homes. This disparity suggests that the bulk of the higher expenditures stem from making people who would currently be

TABLE 15-3. *Number of Elderly Medicaid Patients in Nursing Homes, Base Case and Liberalized Medicaid, Selected Periods, 1986–2020*[a]
Millions of patients

Option	1986–90	2001–05	2016–20
Base case	1.334	2.006	2.343
Liberalized medicaid	1.830	2.650	3.069
Percent change	37.18	32.10	30.99

SOURCE: Brookings-ICF Long-Term Care Financing Model.
a. Ever in a nursing home during the course of a year; assumes a 10 percent increase in nursing home use.

eligible for medicaid under existing rules less impoverished rather than from making new people eligible for medicaid.

Conclusion

Minor and major liberalizations of medicaid are strategies to make the current program less onerous, but still means-tested. Advocates of liberalizing medicaid defend means-tested programs, contending that the proper role of government is to help only those who cannot pay for their own long-term care. Moreover, they assert that incremental change to medicaid is the most politically feasible route to long-term care reform. Others argue, however, that means-tested programs are fundamentally flawed and that the majority of elderly using nursing homes should not have to rely on them. Moreover, the political feasibility of broad reforms, such as social insurance, may improve dramatically over time, making incremental strategies less appealing.

Chapter Sixteen

Public Long-Term Care Insurance

Enacting public long-term care insurance would dramatically change the role of the U.S. government in long-term care financing.* Although most Western European countries and Canada cover long-term care along with acute care under their national health insurance or national health service, the United States makes a sharp distinction between the two kinds of care.[1] Acute care is covered by social insurance under the medicare program, and long-term care is primarily covered by medicaid, a means-tested welfare program.

The rationale for public long-term care insurance is that the use of long-term care is a normal, insurable risk of growing old, but that the private insurance market is unable to provide adequate coverage at a price affordable by most of the elderly. Covering long-term care under a universal public program avoids two problems inherent in the current private insurance market: those people likely to need long-term care insurance may buy it disproportionately, and insurance companies tend

* There are at least five relatively detailed proposals for public long-term care insurance. See Karen Davis and Diane Rowland, *Medicare Policy: New Directions for Health and Long-Term Care* (Baltimore, Md.: Johns Hopkins University Press, 1986); *Medicare Part C: Catastrophic Health Insurance Act of 1986,* H.R. 4287, 99 Cong. 2 sess. (Washington, D.C., February 28, 1986), introduced by Congressman Claude Pepper; Harvard Medicare Project, *Medicare: Coming of Age—A Proposal for Reform* (Cambridge, Mass.: John F. Kennedy School of Government, Center for Health Policy and Management, March 1986); Anne R. Somers, "Long-Term Care for the Elderly and Disabled: A New Health Priority," *New England Journal of Medicine,* July 22, 1982, pp. 221–26; and *Medicare Part C: Catastrophic Health Insurance Act of 1987,* S. 454, 100 Cong. 1 sess. (Washington, D.C., February 4, 1987), introduced by Senator Jim Sasser. In addition, the American Association of Retired Persons, the Villers Foundation, and the Older Women's League are developing a proposal that they hope can be actively discussed in the 1988 presidential election. Some states are considering public-private partnerships that would have elements of public long-term care insurance.

to react by screening out disabled applicants. A universal public program also reduces the high marketing costs associated with private insurance and makes it easier to spread the cost of long-term care over the working-age population as well as the elderly. Covering long-term care under public insurance spares elderly patients the indignity of proving themselves impoverished to establish eligibility for benefits. It also lessens differences in the quality of care and access to services inherent in the current distinction between private pay and welfare patients.

Those who oppose public insurance point out that it would add greatly to the cost of government and the burden on taxpayers. Costs are difficult to estimate and could be larger than initially estimated. Many disabled elderly who now receive no paid services would be entitled to benefits. The reduced out-of-pocket price of services could also lead to increased service use and substitution of paid for unpaid services. Once committed to this type of program, Congress and the president might have great difficulty cutting back, even in the face of rapidly escalating costs.

Public Insurance Design Options

Social insurance provides citizens the opportunity to pool their risk of some costly future event—death, retirement, unemployment, or hospitalization—by paying into a fund from which benefits can be drawn when needed. Benefits are paid as a matter of right or entitlement, not as public charity. A social insurance program for long-term care would involve some form of contributory financing and entitlement to benefits, but many variations in design are possible. Final program design and costs depend on program eligibility, the range of benefits, the degree of cost-sharing, and how the program is administered.

PROGRAM ELIGIBILITY

Eligibility decisions have important implications for equity, cost, and political feasibility. For purposes of this study we have assumed that eligibility for benefits would be limited to disabled people aged 65 and over. There are strong equity and political arguments, however, for including disabled people under 65—the chronically mentally ill, the developmentally disabled including the mentally retarded, and the physically disabled. Although estimates vary, there are probably as many disabled people under age 65 as there are over age 65.* Some of the younger disabled qualify for social security disability insurance and medicare benefits, and some do not.† Given the large number of younger disabled, the costs of serving this group could be high.

RANGE OF BENEFITS

A long-term care insurance program could be limited to nursing home care, which is the form of long-term care most likely to impose catastrophic costs on elderly patients and their families. The varying care requirements of the elderly and their overwhelming desire to stay in their own homes, however, suggest the desirability of covering home care services as well. Decisions would have to be made on the level of disability needed to qualify for benefits and the amount and type of home care covered. Some countries, such as Denmark and Sweden, cover a broad range of home care services for their elderly citizens.[2]

COST-SHARING

A public insurance program could be designed to provide long-term care services at little or no cost to eligible patients or could require cost-sharing through coinsurance or deductibles at various levels. A program that required little cost-sharing would be of great financial assistance to elderly patients and would provide a sense of security to the whole elderly population. No one, not even the poorest elderly, would have to worry about the financial burden of care. The relief would be especially valuable to persons trying to cope with the personal pain and suffering inherent in physical and mental decline. A comprehensive program with low cost-sharing would also enable the government to exert its buying power to control the price of services.[3]

If virtually all costs were covered, no one would require supplemental insurance to achieve adequate financial protection, and the inefficiency

* This estimate includes 6 million people aged 15 to 64 with severe functional limitations and more than 2 million chronically ill children with a limitation in a major activity. U.S. Bureau of the Census, "Disability, Functional Limitation, and Health Insurance Coverage: 1984/85," *Current Population Reports: Household Economic Studies,* series P-70, no. 8 (Washington, D.C.: Department of Commerce, December 1986), p. 11; and U.S. National Center for Health Statistics, "Current Estimates from the National Health Interview Survey: United States, 1986," *Vital and Health Statistics,* series 10, no. 164 (Hyattsville, Md.: DHHS, October 1987), p. 111.

† There are approximately 4 million people receiving social security disability insurance benefits, including spouses and dependents. "Current Operating Statistics," *Social Security Bulletin,* vol. 50 (August 1987), p. 41. Individuals must be on social security disability insurance for twenty-four months before they become eligible for medicare.

of a supplemental insurance market would be avoided. Most current medicare supplemental insurers use an average of 40 percent of premiums for marketing, administrative expenses, and profits.[4] Comprehensive government coverage of the entire elderly population would minimize those costs and could entail economies of scale in processing claims.*

A low cost-sharing program would, however, be expensive. Consumers would have little incentive to economize in the use of services or to be cost conscious in choosing the type of service. Both use of services and provider costs would be likely to go up. In an era when policymakers fear rising costs, such a program lacks political credibility and feasibility. The high cost is likely to impose a significant tax burden on moderate- and lower-income people. A low cost-sharing program would also release people from any sense of personal responsibility to save or plan for their own long-term care needs.

A less costly alternative is a program with fairly substantial coinsurance and deductibles, uniform for all beneficiaries, as in the medicare acute care program. The rationale for such cost-sharing is even more cogent for long-term care than for acute care, since a large part of the nursing home bill is for room and board expenses that people would have even if they were healthy. Because it pays less of the total bill and requires significant out-of-pocket expenditures for services, a moderate cost-sharing program requires fewer public dollars than a low cost-sharing program.

Substantial cost-sharing implies that the proper role of the public sector is to reduce the cost of long-term care to those who need it while preserving people's incentives to provide for themselves or use services sparingly. Cost-sharing fosters private sector initiatives such as insurance for those who want more financial protection or who want services not covered by the public program. This supplemental insurance, however, could undermine the cost-controlling effects of the public program cost-sharing. Although public insurance with substantial

* Administratively, the government appears to run big programs more cheaply than the private sector does. For example, both federal and state administrative costs of the medicaid program were only about 5 percent of total program costs in 1984, compared with administrative costs (including marketing and profits) of 24 percent for group health plans offered by commercial private insurers and 10 percent for Blue Cross and Blue Shield. Data supplied by Betsy Hanczaryk, budget analyst, Division of State Agency Financial Management, HCFA; and "Commercial Insurers' Claims Ratio 'Steadily Declining,'" *Empire Blue Cross and Blue Shield Labor Newsletter,* vol. 9 (September 1985), pp. 1, 7.

cost-sharing provides a role for the private sector, it does not depend on massive expansion of private insurance for its success.

The problem with this type of cost-sharing is setting the proper level. If it is set high enough to reduce government costs substantially and deter middle- and upper-income people from overusing services, it will impose excessive burdens on relatively low-income elderly. Hence a large residual medicaid program may have to be retained, partly defeating the objective of shifting away from means testing.

A possible compromise, making coinsurance and deductibles income-related, would reduce the need for a residual medicaid program, but would make the insurance much more complex to administer. Many social insurance advocates also oppose varying benefits by income because they fear a return to the means test. Political support for this type of program could also erode if higher-income people felt that they were not receiving a high enough "return" on their taxes or premiums.

Another approach would be for the government program to provide full coverage of long-term care only for those who have been in nursing homes for a long period—two years, for example.* The government benefit would thus be limited to the relatively few people who incur catastrophic long-term care expenses. To cover care lasting up to two years, the elderly would be encouraged to purchase private long-term care insurance.

This catastrophic-only approach would encourage private sector involvement by defining the benefit period during which private insurance would be needed. Since private insurance would cover only two years of nursing home care rather than six years or longer, premiums would be lower, so that more elderly could afford policies. Since the gap not covered by the public program would be clearly defined, marketing private insurance should be easier. Moreover, with the public sector covering the relatively uncommon but extremely expensive long nursing home stays, the financial risks to insurers could be reduced.

The principal problem of the catastrophic-only approach is that it places a great deal of faith on the ability of individuals and the private sector to carry the burden for the first two years of care. Most people incur out-of-pocket costs far beyond their means well before they have spent two years in a nursing home. Although these people would need

* This approach is being actively discussed by several states, including Massachusetts, New York, Connecticut, Indiana, Wisconsin, and North Carolina. Mark R. Meiners, University of Maryland, Center on Aging, personal communication, November 12, 1987.

private insurance, it is not certain that insurers would flock to such a market. In addition, although the financial risks of long-stay nursing home patients are of concern to insurers, they have already limited those risks by offering only policies that cover a relatively short, fixed period (typically two to four years). Insurers' risks may thus not be significantly reduced.

Nor would the elderly have any guarantee that they could obtain insurance for the initial two-year period. Although insurance covering only two years of care is more affordable than insurance covering six or more years, it would still be beyond the financial reach of many elderly.* Government subsidies to lower- and middle-income elderly could reduce the out-of-pocket cost of insurance, but such subsidies would be cumbersome to administer. Moreover, insurance companies will not sell policies to the disabled. People unable to obtain insurance will be left with no option other than spending down to medicaid eligibility. Even with insurance, people may be faced with large out-of-pocket costs. Current insurance policies have restrictions that substantially reduce the level of financial protection offered.[5]

PROGRAM ADMINISTRATION

The federal government, through the Health Care Financing Administration of the Department of Health and Human Services, has more than twenty years' experience administering the medicare program. Hence the basic mechanisms for administering a public insurance program are in place. Nonetheless, the additional administrative functions of a long-term care program would require substantial new resources, methods, and routines, creating a major challenge for the federal government. Any new program will need methods for determining and tracking eligibility, authorizing services, assessing quality of care, reviewing use, setting reimbursement rates, and processing claims.[6]

A principal issue is how to capitalize on the states' extensive experience with long-term care. By virtue of the medicaid program, the social services block grant, and their own long-term care programs, states have experience with many of the administrative mechanisms necessary

* HCFA actuaries estimate that cutting the length of nursing home coverage in half from four to two years might reduce premiums only about 20 percent because of the way nursing home length of stays are distributed and because of the fixed costs of research and development, administration, and marketing. Linda Schofield, formerly with the Travelers Insurance Company, personal communication, January 27, 1988.

for a public program and have actively sought to reform the delivery system. The states could play a large role, as do the provinces in Canada.[7] In America, however, states have played a role only in welfare programs. They do not participate at all in the social insurance programs for the elderly—social security and medicare.

By far the most difficult problem in administering a long-term care insurance program would be how to control the use of services. Because many disabled elderly currently receive no paid long-term care services, use of services could increase substantially.[8] Rules governing eligibility for services, especially home care, will be difficult to develop and implement because professional norms regarding these services barely exist. In addition, use of services often depends on social rather than objective medical circumtances.

One approach to administering a long-term care program would be to build on existing administrative structures. The program could, for example, be administered much like the current medicare program, with the federal government establishing the rules and procedures and contracting with intermediaries such as Blue Cross to operate the program. This approach could be implemented by giving additional responsibilities to intermediaries under existing contracts. Or the program could build on the medicaid administrative structure, with contracts signed with state medicaid agencies.

The disadvantage of building on current medicare mechanisms is that the administrative entity could become a distant bureaucracy, embodying the most rigid and undesirable characteristics of the current system. Moreover, current medicare intermediaries know little about long-term care. As a relatively passive bill payer, the intermediary would have little opportunity to reorient the delivery system toward more home care or to improve and coordinate services.

Alternatively, the federal government could contract with case management agencies, which might be state or local governments, to operate the program. Case managers could act as gatekeepers, controlling use of costly long-term care services, screening for need, developing cost-effective care plans, and substituting home-based care for nursing home care where appropriate. The case management agency could even assume the financial risk of keeping expenditures below a specified level.

One difficulty of administration through case management agencies is that it puts agencies in the conflicting position of being responsible for both cost control and client advocacy. If a case management agency is in charge of cost control, it cannot be an effective advocate for the patient, who is thus left with no advocate within the system. Adding to the difficulties, few such agencies exist, and blanketing the country with them would be a huge undertaking. Furthermore, most research on case management, including evaluations of the recent Channeling demonstration, has found it to be ineffective in controlling the use of nursing homes.[9] Whether case managers can control the use of home care is unknown. Finally, case management itself is costly.*

SOURCES OF FINANCING

An essential feature of public insurance is that financing is contributory, meaning that beneficiaries earn their entitlement by paying into the program. Pure public insurance is self-financing. The contributory taxes or premiums, generally paid into a trust fund, pay the full costs of the program, as they do in social security and the hospital portion of medicare. In less pure insurance, such as the physician part of medicare, a portion of the cost of benefits is paid out of general revenues. But with the federal government currently running a large annual deficit, it is imperative that any new social insurance program pay for itself, not add to the deficits.

If a public long-term care insurance program was implemented in the near future, the current elderly population would most likely be eligible for benefits for which they had not contributed much or at all. Thus the program will inevitably result in an intergenerational transfer in which the elderly will receive benefits mostly financed by taxes paid by the working population. Similar transfers occurred when social security and medicare were initiated. Advocates of public insurance argue that while the program will benefit the current elderly, it will also benefit the current working population when they reach old age and face the risk of becoming disabled and using long-term care services. In addition, the children of the elderly will no longer have to worry about their parents' being impoverished by long-term care.

Change from a means-tested to a social insurance program will inevitably provide public benefits to elderly people who currently receive none because they have too much income and assets. Thus,

* The one-time expenses of bringing an eligible client into the Channeling demonstration program (covering outreach, screening, assessment, and care planning) averaged $340 in 1984. The average ongoing cost per client was $89 a month. George J. Carcagno and others, *The Evaluation of the National Long Term Care Demonstration: The Planning and Operational Experience of the Channeling Projects,* vol. 1, report prepared for DHHS (Princeton, N.J.: Mathematica Policy Research, July 18, 1986), pp. 143–48.

unless financing is progressive, shifting to a public long-term care insurance program will result in a net income redistribution from low- and moderate-income workers to upper-middle-income and wealthy elderly. Although elderly advocacy groups have strongly opposed linking medicare benefits to income, financing the program through a progressive tax appears to be more politically palatable to them.

The problem with progressive financing is that it explicitly introduces "welfare" elements into a social insurance program. In fact, some redistribution from higher- to lower-income groups already occurs under medicare, since even with a flat payroll tax, people with higher lifetime earnings pay more for the same medicare benefits than do people with lower earnings. Financing benefits with a progressive tax would increase the redistribution, and might compromise the claim that the insurance is an "earned right" rather than welfare and cause upper-income individuals to oppose the program. Similar arguments about the future rate of return for upper-income groups under social security have proved to be politically divisive.

Contributory Taxes

The United States uses payroll taxes to finance its principal social insurance programs, including the old age, survivors, and disability benefits under social security and hospital insurance under medicare. The payroll tax is, therefore, a familiar method of financing. Resistance to further increases in payroll taxes, however, is likely to be substantial. Combined employer and employee contributions to social security and medicare were already 15.02 percent of payroll in January 1988.[10] Future increases in the payroll tax for social security have already been enacted, and increases for medicare will probably be necessary to keep the hospital trust fund solvent in the 1990s and beyond.[11]

The problem with payroll taxes is that they are regressive; that is, lower-income groups pay a higher proportion of their income in payroll taxes than do higher-income groups. One reason they are regressive is that ceilings are placed on taxable earnings; another is that higher-income groups have asset and other nonsalary income that is not subject to the payroll tax.[12] The increase in social insurance taxes between 1977 and 1984 helped make total federal taxes more regressive, and further increases could raise the effective tax burden on lower-income people even more.[13] Another argument against increased reliance on payroll taxes is that they increase the cost of labor and hence both increase prices and reduce employment in the short run.[14]

It can be argued that payroll taxes make American goods less competitive in international markets by raising production costs.

The federal income tax is more progressive than the payroll tax and does not increase labor costs, but Americans have never used it to fund social insurance programs. Moreover, dedicating income tax funds to specific programs may set an undesirable precedent that could leave many general government functions underfunded.

As an alternative or supplement to a payroll or income tax, the elderly could contribute by paying insurance premiums.* The elderly could reduce the burden on the working population by helping to pay for the program, as they do for the physician portion of the medicare program. With per elderly total expenditures for long-term care already exceeding $1,300 a year, the cost of almost any program, however, is likely to be too great to be shouldered solely by the elderly.[15]

Other Sources of Revenue

Although money to pay for a public insurance program could be raised exclusively through a payroll tax, an income tax surcharge, or premiums paid by the elderly, to do so would require fairly substantial increases in each of these financing mechanisms. To lower the incremental contributory taxes or premium required to finance the program, it would be desirable to draw on other revenue sources. Major candidates for additional funds are state revenues, estate taxes, "sin" taxes, and reduction in other medicare spending.[16]

Because almost any public insurance program would substantially reduce medicaid and other state expenditures for long-term care, it would mean a financial windfall for the states. Requiring continued state contributions for long-term care, albeit at a reduced level, could be an important source of revenue. Such state involvement would also maintain state interest in cost containment, where states have a lot of experience.

Because one result of a public insurance program would be to protect the assets of the elderly, inheritance or estate taxes would also be a logical source of revenue. Current tax law excludes the first $600,000 of estates and gifts from taxation, thus minimizing estate taxes as a source of revenue. It can be argued that the current situation is inequitable because the elderly unlucky enough to end up in a nursing

* Another way would be to increase the taxes of the elderly, either by changing the rates or by treating part of the actuarial value of public insurance benefits as income.

home face a 100 percent "tax" on their assets if they spend down to medicaid eligibility levels, while those who do not enter a nursing home end up paying very little. By spreading the tax over more estates and over a greater proportion of each estate, the effective tax rates could be lower.* Moreover, some analysts argue that an inheritance tax avoids taxing work-related earnings and thus maintains work incentives.[17] Preventing tax evasion through the transfer of assets before death would still be a major problem.

Another possible source of revenue could be increased excise taxes on tobacco and alcohol, which could raise $10 billion to $15 billion in 1989.[18] Because use of these products causes major health problems, raising revenues for health care from these sources seems fair.

Revenue could also be raised through spending cuts in related programs. For example, medicare cost-sharing could be increased and the savings used to finance long-term care services.[19] Such a shift from acute care to long-term care has some appeal, because it can be argued that the older population is overinsured for the former and underinsured for the latter, but it would arouse strong political opposition. Raising cost-sharing under medicare would be especially hard on low-income elderly in need of acute care and would force many of them to turn to medicaid.

Trust Fund Reserves

Benefit claims on a long-term care insurance program will grow as the population ages and will escalate rapidly after about 2020, when the baby boom generation reaches old age. Hence one important question is whether tax rates for long-term care insurance should be high enough to build up reserves to pay for the anticipated increases in claims.

* Total assets held by all elderly expected to die in 1986-90 are an estimated $98 billion. Brookings-ICF Long-Term Care Financing Model. If current patterns of wealth continue, by 2016–20 total assets for elderly who die will increase to $281 billion. Thus, to finance a public insurance program, a flat 20 percent tax on total assets at death could yield $20 billion in 1986–90 and $56 billion in 2016–20. Obviously, revenue would be lower if certain groups were excluded from paying estate taxes. For example, if husbands and wives do not have to pay taxes on assets inherited from their spouses, almost half of total assets would be exempt from taxation. Brookings-ICF Long-Term Care Financing Model. In addition, excluding persons below a certain level of assets could also reduce the revenues from estate taxes. Nonetheless, significant additional revenues could be generated by imposing higher estate taxes on those with relatively large assets. Estate tax returns for those who died in 1982 showed that the top wealthholders (those with gross estates of $300,000 or more) held about $50 billion in assets. Mary F. Bentz, "Estate Tax Returns, 1983," *Statistics of Income Bulletin,* vol. 4 (Fall 1984), pp. 1–12.

The buildup of reserves in public insurance programs would help guarantee that the funds will be perceived as available when needed and would avoid the need for drastic increases in tax rates as the benefit claims escalate in the future. From an economic perspective, however, society will have to pay for services in 2050 out of the economy of 2050. Like many other social programs for the elderly, the economic burden of a public long-term care program will largely depend on the size of the economy at that time. The reserves have economic importance only if they result in net societal savings that can be channeled into productive investments that make the economy grow.

From this perspective, the economic significance of the reserves largely depends on the state of the federal budget. If other government revenues and expenditures are in balance, then the trust fund will buy up existing government debt. Savings can then go into private investments that make the economy grow. But if the government runs a budget deficit, then the trust fund will be used to finance the shortfall, as current surpluses in the social security trust fund are doing. If the reserves are to increase national preparedness to pay for the retirement needs of the baby boom generation, they must add to national saving, not merely offset deficits in the rest of the budget.

Model Results

To estimate the costs of public long-term care insurance, we modeled four different programs. Table 16-1 summarizes eligibility criteria, benefits provided, cost-sharing, and other program characteristics of the different options. Because none of the programs provide free long-term care, some means-tested program for the poor must be retained in all programs. Hence each insurance option includes either the existing or a liberalized medicaid program.

The first option, CATINS, provides catastrophic nursing home coverage with a 10 percent coinsurance after a two-year deductible. People would be encouraged to purchase private insurance to finance their long-term care expenditures during the long deductible period. Medicaid would be retained, but not improved, as a separate program to cover nursing home care for the poor. Home care benefits would not be covered beyond what is currently available.

A second option, HIGHCO, provides a minimal long-term care insurance benefit to all elderly, imposing a high 50 percent coinsurance for nursing home care after a 100-day deductible. This option substan-

TABLE 16-1. *Eligibility Criteria, Benefits, and Program Characteristics of Alternative Public Long-Term Care Insurance Programs*

Option	Medicaid and medicare benefits	Nursing home benefits	Home care benefits	Reimbursement rates
CATINS (including private insurance)[a]	Medicaid not improved; medicare long-term care benefits maintained	Unlimited coverage of skilled nursing and intermediate care facilities; deductible 2 years; coinsurance 10 percent	Current medicare and medicaid home health benefits; no new benefits	Nursing home: 115 percent of medicaid rate; home care: same as current rates
HIGHCO	Medicaid improved: personal needs allowance $200 a month; $15,000 protected assets; home protected; at-home spouse keeps three times SSI level of income. Medicare long-term care benefits maintained	Unlimited coverage of skilled nursing and intermediate care facilities; deductible 100 days; coinsurance 50 percent	Severely disabled elderly;[b] skilled and unskilled care, deductible 1 month; coinsurance 20 percent	Nursing home: 115 percent of medicaid rate; home care: 115 percent of weighted average cost per visit for all noninstitutional services
MODCO	Medicaid not improved; medicare long-term care benefits maintained	Unlimited coverage of skilled nursing and intermediate care facilities; deductible 100 days; coinsurance 25 percent	Severely disabled elderly;[b] skilled and unskilled care; deductible 1 month; coinsurance 20 percent	Nursing home: 115 percent of medicaid rate; home care: 115 percent of weighted average cost per visit for all noninstitutional services
COMPUB	Medicaid improved: pays coinsurance and deductibles for those who cannot afford them; personal needs allowance $60 a month; assets protected after deductible (up to $1,800) is paid; at-home spouse keeps three times the SSI level of income. Medicare long-term care benefits maintained	Unlimited coverage of skilled nursing and intermediate care facilities; deductible and coinsurance vary with income[c]	All disabled elderly; skilled and unskilled care; deductible 1 month; coinsurance varies with income[d]	Nursing home: 120 percent of medicaid rate; home care: 120 percent of weighted average cost per visit for all noninstitutional services

a. Eligibility for purchasing private insurance includes: premiums less than 5 percent of income, at least $10,000 in assets and nondisabled. Private insurance covers two years of nursing home care after twenty-day deductible. Pays $50 a day, not indexed for inflation.

b. People with three or more deficiencies in activity of daily living.

c. For income less than or equal to 200 percent poverty and assets less than or equal to $5,000, no deductible and 10 percent coinsurance. For income less than or equal to 200 percent of poverty and assets more than $5,000, one-month deductible and 10 percent coinsurance. For more than 200 percent poverty, one-month deductible and 30 percent coinsurance .

d. For income less than poverty, no coinsurance. At 100–125 percent poverty, 5 percent coinsurance. At 125–150 percent poverty, 10 percent coinsurance. At 150–200 percent poverty, 15 percent coinsurance. At more than 200 percent poverty, 20 percent coinsurance.

tially liberalizes medicaid, raising the medicaid personal needs allowance and level of protected assets, removing all pressure on patients to sell their homes to pay for nursing home expenses, and allowing the home-based spouse to retain a much higher level of protected income.* Home care is available only for severely disabled people with three or more deficiencies in the activities of daily living.

The third option, MODCO, which has roughly the same level of cost-sharing as the current medicare program, provides nursing home benefits with a moderate coinsurance of 25 percent after a 100-day deductible. Medicaid is retained as a separate program with no improvements. Home care is available only to people with three or more deficiencies in the activities of daily living.

The final option, COMPUB, provides comprehensive public insurance. Coinsurance and deductibles for benefits vary with income, but are low at all but the highest-income level. This program also liberalizes medicaid, raising the personal needs allowance and level of protected assets and allowing the home-based spouse to retain a much higher level of protected income. Home care is available for all disabled elderly.

The availability of public long-term care insurance is likely to increase the use of nursing homes and home care services, but by an amount that is highly uncertain. Yet in projecting the budgetary costs of alternate public insurance programs, it is clearly necessary to make some allowance for increased use. Indeed, meeting some of the unmet demand for care is one of the goals of a public insurance program. The analysis that follows assumes a 20 percent across-the-board increase in nursing home use and expenditures and a 50 percent increase in home care use and expenditures.† None of the estimates include

* The medicaid financial eligibility requirements are the same as those used in LIBMED in chapter 15.

† This assumption of increased service use or moral hazard is different from that in the private sector options, where no increased use was assumed. The assumption that use does not increase for private sector options is consistent with our efforts to estimate the maximum effect of these options on medicaid expenditures and the number of medicaid nursing home patients. For the public insurance options, however, the actual level of expenditures is more relevant to policymakers. Thus we included an assumption of increased use. Expenditures without the moral hazard assumption can be calculated by dividing the nursing home estimates by 1.2, and the home care estimates by 1.5. Expenditures under new assumptions about moral hazard can be calculated by multiplying the expenditures without moral hazard by the new assumption. For example, nursing home expenditures under a 30 percent moral hazard assumption can be calculated by multiplying the expenditures without moral hazard by 1.3.

TABLE 16-2. *Total, Private Out-of-Pocket, and Public Expenditures for Long-Term Care, Base Case and Public Insurance Options, 1986–90, 2016–20*[a]
Billions of 1987 dollars; percent change from base case

Option	Total	Private out-of-pocket[b]	Public[c] Total	Public[c] Nursing home	Public[c] Home care
			1986–90		
Base case	41.602	19.882	21.719	14.730	6.989
CATINS[d]	49.094	14.769	33.373	26.383	6.989
Percent change	18.01	−25.72	53.66	79.11	0.00
HIGHCO	55.549	11.482	44.064	31.635	12.429
Percent change	33.52	−42.25	102.88	114.77	77.84
MODCO	55.057	12.880	42.175	29.746	12.429
Percent change	32.34	−35.22	94.18	101.94	77.84
COMPUB	57.571	10.978	46.589	35.734	10.855
Percent change	38.39	−44.78	114.51	142.59	55.32
			2016–20		
Base case	120.003	54.904	65.096	47.804	17.292
CATINS[d]	144.174	28.461	93.465	76.233	17.292
Percent change	20.14	−48.16	43.58	59.47	0.00
HIGHCO	159.611	35.913	123.690	92.071	31.619
Percent change	33.01	−34.59	90.01	92.60	82.85
MODCO	158.250	36.285	121.959	90.340	31.619
Percent change	31.87	−33.91	87.35	88.98	82.85
COMPUB	166.409	36.237	130.164	103.093	27.071
Percent change	38.67	−34.00	99.96	115.66	56.55

SOURCE: Brookings-ICF Long-Term Care Financing Model.
a. Average annual expenditures. Assumes 20 percent increase in nursing home expenditures and 50 percent increase in home care expenditures.
b. Out-of-pocket includes cash income and assets.
c. Public includes medicaid, medicare, public insurance, and other payer.
d. CATINS includes the effects of both public insurance and private insurance. There is no expansion of home care and no assumed increase in use of home care. In 2016-20 there is an additional $22.244 billion in private insurance expenditures for long-term care.

administrative costs. Since medicare reimbusement rates are higher than medicaid rates for almost all services, the nursing home and home care reimbursement rates under the public insurance programs are assumed to be 10 percent to 20 percent higher than the expected medicaid rate.

EFFECT ON TOTAL EXPENDITURES

Total long-term care expenditures for the four different options during 2016–20 range from $144 billion for CATINS to $166 billion for COMPUB (table 16-2). The estimates represent a 20 percent to 40 percent increase over base-case expenditures of $120 billion and for the most part reflect increased expenditures due to increased use.*

EFFECT ON PUBLIC EXPENDITURES

Public costs increase at a faster rate than total costs. Federal, state, and local costs for all long-term care programs in 1986–90 range from $33 billion for CATINS to $47 billion for COMPUB, compared with $22 billion for the base case, an increase of 54 percent to 115 percent. Longer-run cost estimates for 2016–20 range from $93 billion for CATINS to $130 billion for COMPUB—44 percent to 100 percent more than the base case (table 16-2). Overall, the proportion of nursing home expenditures paid by various public programs ranges from 62 percent for CATINS to 83 percent for COMPUB, compared with 49 percent in the base case in 2016–20 (table 16-3).

In all the options, public programs cover most nursing home expenditures for most elderly demographic and income groups. Every option disproportionately covers those aged 85 and over, the unmarried, women, and the relatively poor (table 16-4). COMPUB and HIGHCO do a better job of covering the most vulnerable elderly, those aged 85 and older, women, and those below the poverty line, because COMPUB requires little cost-sharing and HIGHCO makes medicaid eligibility rules much more generous.

In all the options, the vast majority of public expenditures are for nursing home rather than home care services. Almost three-quarters of public long-term care expenditures in 2016–20 under the base case are for nursing home care. Even with expanded coverage of home care and the assumed increase in use, home care expenditures represent only 19 percent to 26 percent of total public costs in 2016–20 (table 16-2). Thus even with more generous public coverage of home care services, home care costs remain a relatively small part of total long-term care expenditures. If home care use or reimbursement rates were higher than assumed, or if increased coverage of home care resulted in fewer people using nursing homes, then the proportion of expenditures going for home care would be higher.

* The differential across options would grow if they were subject to varying degrees of increased use. For example, COMPUB might induce a 30 percent increase in nursing home use because of the low cost-sharing required; whereas HIGHCO, with a 50 percent coinsurance, might induce only a 10 percent increase in nursing home use. In this case, the differential costs between COMPUB and HIGHCO would be much greater.

TABLE 16-3. *Total Expenditures for Nursing Home Care, by Source of Payment, Base Case and Public Insurance Options, 2016–20*[a]

Billions of 1987 dollars; percent change from base case

Option	Total	Total public[b]	Medicaid[c]	Medicare	Public insurance[d]	Patients' cash income	Patients' assets
Base case	98.117	47.804	46.192	1.612	. . .	27.888	22.423
CATINS	122.305	76.232	19.368	1.934	54.930[e]	16.256	7.568
Percent change	24.65	59.47	−58.07	20.00	. . .	−41.71	−66.25
HIGHCO	120.723	92.071	38.540	1.553	51.978	20.927	7.721
Percent change	23.04	92.60	−16.56	−3.66	. . .	−24.96	−65.57
MODCO	119.362	90.340	11.686	1.934	76.720	21.725	7.295
Percent change	21.65	88.98	−74.70	20.00	. . .	−22.10	−67.47
COMPUB	124.889	103.091	4.135	1.934	97.022	20.393	1.400
Percent change	27.29	115.65	−91.05	20.00	. . .	−26.88	−93.75

SOURCE: Brookings-ICF Long-Term Care Financing Model.

a. Average annual expenditures. Assumes 20 percent increase in nursing home expenditures and 50 percent increase in home care expenditures.

b. Total public includes medicaid, medicare, and public insurance program.

c. Medicaid is income-tested program for lower-income elderly, but varies across options.

d. Public insurance program available to all elderly, without a means test.

e. Under CATINS, there is also $22.244 billion in private insurance expenditures.

TABLE 16-4. *Public Expenditures for Nursing Home Care, by Demographic and Income Groups, Base Case and Public Insurance Options, 2016–20*[a]
Percentage of total payments for nursing home services

Category	Base case	CATINS[b]	HIGHCO	MODCO	COMPUB
Total public share	49.0	62.2	75.1	75.5	82.1
Age					
65–74	31.0	54.1	63.7	70.3	76.6
75–84	46.3	61.7	73.7	73.6	80.8
85 and over	58.9	65.8	80.7	78.9	85.2
Marital status					
Married	36.8	55.7	70.0	70.8	77.6
Unmarried	54.2	64.9	77.1	77.2	83.8
Sex					
Male	34.7	53.7	65.2	69.8	76.1
Female	56.2	66.4	79.8	78.2	85.0
Family income (dollars)[c]					
Under 7,500	84.7	84.2	96.7	89.2	94.6
7,500–14,999	58.5	60.1	79.7	72.4	85.3
15,000–19,999	38.0	52.7	67.5	68.5	75.0
20,000–29,999	26.7	47.4	58.3	66.2	71.2
30,000–39,999	10.8	47.3	48.3	66.5	68.5
40,000–49,999	5.6	44.4	46.3	66.0	68.4
50,000 and over	3.4	45.1	45.6	66.3	68.3

SOURCE: Brookings-ICF Long-Term Care Financing Model.

a. Public expenditures comprise medicare, medicaid, and public insurance. These data are based on the total payments for an admission cohort over the entire length of their stays in a nursing home. For example, for a person who is admitted to a nursing home in 2016–20 for a two-year stay, we totaled two years' worth of nursing home expenditures. We then calculated the proportion of those expenditures paid by each public insurance program.

b. Public payments for nursing home care for CATINS do not include private long-term care insurance payments.

c. Family income is joint income for married persons, individual income for unmarried persons.

EFFECT ON PRIVATE EXPENDITURES

Given the expanded public role in all these options, total private out-of-pocket expenditures for long-term care decline substantially. The reduction in out-of-pocket costs from the base case in 2016–20 ranges from 34 percent for MODCO and COMPUB to 48 percent for CATINS (table 16-2). These reductions are generally much higher than those achieved by any of the private sector options.

More specifically, CATINS reduces out-of-pocket nursing home expenditures from cash income by 42 percent, compared with a 22 percent reduction under MODCO (table 16-3). The reduction is greatest in CATINS because people have double protection against out-of-pocket costs—the first two years in a nursing home covered by private insurance and the remainder covered by the government.* If the elderly

* Without the private insurance covering the first two years, CATINS would reduce nursing home expenditures from cash income by 34 percent.

TABLE 16-5. *Out-of-Pocket Expenditures for Nursing Home Care, by Demographic and Income Groups, Base Case and Public Insurance Options, 2016–20*[a]
Percentage of total payments for nursing home services

Category	Base case	CATINS[b]	HIGHCO	MODCO	COMPUB
Total out-of-pocket share	51.0	20.0	24.9	24.6	17.9
Age					
65–74	69.1	23.6	36.2	29.7	23.4
75–84	53.7	22.1	26.3	26.3	19.2
85 and over	41.2	17.2	19.3	21.2	14.8
Marital status					
Married	63.3	22.1	29.9	29.2	22.4
Unmarried	45.8	19.2	22.9	22.7	16.1
Sex					
Male	65.3	24.3	34.7	30.1	24.0
Female	43.7	18.0	20.1	21.9	15.0
Family income (dollars)[c]					
Under 7,500	15.3	10.6	3.3	10.8	5.4
7,500–14,999	41.5	21.2	20.3	27.6	14.7
15,000–19,999	62.0	24.8	32.5	31.5	25.0
20,000–29,999	73.3	25.6	41.7	33.8	28.9
30,000–39,999	89.1	25.4	51.7	33.6	31.5
40,000–49,999	94.3	29.5	53.6	34.0	31.6
50,000 and over	96.6	26.9	54.4	33.7	31.6

SOURCE: Brookings-ICF Long-Term Care Financing Model.

a. Out-of-pocket payments include cash income and assets. These data are based on the total payments for an admission cohort over the entire length of their stays in a nursing home. For example, for a person who is admitted to a nursing home in 2016–20 for a two-year stay, we totaled two years worth of nursing home expenditures. We then calculated the proportion of those expenditures paid out-of-pocket.

b. Out-of-pocket payments for nursing home care for CATINS do not include private long-term care insurance premiums.

c. Family income is joint income for married persons, individual income for unmarried persons.

purchased supplemental insurance for MODCO, COMPUB, and HIGHCO, as they probably would, then out-of-pocket payments from cash income would drop even lower.

Nursing home expenditures from assets are reduced the most under COMPUB (94 percent from the base case of $22 billion), reflecting this option's conscious policy of protecting assets. In the other three options, asset expenditures fall between 66 percent and 67 percent below the base case. Overall, assets are heavily protected in all options, much more so than in any of the private sector options.

In every option the elderly who are 85 and older, unmarried, female, and low-income pay less out-of-pocket for their care than do other groups (table 16-5). COMPUB best protects these high-risk elderly from having to use their own income and assets to pay for their nursing home care.

TABLE 16-6. *Total Expenditures for Public Long-Term Care as a Percentage of Payroll and Federal Personal Income Tax, Base Case and Public Insurance Options, 1988–2050*[a]

	Payroll tax[b]			Income tax surcharge		
Option	1988	2050	Average, 1988–2050	1988	2050	Average, 1988–2050
Base case						
Total costs	1.57	4.71	2.84	9.87	26.51	16.63
Public costs	0.82	2.93	1.59	5.15	16.51	9.31
CATINS[c]	1.24	3.70	2.22	8.42	21.79	12.97
HIGHCO	1.67	4.97	2.96	10.51	27.98	17.36
MODCO	1.60	5.02	2.94	10.03	28.23	17.19
COMPUB	1.76	5.15	3.11	11.08	28.97	18.19

SOURCE: Brookings-ICF Long-Term Care Financing Model.

a. Assumes a 20 percent increase in nursing home use and expenditures and a 50 percent increase in home care use and expenditures.

b. Combined employee and employer contributions. No ceiling on taxable salaries.

c. Under CATINS, there is no expansion of home care coverage and no assumed increase in home care use.

TAX BURDEN

Table 16-6 shows estimates of the payroll tax and income tax surcharge required to finance the four public long-term care insurance programs modeled. The estimates assume the buildup of reserves rather than a pay-as-you-go system. Obviously the economic burden of the program would vary depending on whether the economy grew faster or slower than assumed in the model.

For the payroll tax, estimates were developed by extrapolating long-term care expenditures of the elderly and wages and salaries of the working population through the year 2050. Annual public long-term care expenditures were calculated as a percentage of total payroll for each year through 2050, and yearly percentages were summed and divided by the number of years in the period.* The payroll tax estimated is unconstrained by current social security taxable salary limits and represents the combined employer and employee contributions.

If, as assumed, there is a 20 percent increase in nursing home expenditures and a 50 percent increase in home care expenditures, the average annual payroll tax for 1988–2050 ranges from 2.22 percent for CATINS to 3.11 percent for COMPUB (table 16-6). For purposes of comparison, if current public long-term care benefits were financed by

* These estimates do not assume that interest is earned on reserves that accumulate. This methodology generally follows that used by the Social Security Administration to determine whether trust funds are in balance. (See the Technical Appendix for a more detailed description of the methodology.)

a payroll tax rather than general revenues, the tax would average 1.59 percent from 1988 through 2050. In 1988 current programs represent 0.82 percent of payroll.

The political feasibility of such a tax increase is hard to anticipate. Opponents argue that the additional payroll tax required would be larger than the tax currently required for medicare hospital benefits and that the payroll tax will certainly have to be increased to pay for the current medicare program. Advocates note that the required increase in tax rate is not high in absolute terms and could be reduced by supplementing it with revenue from other financing sources. Payroll taxes increased from 1979 to 1988 by 2.76 percentage points, with relatively little political opposition or economic consequences.[20]

The program could also be financed by increasing federal personal income tax rates or imposing an income tax surcharge, a flat percentage of the original tax liability. Estimates of the necessary tax increase were based on the assumption that average tax payments by sex and age group for 1987 would increase by the rate of change in real earnings each year through 2050.[21] Again, the buildup of reserves is assumed. Financing a public insurance program between 1988 and 2050 would require an average income tax surcharge ranging from 12.97 percent for CATINS to 18.19 percent for COMPUB (table 16-6). In 1988 current programs would require a 5.5 percent surcharge. The average surcharge for the base case would be 9.31 percent. Including corporate income taxes would reduce the tax burden on individuals, but not by much. In 1986 corporate taxes accounted for only 15 percent of total income taxes.[22]

The payroll or income tax required could be reduced if the elderly had to pay a premium for the insurance. For example, if the elderly were to pay a premium of $20 a year, the payroll tax required would be reduced about 10 percent. In the interests of equity, certain groups, such as younger workers or the low-income population, could be exempt from contributing to the program, but excluding these groups places a heavier financial burden on those who do contribute.

Delivery System Goals

The effect of public insurance on the delivery system varies with program design. The more comprehensive the program, the more directly it seeks to improve the long-term care delivery system. At the same time, the larger the program, the more likely it is to encounter two difficulties that can erode the desired reforms. First, if public expenditures increase substantially more quickly than anticipated or desired, efforts to control these costs may undo some of the improvements. Second, complex and rigid administration may hamper innovative approaches to delivering services.

QUALITY OF CARE

Overall quality of care should improve under a public long-term care insurance program. The program would cover all the elderly, not just the poor, and the middle and upper classes can be expected to demand payment rates higher than those of medicaid. Higher payment rates would provide nursing homes with the funds necessary to upgrade facilities. Furthermore, wealthy and upper-middle-class patients will probably insist on better quality care than is usually provided to low-income patients.

A public system could, however, result in some downward leveling in quality of care. Extremely high-quality facilities may move toward the average if the payments necessary for very high-quality care are deemed excessive by the public insurance program. Moreover, with the exception of a large deductible program design, nursing homes will receive the same reimbursement for most patients because they will all be in the same financing system; facilities will have little incentive to have high quality to attract higher-paying private patients.

BALANCE OF SERVICES

The balance of nursing home and home care services can be directly controlled under a public insurance program. The more comprehensive the coverage of home care services, the more the balance of services could tilt toward home care. If case managers were included in the program, they would generally try to use unpaid support and home and community services, although that strategy may not lead to lower rates of nursing home use.[23] Nevertheless, as shown in the simulations, unless the program covers only minimal nursing home care and comprehensive home care, the bulk of expenditures will still be for nursing home rather than home care services.

FAMILY BURDEN

Emotional and financial strains on patients' families could be relieved by a public long-term care insurance program that covered both nursing home and home care services for the entire elderly population. A fundamental problem for public insurance is how to provide this relief without merely substituting formal, paid care for the care currently provided by families and friends at no cost to the government.[24] To keep costs within bounds and to maximize the quality of life of the disabled elderly, it is critical that high levels of unpaid caregiving be maintained (see chapter 13). Although substitution of paid home care for unpaid care has not been extensively researched, the Channelling demonstration found relatively minor substitution.[25]

ACCESS TO CARE

Access to long-term care services by low-income patients and patients requiring greater than average care would probably improve under a social insurance program in which the entire elderly population was eligible for covered services. Coverage of a broader range of home care services than is currently available should help to improve access. Higher payment rates in the public program combined with universal coverage would reduce the importance of private pay patients, thus improving access for public patients. From the provider's perspective, all income classes of patients would be economically equivalent. If local case management was used to set priorities for use of services, then care-intensive patients might have better access to care.

Although access by certain disadvantaged groups would probably improve under public insurance, the extent of the improvement would depend on the program adopted. For example, under a catastrophic-only public insurance program, private pay patients who pay higher rates would remain a significant source of revenue, leading nursing homes to continue to prefer them to publicly supported patients. In addition, most public insurance proposals require some form of beneficiary cost-sharing to control service use. If the cost-sharing was set too high, it could result in large out-of-pocket expenditures that could deter appropriate service use by the near poor.[26]

A second threat to improved access would be an inadequate supply of services. Demand for services is virtually certain to grow, given the new entitlement to services and reduction in the net cost of services to the elderly. With inadequate service growth, improved access for lower-income and care-intensive patients could be accompanied by reduced access for formerly private pay and easier-to-care-for patients.

FLEXIBILITY TO MEET LOCAL CONDITIONS AND INDIVIDUAL NEEDS

A possible weakness of public insurance is that it may lack flexibility to meet local conditions and individual needs. If designed as a national program with highly centralized administration, public insurance could require extensive uniform regulations for all parts of the country. Regulations would have to be set governing service eligibility, coverage limits, disability qualifications, quality standards, and payment rates. A uniform program would probably have to ignore supply and demand variation among states, as well as the peculiarities of localities and the situation of individual elderly.

In addition, it might be difficult for public insurance to adjust to innovative delivery and cost control systems.[27] There is no conclusive evidence, however, that either the private or the public sector is inherently more innovative than the other. Advocates of the private sector point to the much greater market penetration of health maintenance organizations and preferred provider organizations in the private sector than in medicare and medicaid. Nevertheless medicaid, and to a lesser extent medicare, pioneered in the development of prior authorization of services, rate ceilings, case-mix-adjusted reimbursement systems, hospices, and case management for acute care and long-term care. Several states have developed extensive home care service systems.[28] In addition, private insurance often has coverage rigidities similar to those of any public sector program.

Conclusion

A public insurance program would spread the costs of long-term care over the entire population. Such a program could take a variety of forms but, at the very least, would cover a basic set of nursing home and home care benefits and would require some beneficiary cost-sharing. Beneficiaries would help to pay for the program through a payroll tax, income tax surcharge, or premiums. Other forms of revenue could reduce the contributory tax required to finance the program. To pay for long-term care for the baby boom population, reserves should be accumulated.

Simulation results suggest that total public costs for a long-term care insurance and other programs would range from $94 billion to $130 billion by 2016–20, compared with $65 billion for the base case.

Financing total public costs through 2050 would require a payroll tax of between 2.2 percent and 3.1 percent a year, which could be reduced by partly relying on other financing sources. Most of the expenditures associated with a public insurance program will be incurred by society regardless of whether there is public insurance.* The issue is whether these costs will be borne largely by those who use nursing home and home care or spread more broadly over the entire population.

* Total long-term care expenditures will be $120 billion in 2016-20 even without public insurance. Brookings-ICF Long-Term Care Financing Model.

PART 4
What Should Be Done?

Chapter Seventeen

Recommendations for Financing Long-Term Care

Paying for long-term care is a major problem for older people, their families, and society and will be an increasingly serious problem in the future. Because of greater longevity, many more people face a period of serious disability in old age. Most are cared for informally by relatives and friends, though often at great emotional and sometimes financial costs.

When the disabled elderly and their families seek paid home care or nursing home services, they find, often to their surprise and dismay, that medicare and private insurance do not cover long-term care to any significant extent. Those who need paid care must use their own resources or, once those are exhausted, turn to medicaid, a severely means-tested program for the poor.

The current heavy reliance on individual resources and medicaid creates a two-class system. Medicaid's low reimbursement rates and limited coverage of home care create a bias toward institutional care and sometimes lead to poor quality and an inadequate supply of services.

Over the next several decades this system will become increasingly strained as the number of older people rises. Medical advances that reduce disability in old age are highly desirable but unpredictable. The projections in this study indicate that both public and private spending for long-term care will have to increase substantially to meet expected demand. The question is not whether spending for long-term care will rise, but by whom these costs will be borne. Will they be borne largely by people unlucky enough to need expensive care, or will they be borne by society more broadly? And how will the costs be divided between the public and private sectors?

Principles of Reform

In designing our recommendations, we were guided by six basic principles. First, the most desirable solution (or partial solution) to the problems of long-term care would be medical breakthroughs or lifestyle changes that would appreciably reduce disability at older ages. The federal government should therefore generously support biomedical research designed to reduce the incidence of disabilities and to develop cures and management of diseases requiring considerable long-term care, such as Alzheimer's disease and osteoporosis. However, though advances are possible, a "technological fix" seems quite unlikely and should not be depended on.

Second, long-term care should be treated as a normal risk of growing old. The cost of long-term care should not come as an unpleasant surprise, causing severe financial distress to individuals and families or forcing normally self-sufficient people to depend on public charity. Paying for long-term care should not routinely impoverish people as it does now. Both publicly and privately, Americans need to develop ways to ensure that the elderly and their children will know how they will pay for long-term care if they need it.

Third, risk pooling is an appropriate approach to paying for long-term care. A large majority of the elderly will never incur catastrophic long-term care expenses. Thus pooling the risk of high long-term care expenses over many people through private or public insurance or other mechanisms provides financial protection for long-term care at a far lower cost than having each family bear the risk itself. Because long-term care is not usually needed until very late in life, when people's incomes and assets are relatively low, it is crucial that people begin contributing to this risk-pooling mechanism earlier in life.

Fourth, the financing system should respect the desires of most elderly to remain at home as long as possible and should reinforce the efforts of family and friends to provide informal care. Long-term care financing should cover reasonable amounts of home care, adult day care, respite care, and other noninstitutional services that allow people to remain at home when it is feasible and less costly for them to do so. It should also relieve some of the burden of family caregivers without creating strong incentives to switch to paid care.

Fifth, new payment mechanisms should be designed to improve the quality, flexibility, and efficiency of the delivery system as well as access to it. Payment mechanisms should encourage social/health maintenance organizations, continuing care retirement communities, and other ways of organizing care that may increase patient satisfaction and minimize institutionalization.

Sixth, both the public and private sectors should have major roles in financing long-term care. Reliance on private initiatives has many advantages. It fosters personal responsibility for dealing with the problems of aging, promotes market competition to provide a variety of solutions adapted to consumer demand, and minimizes public costs. Private sector initiatives can also show the feasibility of insurance approaches, demonstrate different administrative techniques, and raise public consciousness about the importance of long-term care. Yet results of this study clearly indicate that the private sector cannot be expected to carry most or even a very large share of the burden of long-term care financing. Most elderly will remain unable to afford comprehensive private sector solutions over the next thirty years.

Our results also show that even under assumptions favorable to the expansion of private insurance and other private sector initiatives, public costs will greatly increase. Hence the question is whether the main public program for financing long-term care should continue to be a severely means-tested welfare program. We believe that it should not, that public as well as private insurance is needed. We therefore propose that social insurance be extended to cover long-term care, even though this would require higher taxes. The public insurance program should be designed to reduce medicaid to a residual program for the very poor, but should still leave a substantial role for private insurance and other private sector initiatives.

In brief, the main recommendations of this study are twofold.

—Private insurance and other private sector risk-pooling mechanisms should be strongly encouraged and should expand to take a larger part in long-term care financing.

—Public insurance should also be enacted and should replace medicaid as the principal public long-term care financing mechanism.

Concern that use of long-term care services, especially paid home care, will escalate if financing is available must be taken seriously, and excessive use guarded against in designing both public and private financing programs. Some additional use is, however, desirable, because many people would function better with more help. Experience in other countries, such as Canada, suggest that increases in use can be held to manageable levels.[1]

The problem of increased use is likely to be less severe for nursing home care than for home care. Surveys show that the elderly prefer home care to nursing home care.[2] Moreover, several studies have found that families place relatives in nursing homes only when unpaid caregiving becomes an overwhelming burden.[3] If this is true, financial benefits will probably not lead to a large increase in use of nursing home care. Use of paid home care, however, could rise rapidly.

Nevertheless, there are other considerations which suggest that a publicly supported insurance program might substantially increase the use of long-term care services. Most disabled elderly are currently cared for at home by family, without any paid services. Unwillingness to accept the stigma of poverty or welfare under the medicaid program may be keeping some elderly out of nursing homes. Over the years a public insurance program might gradually shift the attitudes of family caregivers toward somewhat greater reliance on nursing homes. Moreover, the strong reluctance of the elderly to enter nursing homes would not limit their willingness to use home care services extensively under a public insurance program, especially if those services were available at little out-of-pocket cost.

Taken together, these considerations suggest that while current fears of skyrocketing costs under a public insurance program are probably not warranted, any program must be designed with the possibility of increased use in mind. It would be desirable, for example, to limit benefits to the severely disabled. Substantial cost-sharing should be required. And a variety of other mechanisms, such as case management and social/health maintenance organizations, should be encouraged to limit the use of services to appropriate amounts.

Private Sector

In general, the current absence of private sector financing mechanisms is the result of a lack of effective demand and the reluctance of the private sector to take the necessary risks in making financing options available. It is not the result of major government barriers. Although social/health maintenance organizations, continuing care retirement communities, and home equity conversions should be encouraged, for many reasons they are likely to be of marginal importance in the future financing of long-term care. Private long-term care insurance has the best chance of becoming a significant option.

Government policies to encourage the development of private sector initiatives could be of two types: general support through sponsoring data collection, research, and demonstrations, conducting public education, and establishing a regulatory environment conducive to market growth; and more aggressive strategies such as tax incentives and related approaches.

There are several general steps that federal and state governments should take to encourage the expansion of private sector mechanisms, none of which need be costly. The federal government should fund data collection and research relevant to financing long-term care, including demonstrations to test a variety of innovative financing and delivery approaches. Timely and detailed data on nursing homes and home care are crucial to developing private products. Data on the needs of and service use by the population under age 65 are especially lacking at present.

In addition, government should work with the private sector to educate the public about the risks, costs, and financing options available for long-term care, and about the current limitations of coverage under medicare, medicaid, and medigap insurance. To help solve the problems of affordability and adverse selection, government should urge the sale of group policies for people under age 65 as well as individual policies to the elderly. In this regard, federal and state governments should set an example by making group long-term care insurance available to their own employees and retirees and sharing in the cost.

In regulating long-term care insurance, a balance needs to be struck between protecting the consumer and nurturing new products. In general, regulations proposed by the National Association of Insurance Commissioners seem to be a reasonable middle ground.[4] Some areas, however, need stronger regulation. For example, since almost all insurance products offer only a fixed indemnity benefit, inflation may deeply erode the financial protection of the product. At the very least, this fact needs to be made clear to consumers, and their ability to purchase additional coverage clarified and guaranteed. Likewise, insurers should be required to make clear to consumers that the prior hospitalization requirement of many policies could prevent them from receiving benefits. Moreover, since it is desirable that people purchase policies when they are young, policies must be guaranteed renewable. Under no circumstances should companies be allowed to terminate policyholders who are just reaching the age when they are likely to use benefits. In addition, current restrictions on the types of nursing home care covered by the policies are extremely confusing and need to be greatly simplified.

New measures are also needed to assess the economic value of policies. The simple application of a loss ratio (that is, the proportion of total revenue paid out in benefits during the year) is misleading because it does not take into account future liabilities. Alternative measures can and should be developed that will better gauge whether consumers are receiving reasonable benefits for their expenditures.

Many proposals have been made to provide tax incentives or to subsidize private sector approaches in other ways. As a rule, these proposals benefit only upper-income people and are likely to have small effects on long-term care financing in relation to the amount of federal revenue lost.

In particular, tax deductions or tax credits for individual medical accounts are an ineffective and inefficient way to subsidize long-term care. Few benefits would go to lower- or moderate-income people, and increases in saving would probably be low relative to the cost of care. Even if moderately successful in convincing people to save for their long-term care needs, tax-sheltered savings accounts would result in very large tax losses and would still leave most people unprotected.

Similar arguments apply to tax deductions and tax credits for people who purchase private long-term care insurance. Since it is estimated that only half of the elderly pay any income tax at all, few low- or middle-income elderly would receive any benefit from a tax deduction or credit.[5] In addition, unless the tax credit is exceptionally large, it is unlikely to add greatly to the number of people with insurance.

Some tax changes, however, should be made. Especially for the baby boom population, prefunding of retiree acute care benefits and long-term care insurance as well as pensions should be encouraged as a way of reducing the economic burden on the next generation and of lowering the cost of benefits. Thus, although the revenue loss needs to be estimated, changes in the tax law that would make it more advantageous for employers to prefund retiree acute care and long-term care insurance benefits are desirable in principle. For similar reasons, the tax status of long-term care insurance should be clarified to allow the tax-free buildup of reserves.

Another way to increase the supply of private insurance is to limit through some form of public reinsurance the amount of financial risk that insurers face. In essence, government could limit the financial losses of an insurance company to a predetermined level. While this idea deserves additional investigation, there are reasons to question whether it is either necessary or desirable. Although insurers are clearly worried about their financial risks, they are entering the market in increasing numbers. The principal insurance companies are large financial institutions that have billions of dollars in assets and have no obvious need for additional financial guarantees. Because of the large financial risks, small insurance companies should probably not be encouraged to enter the market for long-term care insurance. More important, owing to the potential risks to the government, the reinsurance approach would require substantial government regulation and oversight to avoid abuse.

Incremental Changes

Proposals abound to "reform" medicaid in a variety of directions. Some people propose making medicaid rules stricter in order to hold down federal spending and increase the incentive to use private sector mechanisms for financing long-term care. Others advocate recognizing that medicaid has become the federal government's main program for financing long-term care and making it less onerous for beneficiaries and providers of care.

Restricting eligibility for medicaid long-term care benefits is likely to cause considerable hardship to moderate-income people without increasing the use of private financing mechanisms appreciably. Tightening medicaid eligibility rules, which would make qualifying for benefits more difficult, would leave unprotected large numbers of moderate-income people who cannot afford private sector initiatives. Similarly, putting a cap on medicaid or substituting a block grant to the states would hold down federal costs, but would not make long-term care more affordable.

One of the themes of this book is that fundamental reform of long-term care requires shifting a large share of the federal financial burden off welfare and onto social insurance. Since comprehensive reform is likely to take some time, however, marginal reforms could be made in existing public programs to improve the current long-term care system in ways not inconsistent with the eventual enactment of a social insurance program.

Several steps should be taken to reduce institutional bias and to support unpaid caregivers. First, home care coverage should be made more available, but the rationale for this initiative should be that people prefer home care, not that it will save money. Specifically, funding for the social services block grant should be increased, restrictions on medicaid home and community-based waivers relaxed, and the medicare home health benefit liberalized. Second, unpaid caregivers should be supported, but not through the use of tax credits, which could result in substantial losses of federal revenue. Tax credits are unlikely to affect behavior or be large enough to be of much help to caregivers. Under extremely limited and controlled circumstances, paying caregivers, as several states are doing, appears to be worthwhile.

Finally, the financial eligibility standards for medicaid should be liberalized. Initiatives that would retain medicaid's means test, but would reduce the level of impoverishment necessary to financially qualify, should include the following: increasing the amount of income that can be retained by spouses of medicaid nursing home patients; raising the medicaid personal needs allowance from its current $30 a month; and allowing medicaid nursing home patients to keep more than $1,900 in assets.

Public Insurance

Our projections show that medicaid expenditures for long-term care will rise rapidly over the next three decades even if the program's rules are not liberalized and even if optimistic assumptions are made about the expansion of private sector financing. The question is, should the federal government continue to rely on a welfare program to finance long-term care for low- and moderate-income people? We believe the answer is no. Continued reliance on medicaid perpetuates a two-class system of long-term care, limits the access of the less affluent to care, and makes it difficult to improve the quality of care.

GENERAL PRINCIPLES

We propose that long-term care for the elderly, like acute care, be covered by medicare, a social insurance program, not a welfare program. The hallmarks of social insurance are that everyone contributes to the program and all contributors are entitled to benefits. Including long-term care under social insurance would eliminate the stigma of means testing and reassure the elderly that, if they need long-term care, they are entitled to the benefits they have earned from contributing to the system. For those people who do end up on medicaid, the program should be liberalized along the lines described above.

It would be a mistake, however, to provide comprehensive benefits for long-term care under medicare without substantial cost-sharing and other controls on use. The risk of increased use is greater for long-term care than for acute care because so many disabled elderly are not now receiving paid care. Moreover, the rationale for cost-sharing is strong, since a large part of the cost of residential care is room-and-board expenses that the patient would have expected to pay anyway. Cost-sharing also reduces the public cost of the program and leaves a role for the private sector.

PUBLIC AND PRIVATE COMBINATIONS

There are at least two main ways in which public programs and private initiatives could fit together. Either would provide a viable financing system, ensuring that most people could finance long-term care without severe hardship or dependence on welfare.

The first option is to rely on the private sector to supply long-term care insurance and other financing mechanisms that provide relatively short-term coverage (for example, the first one to two years of nursing home or home care). The role of the public sector would be to supply coverage after the long deductible period. Thus the public sector would provide both catastrophic insurance for people who had very large long-term care bills and a residual medicaid program. Because of the high costs of even quite short-term nursing home and home care insurance, government should also subsidize participation in the private insurance for lower-income groups. This option depends on the private sector's ability to design and market affordable long-term care insurance products, and would require a public effort to encourage the private sector to do so. If the private sector failed to meet the challenge, most people using long-term care services would continue to be impoverished by the high cost of care. The only effect would be to give substantial fiscal relief to state medicaid programs by transferring costs to the social insurance program.

Another option is to develop a public insurance program that offers more comprehensive benefits but still contains substantial cost-sharing. The goal would be to provide a basic level of financial protection for everyone. Private insurance and other initiatives would be available for those who wanted more services or additional financial protection. This strategy is more like the acute care medicare program (although with higher levels of cost-sharing) supplemented by private medigap policies. Lower levels of cost-sharing (compared with those in the high-deductible public program described above), especially if combined with improved financial protection for the less affluent, would reduce the risk of impoverishment. This approach envisions a substantial role for the private sector, but does not depend on massive expansion of private insurance for its success. A drawback of the approach is that public expenditures would be higher than for the public program with the long deductible period.

Either option should allow participants to use innovative delivery approaches or to obtain better insurance coverage, if possible, in the private market. A person could enroll in a social/health maintenance organization, a continuing care retirement community, or a private insurance program, with the government making a fixed payment that reflected the actuarially expected costs for that person had he or she stayed in the regular public program. The advantages of this approach, which is similar to the one medicare currently uses for health maintenance organizations, are that it allows people to find the delivery system that best suits them, and it encourages innovation. There are also several drawbacks. It is technically very hard to calculate what the proper payment level to the alternate system should be. It is also hard to ensure that people will obtain benefits at least equivalent to those in the standard programs and to guarantee that people will receive adequate quality services.

REVENUE SOURCES

The cost of a public insurance program will be high, but not impossible to finance. Indeed, society will incur most of these long-term care costs under either a public- or private-dominated system. Financing a public insurance program for long-term care through 2050 would probably cost about 3.0 percent of payroll, but continuing the current medicaid program would cost at least half that much.[6] Moreover, total costs need not fall exclusively on the payroll tax. Additional sources of revenue might include premiums paid by the elderly, some level of state financial participation, estate taxes, excise taxes, and income taxes.

Final Thoughts

Totally public and totally private financing of long-term care represent radically different concepts of personal and societal responsibilities. In our view, neither is realistic or desirable. The goal should be a mixed financing system that encourages independence and facilitates personal and family responsibilities, but ensures that all the elderly will obtain care with dignity.

Although financing long-term care has traditionally been viewed as an insolvable issue, it is actually one of the more tractable social problems facing the United States. Indeed, unlike crime, poverty, racism, and teenage pregnancy, financing long-term care has a range of known and feasible solutions. The question is whether we as a society have enough political will and ingenuity to choose among them and put an improved system into place.

Technical Appendix

The Brookings-ICF Long-Term Care Financing Model

The Brookings-ICF Long-Term Care Financing Model simulates the use and financing of nursing home and home care by a nationally representative sample of elderly from 1986 through 2020. A simplified method of extrapolating long-term care expenditures and possible sources of financing from 2020 through 2050 was also developed. The overall objective of the model is to simulate the effects of various financing and organizational reform options on future public and private expenditures for nursing home and home care. A more extensive description of the model and its assumptions is available elsewhere.[1]

Figure A-1 shows a flowchart of the model. The first part of the model, ICF Incorporated's Pension and Retirement Income Simulation Model (PRISM), simulates future demographic (age, sex, and marital status) characteristics, income, and assets of the elderly (figure A-2).[2] In general, PRISM uses mortality and economic assumptions consistent with the Social Security Administration's mid-range II-B assumptions.[3] The second part of the model simulates disability, admission to and use of nursing home and home care, and the methods of financing long-term care services. It is based on analyses of the 1982 National Long-Term Care Survey, the 1977 National Nursing Home Survey, the 1982 National Master Facility Inventory, the 1983 Survey of Consumer Finances, and medicare and medicaid program data from the Health Care Financing Administration. The model uses national data and does not take into account regional, state, or local variations.

The microsimulation model operates on individual records from the May 1979 Current Population Survey Special Pension Supplement. The

FIGURE A-1. **Brookings-ICF Long-Term Care Financing Model**

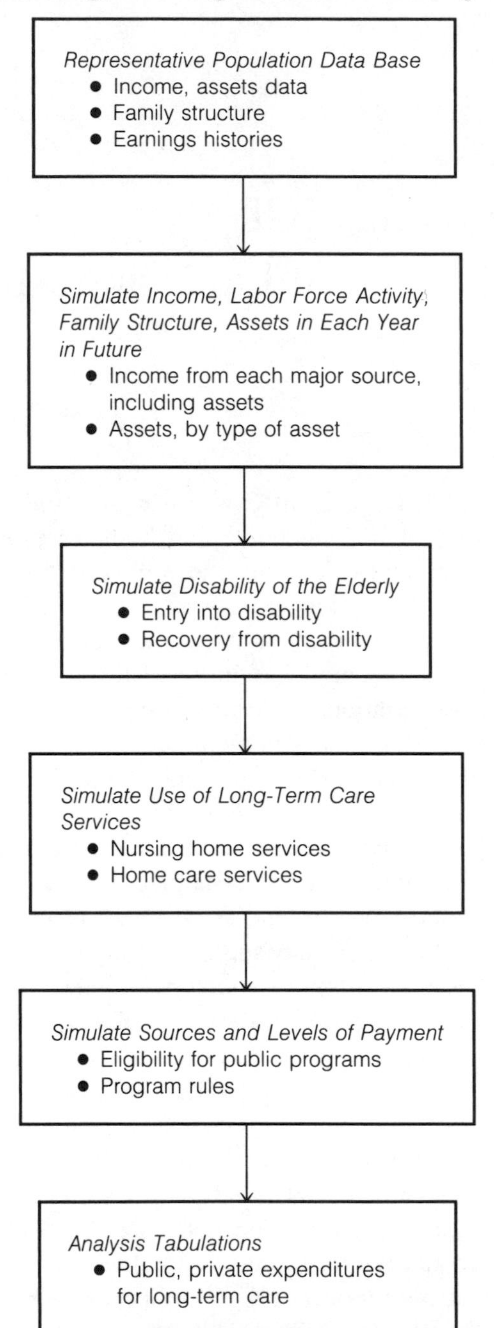

FIGURE A-2. **PRISM Flowchart**

ICF Individual Pension and Social Security Data Base
- Pension coverage in 1979
- Social security covered earnings before 1979
- Employment and demographic data in 1979

ICF Retirement Plan Provisions Data Base
- Normal retirement
- Early retirement
- Vested benefits
- Disability benefits
- Survivor benefits

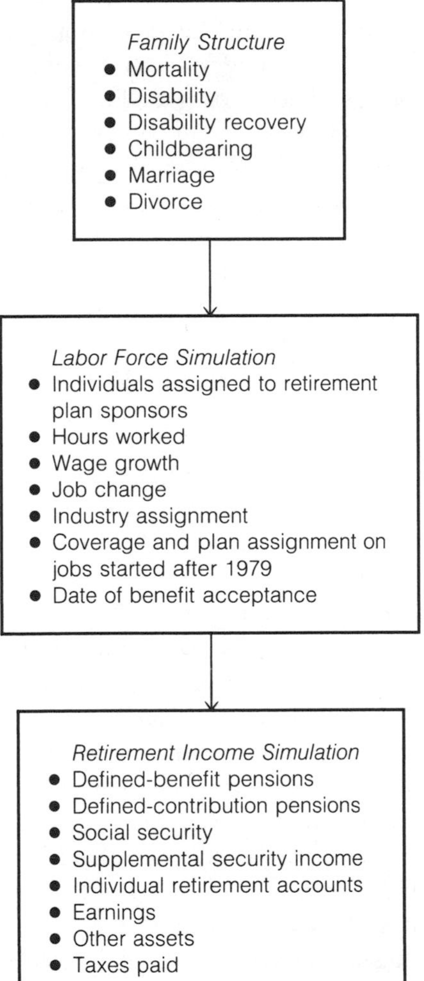

records include earnings history data provided by the Social Security Administration for the surveyed people. Thus the model begins the simulation period with a nationally representative sample of 28,000 adults. To reduce random variation, the data base is run through the model twice. To smooth year-to-year variability of the estimates, results are presented as five-year averages. The final output file from the model provides detailed information for each person aged 65 and older, for each year from 1986 through 2020, on age, marital status, disability, sources and amounts of income, assets, and use of and payment sources for nursing home and home care services.

The detailed model uses a Monte Carlo simulation methodology. For each person in each year in the projection period, it simulates changes in status based on demographic and economic characteristics. Each change in status, such as marriage, admission to a nursing home, and death, is called an event.

The model simulates changes in status, or events, by drawing a random number between zero and one and comparing it with the predetermined probability of that event occurring for a person with particular sociodemographic characteristics. For example, the annual probability of death for an 85-year-old disabled woman who is not in a nursing home is 0.04; that is, 4 out of every such 100 women are expected to die each year. If the random number drawn by the model is less than or equal to 0.04 for this 85-year-old woman, she is assumed to die in that year. If the number drawn lies between 0.04 and 1.0, she is assumed to continue to live during that year.

Demographic Assumptions

For each year in the projection period, the model simulates persons becoming married or divorced, bearing children, becoming disabled or recovering from disability, and dying, based on a variety of assumptions. Changes in marital status are based on vital statistics data from the National Center for Health Statistics; aggregate marriage rates are kept consistent with the Social Security Administration's Alternative II-B (mid-range) forecast.[4] Marriage rates vary by age, sex, education, and previous marital experience (that is, widowed, divorced, never married), and divorce rates vary by age. Marriage and divorce rates stay constant in the simulation period.

Childbearing rates are based on Census Bureau data for 1976–80, and aggregate fertility rates are constrained to the Alternative II-B forecast. Childbearing varies by age, marital status, employment status, and number of children. The model does not follow children as they grow older.

Work disability rates for people under age 65 are based on social security disability insurance data, and working age disability remission rates are for 1979-80 from the same source. Rates for becoming disabled vary by age and sex and remain constant over time. Recovery from disability in the model is based on years since becoming disabled. (For the disability assumptions for persons aged 65 and older, see the later section on Disability Status.)

The overall mortality rates are based on Alternative II-B projections, which assume substantial improvements in longevity over time. For people under age 65, rates vary by age, sex, disability status, and years since becoming disabled. After age 65 the model sets differential age-sex mortality rates for the disabled and the nondisabled and for nursing home residents and people living in the community. The model subtracts the age-sex specific mortality rate for persons who die in a nursing home from the overall Alternative II-B mortality rate for that year and then distributes the residual mortality so that age-sex specific mortality rates for the disabled elderly are twice as high as the age-sex rates for the nondisabled elderly. People entering a nursing home have the highest mortality rates, followed by the chronically disabled still in the community, and finally, the nondisabled in the community.

Labor Force and Economic Assumptions

Using the Pension and Retirement Income Simulation Model, the model simulates an employment history for each person from 1979 through his or her date of retirement. Each year the model calculates wage rates, hours worked, job change, and industry of employment. Aggregate work force and industry composition follow the Bureau of Labor Statistics forecast, and average wage rates are based on the Alternative II-B projections.[5] Inflation increases at the actual and projected consumer price index annual rate specified under Alternative II-B, about 4 percent a year in the long run.

Overall unemployment rates reflect actual data through 1984 and then follow the Alternative II-B projections. Long-run unemployment is assumed to be 6 percent. Labor force participation rates follow Bureau of Labor Statistics age-sex specific forecasts until the year 2000

TABLE A-1. *Assumed Real Wage Growth, 1984–2010*
Percent

Year	Real wage growth	Year	Real wage growth
1984	1.9	1991	1.4
1985	0.0	1992	1.6
1986	0.8	1993	1.6
1987	1.1	1994	1.6
1988	1.1	1995–2009	1.6
1989	1.6	2010 and after	1.5
1990	1.0		

SOURCE: Alternative II-B assumptions from the *1985 Annual Report of the Board of Trustees of the Federal Old Age and Survivors Insurance and Disability Insurance Trust Funds.*

and then remain constant, except for the group aged 62 to 67, as described below.

The Social Security Amendments of 1983, which will eventually raise the age at which full social security benefits are available, are assumed to increase the labor force participation of persons aged 62 to 67 starting in the year 2000. When the normal retirement age increases from 65 to 66, retirement rates for people aged 62 to 65 are assumed to decline 10 percent, and their labor force participation rates are assumed to rise 10 percent. The scheduled increase in retirement age from 66 to 67 due to occur after 2017 is handled the same way in the model.

Given the aggregate levels of labor force participation for different age-sex groups, the model simulates the number of hours each person will work during a year based on Census Bureau employment pattern data that vary by age, sex, marital status, presence of children, hours worked in the previous three years, and pension and social security benefit receipt status. Wage growth reflects aggregate actual rates for 1979-84 and then follows the macroeconomic projections shown in table A-1. Individual hourly wage rate adjustments are based on Census Bureau data. These rates vary by age, sex, and whether the person changed jobs during the year.

Job change rates are based on Census Bureau data on employment patterns for 1979 and vary by age, tenure, and part- or full-time status. These rates remain constant over time. People are assigned to an industry whenever they change jobs or enter or reenter the labor force. This assignment is based on Bureau of Labor Statistics projections of industry work force composition through 1995, remaining constant thereafter. These projections assume an increasing proportion of employment in service industries and a falling proportion in manufacturing. The industry assigned to a person varies by age, part- or full-time status, and prior sector of employment.

Pension Coverage and Retirement Assumptions

As a person changes jobs during the simulation period, the model determines whether he or she is covered by a pension plan and assigns covered workers to an actual plan. The model simulates early, normal, and late retirement. Retirement income sources simulated by the model include private sector defined-benefit pension plans, defined-contribution plans, Keoghs, individual retirement accounts, social security, and supplemental security income. Social security law, including the changes provided by the 1983 amendments, is simulated. Interest rates for defined-contribution plans and individual retirement accounts use the Alternative II-B forecast of interest rates, which vary by year.

Pension coverage rates vary by industry of employment, part- or full-time status, age, and wage rate. Pension coverage rates are based on the May 1979 Current Population Survey Special Pension Supplement and the 1983 Employee Benefit Research Institute–Department of Health and Human Services Current Population Survey Pension Supplement and remain constant after 1983. People are assigned to pension plans on the basis of industry of employment, firm size, social security coverage status, union coverage status, multi- or single-employer plan status, and hourly or salary employee status. Pension plan assignment takes into account the number of people actually covered by that plan sponsor.

Using the actual provisions of the pension plans assigned, the model calculates each person's eligibility and benefit amount. In general, pension plan provisions are assumed to remain unchanged except in instances where plan rules must be changed to come into compliance with the Retirement Equity Act of 1984. Benefit formulas in defined pension plans and salary bend points are indexed to growth in wages. Individual retirement accounts are "new" savings (that is, not transferred from other savings) and converted to an annuity at the time of pension or social security benefit acceptance, but not before age 60.

Private defined-benefit plans are indexed at half the rate of inflation annually (maximum 2 percent a year); early and normal retirement benefits for the public sector retirement plans increase at the rate of inflation (maximum 4 percent a year). These cost-of-living adjustments for pension benefits are based on an analysis by ICF Incorporated of cost-of-living adjustments over a ten-year period for a representative sample of pension plans.

Acceptance of social security benefits is based on 1980 Social Security Administration data. Eligible persons aged 62 or older are automatically assumed to accept benefits when they become disabled, or unemployed, or when they receive an employer pension. Acceptance also varies by age and sex. Social security survivors' benefits accrue to people in the first year they are eligible.

Pension benefit acceptance for employees meeting their assigned plan's eligibility provisions differs between defined-benefit and defined-contribution plans. Pension acceptance also varies by age, sex, and vesting status. In general, the rates are based on data from the Census Bureau's 1979 Current Population Survey Special Pension Supplement.

Levels of Assets

Because assets can be an important source of income for the elderly and therefore a source of financing for their long-term care, the model simulates both the level of housing equity and the value of all other (nonhousing) assets for individuals and couples aged 65 and older. The model assigns actual asset data records from the 1983 Survey of Consumer Finances, adjusted for inflation, to people in the model on the basis of age, marital status, income, and pension receipt status. Assigning the assets provides a distribution of assets rather than just an average amount for different demographic subgroups.

The assigned nonhousing asset holdings are also a source of elderly income in the model. The annual rate of return on nonhousing assets is based upon the Alternative II-B interest rate assumptions, which vary by year. All annual asset income during a year is assumed to be spent during the year.

The asset assignment process in the model has two steps. Beginning in 1979, all family units aged 65 and over are assigned actual asset records that are deflated by the consumer price index change from 1979 to 1982. After 1979, as people reach age 65, the model assigns assets using data from records of persons aged 61 to 69 in the 1983 Survey of Consumer Finances. The value of all assets assigned is adjusted by the actual or expected rate of change in the consumer price index projected under Alternative II-B.

After assets are assigned to persons aged 65 and older in the model,

TABLE A-2. *Disability Prevalence Rates, by Age, Sex, and Marital Status*
Percent

Age	Male		Female	
	Married	Unmarried	Married	Unmarried
65–69	10.37	15.22	10.40	14.74
70–74	14.11	21.33	13.67	18.69
75–79	18.18	25.52	21.11	28.49
80–84	28.87	34.02	30.95	39.13
85–89	38.90	50.69	43.86	52.98
90–94	52.42	75.52	62.15	71.71
95 and over	70.63	90.00	88.07	90.00

SOURCE: ICF calculations using data from the 1982 National Long-Term Care Survey and the 1977 National Nursing Home Survey.

the value of the assigned assets is adjusted. The value of housing equity increases by the actual and projected rates of change in the consumer price index. Nonhousing assets decrease by 2 percent annually for individuals or families with incomes above $15,000 (in 1982 dollars) to reflect some dissaving for most elderly. Nonhousing assets remain constant for retirees with incomes below $15,000. When a person dies, his or her spouse is assumed to receive all assets.

Disability Status

The likelihood of an elderly person using nursing home or home care services is strongly affected by his or her disability status. For people 65 and older, disability rates are derived from population estimates from the 1982 National Long-Term Care Survey, the 1977 National Nursing Home Survey (adjusted to reflect growth in nursing home beds from 1977 to 1982), and the March 1982 Current Population Survey. These rates vary by age, sex, and marital status and remain constant over time (table A-2).

To estimate the disabled elderly population, we grouped nursing home residents and chronically impaired community residents by age, sex, and marital status. The estimates for nursing home residents come from the 1977 National Nursing Home Survey discharged and current resident files (adjusted to 1982). Chronically impaired community resident counts are taken from the 1982 National Long-Term Care Survey. Disability in the 1982 National Long-Term Care Survey was defined as the inability, lasting for at least ninety days, to conduct an activity of daily living or, for health-related reasons, an instrumental

TABLE A-3. *Annual Probability of Recovery from Disability, by Age*[a]
Percent

Age	Nursing home residents	Community residents
65–74	8	20
75–84	6	15
85 and over	3	4

SOURCES: ICF calculations based on data from Laurence G. Branch and others, "A Prospective Study of Functional Status among Community Elders," *American Journal of Public Health,* vol. 74 (March 1984), pp. 266–68; and authors' assumptions.
a. The model actually uses separate rates for each individual year of age.

activity of daily living.* All elderly in the 1977 National Nursing Home Survey were assumed to have been disabled.

Recovery rates from disability status for the elderly in the model are different for people in nursing homes and those living in the community (table A-3). For nursing home residents, recovery rates are assumed to be half those of 1977 National Nursing Home Survey residents who were discharged home and were independent in mobility and continence. Assumptions about recovery by disabled community residents are based on rates from a study by Branch and others, which were reduced by half to reflect the broader, more inclusive definition of disability used in the model.[6] Thus fewer people are assumed to recover completely from disability in the model than in the Branch study.

The model ensures that disability prevalence rates remain constant on the basis of age, sex, and marital status in subsequent years by simulating additional elderly persons becoming disabled. This increase offsets reductions in the numbers of elderly disabled because of death or recovery from disability.

Nursing Home Use

For each year of the simulation, the model selects people, both disabled and nondisabled, to enter a nursing home. The model

* People need long-term care when they have a chronic disease or condition that requires assistance in the basic activities of daily living (ADL), such as bathing, dressing, eating, getting to the toilet, or transferring from a bed or chair. Sidney Katz and others, "Studies of Illness in the Aged—The Index of ADL: A Standardized Measure of Biological and Psychosocial Function," *Journal of the American Medical Association,* September 21, 1963, pp. 914–19. Similarly, chronically disabled persons often require long-term care if they need assistance in the instrumental activities of daily living (IADL), such as shopping, cooking, or housework, in order to maintain themselves. M. Powell Lawton and Elaine M. Brody, "Assessment of Older People: Self-Maintaining and Instrumental Activities of Daily Living," *Gerontologist,* vol. 9 (Autumn 1969), pp. 179–86.

TABLE A-4. *Annual Probability of Entering a Nursing Home, by Age, Sex, and Marital Status*[a]
Percent

Age	Male		Female	
	Married	Unmarried	Married	Unmarried
		Disabled		
65–69	5	30	6	13
70–74	10	30	8	16
75–79	12	30	10	21
80–84	15	30	15	21
85 and over	19	30	15	24
		Nondisabled		
65–69	0.1	1	0.1	0.3
70–74	0.2	1	0.1	0.4
75–79	0.3	1	0.3	1
80–84	1	2	1	1
85 and over	2	4	1	4

SOURCE: ICF calculations using data from the 1977 National Nursing Home Survey, the March 1982 CPS, the 1982 National Long-Term Care Survey, and Mark Meiners and Gordon Trapnell, "Long-Term Care Insurance: Premium Estimates for Prototype Policies," *Medical Care,* vol. 22 (October 1984), pp. 901–11.

a. The model actually uses separate rates for individual years of age from age 65 to age 109. The rates for disabled unmarried men have been pooled because of small sample sizes.

determines the patient's length of stay and whether he or she is discharged dead or alive. The model uses the 1977 National Nursing Home Survey data, adjusted to 1982 bed totals using National Master Facility Inventory data, and the March 1982 Current Population Survey. Nursing home entry rates vary by disability status, age, sex, and marital status. A person can enter a nursing home only once a year.

To obtain a representative sample of annual nursing home admissions, we adjusted the age-specific nursing home admission rates developed by Meiners and Trapnell to take into account growth in the number of nursing home residents and to avoid double counting persons already residing in a nursing home.[7] These admission rates were also adjusted to reflect the sex and marital status of similar age patients in both the current-resident and discharged-resident components of the 1977 National Nursing Home Survey.

People admitted to a nursing home are assumed to have the same distribution of income and assets as those who remain in the community. Separate entry probabilities for disabled and nondisabled elderly are used in the model so that 90 percent of annual nursing home admissions are for long-term disabled, but 10 percent of admissions are for people with short-term disabilities who are not disabled at the beginning of the year (table A-4).

TABLE A-5. *Probability of Nursing Home Length of Stay, by Age at Entry and Mortality Status at Discharge*
Percent

Length of stay (months)	Age at Entry					
	65–74		75–84		85 and over	
	Live	Dead	Live	Dead	Live	Dead
Under 1	17.72	9.68	14.29	9.73	11.66	10.03
1–2	5.68	5.27	6.50	4.73	4.79	6.32
2–3	4.80	3.13	2.97	2.78	2.41	3.76
3–6	5.88	4.63	5.07	6.29	3.99	6.74
6–12	3.86	5.97	4.70	6.30	3.12	7.36
12–24	4.80	5.84	3.15	6.82	2.97	9.70
24–36	2.19	4.56	1.43	4.60	1.26	5.29
36–48	0.99	1.72	1.19	4.05	1.17	6.68
48–60	1.04	1.68	1.09	3.28	0.66	4.15
60–72	0.84	1.29	0.64	3.07	0.18	2.73
73 and over	1.91	6.52	0.74	6.57	0.43	4.59
TOTAL	49.70	50.30	41.77	58.23	32.65	67.35

SOURCE: ICF calculations using data from Meiners and Trapnell, "Long-Term Care Insurance," pp. 901–11.

Both the length of stay assigned by the model to nursing home entrants and the mortality status of residents at time of discharge are based on estimates developed by Meiners and Trapnell from the 1977 National Nursing Home Survey and vary by an entrant's age at admission (table A-5). The Meiners and Trapnell lengths-of-stay probabilities aggregated multiple admissions for patients readmitted to a nursing home soon after being discharged and were further modified to reflect increasing numbers of nursing home residents by age from 1969 to 1977.

All nursing home lengths of stay are assigned the midpoint of the estimate. Nursing home assigned lengths of stay are based on age and remain constant over the simulation period. Previous nursing home residents reenter nursing homes at the same rate as people who have never been institutionalized.

Home Care Use

Noninstitutional services in the model include home health services, chore and homemaker services, personal care, and meal preparation services. Using data from the 1982 National Long-Term Care Survey of noninstitutionalized chronically disabled elderly, the model places disabled people still living at home into one of four groups: those

TABLE A-6. *Probability of Using Home Care Services, by Demographic and Income Groups*
Percentage of noninstitutionalized disabled elderly

Income group and type of service	Age 65–74		Age 75–84		Age 85 and over	
	Married	Unmarried	Married	Unmarried	Married	Unmarried
			Women			
Poor[a]						
Paid only	0.7	6.4	5.6	6.4	8.9	3.7
Unpaid only	66.4	60.8	63.2	58.4	30.6	65.3
Both	24.7	21.6	25.3	28.8	58.5	29.9
None	8.2	11.2	5.9	6.4	2.0	1.1
Nonpoor						
Paid only	3.3	9.8	0.5	11.0	0.0	6.4
Unpaid only	61.4	48.0	57.9	46.3	61.2	59.1
Both	31.0	31.3	38.5	34.2	35.9	31.9
None	4.3	10.9	3.1	8.5	2.9	2.6
			Men			
Poor[a]						
Paid only	0.2	2.4	1.7	4.6	1.7	2.2
Unpaid only	84.0	74.0	70.4	71.7	75.2	64.6
Both	11.9	17.3	25.9	13.6	19.7	29.6
None	3.9	6.3	2.0	10.1	3.4	3.6
Nonpoor						
Paid only	1.3	5.3	2.2	7.3	0.0	10.7
Unpaid only	75.2	53.9	78.0	57.9	73.7	45.9
Both	19.9	28.1	16.7	28.0	26.3	34.7
None	3.6	12.7	3.1	6.8	0.0	8.7

SOURCES: The 1982 National Long-Term Care Survey and ICF calculations.
a. Poor is defined here as having income less than 125 percent of the poverty level.

receiving only paid help, those receiving paid and unpaid help, those receiving only unpaid help, and those receiving no services. As shown in table A-6, the annual probability of entering one of these four groups varies by age, sex, marital status, and income group.

Developing probabilities of annual use of paid home care services was difficult because existing data, such as the 1982 National Long-Term Care Survey, provide only cross-sectional or prevalence estimates. Cross-sectional estimates substantially undercount the number of people using services for a short period. To correct for this undercount, we estimated incidence rates (the number of new service users in a year) by dividing the prevalence rate of paid in-home service use by the duration of use reported in the 1982 National Long-Term Care Survey. Length of paid in-home service use also varies by whether the person receives unpaid care from family and friends (table A-7).

Some nondisabled people are simulated as receiving medicare home

TABLE A-7. *Probability of Duration of Home Care Services for the Disabled Elderly*
Percentage of total receiving services

Duration (months)	Service	
	Paid only	Both paid and unpaid
Under 3	37.1	53.0
3–6	21.1	18.9
6–12	16.5	15.4
12–60	19.3	10.8
61 and over	6.0	1.9
TOTAL	100.0	100.0

SOURCE: Authors' calculations.

health services that are largely provided as short-term, post-acute care. The use of such services by nondisabled people is calculated by subtracting medicare home health use for the disabled (as reported in the 1982 National Long-Term Care Survey) from total medicare home health use (as reported by the Health Care Financing Administration medicare program statistics for 1982). The nondisabled use probabilities vary by age and sex. The number of medicare home health visits each beneficiary receives is taken from medicare program statistics.

People selected by the model to receive family care along with paid in-home care receive eighteen paid visits a month. All other paid home care patients receive nineteen visits a month. Length of use is assumed to be the midpoint of the duration category reported in the 1982 National Long-Term Care Survey (for example, three to six months is assigned 4.5 months) except that people receiving services for less than three months are assumed to receive them for three months, and those who reported receiving services for five years and more are assumed to receive them for five years. The probability of a person using home care in the model is not affected by prior use of nursing home or home care services.

Financing Nursing Home Care

The model simulates expenditures for nursing home care and source of payment for that care for all patients on a month-by-month basis. Expenditures are set equal to a person's simulated number of nursing home days multiplied by payments each day. In the base case, nursing home patients pay for their care with reimbursements from medicare and medicaid, annual income, and assets. Spend-down to medicaid and other financial eligibility requirements are simulated by the model. Each person's payments are accumulated by source.

Daily charges for nursing home care vary by source of payment. The medicare rate is based on average skilled nursing facility rates for 1983, the medicaid daily rate is based upon a weighted average of skilled nursing facility and intermediate care facility rates for fiscal year 1983, and the private pay rate is assumed to be about 30 percent higher than the medicaid rate.[8] The model's nursing home payment rates in 1986 are $95.21 a day for medicare, $62.51 a day for private pay residents, and $47.58 a day for medicaid.

After 1987 all payment rates are assumed to increase 5.8 percent a year. The increase is based on the Social Security Administration Office of the Actuary's long-run assumption that the consumer price index increases 4.0 percent a year, real wages increase 1.6 percent a year, and fringe benefits increase 0.2 percent a year.[9] Implicit in this assumption is that there will be no significant productivity improvements in nursing home care.

Entering nursing home patients generally incur other health care expenses affecting the amount of income and assets they have available to pay for nursing home care. To account for the additional expenses, each nursing home admission is assumed to have out-of-pocket acute health care costs of $85 a month in 1986, which is indexed by the nursing home inflation rate. This includes the medicare part B premium, medicare deductibles and coinsurance, and other health care costs. This expense approximates the cost of a comprehensive medigap policy.

The model assumes that a portion of a patient's income and assets is available to pay the costs of nursing home care. Consistent with current medicaid practice, the entire income of single persons is considered available to pay for their health care expenditures. For married couples, the model assumes that two-thirds of their social security and asset income is available to the institutionalized spouse. All pension and individual retirement account income follows the spouse who earned the benefit.

The model also simulates two intrafamily transfers of income from one spouse to another. When the spouse remaining at home has individual income falling below the federal supplemental security income level, the model assumes an income transfer from the nursing home patient to raise his or her spouse's income to supplemental security income payment levels—$340 a month in 1987, to be increased annually by the consumer price index. Under the medicaid program, some portion of the income of a spouse of a nursing home patient is "deemed" or assumed to be available to pay for nursing home care. In the model, as in most states, a spouse's income is deemed only during the first month of a nursing home stay.

All of a person's nonhousing assets, less the supplemental security income level of protected assets, are assumed to be available for nursing home costs. A married nursing home resident is assumed to have access to two-thirds of the couple's assets. As mandated by the Deficit Reduction Act of 1984, beginning in 1984 the asset limit for single persons increases by $100, and the limit for married couples increases by $150, each year until 1989, when they will be equal to $2,000 and $3,000, respectively. After 1989 the asset limits are assumed to increase at 50 percent of the rate of increase for the Alternative II-B forecast in the consumer price index. No transfer of assets for the purpose of obtaining premature medicaid eligibility is assumed.

In most states the "homestead" is a protected asset under medicaid and need not be used for nursing home expenses. In the model, 10 percent of unmarried people who live in nursing homes longer than one year sell their homes to help finance their care. The value of their housing equity is transferred to nonhousing assets, which can then be spent for nursing home care.

The model simulates nursing home expenditures and sources of payment using the nursing home charges and individual resources described above. The model assumes that 20 percent of nursing home admissions receive full medicare coverage for the first twenty days. For the remainder of the covered stay, medicare pays only for the residual daily costs after a patient pays the required coinsurance (set at one-eighth of the medicare acute inpatient deductible). The medicare coinsurance increases 5.8 percent a year.

For nonmedicare admissions, and when medicare nursing home coverage ends, the model uses patient income and assets (in that order) to pay for care. If a person does not have sufficient income to pay the private payment charge, then the model subtracts remaining expenses to cover the costs from the person's nonhousing assets. Once these nonhousing assets are drawn down to the medicaid asset level, medicaid pays the difference between patient income and the medicaid payment rate less a personal needs allowance ($30 a month in 1986).

TABLE A-8. *Financing of Home Care Services for the Disabled Elderly*[a]
Percentage of total receiving services

Source of funds	Paid services only		Paid and unpaid services	
	Poor[b]	Nonpoor	Poor[b]	Nonpoor
Out-of-pocket (then receive services from other payers)	46.4	64.8	43.1	56.4
Medicare (then receive services from other payers)	11.5	11.5	27.4	27.4
Medicaid	19.0	7.4	19.0	7.4
Other payers	23.1	16.3	10.5	8.8

SOURCE: ICF calculations using data from the 1982 National Long-Term Care Survey and data from the Office of the Actuary, Health Care Financing Administration.
a. Nondisabled persons receive only medicare home health services.
b. Those below 125 percent of the poverty line.

Financing Home Care Services

The model simulates expenditures and sources of payment for home care. Expenditures are set equal to the number of visits multiplied by the price per visit. Nondisabled people receive only medicare home health services. When the model selects a disabled person to start receiving noninstitutional services, it assigns him or her to one of four source-of-payment categories on the basis of age, sex, marital status, and income group. These payment categories are out-of-pocket, medicare, medicaid, and other payer (table A-8). Other payer is a residual home care payment category that includes all funding from state and local programs, Older Americans Act and social services block grant monies, Veterans Administration programs, and charity.

The out-of-pocket price per visit is based on data from the 1982 National Long-Term Care Survey; medicare and medicaid visit rates are based on program data average costs; and other payer rate is a weighted average of the medicare and out-of-pocket rates. For 1986 the charges used by the model are $11.50 a visit for out-of-pocket visits, $47.00 a visit for medicare, $42.50 a visit for medicaid, and $24.00 a visit for other payer. Prices increase 7.6 percent in 1987 and then 5.8 percent a year.

People paying out-of-pocket for home care are assumed to pay up to 50 percent of their income for services and then to use their nonhousing assets. After nonhousing assets are depleted, people are assumed to receive services from other payers. In addition, after nondisabled people stop receiving medicare home health services, they receive no further home care services. Disabled users of medicare home health may continue to receive services that are reimbursed by other payers after medicare home health use ends.

Medicaid coverage of home care services was estimated from the 1982 National Long-Term Care Survey. These probabilities were increased by 4 percent to reflect underreporting of medicaid services when compared with medicaid program data for 1982. No one with a family income greater than $30,000 (in 1986 dollars) receives medicaid home health services.

Extrapolating Long-Term Care Expenditures and Financing through 2050

Although the full model projects nursing home and home care use and expenditures from 1986 through 2020, demand for long-term care by the baby boom cohort will peak well after 2020. One reason for not extending the model past 2020 is that nearly all of the model's 1979 starting population of working-age adults have reached age 65 or died by 2020, leaving too few people to turn age 65 after 2020 for detailed modeling. In addition, behavioral and economic assumption beyond 2020 become highly questionable. Thus, to estimate long-term expenditures for the baby boom cohort, a simplified method for extrapolating long-term care expenditures and potential sources of financing to 2050 was developed.

Estimation of expenditures began by calculating the level of per capita long-term care expenditures in 1986–90 and the rate of growth in these expenditures between 1986–90 and 2016–20 for seven age groups from age 65 to 69 to age 95 and over. The age-specific rate of growth was then applied to the level of expenditures in each age group in 1988 to estimate average per capita expenditures for each year from 1989 through 2050. Using population projections through 2050 from the Bureau of the Census, the age-specific level of expenditures was multiplied by the expected number of elderly in each year between 2020 and 2050.[10] Summing across all age groups produced the estimated annual total long-term care costs.

Alternative options for financing public long-term care expenditures through 2050 include a payroll tax and an income tax surcharge. To estimate the financing potential from wages and salaries of the working population in the period from 1986 through 2050, a similar method was employed. First, the number of wage earners for twelve age groups ranging from age 16 to 17 to age 65 and over was estimated by using

Bureau of Labor Statistics projections through 2000; the number remained constant thereafter. Then Bureau of Labor Statistics data on the distribution of earnings were applied to this population by age and sex. Real wages were assumed to grow at the Alternative II-B rate through 2050. By multiplying the expected number of persons with work force experience by the earnings for each age and sex group in a given year and summing all age groups, an estimate of total annual earnings was derived.

The overall proportion of payroll needed to finance public long-term care expenditures was estimated by calculating annual total public long-term care expenditures as a percentage of all wages and salaries for each year through 2050. The overall average annual percentage of payroll required is assumed to be the sum of the estimated annual percentages from 1988 through 2050 divided by the number of years in the period.

The income tax surcharge estimates are based on average tax payments for 1987 by sex and age group estimated by ICF Incorporated's Household Income and Tax Simulation Model.[11] Future tax payments are assumed to increase by the annual projected change in real earnings under Alternative II-B. The estimate of required payroll taxes or income tax surcharges does not include interest earned on reserves. Thus taxes are somewhat higher than would actually be required.

Notes

Chapter 1

1. U.S. Congressional Budget Office, *Long-Term Care for the Elderly and Disabled* (Washington, D.C., 1977), p. 1; and Pamela Doty, Korbin Liu, and Joshua Wiener, "An Overview of Long-Term Care," *Health Care Financing Review*, vol. 6 (Spring 1985), p. 69. These capacities are known as the "activities of daily living"; see Sidney Katz and others, "Studies of Illness in the Aged: The Index of ADL," *Journal of the American Medical Association*, September 21, 1963, pp. 914–19.

2. Technical Work Group on Private Financing of Long-Term Care for the Elderly, *Report to the Secretary on Private Financing of Long-Term Care for the Elderly* (Washington, D.C.: Department of Health and Human Services, November 1986), chap 2., p. 22.

3. The aged-85-and-older population is projected to increase from 2.7 million in 1985 to 16.0 million in 2050, a rate of growth nearly three times as high as that for the 65–84 age group. As a proportion of the elderly population, the 85-and-older age group will increase from 9 percent in 1985 to 24 percent in 2050. U.S. Bureau of the Census, "Projections of the Population of the United States by Age, Sex, and Race: 1983 to 2080," *Current Population Reports*, series P–25, no. 952 (Washington, D.C.: Department of Commerce, May 1984), table 6.

4. William J. McAuley and Rosemary Blieszner, "Selection of Long-Term Care Arrangements by Older Community Residents," *Gerontologist*, vol. 25 (April 1985), p. 189.

5. U.S. Department of Health and Human Services, 1982 National Long-Term Care Survey, available from the National Technical Information Service, accession nos. PB-86-161775 and PB-86-161783.

6. Robyn Stone, Gail Lee Cafferata, and Judith Sangl, "Caregivers of the Frail Elderly: A National Profile," *Gerontologist*, vol. 27 (October 1987), p. 620.

7. Korbin Liu and Kenneth G. Manton, "Disability and Long-Term Care," paper presented at the Methodologies of Forecasting Life and Active Life Expectancy Workshop, Bethesda, Md., June 25–26, 1985, p. 14. For another estimate of the level of caregiving and its imputed financial value, see Lynn Paringer, "The Forgotten Costs of Informal Long-Term Care," in *Long-Term Care Costs: Project to Analyze Existing Long-Term Care Data*, vol. 6, report

prepared for the Assistant Secretary for Planning and Evaluation, DHHS (Washington, D.C.: Urban Institute, 1983), pp. 50–91.

8. Poulshock found that one of five caregivers evidenced serious stress, half had moderate stress, and all showed some stress. S. Walter Poulshock, "The Effects on Families of Caring for Impaired Elderly in Residence," paper prepared for the Administration on Aging (Cleveland, Ohio: Benjamin Rose Institute, October 1982), p. 5. See also Betsy Robinson and Majda Thurnher, "Taking Care of Aged Parents: A Family Cycle Transition," *Gerontologist,* vol. 19 (December 1979), p. 591; Linda K. George and Lisa P. Gwyther, "Caregiver Well-Being: A Multidimensional Examination of Family Caregivers of Demented Adults," *Gerontologist,* vol. 26 (June 1986), pp. 253–59; and Judith Sangl, "The Family Support System of the Elderly," in Ronald J. Vogel and Hans C. Palmer, eds., *Long-Term Care: Perspectives from Research and Demonstrations* (Washington, D.C.: Health Care Financing Administration, 1983), pp. 320–23.

9. Elaine M. Brody, "Parent Care as a Normative Family Stress," *Gerontologist,* vol. 25 (February 1985), p. 20.

10. Genevieve Strahan, "Nursing Home Characteristics: Preliminary Data from the 1985 National Nursing Home Survey," *Vital and Health Statistics* (advance data), no. 131 (Hyattsville, Md.: National Center for Health Statistics, DHHS, March 27, 1987), p. 2; and American Hospital Association, *Hospital Statistics, 1986* (Chicago, Ill., 1986), p. 10.

11. Daniel R. Waldo, Katharine R. Levit, and Helen Lazenby, "National Health Expenditures, 1985," *Health Care Financing Review,* vol. 8 (Fall 1986), p. 17.

12. George Schieber and others, "Prospective Payment for Medicare Skilled Nursing Facilities: Background and Issues," *Health Care Financing Review*, vol. 8 (Fall 1986), p. 79.

13. Waldo and others, "National Health Expenditures, 1985," p. 17.

14. Brookings-ICF Long-Term Care Financing Model.

15. Ibid.

16. Not much is actually known about the financial characteristics of elderly medicaid nursing home patients and how they became medicaid eligible. A 1976 study of South Dakota found that approximately 30 percent of the medicaid patients in nursing homes at the time of the study had originally been admitted as private patients. U.S. General Accounting Office, *Entering a Nursing Home: Costly Implications for Medicaid and the Elderly,* PAD-80-12 (Washington, D.C., November 26, 1979), p. 38. A GAO study of Minnesota data between 1977 and 1979 suggested that perhaps a quarter of medicaid nursing home residents had originally been private patients. GAO, *Medicaid and Nursing Home Care: Cost Increases and the Need for Services Are Creating Problems for the States and the Elderly,* GAO/IPE-84-1 (Washington, D.C., October 21, 1983), pp. 25–26. Studies of elderly living in the community in the United States found that for elderly living alone 70 percent of those aged 65 and over risked impoverishment after thirteen weeks in a nursing home. *Long Term Care and Personal Impoverishment: Seven in Ten Elderly Living Alone Are at Risk,* Committee Print, House Select Committee on Aging, 100 Cong. 1 sess. (Washington, D.C., July 1985).

17. Most states offer medicaid eligibility to elderly persons with income and assets low enough to qualify for cash welfare assistance under the supplemental security income (SSI) program. The 1988 federal minimum payment level for SSI is $354 a month for an individual and $532 for a couple. *Social Security Bulletin,* vol. 50 (December 1987), p. 2. States may supplement this payment

and provide medicaid to those beneficiaries. The so-called 209(b) states cover only SSI recipients who meet their own more restrictive eligibility criteria for medicaid.

Most states also provide medically needy coverage for people who do not have enough income or assets to meet their medical expenses but who (by welfare standards) have sufficient income and assets to meet basic living expenses. This medically needy income level cannot exceed 133 percent of the aid to families with dependent children payment level and is usually considerably below the SSI payment level. By incurring medical bills in excess of the welfare level, people "spend down" to the allowed income level. The 209(b) states must allow all aged, blind, and disabled persons, including those with too much income to qualify for SSI, to spend down.

To become eligible for medicaid, people must meet certain income and asset tests. They must first use up almost all their liquid assets—bank accounts, stocks, certificates of deposit. In 1988 individuals with assets in excess of $1,900 and couples with incomes in excess of $2,850 are ineligible. As required by the Deficit Reduction Act of 1984, these amounts will increase in 1989 to $2,000 for individuals and $3,000 for couples.

People are precluded from disposing of their assets at less than fair market value to become eligible for medicaid. Persons found to have transferred their assets at less than fair market value within two years of applying for medicaid may be denied medicaid eligibility for up to two years.

The "homestead" is not counted as an asset. Some states, however, contend that after a person has been in a nursing home for an extended period, the nursing home, and not the house, is the person's "home." The house then becomes a piece of real estate, which is a countable asset.

Once an elderly nursing home patient has met the asset criteria, he must also meet an income test. In general, if his income is not adequate to cover medical or nursing home bills, he can qualify for medicaid by "spending down" his income. He must contribute all his income toward the cost of his care, after deducting a small amount for a personal needs allowance (usually $30 a month), and an allowance for spouses or other dependents still at home. If, after using up all his income, he does not have enough to pay the nursing home, then he can qualify for medicaid.

Medicaid pays only the difference between the medicaid rate and the patient's contribution to the cost of the care. For example, in a nursing home costing $1,800 a month, a nursing home patient who has no spouse and whose sole monthly income is a $500 social security check would be allowed to keep $30 each month for expenses such as clothing, telephone, gifts for the grandchildren, trips to the hairdresser, newspapers, books, toothpaste, laundry (in some facilities), and entertainment. The remaining $470 would be paid to the nursing home, and medicaid would pay the difference, or $1,330.

Medicaid eligibility rules can cause financial hardship not only for people in nursing homes but also for their spouses. The most severe and negative consequences of current rules occur in cases in which the nursing home patient has a spouse—usually the wife—who still lives in the community, has little or no independent means of financial support (for example, pension or assets), and is financially dependent on the spouse in the institution. In these cases, virtually all the husband's income and assets must be used to pay for his institutional care, with medicaid paying only the residual amount. The husband is allowed to send only enough money to his wife to keep her income up to the welfare standard—below the poverty level and usually far less than needed to sustain the wife at her customary standard of living. It should be noted that in the rare circumstances in which the financially dependent spouse becomes a medicaid nursing home resident, medicaid rules leave the spouse at home largely free of any obligation to provide financial support for the spouse's nursing home care. For an excellent summary of medicaid eligibility rules and their implications for long-term care, see Edward Neuschler with Claire Gill, *Medicaid Eligibility for the Elderly in Need of Long Term Care,* report prepared for the Congressional Research Service (Washington, D.C.: National Governors' Assocation, September 1987).

18. Neuschler with Gill, *Medicaid Eligibility for the Elderly*, p. 22.

19. Strahan, "Nursing Home Characteristics," p. 2.

20. DHHS, 1982 National Long-Term Care Survey.

21. Gruenberg and Kramer each suggest that disability levels will increase radically. Both argue that medical advances have reduced mortality, but have not changed the age of onset of disability. Hence people will be left in a disabled state for an extended period of time. Ernest M. Gruenberg, "The Failures of Success," *Milbank Memorial Fund Quarterly: Health and Society,* vol. 55 (Winter 1977), pp. 3–24; and M. Kramer, "The Rising Pandemic of Mental Disorders and Associated Chronic Diseases and Disabilities," *Acta Psychiatrica Scandinavica Supplementum,* vol. 62, supplement 285 (1980), pp. 382–96. For other theories regarding the future health status of the elderly, see James F. Fries, "Aging, Natural Death and the Compression of Morbidity," *New England Journal of Medicine,* July 17, 1980, pp. 130–35; B. L. Strehler, "Implications of Aging Research for Society," *Proceedings of the 58th Annual Meeting of the Federation of American Societies for Experimental Biology,* vol. 34 (January 1975), pp. 5–8; and testimony of Roy L. Walford in *Trends in U.S. Life Expectancy,* Hearing before the Subcommittee on Savings, Pensions, and Investment Policy, Senate Committee on Finance, 98 Cong. 1 sess. (Washington, D.C., 1983), pp. 116–31.

22. Charles E. McConnel, "A Note on the Lifetime Risk of Nursing Home Residency," *Gerontologist,* vol. 24 (April 1984), pp. 193–98; ICF Incorporated, *Private Financing of Long-Term Care: Current Methods and Resources, Phase II,* report prepared for the Assistant Secretary for Planning and Evaluation, DHHS (Washington, D.C., January 1985), p. 54; Jersey Liang and Edward Jow-Ching Tu, "Estimating Lifetime Risk of Nursing Home Residency: A Further Note," *Gerontologist,* vol. 26 (October 1986), pp. 560–63; Marc A. Cohen, Eileen J. Tell, and Stanley S. Wallack, "The Lifetime Risks and Costs of Nursing Home Use Among the Elderly," *Medical Care,* vol. 24 (December 1986), pp. 1161–72; and Leticia Vincente, James A. Wiley, and R. Allen Carrington, "The Risk of Institutionalization Before Death," *Gerontologist,* vol. 19 (August 1979), pp. 361–67.

23. Brookings-ICF Long-Term Care Financing Model.

24. DHHS, 1982 National Long-Term Care Survey; and Esther Hing, "Use of Nursing Homes by the Elderly: Preliminary Data from the 1985 National Nursing Home Survey," *Vital and Health Statistics* (advance data), no. 135 (Hyattsville, Md.: NCHS, May 14, 1987), p. 2.

25. Scanlon estimated the price elasticity for private nursing home demand, using two different regression methods (two-stage least squares and ordinary least squares). He reported highly significant negative elasticities for private price (−1.2 and −0.90). In other words, with a 10 percent increase in private price, private demand for nursing home care will decrease 12 percent or 9 percent. William Scanlon, "A Theory of the Nursing Home Market," *Inquiry,*

vol. 17 (Spring 1980), p. 39. Nyman also found that a greater percentage of beds are demanded by private patients when price decreases. John A. Nyman, "A Market-based System for Reimbursing Nursing Homes for Medicaid Patients," University of Iowa, College of Medicine, October 20, 1984, p. 40. Chiswick also found that the nursing home care demanded in a standard metropolitan statistical area is a negative function of price, with an elasticity of −2.3. That is, with a 10 percent rise in price, demand falls 23 percent. Barry R. Chiswick, "The Demand for Nursing Home Care: An Analysis of the Substitution between Institutional and Non-Institutional Care," *Journal of Human Resources,* vol. 11 (Summer 1976), p. 306.

26. Fully 95 percent of the disabled elderly in the community agreed with the statement, "It's better to stay out of nursing homes as long as you can." DHHS, 1982 National Long-Term Care Survey.

27. Robert L. Kane and Rosalie A. Kane, *A Will and a Way: What the United States Can Learn from Canada about Caring for the Elderly* (Columbia University Press, 1985), pp. 230–31.

28. DHHS, 1982 National Long-Term Care Survey; and Hing, "Use of Nursing Homes by the Elderly," p. 2.

29. In one demonstration project, a rich array of paid services produced a modest substitution effect. This finding, however, was attributed more to the withdrawal of friends than family providers. Further, the observed reductions in unpaid care were small and associated with much larger increases in paid care. Jon B. Christianson, *Channeling Effects on Informal Care,* report prepared for DHHS (Princeton, N.J.: Mathematica Policy Research, May 1986), p. v. See also Health Care Financing Administration, "Long-Term Care: Background and Future Directions," Discussion Paper HCFA 81-20047 (Washington, D.C.: DHHS, January 1981), p. 41. One study that reports a large substitution effect is Vernon L. Green, "Substitution Between Formally and Informally Provided Care for the Impaired Elderly in the Community," *Medical Care,* vol. 21 (June 1983), pp. 609–19. However, because of limitations in the measurement of informal support, Green points out his finding may reflect specialization on the part of unpaid caregivers. Ibid., p. 617.

30. Gail Lee Cafferata, "Private Health Insurance Coverage of the Medicare Population," in National Center for Health Services Research, *National Health Care Expenditures Study: Data Preview 18,* (PHS) 84-3362 (Rockville, Md.: DHHS, September 1984), p.6.

31. Task Force on Long-Term Health Care Policies, *Report to Congress and the Secretary by the Task Force on Long-Term Health Care Policies* (Washington, D.C.: DHHS, September 21, 1987), pp. 72–74.

32. American Association of Homes for the Aging, *Continuing Care Retirement Communities: An Industry in Action* (Washington, D.C., 1987), p. 5; Howard E. Winklevoss and Alwyn V. Powell, *Continuing Care Retirement Communities: An Empirical, Financial, and Legal Analysis* (Homewood, Ill.: Richard D. Irwin, 1984), p. 47.

33. See Hirsch S. Ruchlin, "Continuing Care Retirement Communities: An Analysis of Financial Viability and Health Care Coverage," *Gerontologist,* vol. 28 (April 1988), pp. 156–62.

34. Walter N. Leutz, senior research associate, Brandeis University, Heller School, personal communication, September 17, 1987.

35. U.S. Internal Revenue Service, *Statistics of Income, 1984: The Individual Tax Model File* (public use tape). See "Individual Medical Accounts," chap. 7, table 7-1.

36. Brookings-ICF Long-Term Care Financing Model.

37. Letter to authors from Bruce Jacobs, University of Rochester, November 12, 1987.

38. Bruce Jacobs, "The National Potential of Home Equity Conversion," *Gerontologist,* vol. 26 (October 1986), p. 496; and Brookings-ICF Long-Term Care Financing Model.

39. Maurice Weinrobe, Clark University, personal communication, October 6, 1987; Frank Engel, financial planner, American Homestead Mortgage Corporation, Mount Laurel, N.J., personal communication, October 6, 1987; and Sandra Sullivan, formerly of the Rhode Island Housing and Mortgage Finance Authority Corporation, personal communication, October 23, 1987.

40. Technical Work Group on Private Financing of Long-Term Care for the Elderly, *Report to the Secretary on Private Financing of Long-Term Care for the Elderly,* chap. 3, pp. 220–21.

Chapter 2

1. Frank Levy and Richard C. Michel, "Are Baby Boomers Selfish?" *American Demographics,* vol. 7 (April 1985), pp. 38–41.

2. Institute of Medicine, *Improving the Quality of Care in Nursing Homes* (Washington, D.C.: National Academy Press, 1986), pp. 89–91; and Elma Holder, National Citizens Coalition for Nursing Home Reform, personal communication, February 18, 1988.

3. U.S. General Accounting Office, *Medicaid and Nursing Home Care: Cost Increases and the Need for Services Are Creating Problems for the States and the Elderly,* GAO/IPE-84-1 (Washington, D.C., October 21, 1983).

4. Brookings-ICF Long-Term Care Financing Model.

Chapter 3

1. Task Force on Long-Term Health Care Policies, *Report to Congress and the Secretary by the Task Force on Long-Term Health Care Policies* (Washington, D.C.: Department of Health and Human Services, September 21, 1987), pp. 72–74; American Association of Homes for the Aging, *Continuing Care Retirement Communities: An Industry in Action* (Washington, D.C., 1987), p. 5; Howard E. Winklevoss and Alwyn V. Powell, *Continuing Care Retirement Communities: An Empirical, Financial, and Legal Analysis* (Homewood, Ill.: Richard D. Irwin, 1984), p. 47; Maurice Weinrobe, Clark University, personal communication on HECs, October 6, 1987; Frank Engel, financial planner, American Homestead Mortgage Corporation, Mt. Laurel, N.J., personal communication on HECs, October 6, 1987; and Walter N. Leutz, senior research associate, Brandeis University, Heller School, personal communication on S/HMOs, September 17, 1987.

2. Jay N. Greenberg, Lifeplans, Inc., Waltham, Mass., personal communication, November 21, 1987.

3. U.S. Congressional Budget Office, *Long-Term Care for the Elderly and Disabled* (Washington, D.C., January 1977); U.S. Health Care Financing Administration, *Long-Term Care: Background and Future Directions,* pub. 81–20047 (Washington, D.C.: Department of Health and Human Services, January 1981); and James J. Callahan, Jr., and Stanley S. Wallace, eds., *Reforming the Long-Term Care System* (Lexington, Mass.: Lexington Books, 1981).

4. Edward F. Lawlor and William Pollak, "Financing Long-Term Care: Problems and Prospects," paper presented at the Annual Meeting of the Association for Public Policy Analysis and Management, Washington, D.C., October 1985.

5. U.S. Bureau of the Census, "Money Income and Poverty Status of Families and Persons in the U.S., 1985," *Current Population Reports* (advance data), series P–60, no. 154 (Washington, D.C.: Department of Commerce, 1986), p. 22.

6. Sheldon Danzinger and others, "Implications of the Relative Economic Status of the Elderly for Transfer Policy," in Henry J. Aaron and Gary Burtless, eds., *Retirement and Economic Behavior* (Brookings, 1984), p. 179.

7. Michael J. Hurd and John B. Shoven, "Real Income and Wealth of the Elderly," *American Economic Review,* vol. 72 (May 1982, *Papers and Proceedings, 1981*), pp. 314–18.

8. Sheila R. Zedlewski, "The Private Pension System to the Year 2000," in Aaron and Burtless, eds., *Retirement and Economic Behavior,* pp. 315–41.

9. Bruce Jacobs and William Weissert, "Using Home Equity to Finance Long-Term Care," *Journal of Health Politics, Policy and Law,* vol. 12 (Spring 1987), pp. 77–95.

10. Technical Work Group on Private Financing of Long-Term Care for the Elderly, *Report to the Secretary on Private Financing of Long-Term Care for the Elderly* (Washington, D.C.: Department of Health and Human Services, November 1986), chap 3, pp. 186–247.

Chapter 4

1. Task Force on Long-Term Health Care Policies, *Report to Congress and the Secretary by the Task Force on Long-Term Health Care Policies* (Washington D.C.: Department of Health and Human Services, September 21, 1987), pp. 72–74.

2. Daniel R. Waldo, Katherine R. Levit, and Helen Lazenby, "Nursing Home Expenditures, 1985," *Health Care Financing Review,* vol. 8 (Fall 1986), p. 17.

3. Task Force on Long-Term Health Care Policies, *Report to Congress and the Secretary,* pp. 72–74. In 1983 Meiners estimated that there were sixteen long-term care insurance products. Mark R. Meiners, "The State of the Art in Long-Term Care Insurance," in Patrice Hirsch Feinstein, Marian Gornick, and Jay N. Greenberg, eds., *Long-Term Care Financing and Delivery Systems: Exploring Some Alternatives* (Washington, D.C.: DHHS, Health Care Financing Administration, January 24, 1984), p. 16.

4. Task Force on Long-Term Health Care Policies, *Report to Congress and the Secretary,* pp. 72–74; and National Association of Insurance Commissioners, Advisory Committee on Long Term Care, *Long Term Care Insurance: An Industry Perspective on Market Development and Consumer Protection,* report submitted to NAIC Medicare Supplement, Long Term and Other Limited Benefit Plans Task Force (Kansas City, Mo.: NAIC, December 1986). Several state commissions have recently issued reports on long-term care insurance.

5. Rose M. Rubin, Joshua M. Wiener, and Mark R. Meiners, "Private Long Term Care Insurance: Simulations of an Emerging Market," Brookings, August 1987, pp. 11–12.

6. The discussion in this section was drawn from Joshua M. Wiener, Deborah A. Ehrenworth, and Denise A. Spence, "Private Long-Term Care Insurance: Cost, Coverage and Restrictions," *Gerontologist,* vol. 27 (August 1987), pp. 487–93.

7. Esther Hing, "Use of Nursing Homes by the Elderly: Preliminary Data from the 1985 National Nursing Home Survey," *Vital and Health Statistics* (advance data), no. 135 (Hyattsville, Md.: National Center for Health Statistics, DHHS, May 14, 1987).

8. Brookings-ICF Long-Term Care Financing Model.

9. Group Health Cooperative of Puget Sound (a large health maintenance organization) has contracted with Metropolitan Life of New York to offer a service benefit long-term care insurance policy to Group Health's older members. Mark Stensager, Group Health Cooperative of Puget Sound, "Draft Long-Term Care Security Care Plan," paper presented at the 33d Annual Meeting of the American Society on Aging, Salt Lake City, Utah, March 15, 1987; and Lynn Wagner, "Seattle HMO, Insurer Offer Long-Term Care Option," *Modern Healthcare,* April 10, 1987, p. 92. Blue Cross of Washington and Alaska has offered a policy since July 1986 that pays the usual, customary, and reasonable rates set by the insurance company with either 80 percent or 100 percent coverage. David D. Strachan, "Long-Term Care Financing Products," paper presented at the Private Long Term Care Insurance Conference on the Maturing Market, San Antonio, Texas, January 13–14, 1987.

10. Even a majority (53.3 percent) of low-income (up to twice the poverty level) elderly had private insurance in addition to medicare in 1977. Gail Lee Cafferata, "Private Health Insurance Coverage of the Medicare Population," in National Center for Health Services Research, *National Health Care Expenditures Study: Data Preview 18,* (PHS) 84-3362 (Rockville, Md.: DHHS, September 1984), p. 6.

11. More than 70 percent of purchasers of the AARP-Prudential insurance policy cited "security, protection, precaution" as the main reason for buying. Data Group, "Long Term Care Study (Wave II)," Draft 2, survey conducted for AARP and Prudential, Elkins Park, Pa., April 1987, p. 13. The Blue Cross and Blue Shield survey reported that 42 percent cited financial security as the primary reason for buying insurance; the second most frequently cited reason was to protect savings. Results of the survey are presented in Strachan, "Long-Term Care Financing Products." "To assure having a choice in the type of care and place where it is received," "avoidance of the need to depend on family for support," "assurance of receiving all needed care," and "protection of income and assets" were cited most frequently in the medicare supplemental policyholder survey as the most important reasons for wanting to buy long-term care insurance. Mark R. Meiners and Arlene K. Tave, "Consumer Interest in Long-Term Care Insurance: A Survey of the Elderly in Six States," NCHSR, Rockville, Md., December 7, 1984, p. 12.

12. AARP, "Long-Term Care Research Study," Washington, D.C., January 30, 1984, p. 3. Morris and others found that more than 40 percent of the elderly respondents of the Massachusetts survey expressed interest in purchasing long-term care insurance to cover services either in the home or in high-quality institutions. John N. Morris and others, "Interest in Long-Term Care Insurance," paper prepared for HCFA, Hebrew Rehabilitation Center for Aged, Department of Social Gerontological Research, Boston, Mass., June 1987, pp. 17–18. A 1982 survey of medicare supplemental insurance policyholders showed that 70 percent of respondents expressed some interest in buying a long-term

care insurance policy; 28 percent said they would be very likely to purchase such a policy. Meiners and Tave, "Consumer Interest in Long-Term Care Insurance," p. 13. The Blue Cross and Blue Shield survey of people aged 40 and over found that 55 percent of them said they would be likely to purchase long-term care insurance. See Strachan, "Long-Term Care Financing Products."

13. ICF Inc., *The Role of Medicare in Financing the Health Care of Older Americans,* report prepared for AARP (Washington, D.C., July 1985), p. 26. ICF estimates that in 1985 the noninstitutionalized elderly already spent an average of 12 percent of their income on health care. Ibid., p. 36.

14. The Congressional Budget Office estimated that the average medicare supplemental policy cost $542 in 1987. Sandra Christensen, Stephen H. Long, and Jack Rodgers, "Acute Health Care Costs for the Aged Medicare Population: Overview and Policy Options," CBO, Washington, D.C., May 1987, p. 22.

15. In a survey of medicare supplemental policyholders, almost half (48.2 percent) of the respondents cited "can't afford insurance" as the most important reason for not purchasing long-term care insurance. Meiners and Tave, "Consumer Interest in Long-Term Care Insurance," table 18. Seventeen percent of nonbuyers of the AARP-Prudential policy from the direct mail marketing group and 53 percent of nonbuyers from those inquiring about the policy said they did not buy the policy because it was "too expensive, can't afford it." Data Group, "Long Term Care Study (Wave II)," p. 13. Meiners and Tave found that interest in purchasing long-term care insurance was lower among persons with lower income and assets. Mark R. Meiners and Arlene K. Tave, "Predicting the Determinants of Demand for Long-Term Care Insurance," draft, NCHSR, Rockville, Md., December 7, 1984, p. 9. Morris and others found that the relatively more affluent elderly were more interested in long-term care insurance than those who had low incomes and those who received supplemental security income or medicaid. Morris and others, "Interest in Long-Term Care Insurance," p. 22.

16. About 62 percent of the respondents of the survey of medicare supplemental policyholders said in 1982 that they could afford to pay $30 or less a month for insurance. Meiners and Tave, "Consumer Interest in Long-Term Care Insurance," table 20. In the Massachusetts survey, 78 percent of the elderly interested in long-term care insurance said they could afford to pay $25 a month for such coverage, and the rest indicated that $25 was too much. Morris and others, "Interest in Long-Term Care Insurance," p. 31.

17. When asked to choose between a cheaper plan that covers only nursing home care and a plan that was 50 percent more expensive but covered both nursing home and home health care, 65 percent of those questioned in the survey of medicare supplemental insurance policyholders chose the plan that included home health. Almost half of those surveyed said they would still prefer the home health plan even if premiums were twice as high as the nursing home only plan. Meiners and Tave, "Consumer Interest in Long-Term Care Insurance," pp. 14–15. A survey of AARP's membership also showed a strong preference for plans that covered home care, with 80 percent of survey respondents preferring long-term home health care to long-term nursing home care. AARP, "Long-Term Care Research Study," p. 2.

18. Fifty-five percent of nonbuyers of the AARP-Prudential long-term care insurance policy indicated that "lack of need" was the main reason for not purchasing. It is unclear whether this response means that they are strongly denying the possibility of ever using services, whether they believe they can afford to pay for long-term care without insurance, or whether they think they

already have insurance coverage. Data Group, "Long Term Care Study (Wave II)," p. 13.

19. Analysis of the survey of medicare supplemental policyholders in 1982 showed that 15 percent considered the risk of needing long-term care very likely for themselves. Meiners and Tave, "Consumer Interest in Long-Term Care Insurance," p. 9. Among a sample of AARP members, less than 1 percent had been in a nursing home in the past five years, and only 5 percent had used home health services in the past five years. AARP, "Long-Term Care Research Study," p. 2. A survey of retirees and current employees conducted by Equicor found that 55 percent of retirees had thought about the possibility of needing to enter a nursing home, but only 21 percent had given it "a lot of thought." That same survey found that only 15 percent of retirees and 3 percent of employees had seriously considered how they would pay for nursing home care if they needed it. Equicor, *The Equicor Health Care Survey–VI: Looking to the Future of Retiree Health Benefits* (New York, June–August 1986), pp. 47–50.

20. Results from test marketing of the AARP-Prudential long-term care product found that more direct mail buyers than nonbuyers (43 percent versus 25 percent) had a relative or friend in a nursing home. Data Group, "Long Term Care Study (Wave II)," p. 17.

21. Elaine M. Brody, "Parent Care as a Normative Family Stress," *Gerontologist,* vol. 25 (February 1985), pp. 19–29.

22. A telephone survey of 1,000 registered voters in 1987 found that 60 percent of respondents had had some experience with the need for long-term care, and of those without experience 20 percent expected a long-term care problem in their families within the next five years. R L Associates, *The American Public Views Long Term Care,* survey conducted for AARP and the Villers Foundation (Princeton, N.J., October 1987), p. 5.

23. AARP, "Long-Term Care Research Study," p. 3.

24. Thirty-five percent of the AARP members surveyed believed their current private insurance policies covered extended nursing home stays, but these were with companies that AARP was certain did not cover such care. Ibid., pp. 3–4. Among medicare supplemental insurance policyholders not interested in buying long-term care insurance, 38 percent felt that medicare and other insurance would adequately cover long-term care costs. Meiners and Tave, "Consumer Interest in Long-Term Care Insurance," p. 12. In a survey of the elderly, 23 percent reported incorrectly that private insurance would pay for nursing home costs, and 15 percent believed that medicare would pay. Louis Harris and Associates, *Problems Facing Elderly Americans Living Alone,* a national survey conducted for the Commonwealth Fund Commission on Elderly People Living Alone (New York, 1986), p. 42. In the Equicor survey, 10 percent of retirees and 24 percent of employees believed that employer-provided insurance would cover nursing home costs, and 15 percent of retirees and 13 percent of employees believed that medicare would cover those costs. Equicor, *Equicor Health Care Survey–VI,* p. 50. In the Blue Cross and Blue Shield survey, 49 percent of all respondents incorrectly believed they were covered for long-term care expenses. Among retirees, 54 percent believed they were already covered, many expecting medicare to pay the bill. Terri Gendel, David Strachan, and Peter Lopatin, "Blue Cross and Blue Shield Association Long-Term Care Project," Blue Cross and Blue Shield, Chicago, Ill., December 1986, p. 5. Most recently, the AARP-Villers survey reported that 11 percent of a sample of

registered voters aged 65 and over said medicare covered "most but not all nursing home care," 4 percent said it covered "all nursing home care whenever needed," and 34 percent did not know. R L Associates, *American Public Views Long Term Care,* p. 7.

25. Health Insurance Association of America, *Long Term Care: The Challenge to Society* (Washington, D.C., 1984), p. 4.

26. A survey of retirees and employees found that only 3 percent believed medicaid would pay for nursing home costs. Equicor, *Equicor Health Care Survey–VI,* p. 50. Another survey of the elderly had the same results. Louis Harris and Associates, *Problems Facing Elderly Americans Living Alone,* p. 42. Only 19 percent of medicare supplemental policyholders responded that they would not purchase private long-term care insurance, because they thought medicaid and other welfare coverage were adequate. Meiners and Tave, "Consumer Interest in Long-Term Care Insurance," p. 13.

27. Survey data from HIAA indicate that the private insurance industry experienced net underwriting losses from 1965 to 1979, with the exception of net gains in 1972 and 1973. In 1979 the industry experienced a $1.4 billion net underwriting loss. This trend continued because companies set premium rates lower than costs to prevent losing business from large corporations and unions. Moreover, companies subsidized health insurance through other lines of insurance and through investment income earned on premium dollars. Marjorie Smith Carroll and Ross H. Arnett III, "Private Health Insurance Plans in 1978 and 1979: A Review of Coverage, Enrollment, and Financial Experience," *Health Care Financing Review,* vol. 3 (September 1981), p. 70.

28. The AARP-Prudential long-term care insurance policy obtained approval to be sold in fifty states in 1987. Gary Claxton, insurance issues analyst, AARP, personal communication, August 3, 1987.

29. For discussion of long-term care insurability, see Arthur Lifson, "A View from the Private Sector," in Mal Schechter, ed., *Long-Term Care Insurance: If Not Now, When?* (New York: Mount Sinai Medical Center, April 21, 1983), pp. 20–21; and HIAA, *Long Term Care,* pp. 5–6.

30. NCHS, *Health, United States: 1984,* (PHS) 85-1232 (Hyattsville, Md.: DHHS, December 1984), p. 30.

31. Deductibles and coinsurance prevent moral hazard by requiring an out-of-pocket expense, which may make people more reluctant to use services. For example, Link and others concluded that medicare cost-sharing for acute care services, in the absence of private or public supplementation, reduces use of medical services and thus costs to the program. Charles R. Link, Stephen H. Long, and Russell F. Settle, "Cost Sharing, Supplementary Insurance, and Health Services Utilization among the Medicare Elderly," *Health Care Financing Review,* vol. 2 (Fall 1980), p. 30.

32. Wiener and others, "Private Long-Term Care Insurance."

33. NAIC, *Long Term Care Insurance,* p. 16.

34. Laurence F. Lane, "Shaping Long Term Care Insurance in the States," *American Health Care Association Journal,* vol. 11 (October 1985), p. 25.

35. NAIC, *Long Term Care Insurance,* p. iv.

36. Wiener and others, "Private Long-Term Care Insurance," p. 492.

37. Technical Work Group on Private Financing of Long-Term Care for the Elderly, *Report to the Secretary on Private Financing of Long-Term Care for the Elderly* (Washington D.C.: DHHS, November 1986), pp. 220–21.

38. John E. Wennberg, "Dealing with Medical Practice Variations: A

Proposal for Action," *Health Affairs,* vol. 3 (Summer 1984), pp. 6–32; and John E. Wennberg, "Population Illness Rates Do Not Explain Population Hospitalization Rates," *Medical Care,* vol. 25 (April 1987), pp. 354–59.

39. Howard N. Fullerton, "Labor Force Projections, 1986 to 2000," *Monthly Labor Review,* vol. 110 (September 1987), pp. 24–25; and Deborah Chollet, Employee Benefit Research Institute, "Employer Sponsored Retiree Health Insurance Plans: Benefits, Entitlements, Funding and Potential Effects of Regulation," testimony before House Select Committee on Aging, Washington, D.C., July 24, 1987, p. 2.

40. Burton E. Burton, Aetna Life and Casualty, personal communication, March 5, 1986.

41. Burton E. Burton, "Statement of the Health Insurance Association of America on the Financing of Long Term Care," testimony before the Subcommittee on Health, Senate Committee on Finance, Washington, D.C., June 12, 1987, p. 5; Travelers Corporation, "Long-Term Care Insurance Plan Now Available to Large Corporate Customers," news release, Hartford, Conn., December 17, 1986. These policies are not true group policies because not everyone in the group is enrolled. More precisely, they are individual insurance policies sold in group settings.

42. Letter to authors from Susan Van Gelder, associate director, Research and Policy Division, HIAA, November 23, 1987; and Burton, "Statement of the Health Insurance Association of America on the Financing of Long Term Care," p. 5.

43. U.S. Office of Personnel Management, "Long-Term Care Insurance: A National Need . . . A Response," news release, Washington, D.C., September 1987.

44. Surveys show that about 30 percent of all employers and 77 percent of large employers have expressed interest in offering long-term care insurance in the next five years. Of these, most are interested in entirely employee- or retiree-paid policies. Washington Business Group on Health, *The Corporate Perspective on Long Term Care: Survey Report* (Washington D.C., December 1987); and David D. Strachan, director of product development, Blue Cross and Blue Shield Association, Chicago, personal communication, May 20, 1987.

45. Letter to the authors from Robert Friedland, research associate, Employee Benefit Research Institute, Washington, D.C., November 23, 1987.

46. Chollet estimates that in 1984, 21 percent of the elderly aged 65 and over were covered by an employer-sponsored retiree health plan. Chollet, "Employer Sponsored Retiree Health Insurance Plans," p. 2. Short and Monheit estimate that 31 percent of the elderly enrolled in medicare in 1983 were covered by an employer-sponsored retiree health plan. Pamela Farley Short and Alan C. Monheit, "Employers and Medicare as Partners in Financing Health Care for the Elderly," NCHSR, Rockville, Md., December 1987, p. 3. See also Anna M. Rappaport and Robert W. Kalman, "The Future of Employer-Sponsored Retiree Medical Plans," *Inquiry,* vol. 24 (Spring 1987), p. 27.

47. Jay N. Greenberg, Don S. Westwater, and Walter N. Leutz, "Long-Term Care Insurance: How Will It Sell?" *Business and Health,* vol. 3 (November 1986), p. 26; and Bert Seidman, director, Occupational Safety, Health, and Social Security Department, AFL-CIO, personal communication, February 25, 1985.

48. Equicor, *Equicor Health Care Survey–VI,* p. 51.

49. After examining the possibility of immediately insuring retirees against the cost of long-term care, Harvard University found that it could not afford

a plan it had devised. This plan, which would have covered 80 percent of nursing home or home health care costs for retirees and their spouses, would have cost about 5 percent of the university's annual payroll expenses. Katherine S. Mangan, "Cost of Providing Long-Term Health Care for Retirees Too Expensive, Harvard Finds," *Chronicle of Higher Education,* February 25, 1987, pp. 14, 16.

50. These estimates assume that reserves are allowed to accumulate on a tax-free basis. If the reserves were taxed, the premiums would be substantially higher, especially for policies issued at age 30. Technical Work Group on Private Financing of Long-Term Care for the Elderly, *Report to the Secretary,* chap. 3, table 18 and p. 231.

51. Leading cases on both sides are summarized in U.S. Department of Labor, Office of Policy and Research, Pension and Welfare Benefits Administration, "Employer-Sponsored Retiree Health Insurance," Washington, D.C., May 1986, pp. 22–32. See also T. Timothy Ryan, Jr., "Overview of an Employer's Right to Modify Health and Welfare Benefits for Active and Retired Employees," Pierson, Ball and Dowd, Washington, D.C., paper accompanying testimony of Willis B. Goldbeck, president, Washington Business Group on Health, in *Retiree Health Benefits: The Fair-Weather Promise,* Hearing before the Senate Special Committee on Aging, 99 Cong. 2 sess. (Washington, D.C., August 7, 1986), pp. 51–54.

52. Department of Labor, "Employer-Sponsored Retiree Health Insurance," p. 35.

53. The current liability of RCA for retiree health benefits is 1 percent to 2 percent of payroll. Assuming no prefunding, this liability is projected to grow to more than 20 percent over the next twenty years. Testimony of Willis B. Goldbeck in *Retiree Health Benefits,* Hearing, p. 42. In 1984 the Financial Accounting Standards Board adopted an interim rule effective in 1985 that required publicly traded companies to disclose annual retiree health and welfare benefits with their yearly financial statement. See Task Force on Long-Term Health Care Policies, *Report to Congress and the Secretary,* p. 137. The board is developing more comprehensive accounting rules that are expected to be released in 1988. Rappaport and Kalman, "Future of Employer-Sponsored Retiree Medical Plans," p. 30.

54. For example, by 1985 RCA had $180 million in a fund to pay for future retiree medical benefits. As a result of the Deficit Reduction Act of 1984, the company paid $6 million in taxes in the first year, which was 50 percent of its entire retiree health benefit costs for the year. Testimony of Willis B. Goldbeck in *Retiree Health Benefits*, Hearing, p. 42. See also Department of Labor, "Employer-Sponsored Retiree Health Insurance," p. 38; and Rappaport and Kalman, "Future of Employer-Sponsored Retiree Medical Plans," pp. 29–30.

55. See Department of Labor, "Employer-Sponsored Retiree Health Insurance," p. 39; and Employee Benefit Research Insitute, "Employer-Paid Retiree Health Insurance: History and Prospects for Growth," Issue Brief 47, Washington, D.C., October 1985, pp. 5–8.

56. Debra J. Lipson, "State Legislation and Regulations Related to Long-Term Care Insurance," *Focus on . . . ,* no. 15 (Washington D.C.: Intergovernmental Health Policy Project, February 1987), p. 4.

57. Marilu Halamandaris, "The Medi-Scare Insurance Scandal," *Caring,* vol. 4 (March 1985), pp. 42–46; and Val Halamandaris, "Editor's Note," ibid., p. 42.

58. Helen Darling, "Private Long-Term Care Insurance: A Summary of a

Government Research Corporation Roundtable," Government Research Corporation, Washington, D.C., July 17, 1985, p. 9.

59. Lipson, "State Legislation and Regulations Related to Long-Term Care Insurance," pp. 4–5.

60. NAIC, *Long-Term Care Insurance,* pp. 205–10.

61. James Knickman and others, *Increasing Private Financing of Long-Term Care: Opportunities for Collaborative Action* (Menlo Park, Calif.: SRI International, March 1986), pp. 33–34; and NAIC, *Long-Term Care Insurance,* pp. 26–27 and app. H. For example, until the law was modified in 1987, Wisconsin required that policies cover care in all licensed Wisconsin nursing homes, a benefit that far exceeds the coverage of existing policies. See Wisconsin Department of Health and Social Services, "Long-Term Care Financing: The Role of Private Insurance," Document Digest, Madison, Wis., December 28, 1984, p. 10. Similarly, Kentucky prohibits any prior hospitalization requirement to qualify for nursing home or home care benefits. Lipson, "State Legislation and Regulations Related to Long-Term Care Insurance," p. 11.

62. NAIC, *Long-Term Care Insurance,* pp. 208–09. The model act does not allow definitions of preexisting disease to be more restrictive than the following: those symptoms for which medical advice or treatment was sought or for which a reasonable person would have sought treatment, and symptoms that must have been present twelve months preceding the date of coverage for persons 65 and over and twenty-four months for persons under 65. Insurers can exclude coverage for preexisting conditions beginning within twelve months following date of coverage for those 65 and older and within twenty-four months for those under 65. The model act does not allow benefits that require prior institutionalization to be dependent on receiving services within a period of less than fourteen days after discharge from the institution. Prior institutionalization requirements are not allowed to depend on admission to a facility for the same or related condition of the prior institutionalization. Ibid.

63. In a six-state survey in 1985, Kirsch and Robertson found that regulators in four states were applying minimum-loss ratio requirements in the range of 50 percent to 65 percent. Lawrence J. Kirsch and Peter Robertson, "A Preliminary Reconnaissance of Long-Term Care Insurance," report to Commissioner Peter Hiam, Division of Insurance, Commonweath of Massachusetts (Boston, Mass.: Consumer Health Advocates, March 1985), p. 28. In an eight-state survey, Knickman and others found that two states were using medicare supplemental insurance standards as a basis for setting long-term care insurance loss ratios (60 percent for individual policies and 75 percent for group policies). Standards in most states were in the 50 percent to 60 percent range. Knickman and others, *Increasing Private Financing of Long-Term Care,* pp. 33–34; and NAIC, *Long-Term Care Insurance,* p. 27.

64. Carol C. Oviatt, "Private Health Insurance Coverage for Long-Term Care Services," Institute for Health Planning, Madison, Wis., December 1983, p. 12; and Lawrence J. Kirsch, "Highlights of the Massachusetts Survey of Long-Term Care Insurance Regulation," Consumer Health Advocates, Boston, Mass., December 12, 1985, p. 12.

65. NAIC, *Long-Term Care Insurance,* pp. 26–28.

66. Ibid., p. 208.

67. This section is partly drawn from Rubin and others, "Private Long Term Care Insurance."

68. Unpublished Bureau of Labor Statistics data supplied by William Parks, February 25, 1988.

69. Technical Work Group on Private Financing of Long-Term Care for the Elderly, *Report to the Secretary,* chap. 3, table 18.

70. Ibid.

71. For discussion of these issues see Burton, "Statement of the Health Insurance Association of America on the Financing of Long Term Care," p. 9; Mary Nell Lehnhard, "Testimony of the Blue Cross and Blue Shield Association on Long Term Care," testimony before the Subcommittee on Health, Senate Committee on Finance, Washington, D.C., June 12, 1987, p. 11; and Robert Maxwell, "Statement of the American Association of Retired Persons on Long Term Care Financing," testimony before the Subcommittee on Health, Senate Committee on Finance, Washington, D.C., June 12, 1987, p. 6.

Chapter 5

1. A few studies of environments similar to CCRCs have attempted to measure how such campus living affects the quality of life. Like CCRCs, the housing arrangements that were studied offer peer living and some shared services. Sherwood and others found that both medically oriented congregate housing and foster-type home care arrangements with case management have positive effects on the quality of life. Sylvia J. Sherwood, John N. Morris, and Clarence C. Sherwood, "Supportive Living Arrangements and Their Consequences," in Robert J. Newcomer, M. Powell Lawton, and Thomas O. Byerts, eds., *Housing an Aging Society: Issues, Alternatives, and Policy* (Van Nostrand Reinhold, 1986), pp. 104–15. Residents in these settings scored better than comparison groups with respect to emotional status, satisfaction with the living arrangements, and participation in activities. Other positive quality-of-life effects of semi-shared housing reported by Streib and Hilker are a sense of independence and of belonging to a community. Gordon F. Streib and Mary Anne Hilker, "The Cooperative 'Family,'" *Alternative Lifestyles,* vol. 3 (May 1980), p. 170. If a CCRC resident must use the community's health and nursing home facilities, having these services on campus may reduce the negative effects of relocating from familiar surroundings. Lawton found that relocation, especially involuntary relocation because of health or income problems, negatively affects the health of the rehoused. M. Powell Lawton, *Environment and Aging* (Monterey, Calif.: Brooks Cole, 1980). But other studies of moving the elderly into nursing homes show mixed results and often no negative effects. Jerry H. Borup, "Relocation Mortality Research: Assessment, Reply, and the Need to Refocus on the Issues," *Gerontologist,* vol. 23 (June 1983), pp. 235–42.

2. Sherwood and others found that, compared with a control group, residents in foster-type home care arrangements were more likely to have their service needs met. They also found that shared housing arrangements reduced nursing home care of elderly residents. Sherwood and others, "Supportive Living Arrangements," pp. 108, 112.

3. American Association of Homes for the Aging, *Continuing Care Retirement Communities: An Industry in Action* (Washington, D.C., 1987), p. 5; and Howard E. Winklevoss and Alwyn V. Powell, *Continuing Care Retirement Communities: An Empirical, Financial, and Legal Analysis* (Homewood, Ill.: Richard D. Irwin, 1984), p. 47.

4. Winklevoss and Powell, *Continuing Care Retirement Communities: An*

Empirical, Financial, and Legal Analysis, p. 30; and Susan Brecht and Michael J. Fogel, "The Proprietary Lifecare Community Comes of Age," in Laventhol and Horwath, *Fourth Annual Report on the Lifecare Industry in the United States* (Philadelphia, Pa., 1984), pp. 6–7.

5. Eileen J. Tell and others, "Assessing the Elderly's Preferences for Lifecare Retirement Options," *Gerontologist,* vol. 27 (August 1987), pp. 503–09.

6. AAHA, *Continuing Care Retirement Communities: An Industry in Action,* pp. 5–24 (AAHA–Ernst and Whinney Study); and Winklevoss and Powell, *Continuing Care Retirement Communities: An Empirical, Financial, and Legal Analysis,* p. 22 (Wharton School study).

7. Harvey E. Pies, "Life Care Communities for the Aged: An Overview," in Patrice H. Feinstein, Marian Gornick, and Jay N. Greenberg, eds., *Long-Term Care Financing and Delivery Systems: Exploring Some Alternatives* (Washington, D.C.: Health Care Financing Administration, January 24, 1984), pp. 41–52; and James F. Sherman, "An Introduction to Lifecare Industry, 1984," in Laventhol and Horwath, *Fourth Annual Report on the Lifecare Industry,* p. 2.

8. Lloyd W. Lewis, "Long-Term Care for the Elderly," testimony before the Subcommittee on Health and the Environment, House Committee on Energy and Commerce, Washington, D.C., October 18, 1985, p. 8; and Winklevoss and Powell, *Continuing Care Retirement Communities: An Empirical, Financial, and Legal Analysis,* p. 12.

9. AAHA, *Continuing Care Retirement Communities: An Industry in Action,* p. 17. Because the fees reported in the AAHA–Ernst and Whinney survey were for 1986, we inflated them to 1987 dollars using our projected annual long-term care inflation rate of 5.8 percent.

10. Ibid., p. 19.

11. Refundable entry fees may have a limited future in light of a pending Internal Revenue Service ruling. The Deficit Reduction Act of 1984 (DEFRA) made imputed interest income on below-market-rate loans taxable. The provision was meant to curb abuses of intrafamily transfers of large amounts of money through interest-free loans designed to avoid full taxation of income. Although rules were never promulgated, the IRS announced its intent to consider refundable entry fees to be below-market loans to the CCRC. Thus the provision would make residents pay income taxes on imputed interest on refundable entry fees, even though no interest payments are actually received and even though the entry fee may not be refunded. CCRCs opposed this tax provision because refundability is quite attractive to potential residents and taxing such fees could hurt marketing efforts. "Life Care Gets Break on Imputed Interest," in *Long-Term Care Management* (Washington, D.C.: McGraw-Hill Health Care Management Center, June 1985), p. 3; and AAHA, "Application of Section 7872 to Entry Fees of Continuing Care Retirement Communities," comments submitted to the Internal Revenue Service, October 21, 1985, p. 8. In 1985 an amendment to DEFRA (P.L. 99-121) clarified that refundable entry fees of up to $90,000 to qualifying CCRCs were exempt from taxation. However, as of February 1988 the Internal Revenue Service had not published final rules indicating whether any entry fees will be subject to any imputed interest provisions. Valerie Wilbur, assistant director for corporate planning, AAHA, personal communication, February 12, 1988.

12. AAHA, *Continuing Care Retirement Communities: An Industry in Action,* p. 17.

13. For discussions of refundable entry fees, see AAHA, "Applications of

Section 7872 to Entry Fees," p. 8; Pies, "Life Care Communities for the Aged," p. 43; Winklevoss and Powell, *Continuing Care Retirement Communities: An Empirical, Financial, and Legal Analysis,* p. 42; and AAHA, *Continuing Care Retirement Communities: An Industry in Action,* pp. 17–18. According to the 1986 AAHA–Ernst and Whinney survey, facilities opened after 1984 or then under construction were shifting away from declining refunds and toward full or partial unconditional refunds.

14. AAHA, *Continuing Care Retirement Communities: An Industry in Action,* pp. 18–19. Because the fees reported in the AAHA–Ernst and Whinney survey were for 1986, we inflated them to 1987 dollars using our projected annual long-term care inflation rate of 5.8 percent.

15. Pies, "Life Care Communities for the Aged"; Sherman, "Introduction to Lifecare Industry 1984," p. 2; and AAHA, *Continuing Care Retirement Communities: An Industry in Action,* p. 40.

16. Christine E. Bishop, "Use of Nursing Care in Continuing Care Communities," Brandeis University, Health Policy Center, May 1985, p. 14.

17. Christine E. Bishop, "Design of Low-Cost Continuing Care Retirement Communities: Learning from Cost Analysis," Brandeis University, Health Policy Center, March 1985, p. 33.

18. Alwyn Powell, consulting actuary, Tillinghast/Tower Perrin, Atlanta, personal communication, December 18, 1987.

19. Winklevoss and Powell, *Continuing Care Retirement Communities: An Empirical, Financial, and Legal Analysis,* p. 62.

20. According to the AAHA–Ernst and Whinney survey, for 35 percent of CCRCs the length of time on a waiting list for a one-bedroom unit was a year or more. Only 24 percent of facilities had one-bedroom units immediately available. Waiting time for a two-bedroom unit was even longer. AAHA, *Continuing Care Retirement Communities: An Industry in Action,* p. 30. See also Randall A. Smith and Aaron M. Rose, "The Lifecare Industry—1984," in Laventhol and Horwath, *Fourth Annual Report on the Lifecare Industry,* p. 18.

21. Valerie Wilbur, personal communication, January 15, 1987; and John Goodwin, director, EMA Management Inc., subsidiary of Fairhaven Lifecare Community, Sykesville, Maryland, personal communication, February 3, 1987.

22. Winklevoss and Powell, *Continuing Care Retirement Communities: An Empirical, Financial, and Legal Analysis,* pp. 27, 62, 51.

23. Statutes in both Illinois and Connecticut limit the ability of CCRC residents to qualify for medicaid benefits. Ibid., p. 253.

24. The AAHA–Ernst and Whinney data base shows an increase in the proportion of residents over age 82 in 1986, as compared with data on CCRC residents collected in 1982 by the Wharton School. AAHA, *Continuing Care Retirement Communities: An Industry in Action,* pp. 27–30.

25. Tell and others, "Assessing the Elderly's Preferences for Lifecare Retirement Options," p. 506; and Maria B. Dwight, "Affluent Elderly Want to Live Where Quality Care's Readily Available," *Modern Healthcare,* April 26, 1985, pp. 74–76.

26. Tell and others, "Assessing the Elderly's Preferences for Lifecare Retirement Options," p. 506.

27. American Association of Retired Persons, *Understanding Senior Housing: An American Association of Retired Persons Survey of Consumers' Preferences, Concerns, and Needs* (Washington D.C., n.d.), p. 22; and Steven F. Venti and David A. Wise, "Aging, Moving, and Housing Wealth," Working Paper 2324 (Cambridge, Mass.: National Bureau of Economic Research, July 1987), p. 4.

28. Pies, "Life Care Communities for the Aged," p. 44.

29. Even Winklevoss found that of the fifteen communities he studied, half were not financially sound. Howard E. Winklevoss, "Continuing Care Retirement Communities: Issues in Financial Management and Actuarial Prediction," in Ian A. Morrison and others, eds., *Continuing Care Retirement Communities: Political, Social, and Financial Issues* (New York: Haworth Press, 1986), p. 58. Piecing together data from a variety of sources, Topolnicki reported that at least forty communities have had financial problems since the mid-1970s, about 10 percent to 20 percent of the remaining CCRCs have defaulted on their debts, and about 14 percent are failing to meet projected occupancy rates. Denise M. Topolnicki, "The Broken Promise of Life-Care Communities," *Money,* April 1985, pp. 150–57.

30. Hirsch S. Ruchlin, "Are CCRCs Facing a Promising Future or Potential Problems?" *Healthcare Financial Management,* vol. 41 (October 1987), p. 56.

31. Robert Ball, visiting scholar, Center for the Study of Social Policy, Washington, D.C., personal communication, November 15, 1987.

32. "Maintaining Reserves," in Lois Jenkins Wasser and Deborah A. Cloud, eds., *Continuing Care: Issues for Nonprofit Providers* (Washington, D.C.: AAHA, 1980), pp. 73–75.

33. Letter to the authors from Valerie Wilbur, December 17, 1987.

34. David L. Cohen, "Legal Regulations of the Continuing Care Retirement Community Industry as a Whole," in Morrison and others, eds., *Continuing Care Retirement Communities: Political, Social, and Financial Issues,* p. 38. In New York state nursing home operators are prohibited by law from entering into "lifecare" contracts or accepting prepayment for services for more than three months. In New York it is recognized that the legislation was intended to prohibit a certain type of financially risky CCRC, that the legislation is outdated, and that it eventually will be changed. Lloyd Nurick, "The Prospect for the Future of Continuing Care Retirement Communities in New York State," in ibid., pp. 115–20.

35. Areas of regulation include language regarding definitions, reserve requirements, refund provisions, rights of residents to self-organize, registration and certification by relevant state authorities, financial disclosure to residents, form and content of contract agreement, resident contract termination rights, regulation of advertising, and state agency responsible for overseeing regulation. AAHA, *Current Status of State Regulation of Continuing Care Retirement Communities* (Washington D.C., May 1987), p. 1.

36. In 1983 the FTC issued an order against Christian Services Inc., a proprietary corporation involved in the management of fifty lifecare facilities, which required adequate disclosure to prospective residents of the financial risks in contracting for life care. Alpha Center, "Long-Term Care Alternatives: Continuing Care Retirement Communities," in *Alpha Centerpiece* (Bethesda, Md., January 1984), p. 3.

37. The CCAC's evaluation includes a review of the financial position of candidates, among other criteria. Continuing Care Accreditation Commission, *Information Guide and Standards* (Washington, D.C.: AAHA, January 1987). As of December 1987, the CCAC had accredited twenty-seven communities and is scheduled to evaluate fifty new facilities in 1988. Letter to the authors from Valerie Wilbur, December 17, 1987.

38. To encourage CCRCs, New Jersey exempts them from its certificate-of-need review. Alpha Center, "Long-Term Care Alternatives," pp. 3, 5.

39. Rep. Doug Walgren of Pennsylvania, "Legislation to Protect Elderly Residents of Life Care Homes," *Congressional Record,* April 15, 1985, pp. E1449–51.

40. Age 76 was the average age of entry in the Winklevoss and Powell study. Winklevoss and Powell, *Continuing Care Retirement Communities: An Empirical, Financial, and Legal Analysis,* p. 101.

41. For example, 42 percent of CCRCs with "all-inclusive" contracts cover one meal a day in the facility, and 36 percent cover three meals a day. AAHA, *Continuing Care Retirement Communities: An Industry in Action,* p. 19.

42. This is a generous assumption in light of the results of a national survey showing that 85 percent of elderly people disagreed with the statement, "What I'd really like to do is move from here," and 70 percent agreed with the statement, "What I'd really like to do is stay in my home and never move." AARP, *Understanding Senior Housing,* p. 22.

43. ICF Inc., *Private Financing of Long-Term Care: Current Methods and Resources, Phase I,* Final Report to the Assistant Secretary for Planning and Evaluation, Department of Health and Human Services (Washington, D.C., June 1984), p. 74.

44. Marc A. Cohen and others, "The Financial Capacity of the Elderly to Insure for Long-Term Care," *Gerontologist,* vol. 27 (August 1987), pp. 494–502.

45. Winklevoss and Powell, *Continuing Care Retirement Communities: An Empirical, Financial, and Legal Analysis,* p. 253.

46. AAHA, *Continuing Care Retirement Communities: An Industry in Action,* p. 20.

Chapter 6

1. Harold S. Luft, *Health Maintenance Organizations: Dimensions of Performance* (John Wiley and Sons, 1981), pp. 1–10.

2. Margaret Stassen and John Holahan, *A Comparative Analysis of Long-Term Care Demonstrations and Evaluations,* draft report prepared for the Administration on Aging (Washington, D.C.: Urban Institute, 1980), pp. 193–94; Brenda Haskins and others, *Evaluation of Coordinated Community-Oriented Long-Term Care Demonstration Projects,* report prepared for the Health Care Financing Administration (Berkeley, Calif.: Berkeley Planning Associates, May 1985), pp. 284–85; Judith R. Lave, "Cost Containment Policies in Long-Term Care," *Inquiry,* vol. 22 (Spring 1985), p. 20; John A. Capitman, "Community-based Long-Term Care Models, Target Groups, and Impacts on Service Use," *Gerontologist,* vol. 26 (August 1986), p. 396; John A. Capitman, Brenda Haskins, and Judith Bernstein, "Case Management Approaches in Community-Oriented Long-Term Care Demonstrations," *Gerontologist,* vol. 26 (August 1986), p. 403; Peter Kemper, Robert Applebaum, and Margaret Harrigan, "Community Care Demonstrations: What Have We Learned?" *Health Care Financing Review,* vol. 8 (Summer 1987), pp. 87–100; and Craig Thornton and Shari Miller Dunstan, *The Evaluation of the National Long-Term Care Demonstration: Analysis of the Benefits and Costs of Channeling,* report prepared for the Department of Health and Human Services (Princeton, N.J.: Mathematica Policy Research, May 1986), pp. xiii, 121–27.

3. Judith Wooldridge and Jenifer Schore, *Evaluation of the National Long-*

Term Care Demonstration: Channeling Effects on Hospital, Nursing Home, and Other Medical Services, report prepared for DHHS (Princeton, N.J.: Mathematica Policy Research, May 1986), p. xvii.

4. The Channeling demonstration tested two different case management models. The basic model, which did not offer a significant expansion of home care, increased total costs by 6 percent per client above the costs that would be expected without case management. The financial control model, which offered significantly more home care services, increased total costs by 18 percent over those that would otherwise be expected. Peter Kemper and others, *The Evaluation of the National Long-Term Care Demonstration: Final Report,* report prepared for DHHS (Princeton, N.J.: Mathematica Policy Research, May 1986), pp. 128–29.

5. George J. Carcagno and others, *The Evaluation of the National Long-Term Care Demonstration: The Planning and Operational Experience of the Channeling Projects,* report prepared for DHHS (Princeton, N.J.: Mathematica Policy Research, July 18, 1986), vol. 1, pp. 143–48.

6. Mark Schlesinger, "On the Limits of Expanding Health Care Reform: Chronic Care in Prepaid Settings," *Milbank Quarterly,* vol. 64 (Spring 1986), pp. 194–95.

7. Walter N. Leutz, senior research associate, Brandeis University, Heller School, personal communication, September 17, 1987.

8. Social/Health Maintenance Organizations Research Consortium, "First Returns Data from the Social/Health Maintenance Organizations Research Consortium," data presented at the National Health Policy Forum, Washington, D.C., November 17, 1986.

9. Testimony of Merwyn R. Greenlick in *Hearings on Catastrophic Health Insurance,* Hearings before the Subcommittee on Health and Long-Term Care, House Committee on Aging, 99 Cong. 2 sess. (Washington, D.C., 1987), table 4.

10. Cost-sharing in the demonstration is used to help control use and not to provide significant net revenues.

11. Medicare capitation rates are roughly twice as high for institutionalized beneficiaries as for those outside a nursing home. Walter N. Leutz and others, *Changing Health Care for an Aging Society: Planning for the Social/Health Maintenance Organization* (Lexington, Mass.: Lexington Books, 1985), p. 182.

12. This result assumes continuation of the current reimbursement practice used in the HCFA demonstration, which sets rates at 100 percent of the AAPCC.

13. Social/Health Maintenance Organizations Research Consortium, "First Returns Data"; and "The Clock Is Ticking for S/HMOs," *Long-Term Care Management,* April 30, 1987, p. 6.

14. Many medicaid recipients are not eligible for medicaid at the time of nursing home admission; instead, they spend down to medicaid eligibility over time.

15. U.S. General Accounting Office, *Medicaid and Nursing Home Care: Cost Increases and the Need for Services Are Creating Problems for the States and the Elderly,* GAO/IPE–84–1 (Washington, D.C., October 21, 1983), p. 17.

16. Leutz and others, *Changing Health Care,* p. 197.

17. The Metropolitan Life Insurance Company of New York and Group Health Cooperative of Puget Sound recently entered into a contract to offer a long-term care insurance policy to members of the health maintenance

organization. Lynn Wagner, "Seattle HMO, Insurer Offer Long-Term Care Option," *Modern Healthcare,* April 10, 1987, p. 92.

Chapter 7

1. See U.S. Department of Health and Human Services, *Catastrophic Illness Expenses: Report to the President* (Washington, D.C., November 1986); Peter J. Ferrara, "Medicare Solution: The Health Bank IRA," *Journal of the Institute for Socioeconomic Studies,* vol. 10 (Spring 1985), pp. 78–87; Harold J. Simon and Barbara L. Brody, "Independent Health Security Account Plan: An Option for Private Financing of Long Term Care for the Elderly," University of California at San Diego, Department of Community and Family Medicine, 1984, pp. 1–5; and Joseph Lipscomb and William G. Analyan, Jr., "The National Health Care Trust Plan," *Health Affairs,* vol. 4 (Fall 1985), pp. 5–31.

2. H.R. 955, 100 Cong. 1 sess., introduced by Congressman D. French Slaughter, Jr.; and H.R. 2997, 100 Cong. 1 sess., introduced by Congressman Hal Daub.

3. Mark R. Meiners and Arlene K. Tave, "Consumer Interest in Long-Term Care Insurance: A Survey of the Elderly in Six States," National Center for Health Services Research, Washington, D.C., 1984; and Equicor, *The Equicor Health Care Survey–VI: Looking to the Future of Retiree Health Benefits* (New York, 1986), pp. 44–59.

4. Data from the Brookings Tax Model supplied by Charles Byce. The Brookings Tax Model is a simulation model of the federal individual income tax system. It uses a representative sample of taxpayers to estimate the tax liabilities for all taxpayers under current law and under policy alternatives.

5. U.S. Internal Revenue Service, *Statistics of Income, 1984: The Individual Tax Model File* (public use tape).

6. Harvey Galper and Charles Byce, "Individual Retirement Accounts: Facts and Issues," *Tax Notes,* June 2, 1986, pp. 917–21.

7. Ibid., table 2.

8. *Economic Report of the President, January 1987,* p. 274.

9. Steven F. Venti and David A. Wise, "Have IRAs Increased U.S. Saving? Evidence from Consumer Expenditure Surveys," Hoover Institution Working Papers in Economics E-87-13 (Stanford University, March 1987), p. 36.

10. DHHS, *Catastrophic Illness Expenses,* pp. 107–09.

11. The participation in individual medical accounts and the average account balance for IMA4.4 are projected to be the same as for IMA5.8.

12. Assuming inflation is 5.8 percent a year, by 2020 a year of nursing home care will cost roughly $44,000 in constant 1987 dollars.

13. Data from the Brookings Tax Model supplied by Charles Byce. The tax loss was estimated in a three-step process using the rules of the Tax Reform Act of 1986. First, we determined expected tax revenues using current law. Second, we estimated tax revenues allowing taxpayers to contribute $1,000 to an IMA. Only those taxpayers who would have been expected to contribute the maximum allowable amount to an IRA under pre-tax-reform rules contribute to an IMA. The tax loss equals tax revenues without an IMA minus tax revenues with an IMA. See also table 7-5.

14. Technical Work Group on Private Financing of Long-Term Care for

the Elderly, *Report to the Secretary on Private Financing of Long-Term Care for the Elderly* (Washington, D.C.: DHHS, November 1986), chap. 3, pp. 21–23.

Chapter 8

1. Brookings-ICF Long-Term Financing Model.

2. Bruce Jacobs and William Weissert, "Using Home Equity to Finance Long-Term Care," *Journal of Health Politics, Policy and Law,* vol. 12 (Spring 1987), p. 79.

3. The average annual payment for current reverse mortgages ranges from $6,000 to $7,800. Maurice D. Weinrobe, personal communication, December 14, 1987; and Frank Engel, personal communication, December 14, 1987. The average cost of a year in a nursing home in 1986 was about $22,000.

4. Ken Scholen, "An Overview of Home Equity Conversion Plans," in *Home Equity Conversion: Issues and Options for the Elderly Homeowner*, Committee Print, Joint Briefing by the Subcommittee on Housing and Consumer Interests, House Select Committee on Aging, and the Senate Special Committee on Aging, 99 Cong. 1 sess. (Washington, D.C., 1985), p. 11.

5. Letter to the authors from Ken Scholen, director, National Center for Home Equity Conversion, November 11, 1987.

6. Peter Wessel, "IRMA: A Long-Term Home-Equity Conversion Program," *Pride Institute of Long Term Home Health Care*, vol. 4 (Spring 1985), pp. 29–31; and Ken Scholen, Maurice Weinrobe, and William Perkins, *A Financial Guide to the Century Plan*, 4th ed. (Madison, Wis.: NCHEC, April 1986), pp. 11–15.

7. Scholen, "Overview of Home Equity Conversion Plans," p. 21.

8. Bruce Jacobs, "The National Potential of Home Equity Conversion," *Gerontologist,* vol. 26 (October 1986), p. 496.

9. Data from the Retirement History Study showed that in 1975 median home equity accounted for 70 percent of the elderly's total assests. Joseph Friedman and Jane Sjogren, "Assets of the Elderly as They Retire," *Social Security Bulletin,* vol. 44 (January 1981), p. 28.

10. Brookings-ICF Long-Term Care Financing Model. Aggregate is calculated by multiplying $54,000 average home equity by 14.4 million elderly homeowners.

11. Letter to the authors from Bruce Jacobs, University of Rochester, November 12, 1987.

12. Jacobs and Weissert, "Using Home Equity to Finance Long-Term Care," p. 79.

13. Douglas Nelson, "A Profile of Elderly Homeowners," in Ken Scholen and Yung-Ping Chen, eds., *Unlocking Home Equity for the Elderly* (Cambridge, Mass.: Ballinger, 1980), pp. 14–17.

14. Louis Harris and Associates, *Problems Facing Elderly Americans Living Alone,* a national survey conducted for the Commonwealth Fund Commission on Elderly People Living Alone (New York: Louis Harris and Associates, 1986), p. 59; and American Association of Retired Persons, *Understanding Senior Housing: An American Association of Retired Persons Survey of Consumers' Preferences, Concerns, and Needs* (Washington D.C., n.d.), p. 26.

15. James B. Davies, "Uncertain Lifetime, Consumption, and Dissaving in Retirement," *Journal of Political Economy,* vol. 89 (June 1981), pp. 561–77; Thad W. Mirer, "The Wealth-Age Relation among the Aged," *American Economic*

Review, vol. 69 (June 1979), pp. 435–43; and B. Douglas Bernheim, "Dissaving after Retirement: Testing the Pure Life Cycle Hypothesis," Working Paper 1409 (Cambridge, Mass.: National Bureau of Economic Research, July 1984).

16. Steven F. Venti and David A. Wise, "Aging, Moving, and Housing Wealth," Working Paper 2324 (Cambridge, Mass.: NBER, July 1987), p. 4.

17. Scholen and others, *Financial Guide to the Century Plan,* p. 11.

18. A. Frank Thompson, Jr., "Homeowner's Equity: Providing Lifetime Annuities for the Elderly," *Federal Home Loan Bank Board Journal,* vol. 13 (December 1980), p. 24.

19. Judith Feder and William Scanlon, "Financing Long-Term Care for the Elderly: Whose Job Is It?" paper presented at the American Hospital Association Forum on Strategies, Services, Structures, February 13, 1984.

20. Maurice D. Weinrobe, "An Economic Analysis of Reverse Mortgage Insurance," in *Home Equity Conversion,* Committee Print, p. 43; and *Turning Home Equity into Income for Older Homeowners,* Committee Print, Senate Special Committee on Aging, 98 Cong. 2 sess. (Washington, D.C., July 1984), p. 14.

21. Feder and Scalon, "Financing Long-Term Care for the Elderly."

22. Housing and Community Development Act of 1987, P.L. 100-242.

23. *Economic Report of the President, January 1987,* p. 310.

24. Brookings-ICF Long-Term Care Financing Model.

Chapter 9

1. Some researchers contend that the quality of nursing home care is higher the greater the size of the private pay market relative to the medicaid market. Paul J. Gertler, "Regulated Price Discrimination and Quality: The Implications of Medicaid Reimbursement Policy for the Nursing Home Industry," Working Paper 1667 (Cambridge, Mass.: National Bureau of Economic Research, July 1985), p. 1; and John A. Nyman, "A Market-Based System for Reimbursing Nursing Homes for Medicaid Patients," University of Iowa, College of Medicine, October 20, 1984, p. 40. Others contend there is only weak evidence of a link between the quality of care and the proportion of a nursing home's beds that are filled with private pay patients. See David Zimmerman and others, *Evaluation of the Three State Demonstrations in Nursing Home Quality Assurance Processes: Final Report,* prepared for the Health Care Financing Administration (Madison, Wis.: Mathematica Policy Research, September 1985), pp. 99–130. Conventional wisdom holds that predominantly private pay nursing homes provide better quality care.

2. David H. Gustafson and David Zimmerman, "The Potential for Incentives to Improve Quality of Care in Nursing Homes," University of Wisconsin, November 4, 1984, p. 23.

3. Ibid.

4. Paul J. Gertler, "Subsidies, Quality, and Regulation in the Nursing Home Industry," Working Paper 1691 (Cambridge, Mass.: NBER, August 1985), p. 17.

5. Nyman, "Market-Based System for Reimbursing Nursing Homes," p. 13.

6. Joshua M. Wiener, "A Sociological Analysis of Government Regulation: The Case of Nursing Homes" (Ph.D. dissertation, Harvard University, 1981), p. 291.

7. Although the original intention of certificate of need (CON) legislation

was to assist planning agencies in restructuring health care delivery, CON programs have been used as cost containment tools to limit the supply of nursing homes, and in more recent years to achieve specific quality of care and access-related goals. James B. Simpson, "State Certificate-of-Need Programs: The Current Status," *American Journal of Public Health,* vol. 75 (October 1985), pp. 1225–29. See also Judith Feder and William Scanlon, "Regulating the Bed Supply in Nursing Homes," *Milbank Memorial Fund Quarterly: Health and Society,* vol. 58 (Winter 1980), pp. 54–88.

8. Joshua M. Wiener, Deborah A. Ehrenworth, and Denise A. Spence, "Private Long-Term Care Insurance: Cost, Coverage, and Restrictions," *Gerontologist,* vol. 27 (August 1987), p. 491; and Institute of Medicine, Committee on Nursing Home Regulation, *Improving the Quality of Care in Nursing Homes* (Washington D.C.: National Academy Press, 1986), p. 21.

9. William J. McAuley and Rosemary Blieszner, "Selection of Long-Term Care Arrangements by Older Community Residents," *Gerontologist,* vol. 25 (April 1985), p. 190; Mark R. Meiners and Arlene K. Tave, "Consumer Interest in Long-Term Care Insurance: A Survey of Elderly in Six States," National Center for Health Services Research, Rockville, Md., December 7, 1984, p. 14; and Marvin Cetron, "The Public Opinion of Home Care: A Survey Report Executive Summary," *Caring,* vol. 4 (October 1985), p. 13. In 1982, 95 percent of the chronically disabled elderly in the community agreed that it is better to stay out of a nursing home as long as you can. U.S. Department of Health and Human Services, 1982 National Long-Term Care Survey, available from the National Technical Information Service, accession nos. PB-86-161775 and PB-86-161783.

10. John F. Holahan and Joel W. Cohen, *Medicaid: The Trade-off between Cost Containment and Access to Care* (Washington, D.C.: Urban Institute, 1986), p. 121.

11. Robert Morris and Paul Youket, "The Long-Term-Care Issues: Identifying the Problems and Potential Solutions," in James J. Callahan, Jr., and Stanley S. Wallack, eds., *Reforming the Long-Term Care System* (Lexington, Mass.: Lexington Books, 1981), p. 14.

12. Wiener and others, "Private Long-Term Care Insurance," p. 493. Criteria for obtaining home care services, however, usually include a prior hospital or nursing home stay.

13. Based on results from the Brookings-ICF Long-Term Care Financing Model for 2016–20. The average IMA balance is projected to be $14,777 in 2016–20. This amount could purchase 246 home visits at $60 a visit, or about 2.4 years of in-home care assuming 2 visits a week. For HECs the average yearly income from a shared appreciation loan in 2016–20 is $2,182, which could purchase 36 home visits a year at the same cost per visit.

14. U.S. General Accounting Office, *Medicaid and Nursing Home Care: Cost Increases and the Need for Services Are Creating Problems for the States and the Elderly,* GAO/IPE-84-1 (Washington, D.C., October 21, 1983), pp. 107–27; and William G. Wiessert and others, "Care for the Chronically Ill: Nursing Home Incentive Payment Experiment," *Health Care Financing Review,* vol. 5 (Winter 1983), pp. 41–49.

15. William J. Scanlon, "A Theory of the Nursing Home Market," *Inquiry,* vol. 17 (Spring 1980), p. 39.

16. Wiessert and others, "Care for the Chronically Ill," pp. 41–49.

17. Pamela Doty, "Family Care of the Elderly: The Role of Public Policy," *Milbank Quarterly,* vol. 64, no. 1 (1986), pp. 49–53; and Marjorie H. Cantor,

"Strain among Caregivers: A Study of Experience in the United States," *Gerontologist,* vol. 23 (December 1983), pp. 597–604.

18. Eileen J. Tell and others, "Assessing the Elderly's Preferences for Lifecare Retirement Options," *Gerontologist,* vol. 27 (August 1987), p. 505.

19. David L. Cohen, "Legal Regulations of the Continuing Care Retirement Community Industry as a Whole," in Ian A. Morrison and others, eds., *Continuing Care Retirement Communities: Political, Social, and Financial Issues* (New York: Haworth Press, 1986), pp. 37–56. See also F. Ellen Netting and Cindy C. Wilson, "Current Legislation Concerning Life Care and Continuing Care Contracts, *Gerontologist,* vol. 27 (October 1987), pp. 645–51; and Hirsh S. Ruchlin, "Are CCRCs Facing a Promising Future or Potential Problems?" *Healthcare Financial Management,* vol. 41 (October, 1987), pp. 54–61.

Chapter 10

1. Brookings-ICF Long-Term Care Financing Model.

2. Bruce C. Vladeck, *Unloving Care: The Nursing Home Tragedy* (Basic Books, 1980), pp. 48–50.

3. See Thomas Rice and Jon Gabel, "Protecting the Elderly against High Health Care Costs," *Health Affairs,* vol. 5 (Fall 1986), pp. 5–21.

4. *1987 Annual Report of the Board of Trustees of the Federal Supplementary Medical Insurance Trust Fund,* table 6.

Chapter 11

1. Stuart M. Butler, Michael Sanera, and W. Bruce Weinrod, *Mandate for Leadership II: Continuing the Conservative Revolution* (Washington, D.C.: Heritage Foundation, 1984), pp. 100–01; Daniel J. Evans and Charles S. Robb, *To Form a More Perfect Union,* Report of the Committee on Federalism and National Purpose (Washington, D.C.: National Conference on Social Welfare, 1985), p. 9; and National Study Group on State Medicaid Strategies, *Restructuring Medicaid: An Agenda for Change* (Washington, D.C.: Center for the Study of Social Policy, January 1983).

2. Carroll L. Estes, Robert J. Newcomer, and associates, *Fiscal Austerity and Aging: Shifting Government Responsibility for the Elderly* (Beverly Hills, Calif.: Sage Publications, 1983); and Robert B. Hudson, "Restructuring Federal/State Relations in Long-Term Care: The Bloc Grant Alternative," in James J. Callahan, Jr., and Stanley S. Wallack, eds., *Reforming the Long-Term Care System* (Lexington, Mass.: Lexington Books, 1981), pp. 31–59.

3. Joseph A. Pechman, *Federal Tax Policy,* 5th ed. (Brookings, 1987), p. 290.

4. See P.L. 97-35. The nine block grants are for community development; low income home energy assistance; social services; elementary and secondary education; primary care; alcohol, drug abuse, and mental health; community services; maternal and child health; and preventive health and health services. U.S. General Accounting Office, *Lessons Learned from Past Block Grants: Implications for Congressional Oversight,* GAO/IPE-82-8 (Washington, D.C., September 23, 1982), pp. 1, 10–11.

5. Butler and others, *Mandate for Leadership II,* p. 103; Evans and Robb, *To Form a More Perfect Union,* p. 9; and National Study Group on State Medicaid Strategies, *Restructuring Medicaid,* pp. 36–58.

6. Robert L. Kane and Rosalie A. Kane, *A Will and a Way: What the United States Can Learn from Canada about Caring for the Elderly* (Columbia University Press, 1985), pp. 1–63.

7. Bruce C. Vladeck, *Unloving Care: The Nursing Home Tragedy* (Basic Books, 1980), p. 76.

8. Ibid., pp. 75–77.

9. Estes and others, *Fiscal Austerity and Aging.*

10. For example, Congress and the executive branch have cut the indexing of the medicare hospital prospective payment system below the hospital inflation rate in each fiscal year since the inception of the program in 1984. Judy Moore, Prospective Payment Advisory Commission, Washington, D.C., personal communication, January 21, 1988.

11. The seven block grants created by OBRA were maternal and child health; preventive health and health services; alcohol, drug abuse, and mental health services; low income home energy assistance; social services; community services; and education. GAO, *Block Grants Brought Funding Changes and Adjustments to Program Priorities,* GAO/HRD-85-33 (Washington, D.C., February 11, 1985), pp. 3, 6.

12. Ibid., p. ii.

13. Federal requirements, for example, prohibit the use of medicaid funding for social services, with only minor exceptions.

14. GAO, *States Use Added Flexibility Offered by the Preventive Health and Health Services Block Grant,* GAO/HRD-84-41 (Washington, D.C., May 8, 1984), pp. 17–23.

15. Joshua M. Wiener, "A Sociological Analysis of Government Regulation: The Case of Nursing Homes" (Ph.D. dissertation, Harvard University, 1981), pp. 126–55.

16. GAO, *Lessons Learned from Past Block Grants.*

17. GAO, *Block Grants: Overview of Experience to Date and Emerging Issues,* GAO/HRD-85-46 (Washington, D.C., April 3, 1985), pp. 20–21.

18. *Budget of the United States Government, Fiscal Year 1988: Appendix,* p. I-K27.

19. Butler and others, *Mandate for Leadership II.*

20. Draft legislative specifications developed by the Department of Health and Human Services for a long-term care block grant included allowing states to reinstate family financial responsibility for nursing home patients and making it easier to force the sale of the home. Policy memorandum by Joshua Wiener and George Greenberg, Health Care Financing Administration and Office of the Assistant Secretary for Planning and Evaluation, DHHS, October 20, 1981.

21. Estes and others, *Fiscal Austerity and Aging*; and Hudson, "Restructuring Federal/State Relations in Long-Term Care."

22. GAO, *Community Services Block Grant: New State Role Brings Program and Administrative Changes,* GAO/HRD-84-76 (Washington, D.C., September 28, 1984).

23. Wiener, "Sociological Analysis of Government Regulation," pp. 216–325.

24. Helen L. Smits, "Quality of Care," in Joshua M. Wiener, ed., *Swing Beds: Assessing Flexible Health Care in Rural Communities* (Brookings, 1987), p. 105.

25. Institute of Medicine, Committee on Nursing Home Regulation, *Improving the Quality of Care in Nursing Homes* (Washington, D.C.: National Academy Press, 1986), p. 21.

26. Theoretically, this problem could be mitigated by regulations that tied the level of services to patient disability. Developing such a system, however, would not be easy and would be a substantial regulatory burden on states and facilities.

Chapter 12

1. Alvin Schorr, . . . *Thy Father and Thy Mother . . . A Second Look at Filial Responsibility and Family Policy,* SSA 13-11953 (Washington, D.C.: Social Security Administration, Office of Policy, July 1980), pp. 7–8.

2. In the 1950s sixteen states required no financial support of a parent by his or her offspring, and another twenty-one required some support but did not count the child's contribution against the elder's old age assistance payment. But in the remaining fourteen states, OAA payment was reduced or entirely withheld when the child did not contribute. Alvin Schorr, *Filial Responsibility in the Modern American Family* (Baltimore, Md.: Social Security Administration, Division of Program Research, June 1960), pp. 23–24.

3. Marshall B. Kapp, "Residents of State Mental Institutions and Their Money (or, The State Giveth and the State Taketh Away)," *Journal of Psychiatry and Law,* vol. 6 (Fall 1978), pp. 305–08.

4. Several states do collect family payments from spouses. General Accounting Office, *Entering a Nursing Home: Costly Implications for Medicaid and the Elderly,* PAD-80-12 (Washington, D.C., November 26, 1979), pp. 46–47.

5. *Compilation of the Social Security Laws, Including the Social Security Act, as Amended, and Related Enactments through April 1, 1984,* Committee Print, House Committee on Ways and Means, 98 Cong. 2 sess. (Washington, D.C., 1984), pp. 710–11. The legislative intent is discussed in *Social Security Amendments of 1965: Report of the Senate Finance Committee to Accompany H.R. 6675,* S. Rept. 404, pt. 1, 89 Cong. 1 sess. (Washington, D.C., 1965), pp. 77–78.

6. In the thirty-five states that follow supplemental security income eligibility guidelines, spouses are not responsible for contributing to the cost of care after their marriage partner has spent one month in a nursing home (six months if both are eligible for SSI). In the remaining so-called 209(b) states, spouses can be considered financially responsible after the one month cutoff provided that such a policy was in effect before January 1972. In practice, however, few states employ more restrictive policies for considering income and resources that may not be directly available to the applicant. Brian O. Burwell, "Shared Obligations: Public Policy Influences on Family Care for the Elderly," Medicaid Program Evaluation Working Paper 2.1 (Baltimore, Md.: Health Care Financing Administration, Office of Research and Demonstrations, May 1986), pp. 110–12. In general, when the spouse outside the nursing home has most or all of the income in his or her name (for example, a pension), he or she does not face a large financial burden. However, when the situation is reversed, real hardship can result. When the medicaid-eligible institutionalized marriage partner has most or all of the retirement income in his or her name, all of that income will go to the nursing home to cover the costs of care, and medicaid picks up the balance of the charges. Only some small amount, up to the SSI level, is returned to the spouse in the community. Edward Neuschler with Claire Gill, *Medicaid Eligibility for the Elderly in Need of Long Term Care,* report prepared for the Congressional Research Service (Washington, D.C.: National Governors' Association, September 1987). Some states are also

currently collecting payments from the husband or wife of a medicaid nursing home patient through generally applicable state laws of spousal financial responsibility. For example, in New York the spouse remaining in the community is legally responsible for his or her mate in a nursing home under state family law. But as a practical matter, the approach is difficult to enforce. "Nursing Home Care: A Guide Provides Step-by-Step Advice," *New York Times,* November 27, 1982.

7. Burwell, "Shared Obligations," p. 99.

8. A recent attitude survey conducted in Massachusetts found that 62 percent of the adult children providing care to an aged parent were opposed to legally mandating family responsibility. Claire E. Gutkin, John N. Morris, and Clarence C. Sherwood, "The Responsibility of Children for Financing Institutional Care," paper presented at the 39th Annual Scientific Meeting of the Gerontological Society of America, Chicago, November 21, 1986.

9. *Medicaid and Family Responsibility: Who Pays?* Committee Print, Briefing by the Subcommittee on Human Services, House Select Committee on Aging, 98 Cong. 1 sess. (Washington, D.C., 1983), p. 4.

10. Burwell, "Shared Obligations," pp. 131–32.

11. Ibid., p. 106; and Robert Koskela, *Child Responsibility for Supporting Parents in Nursing Homes,* Supports for Natural Caregivers Report 2 (Madison, Wis.: Wisconsin Department of Health and Human Services, Bureau of Collections, December 1983), pp. 23–26.

12. Burwell, "Shared Obligations," pp. 128–29.

13. U.S. Bureau of the Census, "1976 Survey of Institutionalized Persons: A Study of Persons Receiving Long-Term Care," *Current Population Reports,* Special Studies, series P–23, no. 69 (Washington, D.C.: Department of Commerce, June 1978), tables III–211, III–212. Authors inflated dollar figures by the personal consumption expenditure deflator taken from the *Economic Report of the President, January 1987,* p. 248.

14. Burwell, "Shared Obligations," p. 130.

15. Koskela, *Child Responsibility for Supporting Parents,* pp. 18–21.

16. U.S. National Center for Health Statistics, "1977 National Nursing Home Survey: 1977 Summary for the United States," *Vital and Health Statistics,* series 13, no. 43 (Hyattsville, Md.: Department of Health, Education, and Welfare, July 1979), pp. 99–101.

17. Bureau of the Census, "1976 Survey of Institutionalized Persons," tables III–211 and III–212. Dollar amounts inflated by the authors.

18. Burwell, "Shared Obligations," p. 108.

19. Schorr, *Filial Responsibility,* pp. 22–27.

20. Ibid., p. 26.

21. Burwell, "Shared Obligations," p. 138.

22. Marian Smallegan, "There Was Nothing Else to Do: Needs for Care before Nursing Home Admission," *Gerontologist,* vol. 25 (August 1985), pp. 364–69; and Greg Arling and William J. McAuley, "The Feasibility of Public Payments for Family Caregiving," *Gerontologist,* vol. 23 (June 1983), p. 303.

23. *Medicaid and Family Responsibility,* p. 4.

24. Ethel Shanas, "Social Myth as Hypothesis: The Case of Family Relations of Old People," *Gerontologist,* vol. 19 (February 1979), pp. 3–9; Michael A. Smyer, "The Differential Usage of Services by Impaired Elderly," *Journal of Gerontology,* vol. 35 (March 1980), pp. 249–55; Laurence G. Branch and Alan Jette, "Elders' Use of Informal Long-Term Care Assistance," *Gerontologist,* vol. 23 (February 1983), pp. 51–56; and Pamela Doty, "Family Care of the Elderly:

The Role of Public Policy," *Milbank Quarterly,* vol. 64, no. 1 (1986), pp. 34–75.

25. Burwell, "Shared Obligations," p. 131.

26. Stephen Crystal, *America's Old Age Crisis: Public Policy and the Two Worlds of Aging* (Basic Books, 1982), p. 80.

27. National Center for Health Statistics, "1977 National Nursing Home Survey," pp. 99–101.

28. Koskela, *Child Responsibility for Supporting Parents,* p. 37.

29. U.S. Department of Health and Human Services, 1982 National Long-Term Care Survey, available from the National Technical Information Service, accession nos. PB-86-161775 and PB-86-161783.

Chapter 13

1. U.S. Department of Health and Human Services, 1982 National Long-Term Care Survey, available from the National Technical Information Service, accession nos. PB-86-161775 and PB-86-161783.

2. About 86 percent of the older persons receiving informal care in 1982 had received it for more than one year; 40 percent had received it for more than five years. Ibid.

3. Linda S. Noelker and Robert W. Wallace, "The Organization of Family Care for Impaired Elderly," *Journal of Family Issues,* vol. 6 (March 1985), pp. 23–44.

4. Although the empirical effect has never been demonstrated, some elements of current federal policy undoubtedly discourage family care. For example, under the supplemental security income (SSI) program, family members have a disincentive to support their elderly kin financially because the income received from family sources results in a large reduction in SSI benefits. Moreover, obtaining medicaid coverage for help with medical expenses is much easier to do in a nursing home than in the community. Edward Neuschler with Claire Gill, *Medicaid Eligibility for the Elderly in Need of Long Term Care,* report prepared for the Congressional Research Service (Washington, D.C.: National Governors' Association, September 1987).

5. Pamela Doty, "Family Care of the Elderly: The Role of Public Policy," *Milbank Quarterly,* vol. 64, no. 1 (1986), pp. 39–46.

6. Douglas A. Wolf, "Kinship and the Living Arrangements of Older Americans," paper prepared for the National Institute of Child Health and Human Development, DHHS (Urban Institute, Washington, D.C., January 1983), p. 108.

7. Greg Arling and William J. McAuley, "The Feasibility of Public Payments for Family Caregiving," *Gerontologist,* vol. 23 (June 1983), p. 303; Marian Smallegan, "There Was Nothing Else to Do: Needs for Care before Nursing Home Admission," *Gerontologist,* vol. 25 (August 1985), pp. 364–69; and Doty, "Family Care of the Elderly," p. 49.

8. Walter Leutz, "Long-Term Care for the Elderly: Public Dreams and Private Realities," *Inquiry,* vol. 23 (Summer 1986), p. 135.

9. Candace L. Macken, "A Profile of Functionally Impaired Elderly Persons Living in the Community," *Health Care Financing Review,* vol. 7 (Summer 1986), p. 37.

10. William Scanlon and others, *Project to Analyze Existing Long-Term Care Data,* vol. 1: *Summary and Conclusions,* report prepared for the Assistant

Secretary for Planning and Evaluation and the Administration on Aging, DHHS (Washington, D.C.: Urban Institute, 1983), p. 142.

11. Recently, bills to expand the federal and dependent care credit have been introduced by Senator John Heinz III (S. 778) and Congressmen Tom Corcoran (H.R. 2361), Silvio O. Conte (H.R. 644), and Olympia Jean Snowe (H.R. 467).

12. Center for the Study of Social Policy, *Tax Subsidies for Long-Term Care of the Elderly,* final report to the Administration on Aging, DHHS (Washington, D.C., June 1982), pp. 31–32. Under current law, qualified families with incomes below $10,000 can credit 30 percent of their annual care expenses up to $720 for each qualified dependent (up to two). There is a progressive reduction of the credit percentage for families earning more than $10,000 until it reaches 20 percent at earnings of $28,000 or more, up to $480. The credit is nonrefundable.

13. U.S. Internal Revenue Service, *Statistics of Income, 1984: Individual Income Tax Returns* (Washington, D.C.: Statistics of Income Division, 1986) p. 30; and Center for the Study of Social Policy, "Tax Subsidies," p. 32.

14. A more detailed look at eligibility for coverage shows that of the 4.65 million disabled elderly in the community, approximately 1.2 million received formal care in 1982. Just over half that group (0.6 million people) reported that the visits involved some out-of-pocket expense. Since roughly 0.3 million of them lived alone, half the candidates would be ineligible because of living arrangement restrictions. Among the 0.17 million residing with their husband or wife, only 13 percent had a spouse working more than thirty hours a week. For the remaining 0.13 million living with a child or other relative, only 53 percent of the households reported a helper meeting the thirty hour a week employment requirement. Therefore, without even taking into account the financial support restrictions, the current child and dependent care credit probably misses more than nine in ten of the chronically disabled elderly receiving family and formal help. DHHS, 1982 National Long-Term Care Survey.

15. Brian O. Burwell, "Shared Obligations: Public Policy Influences on Family Care for the Elderly," Medicaid Program Evaluation Working Paper 2.1 (Baltimore, Md.: Health Care Financing Administration, Office of Research and Demonstrations, May 1986), p. 93.

16. The states that pay family members for long-term care services provided to elderly kin are California, Colorado, Connecticut, Florida, Kansas, Maine, Maryland, Michigan, Minnesota, North Dakota, Oregon, Virginia, and Wisconsin. Burwell, "Shared Obligations," pp. 47–67. Another study concluded that 74 percent of the states have arrangements for paid family caregiving. Nathan L. Linsk and others, "Paid Family Caregiving: A Policy Option for Community Long Term Care," paper prepared for the Illinois Association of Family Service Agencies, University of Illinois at Chicago, April 1986, p. 21.

17. By regulation, medicaid prohibits the reimbursement of family members as personal care providers. However, three states—Kansas, Minnesota, and Oregon—have used the flexibility of medicaid home and community-based care waiver options granted under section 2176 of the Omnibus Budget Reconciliation Act of 1981 to reimburse family caregivers. Michigan circumvented the need for a waiver by interpreting the restriction as prohibiting reimbursement only of those family members who are legally responsible for support of the recipient. Thus, in Michigan, adult children, siblings, and other relatives are eligible to be personal care providers under existing medicaid

provisions. Burwell, "Shared Obligations," pp. 54, 65–66. A policy change would require altering medicaid regulations for personal care services.

18. Ibid., pp. 67–68.

19. Deborah Kuhn and others, *In-Home Services and the Contribution of Kin: Substitution Effects in Home Care Programs for the Elderly,* report prepared for the Assistant Secretary for Planning and Evaluation, DHHS (Cambridge, Mass.: Urban Systems Research and Engineering, May 1982), pp. 16–18.

20. Burwell, "Shared Obligations," pp. 68–70.

21. Doty, "Family Care of the Elderly," pp. 68–69.

22. For example, national data show that caregivers rate the potential stress involved in placing a relative in a nursing home as ten times higher than the stress produced by all their caregiving activities combined. Nora Schaeffer and Norman M. Bradburn, "Magnitude Scales in the Informal Caregivers Survey," University of Chicago, National Opinion Research Center, November 1983, table 3.

23. Smallegan, "There Was Nothing Else to Do," pp 364–69; and Arling and McAuley, "Feasibility of Public Payments," pp. 300–06. Indeed, some observers suggest that the more common problem may be getting families to relinquish care, even when it is in the best interest of the older relative and the family. Linda S. Noelker, "Family Care of Elder Relatives: The Impact of Policy and Programs," in Alice J. Kethley and Martha K. Parker, eds., *Family Support and Long-Term Care* (Excelsior, Minn.: InterStudy, 1984), pp. 76–77; and Noelker and Wallace, "Organization of Family Care," p. 41.

24. William G. Weissert, "Hard Choices: Targeting Long-Term Care to the 'At-Risk' Aged," *Journal of Health Politics, Policy and Law,* vol. 11 (Fall 1986), p. 479; John A. Capitman, "Community-Based Long-Term Care Models, Target Groups, and Impacts on Service Use," *Gerontologist,* vol. 26 (August 1986), p. 395; Peter Kemper, Robert Applebaum, and Margaret Harrigan, *A Systematic Comparison of Community Care Demonstrations* (Rockville, Md.: National Center for Health Services Research, March 1987), pp. 22–31; Brenda Haskins and others, *Evaluation of Coordinated Community-Oriented Long-Term Care Demonstrations,* report prepared for HCFA (Berkeley, Calif.: Berkeley Planning Associates, May 1985), p. 216; and Margaret Stassen and John Holahan, *A Comparative Analysis of Long-Term Care Demonstrations and Evaluations,* Working Paper 1227-2, prepared for the Administration on Aging (Washington, D.C.: Urban Institute, September 1980), pp. 185–88.

25. Burwell, "Shared Obligations," p. 58.

26. Moreover, evaluations of some service support programs suggest that they do not substantially reduce the caregivers' perceptions of burden. Nancy J. Chapman and Diane L. Pancoast, "Working with the Informal Helping Networks of the Elderly: The Experiences of Three Programs," *Journal of Social Issues,* vol 41, no. 1 (1985), p. 61; Noelker, "Family Care of Older Relatives," p. 79; Linda K. George, *Caregiver Well-Being: Correlates and Relationships with Participation in Community Self-Help Groups,* final report submitted to the American Association of Retired Persons, Andrus Foundation (Washington, D.C.: AARP, December 1983), pp. 11–13; and Noreen M. Clark and William Rakowski, "Family Caregivers of Older Adults: Improving Helping Skills," *Gerontologist,* vol. 23 (December 1983), p. 641.

27. General Accounting Office, *Assessment of the Use of Tax Credits for Families Who Provide Health Care to Disabled Elderly Relatives,* GAO/IPE-82-7 (Washington, D.C., August 27, 1982), p. 12.

28. Ibid.

29. This estimate assumes that the program is available only to older persons receiving supplemental security income. In 1982 just over 1.5 million elderly were receiving SSI. Social Security Administration, *Social Security Bulletin: Annual Statistical Supplement, 1982* (Washington, D.C., 1983), p. 237. From the screening for the 1982 National Long-Term Care Survey, DHHS found that about 19.1 percent of the medicare beneficiaries aged 65 and over had a chronic functional impairment. Macken, "Profile of Functionally Impaired Elderly Persons," p. 37. Hence, assuming the same rate of disability for aged SSI recipients, just under 300,000 elderly nationally might be eligible. Assuming 29 percent have a qualifying family member, as in the California in-home supportive services experience, that leaves close to 100,000 participants nationally. Burwell, "Shared Obligations," p. 52. Assuming each older person receives $265 a month (the 1983 average monthly family provider payment in California's program) for twelve months, payments for family providers of chronically disabled aged SSI recipients would be roughly $300 million annually. This estimate is probably low, since California alone spent approximately $90 million in 1984 on long-term care provided by relatives.

30. Burwell, "Shared Obligations," p. 68.

31. Arling and McAuley, "Feasibility of Public Payments," p. 305.

32. Shirley Whitfield with Brigita Krompholz, *Report to the General Assembly on the Family Support Demonstration Program* (Annapolis, Md.: Maryland Office on Aging, August 31, 1981), p. 29.

33. John M. Grana, "Disability Allowances for Long-Term Care in Western Europe and the United States," *International Social Security Review,* no. 2 (August 1983), p. A-18.

34. John M. Grana and Sandra M. Yamashiro, *An Evaluation of the Veterans Administration Housebound and Aid and Attendance Allowance Program,* final report prepared for the Assistant Secretary for Planning and Evaluation, DHHS (Millwood, Va.: Project HOPE Center for Health Affairs, April 15, 1987), chap. 3, p. 4.

35. Cash grants averaged $1,824 a year. Whitfield with Krompholz, *Report to the General Assembly,* p. 29.

36. Ibid.

37. Arthur M. Okun, *Equality and Efficiency: The Big Tradeoff* (Brookings, 1975).

Chapter 14

1. U.S. Department of Health and Human Services, 1982 National Long-Term Care Survey, available from the National Technical Information Service, accession nos. PB-86-161775 and PB-86-161783.

2. John F. Holahan and Joel W. Cohen, *Medicaid: The Trade-off Between Cost Containment and Access to Care* (Washington, D.C.: Urban Institute, 1986), p. 121.

3. Walter Leutz, "Long-Term Care for the Elderly: Public Dreams and Private Realities," *Inquiry,* vol. 23 (Summer 1986), pp. 134–40.

4. Pamela Doty, "Expanding Home and Community Care: What Is the Goal?" Health Care Financing Administration, Washington, D.C., 1984.

5. *Compilation of the Social Security Laws, Including the Social Security Act,*

as Amended, and Related Enactments through April 1, 1984, Committee Print, House Committee on Ways and Means, 98 Cong. 2 sess. (Washington, D.C., 1984), pp. 759–63.

6. Pamela Doty, "Can Home and Community-Based Services Provide Lower Cost Alternatives to Nursing Homes?" Working Paper (Washington, D.C.: HCFA, Office of Policy Analysis, May 1984), p. 2.

7. Two models of Channeling were tested. The basic model primarily arranged existing services for clients using case management. The financial control model provided a much wider array of home care services at no or low cost to participants. Peter Kemper and others, *The Evaluation of the National Long Term Care Demonstration: Final Report,* prepared for DHHS (Princeton, N.J.: Mathematica Policy Research, May 1986), pp. 2–3

8. Ibid., pp. 115–21; James G. Zimmer, Annemarie Groth-Juncker, and Jane McCusker, "A Randomized Controlled Study of a Home Health Care Team," *American Journal of Public Health,* vol. 75 (February 1985), pp. 134–41; Robert Applebaum, Fredrick W. Seidl, and Carol D. Austin, "The Wisconsin Community Care Organization: Preliminary Findings from the Milwaukee Experiment," *Gerontologist,* vol. 20 (June 1980), pp. 350–55; Gerald M. Eggert, Joyce E. Bowlyow, and Carol W. Nichols, "Gaining Control of the Long Term Care System: First Returns from the ACCESS Experiment," *Gerontologist,* vol. 20 (June 1980), pp. 356–63; William Weissert and others, "Effects and Costs of Day-Care Services for the Chronically Ill: A Randomized Experiment," *Medical Care,* vol. 18 (June 1980), p. 576; F. Albert Skellie, Melton Mobley, and Ruth E. Coan, "Cost-Effectiveness of Community-Based Long-Term Care: Current Findings of Georgia's Alternative Health Services Project," *American Journal of Public Health,* vol. 72 (April 1982), p. 356; and Lawrence J. Weiss and June Okazawa Monarch, "San Francisco Project OPEN: A Long Term Care Health System Development and Demonstration Program for the Elderly," *Pride Institute Journal of Long Term Home Health Care,* vol. 4 (Winter 1983), pp. 13–23.

9. Peter Kemper, Robert Applebaum, and Margaret Harrigan, "Community Care Demonstrations: What Have We Learned?" *Health Care Financing Review,* vol. 8 (Summer 1987), p. 92; Cathleen L. Yordi and Jacqueline Waldman, "A Consolidated Model of Long-Term Care: Service Utilization and Cost Impacts," *Gerontologist,* vol. 25 (August 1985), p. 393; Brenda Haskins and others, *Evaluation of Coordinated Community-Oriented Long-Term Care Demonstration Projects,* report prepared for HCFA (Berkeley, Calif.: Berkeley Planning Associates, May 1985), pp. 189–91; Susan L. Hughes, David S. Cordray, and V. Alan Spiker, "Evaluation of a Long-Term Home Care Program," *Medical Care,* vol. 22 (May 1984), p. 469; and Gary L. Gaumer and others, "Impact of the New York Long-Term Home Health Care Program," *Medical Care,* vol. 24 (July 1986), p. 647.

10. Barry C. Nocks and others, "The Effects of a Community-based Long-Term Care Project on Nursing Home Utilization," *Gerontologist,* vol. 26 (April 1986), p. 153; and Kemper and others, "Community Care Demonstrations," p. 92.

11. Judith Wooldridge and Jennifer Schore, *Evaluation of the National Long Term Care Demonstration: Channeling Effects on Hospital, Nursing Home, and Other Medical Services,* report prepared for DHHS (Princeton, N.J.: Mathematica Policy Research, May 1986), p. 13.

12. Rick T. Zawadski and Marie-Louise Ansak, "Consolidating Community-Based Long-Term Care: Early Returns from the On Lok Demonstration,"

Gerontologist, vol. 23 (August 1983), pp. 367–68; and Yordi and Waldman, "Consolidated Model of Long-Term Care," pp. 393–94.

13. Wooldridge and Schore, *Evaluation of the National Long Term Care Demonstraton: Channeling Effects on Hospital, Nursing Home, and Other Medical Services,* pp. 138, 146; Hughes and others, "Evaluation of a Long-Term Home Care Program," p. 468; Donald K. Blackman, Thomas E. Brown, and R. Max Lerner, "Four Years of a Community Long Term Care Project: The South Carolina Experience," *Pride Institute Journal of Long Term Home Health Care,* vol. 4 (Winter 1983), p. 10; Haskins and others, *Coordinated Community-Oriented Long-Term Care,* p. 203; John A. Capitman, "Community-Based Long-Term Care Models, Target Groups, and Impacts on Service Use," *Gerontologist,* vol. 26 (August 1986), p. 395; and Skellie and others, "Cost-Effectiveness of Community-Based Long-Term Care," p. 356.

14. Wooldridge and Schore, *Evaluation of the National Long Term Care Demonstration: Channeling Effects on Hospital, Nursing Home, and Other Medical Services,* pp. 138, 156.

15. Kemper and others, "Community Care Demonstrations," pp. 93–94; Applebaum and others, "Wisconsin Community Care," p. 353; and Zimmer and others, "Randomized Controlled Study," pp. 139–40.

16. Barbara Hicks and others, "The Triage Experiment in Coordinated Care for the Elderly," *American Journal of Public Health,* vol. 71 (September 1981), p. 998; and Gaumer and others, "Impact of the New York Long-Term Home Health Care Program," pp. 646–47.

17. Eggert and others, "Gaining Control of the Long Term Care System," p. 362; and William G. Weissert and others, "Cost-Effectiveness of Homemaker Services for the Chronically Ill," *Inquiry,* vol. 17 (Fall 1980), p. 241.

18. Judith R. Lave, "Cost Containment Policies in Long-Term Care," *Inquiry,* vol. 22 (Spring 1985), p. 15; Kemper and others, "Community Care Demonstrations," p. 97; and Capitman, "Community-Based Long-Term Care Models," p. 395.

19. Wooldridge and Schore, *Evaluation of the National Long Term Care Demonstration: Channeling Effects on Hospital, Nursing Home, and Other Medical Services,* p. 101. In Channeling all participants were at least aged 65 and were functionally impaired as measured by two moderate deficiencies in activities of daily living, or three severe deficiencies in instrumental activities of daily living, or two severe deficiencies in instrumental activities of daily living plus one severe activity of daily living deficiency, in addition to having unmet needs for at least two services expected to last at least six months or for an unpaid support system that may no longer be able to provide needed care. Ibid., p. xi.

20. Kemper and others, "Community Care Demonstrations," pp. 92–93; Haskins and others, *Coordinated Community-Oriented Long-Term Care,* p. 217; Margaret Stassen and John Holahan, "A Comparative Analysis of Long-Term Care Demonstrations and Evaluations," Working Paper 1227–2 (Washington, D.C.: Urban Institute, September 1980), pp. 185–88; and Capitman, "Community-Based Long-Term Care Models," p. 395.

21. Nocks and others, "Effects of a Community-based Long Term Care Project," pp. 154–55.

22. Doty, "Home and Community-Based Services," pp. 5–11; and HCFA, "Long Term Care: Background and Future Directions," Discussion Paper HCFA 81-20047 (Washington, D.C.: DHHS, January 1981), pp. 35–37.

23. DHHS, 1982 National Long-Term Care Survey.

24. HCFA, "Long Term Care," p. 41. One study that reports a large substitution effect is Vernon L. Green, "Substitution Between Formally and Informally Provided Care for the Impaired Elderly in the Community," *Medical Care,* vol. 21 (June 1983), pp. 609–19. However, because of study limitations in the measurement of unpaid support, Green points out that his finding may reflect redeployment or specialization rather than withdrawal on the part of informal caregivers.

25. Jon B. Christianson, *Channeling Effects on Informal Care,* report prepared for DHHS (Princeton, N.J.: Mathematica Policy Research, May 1986), p. v.

26. Kemper and others, *Evaluation of the National Long Term Care Demonstration: Final Report,* pp. x–xii, xiv.

27. Eggert and others, "Gaining Control of the Long Term Care System," pp. 360–61.

28. Zawadski and Ansak, "Consolidating Community-Based Long-Term Care," pp. 367–68.

29. Doty, "Home and Community-Based Services," pp. 30–32.

30. Kemper and others, "Community Care Demonstrations," p. 94; Haskins and others, *Coordinated Community-Oriented Long-Term Care,* pp. 284–85; and Stassen and Holahan, "Comparative Analysis of Long-Term Care Demonstrations," pp. 188–93.

31. Kemper and others, *Evaluation of the National Long Term Care Demonstration: Final Report,* p. 129.

32. William J. McAuley and Rosemary Blieszner, "Selection of Long-Term Care Arrangements by Older Community Residents," *Gerontologist,* vol. 25 (April 1985), pp. 188–93; Mark R. Meiners and Arlene K. Tave, "Consumer Interest in Long-Term Care Insurance: A Survey of the Elderly in Six States," National Center for Health Services Research, Rockville, Md., December 7, 1984, table 22; and Marvin Cetron, "The Public Opinion of Home Care: A Survey Report Executive Summary," *Caring,* vol. 4 (October 1985), p. 13.

33. DHHS, 1982 National Long-Term Care Survey.

34. See Anselm Strauss, "Health Policy and Chronic Illness," *Society,* vol. 25 (November–December 1987), pp. 33–39.

35. Kemper and others, "Community Care Demonstrations," p. 95; and Robert A. Applebaum and Margaret Harrigan, *Channeling Effects on the Quality of Clients' Lives,* report prepared for DHHS (Princeton, N. J.: Mathematica Policy Research, April 1986), pp. 18–27.

36. At the start of the Channeling demonstration, the majority of respondents in both control and treatment groups reported that they needed help (or additional help) with personal care tasks (that is, dressing, bathing, toileting, or transferring), housekeeping, and meal preparation. Applebaum and Harrigan, *Channeling Effects on the Quality of Clients' Lives,* pp. 18–19.

37. DHHS, 1982 National Long-Term Care Survey.

38. Amy Horowitz and Lois W. Shindelman, "Social and Economic Incentives for Family Caregivers," *Health Care Financing Review,* vol. 5 (Winter 1983), pp. 25–33.

39. Christianson, *Channeling Effects on Informal Care,* p. vii.

40. Kemper and others, "Community Care Demonstrations," p. 98.

Chapter 15

1. For example, at any one time, 25 million Americans today have no health insurance at all. Karen Davis and Diane Rowland, "Uninsured and Underserved: Inequities in Health Care in the United States," *Milbank Memorial Fund Quarterly: Health and Society,* vol. 61 (Spring 1983), p. 152. Many of these people cannot qualify for medicaid, regardless of their medical expenses, because they are not aged, blind, disabled, or living in a family with dependent children.

2. Aaron Wildavsky, "The Annual Expenditure Increment—or How Congress Can Regain Control of the Budget," *Public Interest,* no. 33 (Fall 1973), pp. 84–108.

3. David Donnison, *The Politics of Poverty* (Oxford: Martin Robertson, 1982), pp. 11–12.

4. Federal non-means-tested entitlement spending grew at a 9.9 average annual percentage rate between 1980 and 1984, which was 2.5 percentage points higher than means-tested entitlement spending. *Budget of the United States Government, Fiscal Year 1986: Historical Tables,* tables 8.1, 11.3.

5. Sheila R. Zedlewski and Jack A. Meyer, *Toward Ending Poverty among the Elderly and Disabled: Policy and Financing Options,* report prepared for the Villers Foundation and the Commonwealth Fund Commission on Elderly People Living Alone (Washington, D.C.: Urban Institute, February 27, 1987), pp. 18–23.

6. Jonathan Bradshaw, "A Defence of Social Security," in Philip Bean, John Ferris, and David Whynes, eds., *In Defence of Welfare* (New York: Tavistock, 1985), pp. 247–48; and Alan Deacon and Jonathan Bradshaw, *Reserved for the Poor: The Means Test in British Social Policy* (Oxford: Basil Blackwell and Martin Robertson, 1983), pp. 197–98.

7. "Easing the Burden of Nursing Home Costs," *Business Week,* March 11, 1985, pp. 123–24; and Bernard Sloan, "A Nursing-Home Scandal in the Making," *Wall Street Journal,* August 9, 1983.

8. R L Associates, *The American Public Views Long-Term Care* (Princeton, N.J., October 1987), pp. 16–17.

Chapter 16

1. *Long-Term Care in Western Europe and Canada: Implications for the United States,* Committee Print, Senate Special Committee on Aging, 98 Cong. 2 sess. (Washington D.C., July 1984), p. 12; and Charlotte Nusberg with Mary Jo Gibson and Sheila Peace, *Innovative Aging Programs Abroad: Implications for the United States* (Westport, Conn.: Greenwood Press, 1984), p. 66.

2. Virginia Little, *Open Care for the Aging: Comparative International Approaches* (New York: Springer Publishing, 1982), p. 59; and Birgitte Uldall-Hansen, "Open Care for the Elderly—Denmark," in Anton Amann, ed., *Open Care for the Elderly in Seven European Countries: A Pilot Study in the Possibilities and Limits of Care* (Pergamon Press, 1980), pp. 62–63.

3. Robert L. Kane and Rosalie A. Kane, *A Will and a Way: What the United States Can Learn from Canada about Caring for the Elderly* (Columbia University Press, 1985), pp. 231–32.

4. U.S. General Accounting Office, *Medigap Insurance: Law Has Increased Protection against Substandard and Overpriced Policies,* GAO/HRD-87-8 (Washington, D.C., October 1986), pp. 24–25.

5. Joshua M. Wiener, Deborah A. Ehrenworth, and Denise A. Spence, "Private Long-Term Care Insurance: Cost, Coverage, and Restrictions," *Gerontologist,* vol. 27 (August 1987), p. 490.

6. This section is largely drawn from Lewin and Associates, "Draft Proposal: Long-Term Care/Social Insurance Program (LTC/SIP)," Washington, D.C., June 8, 1987, pp. 25–27.

7. Kane and Kane, *A Will and a Way,* pp. 60–61.

8. Only 25 percent of the chronically disabled community-based elderly receive some paid help. DHHS, 1982 National Long-Term Care Survey, available from the National Technical Information Service, accession nos. PB-86-161775 and PB-86-161783.

9. Judith Wooldridge and Jennifer Schore, *Evaluation of the National Long Term Care Demonstration: Channeling Effects on Hospital, Nursing Home, and Other Medical Services,* report prepared for DHHS (Princeton, N.J.: Mathematica Policy Research, May 1986), pp. xv–xvi; John A. Capitman, Brenda Haskins, and Judith Bernstein, "Case Management Approaches in Coordinated Community-Oriented Long-Term Care Demonstrations," *Gerontologist,* vol. 26 (August 1986), pp. 398–404; and Peter Kemper and others, *The Evaluation of the National Long Term Care Demonstration: Final Report,* report prepared for DHHS (Princeton, N.J.: Mathematica Policy Research, May 1986), pp. 115–25.

10. U.S. Congressional Budget Office, *The Changing Distribution of Federal Taxes, 1975–1990* (Washington, D.C., October 1987), p. 13.

11. *1984 Annual Report of the Board of Trustees of the Federal Old-Age and Survivors Insurance and Disability Insurance Trust Funds,* pp. 8–12.

12. Joseph A. Pechman, *Federal Tax Policy,* 5th ed. (Brookings, 1987), pp. 220–21.

13. CBO, *Changing Distribution of Federal Taxes,* p. xvii.

14. Pechman, *Federal Tax Policy,* p. 224.

15. Brookings-ICF Long-Term Care Financing Model.

16. See, for example, Lawrence Summers, "A Few Good Taxes," *New Republic,* November 30, 1987, pp. 14–16.

17. See, for example, Lynn Etheredge, "Financing Health Services and Long-Term Care for the Elderly: The Case for the Estate Tax," paper presented at the conference on Medicare Reform and the Baby Boom Generation sponsored by Americans for Generational Equity, Washington, D.C., April 1987, p. 3.

18. Henry J. Aaron and others, *Economic Choices 1987* (Brookings, 1986), p. 104.

19. Jack A. Meyer, "Medicare and Medicaid: An Agenda for Reform," New Directions for Policy, Washington, D.C., April 1987, pp. 18–19.

20. CBO, *Changing Distribution of Federal Taxes,* p. 13.

21. Income tax estimates were based on output from ICF's Household Income and Tax Simulation Model. Rate of change in real earnings was based on the social security Alternative II-B assumptions.

22. Pechman, *Federal Tax Policy,* p. 369.

23. An evaluation of the Channeling case management demonstration project found that there were virtually no differences in rates of nursing home use between those receiving case management services and the control group. Kemper and others, *Evaluation of the National Long Term Care Demonstration: Final Report,* pp. 115–25.

24. Dorothy P. Rice and Saul Waldman, "Issues in Designing a National Program of Long-Term Care Benefits," *Medical Care,* vol. 14 (May 1976,

Supplement), p. 103; and Karen Davis and Diane Rowland, *Medicare Policy: New Directions for Health and Long-Term Care* (Baltimore, Md.: Johns Hopkins University Press, 1986), p. 107.

25. Kemper and others, *Evaluation of the National Long Term Care Demonstration: Final Report,* pp. 108–13.

26. Davis and Rowland, *Medicare Policy,* p. 108.

27. Some observers argue that reliance on the private sector is likely to provide for a more innovative service delivery system and ways of controlling costs. Jay N. Greenberg, Lifeplans, Inc., Waltham, Mass., personal communication, November 21, 1987.

28. Diane Justice, "State Initiatives in Reforming Long-Term Care," *Business and Health,* vol. 4 (December 1986), pp. 14–19.

Chapter 17

1. Robert L. Kane and Rosalie A. Kane, *A Will and a Way: What the United States Can Learn from Canada about Caring for the Elderly* (Columbia University Press, 1985), p. 231.

2. William J. McAuley and Rosemary Blieszner, "Selection of Long-Term Care Arrangements by Older Community Residents," *Gerontologist,* vol. 25 (April 1985), p. 190; Mark R. Meiners and Arlene K. Tave, "Consumer Interest in Long-Term Care Insurance: A Survey of Elderly in Six States," National Center for Health Services Research, Rockville, Md., December 7, 1984, p. 14; and Marvin Cetron, "The Public Opinion of Home Care: A Survey Report Executive Summary," *Caring,* vol. 4 (October 1985), p. 13.

3. Greg Arling and William J. McAuley, "The Feasibility of Public Payments for Family Caregiving," *Gerontologist,* vol. 23 (June 1983), p. 304.

4. National Association of Insurance Commissioners, Advisory Committee on Long Term Care, *Long Term Care Insurance: An Industry Perspective on Market Development and Consumer Protection,* report submitted to NAIC Medicare Supplement, Long Term and Other Limited Benefit Plans Task Force (Kansas City, Mo.: NAIC, December 1986).

5. Data from ICF Inc., Household Income and Tax Simulation Model, furnished by John Gist of the American Association of Retired Persons.

6. Brookings-ICF Long-Term Care Financing Model.

Technical Appendix

1. David L. Kennell and John F. Sheils, "Summary of Methodology and Assumptions for Base Case Long-Term Care Financing Simulations," ICF Inc., Washington, D.C., April 1986.

2. David L. Kennell and John F. Sheils, *The ICF Pension and Retirement Income Simulation Model (PRISM) with the Brookings/ICF Long-Term Care Financing Model: Draft Technical Documentation* (Washington, D.C.: ICF, September 1986).

3. *1985 Annual Report of the Federal Old-Age and Survivors Insurance and Disability Insurance Trust Funds.*

4. Marriage partners are chosen by age and educational status. See U.S. Bureau of the Census, "Educational Attainment in the U.S., March 1979," *Current Population Reports,* series P–20, no. 356 (Washington, D.C.: Department of Commerce, 1980), table 4.

5. Howard N. Fullerton, Jr., "1995 Labor Force: BLS' Latest Projections," in U.S. Bureau of Labor Statistics, *Employment Projections for 1995: Data and Methods,* bulletin 2253 (Washington, D.C.: Department of Labor, April 1986), pp. 16–24.

6. Laurence G. Branch and others, "A Prospective Study of Functional Status among Community Elders," *American Journal of Public Health,* vol. 74 (March 1984), pp. 266–68.

7. Mark Meiners and Gordon Trapnell, "Long-Term Care Insurance: Premium Estimates for Prototype Policies," *Medical Care,* vol. 22 (October 1984), pp. 901–11.

8. Medicare rate provided by Margaret Sulvetta, Urban Institute, Washington, D.C., personal communication, March 25, 1986. Medicaid rate from La Jolla Management Corporation, *Analysis of State Medicaid Program Characteristics, 1983* (Rockville, Md., 1983), pp. 126–27, 130–31.

9. *1985 Annual Report of Federal Old-Age and Survivors Insurance and Disability Insurance Trust Funds.* This means inflation-adjusted (or constant-dollar) nursing home prices increase at 1.8 percent annually in the model, except as noted in chapter 2 ("Assumptions and Base Case").

10. U.S. Bureau of the Census, "Projections of the Population of the United States by Age, Sex, and Race: 1983–2080," *Current Population Reports*, series P–25, no. 952 (Washington, D.C.: Department of Commerce, May 1984).

11. Joseph M. Anderson and John F. Sheils, "The Household Income and Tax Simulation Model (HITSM) Methodology and Documentation," ICF, Washington, D.C., March 1985.

Index